LANGUAGE AND COMMUNICATION IN MENTALLY HANDICAPPED PEOPLE

There have been many recent advances in our knowledge of normal language processes in mentally handicapped people. As a result we are beginning to recast the language problems of mental handicap within a communicative mould. We are also able to give a clearer account of the role of language in the cognitive and social development of mentally handicapped persons. This book presents an up-to-date picture of current research into their language processes. The topics range from the development of phonology through to the acquisition and use of subtle conversational devices. This book as a whole presents mentally handicapped people as active users of language with access to their own patterns of development and meaning. The authors make the linguistic issues clear to the non-specialist while retaining a firm basis in current research. The aim is to show that the study of language and communication can do more than provide a framework for training programmes for mentally handicapped persons. It can also help us understand and relate to them in their daily lives. The book will be of interest to anyone who has regular contact with people with mental handicap or to academics involved in language acquisition or remediation.

To Pixie and Pippa and to Alicia Conti
for helping, caring and giving.

LANGUAGE AND COMMUNICATION IN MENTALLY HANDICAPPED PEOPLE

Edited by Michael Beveridge,
Gina Conti-Ramsden
and Ivan Leudar

London New York
CHAPMAN AND HALL

First published in 1989 by Chapman and Hall Ltd
11 New Fetter Lane, London EC4P 4EE

Published in the USA by Routledge, Chapman and Hall
29 West 25th Street, New York NY 10001

Set in 10/12pt Times by Leaper & Gard
Printed in Great Britain by
T.J. Press (Padstow) Ltd, Padstow, Cornwall

ISBN 0 412 32390 7

British Library Cataloguing in Publication Data

Language and communication in mentally handicapped
    people.
    1. Mentally handicapped persons. Language skills
    I. Beveridge, Michael   II. Conti-Ramsden, Gina
    III. Leudar, Ivan
    401′.9
    ISBN 0 412 32390 7

Library of Congress Cataloging in Publication Data

Applied for.

Contents

Contributors

Dr Martyn D. Barrett. Lecturer at Royal Holloway and Bedford New College, London University. Formerly taught at Roehampton Institute, London.

Dr Michael Beveridge. Senior lecturer in psychology in the Department of Education, University of Manchester. Formerly a Research Fellow in the Hester Adrian Research Centre.

Dr Sue Clarke. Trainee clinical psychologist in Wessex. Worked with Paul Light and Bob Remington on sign acquisition, in the Department of Psychology, University of Southampton.

Dr Gina Conti-Ramsden. Lecturer in the Department of Education, University of Manchester. Previously at the universities of Texas and Cambridge, and is currently spending two years at the Harvard Graduate School of Education.

Fernando A. Diniz. Principal lecturer and the Head of the Division of Special Educational Needs at the Faculty of Education, Thames Polytechnic, London.

Dr Barbara Dodd. Senior lecturer at the Speech, Language and Hearing Research Centre, School of English and Linguistics, Macquarie University, Sydney, Australia. Formerly Scientific Officer, MRC Developmental Psychology Unit, London, and lecturer in the Department of Speech, University of Newcastle upon Tyne.

Dr Alan G. Kamhi. Associate professor in the Department of Audiology and Speech Pathology, Memphis State University, Tennessee, USA. Formerly at Indiana University and Case Western Reserve University in Cleveland, Ohio.

Dr Keith T. Kernan. Associate professor of anthropology in the Department of Psychiatry and Biobehavioural Sciences at UCLA. Current research interests are concerned with the communicative competence of mentally retarded adults who reside in the community; research also conducted on the acquisition of language by children and on the use of language by speakers of Belizean Creole.

Judy Leahy. Research speech pathologist at the Speech, Language and

Hearing Research Centre, Macquarie University, Sydney, Australia. Formerly a Clinical Supervisor at the School of Human Communication Disorders, Cumberland College of Advanced Education, Sydney.

Dr Ivan Leudar. Lecturer in psychology at the University of Manchester. Previously researched into language processing at the universities of London and St Andrews.

Dr Paul Light. Professor and Director of the Centre for Human Development and Learning at the Open University, Milton Keynes. Formerly at the universities of Cambridge and Southampton.

Dr Julie J. Masterson. Assistant professor in the Department of Communication Disorders, Whittier College, Los Angeles, USA. Received PhD from Memphis State University and subsequently taught at Lamar University, Texas.

Dr Robert Owens. Associate professor at the State University, College of Arts and Sciences, Genesco, New York.

Dr Penny Price. Lecturer in the School of Education at Macquarie University, Sydney, Australia, where she researches into parent training in language facilitation.

Dr Douglass Price-Williams. Professor in the Department of Psychiatry and Anthropology, Centre for Health Sciences, Los Angeles, USA.

Dr Bob Remington. Senior lecturer in psychology at the University of Southampton. Formerly a Research Fellow in the Hester Adrian Research Centre and at the University of Exeter.

Dr Sharon Sabsay. Assistant Research Linguist in the Department of Psychiatry and Biobehavioural Sciences at UCLA. Teaches courses on Culture and Communication and is Assistant Editor of the Socio-behavioural Group Working Papers series.

Dr Julia Watson. Teacher for children with special needs. Worked with Paul Light and Bob Remington on sign acquisition at the University of Southampton.

Dr Anthony Wootton. Senior lecturer in the Department of Sociology, University of York.

Preface

This book shows how our increased understanding of normal language development is influencing research into the language processes of mentally handicapped people. One result is the recasting of their language problems within a communicative framework. We are also able to give a clearer account of the role of language in the cognitive and social development of mentally handicapped persons.

This book presents an up-to-date picture of current research into the language processes of mentally handicapped people. The topics range from the development of phonology through to the acquisition and use of subtle conversational devices. The book as a whole presents people with mental handicaps as active users of language with complex patterns of development and meaning. We aim to make the issues clearer to the non-specialist while retaining a firm basis in current research. The aim is to show that the study of language and communication can do more than provide a framework for training programmes for mentally handicapped people. This approach can also help us to relate to and understand them in their daily lives.

The contributors have been invited because of their combination of high-quality research and their concern to see that research benefits mentally handicapped people. All of us believe that unless research has a well-founded theoretical base, it will produce little of lasting use. Furthermore, in the hands of educational practitioners, good theory generates good practice. Readers wishing for simple answers which require little reflection may find this book difficult. On the other hand, all the contributors have particular skills in communicating difficult issues. Our view is that they have used these skills in their present chapters.

The book is organized into four sections. The first section contains up-to-date reviews of the way that people with mental handicaps acquire phonology, lexis and sign systems. Despite this knowledge being fundamental to the entry of this population into a communicative world, there have been few attempts to synthesize these areas. Part I reveals that previous theories of development of communication should be re-evaluated.

In Part II we examine the interrelationships between language, communication and cognition. This is a crucial area for a population whose capacity to think and reason is regarded as their primary difficulty. The chapters in this part put the cognition and language question into current psychological perspectives. Communication emerges as a process which is not just interpersonal, but also intrapersonal. Discourse is shown to have a constitutive role in the cognitive development of mentally handicapped people.

Part III looks, in detail, at the interactive processes between mentally handicapped children, parents and other adults. Again, previous claims both for causality and intervention are carefully examined. Techniques for the analysis of interactions are illustrated, and their evidence is discussed in the light of current theory.

In Part IV we look at the complexity of the communications in which adult mentally handicapped persons participate. New theories of conversational analysis are applied with revealing results. The focus is both on the individual's communicative abilities and on the contexts in which these abilities are exercised. The way mentally handicapped people reveal their personalities and feelings through language is brought into focus.

Overall, then, this volume takes a wide-ranging view of what communication does for (and to) people with mental handicaps. In one volume many different and crucial issues are addressed for the first time. We hope that this book will play a part in the process of increasing understanding of the lives of mentally handicapped people.

Michael Beveridge
Gina Conti-Ramsden
Ivan Leudar
Manchester
1988

PART I

The Acquisition of
Sounds, Words and Signs

Part I contains chapters which look at the ways that people with mental handicaps acquire the three basic units out of which communication can be constructed: namely, sounds, words and signs. Developmental psycholinguistics has shown that non-intellectually impaired children acquire rules which provide the basis for the production and comprehension of these basic communicative units. Chapters 1–3 in this section examine the rules of acquisition of phonology, lexis and sign systems by mentally handicapped people. Differences and similarities with other children are noted and discussed. The implications for intervention are also drawn out. All three chapters refer to the authors' own recent work. The chapters show how appropriate research methods can reveal both gaps and confusions in previous theories. The authors also show that even at these fundamental levels of language, we must not forget the communicative purposes that linguistic rules must serve.

Lexical Development in Mentally Handicapped Children

Martyn D. Barrett and Fernando A. Diniz

How do mentally handicapped children learn the meanings of words? How do mentally handicapped children represent their knowledge of word meanings in their mental lexicons? And how do these children acquire and mentally represent their knowledge of the semantic relationships which exist between the meanings of different words?

These three questions all concern different aspects of the lexical development of mentally handicapped children (MHC). In this chapter, we review the research which has been conducted to date which serves to cast some light upon such questions. However, as we shall see in the course of this review, we are still a very long way from being able to provide adequate answers to any of the above questions.

In the first two sections of this chapter we examine those studies which have reported information which enables us to compare the overall pattern of lexical development in MHC with the overall pattern of lexical development in non-handicapped children (NHC), and those studies which have reported information relating to the possibility that MHC with different syndromes display different patterns of lexical development. The third section is then devoted to a more detailed consideration of our current knowledge concerning the acquisition and mental representation of the meanings of particular types of words by MHC. In the fourth section we review those studies which have addressed the issue of how MHC acquire a knowledge of superordinate and subordinate lexical relations. The chapter concludes with some general observations which can be drawn from the four preceding sections.

1.1 THE OVERALL PATTERNS OF LEXICAL DEVELOPMENT IN THE MHC AND NCH COMPARED

Studies which have compared MHC and NHC using one or more lexical measures in such a way that they enable us to compare the overall patterns of lexical development in these two populations are summarized in Table 1.1. These studies are arranged in the table in the approximate order of the

Table 1.1: Studies which enable comparisons to be drawn between the overall patterns of lexical development in mentally handicapped children (MHC) and non-handicapped children (NHC)

Reference	N	CA	MA	Subjects	Findings
Glenn and Cunningham (1982)	9	12.4 (9.2–15.5) mth	9.1 (7.5–13.0) mth	DS	MHC respond appropriately to the same number of verbal requests (2) as MA-matched NHC; i.e. word comprehension begins at same MA in MHC and NHC
Cardoso-Martins, Mervis and Mervis (1985)	6	17–19 mth at start of study	8–14 mth at start of study	DS	(i) MHC first comprehend object names at same MA (14 mth) and at same level of sensorimotor development as NHC (ii) MHC first produce object names at same MA (19 mth) and at same level of sensorimotor development as NHC (iii) MHC have the same sized vocabularies (in both production and comprehension) as MA-matched NHC (when MA is between 13 and 21 mth) (iv) MHC have smaller vocabularies (in both production and comprehension) than NHC matched for level of sensorimotor development
Gopnik (1987)	31	12–36 mth	–	DS	MHC and NHC exhibit a similar pattern of early vocabulary development, with both groups acquiring social words and a few object names at first, and only later acquiring relational words and many object names
Cardoso-Martins and Mervis (1985)	5	31.4 (21.5–37.1) mth	15.7 (13.4–17.0) mth	DS	MHC not yet producing their first word, unlike MA-matched NHC; i.e. onset of word production delayed in MHC
Gillham (1979)	4	–	–	DS	Little difference in the first 50-word vocabularies which are acquired by MHC and by NHC (both in terms of word types and in terms of actual words acquired)

Reference	N	CA	MA	Subjects	Findings
Dooley (1976)	2	3.8 and 5.2 yr	2.4 and 2.9 yr	DS (IQs: 51 and 44)	MHC have similar-sized vocabularies to NHC with similar MLUS (1.48–1.84 morphemes); however, MLUs are low for these MAs, implying that MHC have smaller vocabularies than NHC of same MA
Rondal (1978)	21	3–12 yr	–	DS	The speech of MHC has a higher type-token ratio than the speech of MLU-matched NHC
Thompson (1963)	29	5–6 yr	2.7 (1.8–3.8) yr	DS (IQs: 29–61)	MHC have impoverished vocabularies compared with NHC of same MA, with no MHC yet using words which denote spatial relationships (e.g. *in* and *on*)
Cunningham and Sloper (1984)	44	5.1 (3.1–7.5) yr	3.0 (0.9–5.3) yr	DS	The object name vocabularies acquired by MHC have a similar content to those acquired by NHC
Ryan (1975, 1977)	31	5–9 yr	3.1 (2.5–3.5) yr	DS and others of varied aetiology (mean IQ: 40)	(i) MHC equal to or better than MA-matched NHC on comprehension and production of nouns (ii) MHC worse than MA-matched NHC on comprehension of prepositions (iii) MHC and MA-matched NHC exhibit equal improvement in vocabulary testing scores when retested after MAs have increased by 3.5 mth
Miller, Chapman and MacKenzie (1981)	42	–	0.6–7.0 yr	Multiply handicapped, moderately and severely retarded children	The speech of MHC has a higher type-token ratio than the speech of NH MA comparisons
Lyle (1961)	58	6.5–13.5 yr	3.6 yr (median)	DS and non-DS (mean IQ: 36.7)	(i) MHC and MA-matched NHC similar on comprehension and production of object names and action names (ii) MHC less able than MA-matched NHC on word-definition task

Reference	N	CA	MA	Subjects	Findings
Rogers (1975)	37	10 (4.4–16.1) yr	3.9 (1.7–7.7) yr	DS and others of varied or uncertain aetiology	68% MHC have lower scores than NH MA comparisons on the expressive vocabulary subscale of the Reynell Scales
Bartel, Bryen and Keehn (1973)	–	11.2 (9.1–12.9) yr	4.2 (2.7–6.0) yr	Trainable retarded children (mean IQ: 37.4)	MHC usually comprehend particular words either at the same MA or at a later MA than NH MA comparisons
Mein and O'Connor (1960)	80	20.8 (10–30) yr	4.9 (3–7) yr	DS and others of varied or unclassified aetiology	(i) Size of vocabulary correlates with both MA and CA, but is more closely related to MA than to CA (ii) MHC have larger vocabularies than NH MA comparisons (iii) Vocabularies of MHC contain more core words but fewer fringe words than those of NH MA comparisons (iv) The speech of MHC has a higher type-token ratio than the speech of NH MA comparisons
Mein (1961)	40	10–30 yr	5.0 (3.0–6.9) yr	DS and others of varied or unclassified aetiology	The proportion of nouns occurring in MHC's conversational speech decreases as MA increases, but at a later stage than in NH MA comparisons
Lozar, Wepman and Hass (1972)	27	5.5 14.5 yr	4.2–9.1 yr	Mentally retarded children (IQs: 46–78)	A comparable percentage of words (84%) in the speech of both MHC and NHC consists of the same basic dictionary of 359 words
Lozar, Wepman and Hass (1973)	20	11.5 yr	7.0 yr	Mentally retarded children (mean IQ: 61.2)	Little difference in the vocabularies which are used by MHC and by CA-matched NHC
Beier, Starkweather and Lambert (1969)	30	19 (11–24) yr	–	Mentally retarded children (IQs: 23–75)	(i) The same number of words (40) accounts for 50% of the speech of both MHC and slightly younger NHC

Reference	N	CA	MA	Subjects	Findings
					(ii) Little difference in the vocabularies which are used by MHC and by slightly younger NHC (iii) The speech of MHC has a lower type-token ratio than the speech of slightly younger NHC
Bless, Swift and Rosen (1985)	9	–	5–8 yr	DS	MHC's vocabulary production and comprehension both developmentally delayed compared with non-verbal cognitive status
Papania (1954)	250	12.3 (9–16) yr	8.4 (6–10) yr	Non-brain-injured mentally retarded children (mean IQ: 70.2)	When asked to define Stanford-Binet vocabulary items: (i) MHC produce more abstract and fewer concrete word definitions as MA increases (ii) MHC produce fewer abstract and more concrete word definitions than NH MA comparisons
Winters and Brzoska (1975)	24	11.9 yr	8.5 yr	Mentally retarded children (mean IQ: 71.6)	(i) Ability to correctly label pictures with nouns correlates with both MA and CA, but is more closely related to MA than to CA (ii) MHC lag behind NH MA in comparisons their ability correctly to label pictures with nouns
Furth and Milgram (1965)	38	12.9 (11.5–13.5) yr	9.0 (8.5–9.5) yr	Educable retarded children (mean IQ: 70)	(i) MHC perform less well than MA-matched NHC on a word-sorting task which involves the selection of words which are semantically related (ii) MHC perform less well than MA-matched NHC on a word-verbalization task which involves explaining the nature of the semantic relationship linking a set of words

mental ages of the subjects which they employed. The findings of these studies seem to suggest the following general picture.

First of all, it would appear to be the case that, as assessed by comprehension measures, lexical development begins at the same mental age (MA) in MHC and in NHC (Glenn and Cunningham, 1982; Cardoso-Martins, Mervis and Mervis, 1985). However, the indications are that MHC soon start to fall behind NHC in their lexical development, a finding which has emerged both when MHC and NHC are matched for MA (Cardoso-Martins and Mervis, 1985) and when they are matched for level of sensorimotor development (Cardoso-Martins, Mervis and Mervis, 1985). (However, it should be noted that all of the studies which have been conducted with very young MHC have only included Down's syndrome (DS) children as subjects; consequently, further studies are really required to ascertain the extent to which these particular conclusions might also apply to MHC with other aetiologies.)

The studies which have been conducted on older MHC indicate that these children continue to lag behind NHC of similar MAs in their lexical development. This general conclusion emerges from a variety of studies which have used all sorts of different lexical measures and children with a variety of different aetiologies (Dooley, 1976; Thompson, 1963; Lyle, 1961; Rogers, 1975; Bartel, Bryen and Keehn, 1973; Mein, 1961; Bless, Swift and Rosen, 1985; Papania, 1954; Winters and Brzoska, 1975; Furth and Milgram, 1965). There are only three findings in Table 1.1 which do not accord with this general conclusion: these are the first finding of Lyle (1961), and the first and third findings of Ryan (1975, 1977). However, Lyle's comprehension and production measures were not only theoretically unmotivated, but also rather crude in nature; it is therefore possible that they were not sufficiently sensitive. By contrast, Ryan fails to report any procedural information, quantitative results or statistical analyses from her study; as a consequence, it is impossible to evaluate the status of her findings.

However, although the bulk of the studies shown in Table 1.1 indicate that MHC tend to lag behind NHC of a comparable MA in their lexical development, there is one finding (obtained by both Mein and O'Connor, 1960, and Winters and Brzoska, 1975) which indicates that a very important qualification should perhaps be added to this general conclusion: this is the finding that lexical measures obtained from MHC correlate not only with MA, but also with chronological age (CA). For if lexical development does indeed correlate with CA (independently of MA), then it is possible that, with increasing years, the vocabularies of some MHC may continue to grow until they eventually begin to exceed the vocabularies of NHC of a comparable MA. It is therefore relevant to note that in the study by Mein and O'Connor (1960), in which severely handicapped persons with relatively high CAs were tested (see Table 1.1), it was found that these persons

8

did have larger vocabularies than NHC of similar MAs. However, much more systematic life-span studies of lexical development in mentally handicapped adults are really required in order to explore this matter properly (indeed, given the current trend towards the provision of continuing education for young mentally handicapped adults, the need for such studies which could be used to inform the design of appropriate lexical remediation programmes for these people is now particularly acute).

Thus the studies which are listed in Table 1.1 would seem to indicate that lexical development proceeds at different rates in MHC and in NHC. However, it is also clear from many of the studies which are shown in Table 1.1 that the actual words which are acquired by MHC are very similar to the words which are acquired by NHC (Gopnik, 1987; Gillham, 1979; Cunningham and Sloper, 1984; Bartel, Bryen and Keehn, 1973; Lozar, Wepman and Hass, 1972, 1973; Beier, Starkweather and Lambert, 1969).

It should be noted that the overall picture of lexical development in MHC which has just been sketched accounts for virtually all of the findings listed in Table 1.1, with just one major exception: this concerns the type-token ratios (TTRs) which have been found to characterize the speech of MHC.[1] Rondal (1978), Miller, Chapman and Mackenzie (1981), and Mein and O'Connor (1960) all found the speech of MHC to have higher TTRs than the speech of NHC; Beier, Starkweather and Lambert (1969) obtained the converse result. Thus, if TTR reflects vocabulary size, then three out of these four studies suggest that MHC have larger vocabularies than NHC. However, it is arguable that TTRs should only be interpreted as indexing lexical usage rather than lexical knowledge (an argument which would be supported by the findings of the studies in Table 1.1, which overwhelmingly indicate that the MHC lag behind NHC of equivalent MA in terms of their lexical knowledge, even though MHC are often ahead of these NHC in their lexical usage as indexed by their TTRs). It is also arguable that the higher TTRs exhibited by MHC are simply a result of the greater distractability of these children. Nevertheless, this is a curious finding, given the consistency of the picture which otherwise emerges from the studies listed in Table 1.1.

Of course, the above sketch must be regarded as extremely provisional and tentative. This is because the studies upon which this sketch is based differ from one another in a variety of ways. The subjects in these studies differ in terms of their ages, their aetiologies, the severity of their handicaps, the degree to which they were institutionalized, and in terms of the type of educational provision and degree of remediation which they received. In addition, the methodologies of these studies differ in terms of the methods which were used to establish a sample from the non-handicapped population for the purposes of comparison, the tools which were used to assess MA, and the lexical measures which were taken. Indeed, given all these differences, it is perhaps rather surprising to have

9

found any consistent picture at all emerging from this particular set of studies (cf. Kamhi and Masterson, in Chapter 4 in this volume).

1.2 POSSIBLE SYNDROMIC DIFFERENCES IN THE LEXICAL DEVELOPMENT OF MHC

Studies which have reported information relating to the question of whether MHC with different syndromes display different patterns of lexical development are summarized in Table 1.2. It can be seen from the table

Table 1.2: Studies which have reported information relating to the possibility of syndromic differences in the lexical development of mentally handicapped children

Reference	N	CA	MA	Subjects	Findings
Ryan (1975, 1977)	31	5–9 yr	3.1 (2.5–3.5) yr	DS vs others of varied aetiology (mean IQ: 40)	No differences between DS and non-DS on comprehension and production of nouns, or on comprehension of prepositions
Lyle (1960)	77	6.5–14.0 yr	2.5–5.5 yr	DS vs non-DS (IQs: 20–54)	(i) No differences between DS and non-DS on comprehension and production of object names and action names (ii) DS less able than non-DS on word-definition task
Lyle (1961)	58	6.5–13.5 yr	3.6 yr (median)	DS vs non-DS (mean IQ: 36.7)	No differences between DS and non-DS on comprehension and production of object names and action names, or on word-definition task
Rogers (1975)	37	10.0 (4.4–16.1) yr	3.9 (1.7–7.7) yr	DS vs others of varied or uncertain aetiology	DS tend to have lower scores on the expressive vocabulary subscale of the Reynell Scales than non-DS, but no statistical analyses are reported
Mein (1961)	22	20.6 yr	4.7 yr	DS vs non-DS	(i) DS and non-DS have same size vocabularies (ii) In a picture-description task DS use a higher percentage of nouns and a lower percentage of articles than non-DS

that the available data-base addressing this question is extremely weak on several counts. First, there only seem to be five studies which have attempted to address this question; secondly, these five studies have all only attempted to compare DS with non-DS MHC; thirdly, in all five studies, the non-DS population is treated as homogeneous for the purposes of comparison despite the fact that it is actually heterogeneous; and finally, the procedures which are used in these studies to measure lexical development are not very sophisticated from a theoretical point of view. Nevertheless, the picture which seems to emerge from these studies is that DS and non-DS MHC do not differ radically in their lexical development, although there are some findings which are suggestive of the possibility that DS children may lag slightly behind non-DS MHC in their lexical development (Lyle, 1960; Rogers, 1975; Mein, 1961).

1.3 THE ACQUISITION AND MENTAL REPRESENTATION OF THE MEANINGS OF WORDS BY MHC

In this section we review what is currently known about how MHC acquire and mentally represent the meanings of particular types of words. We begin with a fairly extensive discussion of object names as these are the words about which most is known at the present time; we will then pass on to much briefer discussions of action names, personal-social words, formulaic phrases, adjectives, prepositions, proforms, demonstratives and connectives.

(a) Object names

Much of the research which has been conducted into the acquisition of the meanings of object names by MHC has been based upon theoretical ideas drawn from the literature on the acquisition of the meanings of these words by NHC and, in particular, upon ideas deriving from prototype theory (which was originally developed by Rosch, 1977, 1978, but which is perhaps most clearly articulated in the context of lexical development in NHC by Bowerman, 1978). According to this theory, when children acquire the meaning of an object name, they acquire and mentally represent that meaning in the form of prototypical referential exemplar. This prototypical exemplar effectively functions as a specification of the most typical and clearest example of the kind of object which can be referred to by means of that word. The word is then used to refer to actual objects which share attributes with this mentally represented prototypical exemplar. Depending upon how many attributes a particular object shares with the prototypical exemplar, that object may be a more or less typical

11

referent of the word. Thus an object which shares many attributes with the prototype would be a highly typical referent of the word; an object which shares relatively few attributes with the prototype would be an atypical or peripheral referent of the word.

Because prototype theory postulates that a word will be extended to label a particular object on the basis of the attributes which that object shares with the prototypical exemplar of the word, and because typical referents share many attributes with this prototype whereas peripheral referents share relatively few attributes with the prototype, this theory predicts that the degree of typicality/peripherality exhibited by potential referents can have an important effect upon the actual use of the word. Consequently, many studies have been conducted with NHC in order to establish whether or not such typicality effects occur; the findings of these studies have revealed that both the production and the comprehension of object names by NHC are subject to these effects.

For example, in production, NHC sometimes make errors in their use of object names, either by underextending these names (i.e. by using them to refer to only a subset of the full range of objects which are properly labelled with those words in the adult language) or by overextending these names (i.e. by using them not only to refer to all of the objects which are properly labelled with those words in the adult language, but also to refer to some further objects as well). Kay and Anglin (1982) have shown that NHC's production of underextensions is in fact based upon the exclusion of peripheral rather than typical referents from the extension of the word, while Bowerman (1978) and Barrett (1982, 1986) have shown that NHC's production of overextensions is based upon the use of object names for referring to inappropriate objects which nevertheless share certain attributes with the most typical (but not necessarily with the more peripheral) referents of these words. Similarly, Kuczaj (1982) has shown that NHC respond in lexical comprehension tasks by first selecting the most typical referents of object names and only subsequently selecting more peripheral referents. As all of these effects of typicality are readily explicable in terms of prototype theory, they can be interpreted as providing strong empirical support for this theory (see Barrett, in press (a), for a more extended discussion of these findings).

Turning now to the research which has been conducted into MHC's knowledge of object names, there have been several studies to date which have indicated that MHC's comprehension and production of these words are also subject to typicality effects. For example, in one study, Mervis (1984) tested the comprehension of object names by six DS children (these were the same six children who formed the sample for the study by Cardoso-Martins, Mervis and Mervis, 1985; see Table 1.1). Mervis found that just as in the case of NHC, these MHC sometimes underextended their object names by excluding the more peripheral (rather than the more typical) referents from the extensions of these words. She also found that these children sometimes overextended their object names, by including within their extensions inappropriate referents which shared either perceptual or functional attributes with the more typical referents of the words.

Similar findings have also been reported by Tager-Flusberg (1985), who tested the lexical comprehension abilities of a group of 14 MHC with various aetiologies (CA = 11.5 years, MA = 4.9 years, IQ = 44). She too found that these children were more likely to include typical rather than peripheral exemplars within the extension of an object name; thus when underextension occurred, it was the peripheral rather than the typical exemplars which were excluded from the extension of the word. Furthermore, when they selected the referents for object names in the comprehension task, these children tended to select the most typical referents first and the more peripheral referents only subsequently. Tager-Flusberg reports that, in the case of both of these two findings, the performance of the MHC was identical to that of a group of MA-matched NHC.

Tager-Flusberg (1986) also employed tests of object name production with this same sample of MHC. In these tests she used pictures which represented referents for the words *boat, bird, fish* and *house.* For each of these four words, both typical and peripheral referents were included. Tager-Flusberg found that when the children were labelling these pictures, the typicality of the referents influenced the children's behaviour. For example, they made more naming errors when they were labelling the peripheral referents than when they were labelling the typical referents. The children were also more likely to use a more specific name (e.g. *penguin* rather than *bird*) when labelling the peripheral referents than when labelling the typical referents. One again, Tager-Flusberg reports that the performance of the MHC on both counts was identical to that of the group of MA-matched NHC.

It should be noted that the findings of Mervis were obtained using a sample of DS children who were aged $1^{1}/_{2}$ to 3 years old, whereas Tager-Flusberg's findings were obtained using a group of MHC displaying various aetiologies with a mean age of 11.5 years and a mean IQ of 44. In addition, educable mentally retarded adolescents (aged approximately 17 years and with IQs between 50 and 70) have also been found to be subject to typicality effects when producing object names; for example, when these adolescents are asked to label objects as rapidly and as accurately as possible, they label typical referents faster than peripheral referents (Weil, McCauley and Sperber, 1978; Davies, Sperber and McCauley, 1981).

Thus the evidence which has been obtained from MHC of different ages, different aetiologies and different degrees of severity of handicap would seem to indicate the following situation. As in the case of NHC, MHC also acquire and mentally represent the meanings of object names in the form of prototypical referential exemplars. These children then extend those names to objects on the basis of their degree of similarity to the prototypes, with highly similar (i.e. highly typical) objects being more readily identifiable as the referents of names than less similar (i.e. more peripheral) objects.

Notice that these conclusions have important implications for remedial programmes which attempt to teach the meanings of object names to MHC. For if the meanings of these words consist of prototypical referents, then it should be easier for MHC to acquire a knowledge of the meanings of these words from experience with highly typical referents (which bear a high degree of resemblance to the prototypical exemplars) than from experience with more peripheral referents. In addition, word meaning acquisition (and the subsequent extension of the word to both typical and peripheral referents) should be easier for MHC if they initially experience the word only in conjunction with highly typical referents rather than in conjunction with a mixture of both typical and peripheral referents. This is because the former should facilitate the acquisition of the appropriate prototype (which then provides the basis for the subsequent extension of the word) much more readily than the latter (even though the latter situation actually models the extension of the word to peripheral referents).

These implications of prototype theory have been tested by Hupp and Mervis (1982), but only using a group of six severely handicapped children whose ages ranged from 8 to 18 years. None of these children was able to communicate using either spoken or sign language, but all had cognitive-developmental levels of at least sensorimotor stage 5 of means–ends relationships and sensorimotor stage 6 on object permanence. These children were each trained to produce six different signed labels. These labels were taught by reference to either one typical referent, three typical referents, or three varied referents (one typical, one intermediate and one peripheral). After this training, the children's comprehension of the labels was tested; in particular, the extent to which the children had generalized these labels to novel referents was examined. It was found that when training had been based only on typical referents, this procedure had led to more accurate generalization than when training had been based on varied referents (with no evidence that the latter had produced any generalization at all). It was also found that the training based on three typical referents had led to more accurate generalization than the training based on just one typical referent (with the former procedure resulting in the acquisition of broad, accurate extensions for the signed labels, and the latter procedure resulting in restricted extensions for the labels which were limited primarily to just typical referents).

Given the extreme characteristics of the sample, and the fact that these children were trained in the use of signed rather than spoken labels, further research is clearly required in order to ascertain whether or not similar findings would apply in the case of children who are not so severely handicapped and who are taught spoken as opposed to signed labels. Additional caution is required in the light of the findings of a follow-up study conducted by Hupp *et al.* (1986). In this study a similar group of six severely retarded children were initially trained either to produce or to comprehend signed labels by reference to three typical referents. When the extent to which those labels were then generalized to novel referents was examined (using a comprehension test procedure), it was found that the production training had not led to any generalization (contrary to the findings of the previous study), and that only the comprehension training had resulted in the generalization of the labels. However, despite this need for caution, the findings of the study by Hupp and Mervis do seem to suggest that when designing lexical remediation programmes for MHC, the basic principles of prototype theory ought to be taken into account if the effectiveness of those programmes is to be maximized.

So far in this discussion we have only considered the way in which studies of typicality effects have served to indicate that MHC are essentially similar to NHC in how they acquire and mentally represent the meanings of object names. The same conclusion emerges, however, from a consideration of the findings of studies into many other aspects of the acquisition of object names by MHC. For example, Gillham (1979) has examined the characteristics of the early object name vocabularies which DS children acquire (see Table 1.1). He found that the early object names which these children acquire consist predominantly of the names of dynamic objects (e.g. people, animals, vehicles, etc.), objects which the child can manipulate (e.g. toys, foodstuffs, items of clothing, etc.), and body parts. These are exactly the same kinds of object name as NHC tend to acquire during the early stages of lexical development (Nelson, 1973). Similarly, Gopnik (1987) (see Table 1.1) has reported that young DS children tend to acquire just a few object names at the very outset of lexical development, but subsequently exhibit a sudden spurt in the growth of their vocabularies which entails the relatively rapid acquisition of many new object names. Again, this is similar to the pattern of development which occurs in NHC (Nelson, 1973; Benedict, 1979).

Another finding which supports the view that MHC acquire the meanings of object names in a similar way to NHC has been reported by Mervis (1984). As we have already seen, Mervis found that the young DS children who were examined in her study sometimes overextended their object names, by using some of these names to label inappropriate objects which happened to share certain attributes with the more typical referents of the words. Mervis also examined the manner in which these children subsequently rescinded their overextensions of these names. She found that this usually occurred in the following way. The child would begin by acquiring a new and more appropriate object name for labelling the previously misnamed object; at this point, the object would be simultaneously included within the extensions of both the old overextended word and the new, more appropriate, word. At a subsequent point in time, the child would then completely transfer the object from the extension of the old word to the extension of the new word, with the two words acquiring mutually exclusive extensions. Mervis reports that both the DS children and the NHC who were included in her study corrected their overextensions in this way, indicating that both of these groups of children were acquiring and subsequently adjusting the meanings of their object names in a similar manner (see Barrett, in press (b), for a theoretical account of why overextensions should be rescinded in this way).

Thus it was now apparent from a variety of studies that MHC acquire and mentally represent the meaning of object names in a similar manner to NHC. That said, however, there is still a great deal that we do not know about the acquisition of the meanings of these words by MHC. For example, it has been discovered that when NHC acquire their earliest object names (between approximately 12 and 18 months of age), these words are often used initially only in very limited and specific behavioural contexts by these children (for example, the word *bird* might only be used initially while the child looks up at birds flying about in the sky, and never in any other situation; the word *dog* might only be used initially while the child points at one particular picture of a dog; etc.). At a subsequent point in time, these early context-bound object names are decontextualized by NHC; these words are then used for referring to objects in a variety of different situations (see Barrett, in press (a), for detailed discussions of these two phenomena of context-bound word usage and decontextualization in NHC). However, the studies which have been conducted into the early acquisition of object names by MHC (e.g. Gillham, 1979; Mervis, 1984) have not attempted to document details of the behavioural contexts in which young MHC use their earliest object names. Consequently, it is still unknown whether MHC exhibit these two phenomena of context-bound word usage and decontextualization, or whether MHC (perhaps because of their greater CA) begin to use their earliest object names in a decontextualized manner right from the outset. The resolution of this particular issue is obviously very important for attempts to devise appropriate lexical remediation programmes for these children, for if very young MHC are only capable of using object names in a context-bound manner, it would clearly be inappropriate to try to teach them to use these words in a decontextualized manner at this early stage in their language development.

In addition, as we have already noted in connection with the study by Hupp and Mervis (1982), further studies are still required to test out the various possibilities for lexical remediation which are suggested by prototype theory. Thus we still need to ascertain how object names can be most effectively taught to moderately and mildly (as opposed to severely) handicapped children. In particular, we need to ascertain whether, with these children, it is more effective to use a small group of highly typical referential exemplars for each object name which is taught, or whether it is more effective to use just a single typical exemplar instead. We also need to ascertain whether lexical remediation programmes for such children should employ production or comprehension training (or both) in order to maximize their effectiveness.

But although there is still this need for further investigation in this area, we are at least beginning to gain some sort of understanding of how MHC acquire the meanings of object names. By comparison, we have virtually no understanding at all of how MHC acquire the meanings of any other types of words, as we shall now see.

(b) Action names

In the case of action names, there are only two studies in the literature which have reported information concerning the acquisition of these words by MHC. In one of these studies, Gillham (1979) examined the first ten words which were acquired by four young DS children; his data indicate that, very occasionally, action names (e.g. *kick*) may be included within these children's ten-word vocabularies (an acquisition pattern which is comparable to that displayed by NHC). However, Gillham does not provide any details of the behavioural contexts in which these early action names were produced, nor does he give any indication of the precise types of action which were labelled with these words by the children.

Bartel, Bryen and Keehn (1973) (see Table 1.1) have also reported some information concerning the acquisition of action names by MHC. They administered the Carrow Auditory Test of Language Comprehension to a sample (of unspecified size) of trainable mentally handicapped children; the CAs of these children ranged from 9.1 to 12.9 years, and their MAs ranged from 2.7 to 6.0 years. The Carrow Test measures comprehension of a range of lexical items; no language production is required for responding to these items as the child merely has to point to one of three pictures which are presented for each item. The test includes the following action names as items: *jump, run, hit, catch* and *give*. Using this procedure, Bartel, Bryen and Keehn found that the MHC comprehended the words *jump, run* and *catch* at higher MAs than NHC, the word *hit* at the same MA as NHC, and the word *give* at a lower MA than NHC.

Because these two studies both provide only minimal information concerning the acquisition of action names by MHC, it is not really possible to draw any very meaningful conclusions from either study about either the acquisition or the mental representation of the meanings of these words by MHC.

(c) Personal-social words and formulaic phrases

Personal-social words are those which are used within the context of particular interactional exchanges to fulfil specific social or expressive functions (e.g. *no, want, ta, please*, etc.). Studies of early language development in NHC (e.g. Nelson, 1973; Barrett, 1981) have shown that NHC usually begin to acquire such words at a very early point in their development, often by the time that they have acquired a ten-word vocabulary. These studies have also revealed that NHC's early personal-social words sometimes consist of whole phrases of adult language (e.g. *here-you-are, you-do-it, I-want-it*, etc.) which are used in an unanalysed formulaic manner for these social-expressive functions (see Barrett, in press (a), for a discussion of the acquisition and subsequent development of formulaic phrases in NHC).

As far as MHC are concerned, we know from the study by Gillham (1979) that personal-social words are sometimes included in the ten-word vocabularies of DS children (for example, he reports that the words *no, ta* and *boo* were present in the ten-word vocabularies of the four DS children that he studied). In addition, both Dooley (1976) and Ryan (1975) have reported the use of formulaic phrases by MHC (see Table 1.1 for details of the samples in these two studies). However, none of these studies provides any detailed information concerning the behavioural contexts in which these words or phrases were produced, nor do they provide any information about the changes which presumably occurred in the use of the words and phrases over time. Consequently, although it is apparent that MHC acquire and use both personal-social words and formulaic phrases, we cannot really draw any specific conclusions about how MHC acquire these words and phrases from these particular studies.

(d) Adjectives

We also have little evidence available concerning the acquisition of adjectives by MHC. Gillham (1979) reports that the occasional adjective (e.g. *hot*) was sometimes included in the ten-word vocabularies of the DS children that he studied (an acquisition pattern comparable to that shown by NHC), but again he fails to provide any information concerning the actual use of these words by these children. Bartel, Bryen and Keehn (1973) report that their sample of MHC comprehended (on the Carrow Test) the adjectives *little, big, fast, slow, red, two, some, many* and *middle* at higher MAs than NHC and the adjectives *tall, short, black, yellow, more, four* and *few* at the same MAs as NHC but only the adjectives *left* and *right* at lower MAs than NHC. They also report that their MHC failed to comprehend the adjectives *alike, different* and *fourth*, even at a MA of six years (the highest MA at which these subjects were tested), whereas 60% of NHC are able to comprehend these particular adjectives by this age.

In addition, Cook (1977) has reported some evidence suggesting that DS children comprehend *big* before *long* (which is also the order of acquisition exhibition by NHC). This last finding could be interpreted as indicating that MHC (like NHC) begin by acquiring those dimensional adjectives which are not tied to a particular dimension (such as *big* and *little*), and only then go on to acquire those dimensional adjectives which refer to size as measured along a single dimension (such as *long* and *short*); see Carey (1982) and Clark (1983) for detailed discussions of this interpretation of the data from NHC. However, considerable caution is needed in interpreting Cook's finding as Bartel, Bryen and Keehn obtained the converse result, with their subjects comprehending *tall* and *short* at a much lower MA than *big* and *little*.

(e) Prepositions

The same rather minimal level of evidence also characterizes our knowledge of how MHC acquire and mentally represent the meanings of prepositions. Thompson (1963) (see Table 1.1) reports that the acquisition of *on* and *in* was delayed with respect to MA in the group of DS children that she examined. Similarly, Bartel, Bryan and Keehn (1973) report that their sample of MHC comprehended (on the Carrow Test) not only *on* and *in*, but also *up, down, by* and *between* at higher MAs than NHC; in addition, these children failed to comprehend *under* and *in front of* at even the highest MA at which they were tested (i.e. at an MA of six years; 60% of NHC can comprehend these two items on the Carrow Test by 3 and 4 years of age respectively). The results from these two studies therefore suggest that MHC may experience particular difficulties in acquiring prepositions.

And finally, Cook (1977) has reported evidence suggesting that DS children comprehend *on* before *in* before *under*, an order which is also exhibited by NHC (see Clark 1973, 1983). Bartel, Bryen and Keehn (1973) also found that the goup of MHC which they tested comprehended *on* at a lower MA than *in*. Taken together, these findings could be interpreted as indicating that MHC acquire the meanings of these prepositions in a similar manner to NHC; however, further more detailed evidence is really required on both the production and the comprehension of these words by MHC before any firm conclusions can be drawn concerning their acquisition.

19

(f) Proforms

There are only two studies which have reported information on the acquisition of proforms by MHC. Dooley (1976) reports that the two DS children that he studied (see Table 1.1) both used proforms (e.g. *it, they, here, there* and *do*) at an early point in their language development (when their mean lengths of utterance (MLUs) were approximately 1.5–1.8 morphemes). The early appearance of proforms in the language productions of these two children may have been due to the fact that both had already acquired many formulaic phrases; the formulaic phrases which are acquired by NHC (e.g. *here-you-are, you-do-it, I-want-it*, etc.) frequently contain proforms as constituents, and these phrases are often subsequently analysed by these children into their constituent words, some of which are then used independently as genuine proforms (see Barrett, in press (a)).

In addition, Bartel, Bryen and Keehn (1973) report the following results from their administration of the Carrow Test to their sample of MHC: these children comprehended *he, she, they, her, him* and *them* at higher MAs than NHC, while they failed to comprehend *his, her* and *their* at even the highest MA at which they were tested (i.e. at an MA of six years; 60% of NHC can comprehend these particular items on the Carrow Test at 4 years of age).

Thus these two studies would seem to indicate that although MHC can acquire some proforms at an early point in their development, they may encounter some difficulty in mastering the full set of proforms which are available in the language which they are acquiring. Apart from this conclusion, however, we do not really have sufficient information from either of these two studies to be able to draw any further conclusions about either the acquisition or the mental representation of the meanings of these words by MHC.

(g) Demonstratives

We have even less information concerning the acquisition of demonstratives by MHC. Bartel, Bryen and Keehn (1973) report that their sample of MHC comprehended *these* and *those* at a much lower MA than NHC, but *this* and *that* at a slightly higher MA than NHC. In addition, Coggins (1979), who analysed the two-word speech produced by a sample of four DS children (whose CAs ranged from 3.8 to 6.3 years, and whose MLUs ranged from 1.22 to 2.06 morphemes), reports that all four of these children produced two-word combinations containing a demonstrative word and the name of an entity (e.g. *that chair*). Thus it appears to be the case that MHC can acquire demonstratives at an early stage in their language development; however, no more than this is known about the acquisition of demonstratives by MHC at the present time.

(h) Connectives

Finally, there are two studies which have reported information on the acquisition of connectives by MHC. Bartel, Bryen and Keehn (1973) report that 60% of their subjects could comprehend *and* and *or* at a MA of 4 years (60% of NHC do not comprehend these two items on the Carrow Test until they are aged 4½ years). And Kamhi and Johnston (1982), who examined the linguistic productions of ten educable mentally retarded children (CA = 8.3, IQ = 63.1), report that the productive use of *and* in conjunctions was well established in the speech of these children, whose mean MA was 5.2 years; seven of these ten children were also found to be using other connectives in their spontaneous speech (e.g. *because*, *so*, etc.). However, there is no other information available in the literature which serves to cast any further light upon either the acquisition or the use of these words by MHC.

(i) Conclusions

It is clear from the preceding review that, apart from the notable exception of object names, we still know very little about the acquisition and mental representation of the meanings of words of MHC. (Indeed it should be noted that there are several other types of words — e.g. place names, abstract nouns, mental verbs, etc. — which we have not even mentioned in the preceding review, mainly because there appears to be no information at all in the available literature concerning their acquisition by MHC.) Our ignorance is further compounded by the fact that many of the studies which we have just reviewed have failed to address a crucial question, namely to what extent are the word meanings which are acquired by MHC the same as the meanings which are acquired by NHC? For example, we know from the study by Bartel, Bryen and Keehn (1973) that MHC acquire prepositions such as *on* and *up* at a slightly higher MA than NHC; however, we do not know from this study whether these children then begin to use and understand these words in exactly the same way as NHC, or whether there are subtle differences in the ways in which MHC and NHC use and understand these words.

Thus it is readily apparent that this field requires much more extensive investigation. In particular, properly detailed longitudinal observational studies are required to ascertain how all these different types of words are actually used by MHC in naturalistic contexts. These studies need to be conducted at a sufficiently detailed level to provide precise information about the linguistic and non-linguistic contexts in which these various words are produced by MHC during the course of their development, and about the types of spontaneous errors which MHC make when using these words. Such studies would, at least, provide a data-base which could then be used to assist in the initial formulation of hypotheses about MHC's lexical development.

In addition, once some initial information of this sort has been obtained, there are at least two types of experimental study which will then become necessary. First, it will be necessary to conduct experiments to establish the full range of circumstances (as opposed to just the naturally occurring circumstances) in which particular words are produced by MHC. Secondly, it will be necessary to conduct experiments to examine MHC's comprehension of particular words under controlled conditions, so that a detailed comparison can be made between MHC's production and comprehension of specific words. Until studies of this sort have been conducted, our knowledge of MHC's lexical development will inevitably remain rudimentary.

Nevertheless, from the preceding review, it is possible to draw three tentative conclusions. First of all, as far as object names are concerned, it would appear to be the case that, just like NHC, MHC also acquire and mentally represent the meanings of these words in the form of prototypical referential exemplars (with the consequence that MHC's production and comprehension of object names are subject to typicality effects). Secondly, it seems to be the case that MHC experience particular difficulties in acquiring prepositions and proforms. And thirdly, it would appear that we now have to qualify still further the general conclusion which we drew earlier on in this chapter to the effect that MHC tend to lag behind MA equivalent NHC in their overall lexical development. For as we have just seen, whereas MHC may indeed exhibit such an overall lag, this lag may be much more pronounced in some lexical domains (e.g. prepositions and pronouns) than in others (e.g. object names and connectives). Consequently, the growth of the vocabulary in MHC is not just slower than it is in NHC; the growth of the vocabulary in MHC is uneven when compared with the norm provided by NHC's vocabulary growth. And therefore, at any given point in development, the total lexical resources of a mentally handicapped child may be rather different from those of a younger non-handicapped child.

1.4 MHC's KNOWLEDGE OF SUPERORDINATE AND SUBORDINATE LEXICAL RELATIONS

In acquiring their lexical knowledge children do not only acquire a knowledge of the meanings of words, but also acquire a knowledge of the relationships that exist between the meanings of different words. There are many kinds of lexical relation that can exist between the meanings of different words, including synonymy (e.g. *hide: conceal*), antonymy (e.g. *big: little*) hyponymy (e.g. *dog: animal*) and cohyponymy (e.g. *dog: cat*) (see Lyons, 1977). The only lexical relation to have received any explicit attention in studies of MHC is hyponymy, that is the subordinate–superordinate relationship.

Perhaps the most useful theoretical account of subordination and superordination currently available in the psychological literature is that provided by Rosch (1977, 1978). Rosch points out that although objects can be categorized at a variety of different levels of generality (e.g. a kitchen table can be called either a *kitchen table*, a *table* or *furniture*), there is one particular level of categorization which seems to have a privileged position in the hierarchy; Rosch calls this privileged level the 'basic-level' of categorization. A basic-level category is the most general category in a categorical hierarchy to contain objects sharing many attributes (thus *table* is the basic-level category in the preceding hierarchy). The objects which are included in a basic-level category also share very few attributes with objects which belong to other adjacent basic-level categories (e.g. *chair, wardrobe,* etc.). Superordinate categories (e.g. *furniture*), which are more general than basic-level categories, contain many different kinds of object (e.g. tables, chairs, wardrobes, etc.) which tend to have very few attributes in common with one another. Subordinate categories (e.g. *kitchen table*), which are more specific than basic-level categories, resemble basic-level categories, in that they too include objects which have many attributes in common with one another; however, they differ from basic-level categories, in that these same attributes are also shared with objects which belong to other adjacent subordinate categories (e.g. *dining-room table*).

Rosch argues that basic-level categories are psychologically privileged because their particular attribute structure makes them much easier to distinguish and to process than either superordinate or subordinate categories. Consequently, they are the categorical level at which objects are usually first recognized during perception, and they are the level at which objects are most frequently named. In addition, Rosch argues that a basic-level category is also privileged from a psychological point of view because it is the most general category in a hierarchy for which a mental image can be formed which is representative of all the objects within that category, and because it is the most general category in a hierarchy to contain a set of objects which all permit similar actions to be performed upon them.

If superordinate and subordinate categories are more difficult to distinguish and to process than basic-level categories, then one question which arises in connection with the lexical knowledge of MHC is: do MHC experience particular difficulties with words denoting superordinate and subordinate categories (over and above any difficulties which they experience with words denoting basic-level categories)? One study which provides some evidence addressing this question has been conducted by Winters and Brzoska (1976). They showed pictures of objects to 24 mentally handicapped children ($CA = 11.9$ years, $MA = 8.5$ years, $IQ =$

71.6), and asked them to name the object in each picture and then to categorize it (i.e. to name the group to which the pictured object belonged). The same tasks were also given to NHC of variable MAs. It was found that the MHC performed similarly to NHC of a comparable MA on the labelling task (which would have drawn largely upon their knowledge of basic-level names), whereas they did not perform as well as NHC of a comparable MA on the categorization task (which drew more upon their knowledge of superordinate names).

Similar findings have also been obtained by Harrison, Budoff and Greenberg (1975). In their study a verbal association task was administered to 32 educable mentally handicapped children (CA = 14.4, IQ = 70); each child had to produce 25 verbal associations to ten different stimulus words. It was found that, in response to these stimulus words, the MHC produced as many synonyms and cohyponyms as a group of CA-matched NHC, but fewer superordinate and subordinate words than the NHC. It was also found that the MHC took longer to produce their verbal associations than the NHC.

Both of these studies therefore indicate that MHC may indeed experience particular difficulties with superordinate and subordinate words. Nevertheless, it should be noted that in these studies the MHC did still manage to produce some superordinate and subordinate words. Consequently, the question arises as to whether or not MHC mentally represent the meanings of the superordinate and subordinate words which they do acquire in a similar manner to NHC. The studies by Tager-Flusberg (1985, 1986), to which we have already referred, provide some evidence which addresses this question.

It will be recalled that Tager-Flusberg examined the lexical knowledge of a group of 14 MHC with various aetiologies (CA = 11.5 years, MA = 4.9 years, IQ = 44). To this end, she tested not only their production and comprehension of basic-level names (e.g. *boat* and *bird*), but also their production and comprehension of superordinate names (e.g. *food* and *tool*). She found that on all the tests involving superordinate names the MHC performed identically to a group of MA-matched NHC (e.g. the two groups of children were subject to exactly the same typicality effects when comprehending the superordinate names). In addition, Tager-Flusberg reports that exactly the same factors led both groups of children to produce subordinate names in her experiments (e.g. both groups of children were more likely to use subordinate names when labelling peripheral rather than typical exemplars of basic-level categories). These findings therefore suggest that MHC mentally represent the meanings of superordinate and subordinate names in a similar way to NHC (with the result that the production and the comprehension of these words by MHC and by NHC are subject to similar influences).

Given these two conclusions, that some MHC do acquire at least some superordinate and subordinate words and that these children mentally represent the meanings of these words in a similar way to NHC, a further question can then be asked: to what extent do these MHC also know about the semantic relationships which exist between the meanings of these superordinate and subordinate words and the meanings of basic-level words? One study which has addressed this particular question in a much more direct manner than any of the studies which have been described so far was conducted by Bender and Johnson (1979). They gave the following task to 54 educable mentally handicapped children (CA = 13.2 years, MA = 8.2 years, IQ = 62.2). Each child was first shown a series of pictures of objects and had either to say or to learn the appropriate (basic-level) name of each depicted object. The pictures were then removed, and the child had to recall the names of the objects when given another word as a retrieval cue. The cue words related to the target words in one of four different ways (see Figure 1.1): they could either be a close cohyponym (CC), a remote cohyponym (RC), a close superordinate (CS) or a remote superordinate (RS) (for example, when the target word was *apple*, the CC was *banana*, the RC was *hot-dog*, the CS was *fruit* and the RS was *food*).

Bender and Johnson found that retrieval of the target word was best when CS words were used as cues, next best when either CC or RS words were used and poorest of all when RC words were used. These results suggest that the children were using the cue words as points of entry to a hierarchically organized mental structure, with the effectiveness of each cue word being determined by its precise semantic relationship to, and distance

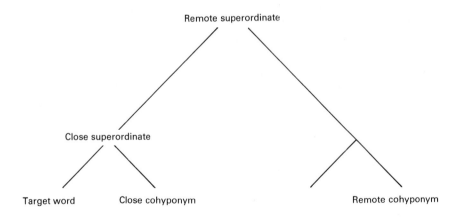

Figure 1.1: The semantic relationships between the cue words and the target words in the experiment by Bender and Johnson (1979).

from, the target word within that structure (see Figure 1.1). Thus it does indeed appear to be the case that at least some MHC have mental structures embodying a knowledge of superordinate–subordinate relationships. In addition, it should be noted that exactly the same results have also been obtained in another study in which NHC were used as subjects (Steinberg and Anderson, 1975); this would therefore seem to indicate that when MHC do acquire a knowledge of superordinate–subordinate relationships, they mentally represent that knowledge in a similar way to NHC.

The same conclusion also emerges from another study conducted by Davies, Sperber and McCauley (1981). They gave 20 educable mentally handicapped children (CA = 16.8 years, MA = 9.8 years, IQ = 67) two tasks to perform. In the first task children had to name pictures of objects as rapidly and as accurately as possible. Immediately prior to the presentation of each picture, the children heard one of two types of verbal prime — either a sentence which contained an appropriate superordinate word (e.g. *This is an animal*) or a sentence which expressed a neutral statement (*There is no clue for this*). It was found that the MHC labelled the pictures faster when they were preceded by a superordinate prime than when they were preceded by a neutral prime. Thus these children appeared to have a knowledge of the semantic relationship which existed between the superordinate words and the basic-level and subordinate names with which they were labelling the pictures (with the consequence that the perception of the superordinate word could prime the lexical entries of those basic-level and subordinate names for more rapid access).

The second task which Davies, Sperber and McCauley gave to these MHC used the following procedure. Each child was presented with a sentence which contained either a basic-level description of a picture (e.g. *This is a dog*) or a superordinate description of a picture (e.g. *This is an animal*). A picture was then presented and the child had to say as rapidly and accurately as possible either 'yes' (if the sentence correctly described the picture) or 'no' (if the sentence did not correctly describe the picture). It was found that the children could verify the basic-level descriptions faster than the superordinate descriptions; this finding supports the idea that, for these children, basic-level names are psychologically privileged compared to superordinates.

Davies, Sperber and McCauley also gave both these two tasks to a group of CA-matched NHC. They found that the NHC performed similarly to the MHC, that is they also exhibited superordinate priming and verified the basic-level descriptions faster than the superordinate descriptions. These two findings therefore provide further support for the idea that when MHC acquire a knowledge of superordinate–subordinate lexical relationships, that knowledge is essentially similar to the knowledge which is acquired by NHC.

However, Davies, Sperber and McCauley also report that, as a general rule, the NHC responded more quickly than the MHC, both on the picture labelling task and on the description verification task. It will be recalled that a similar finding was also obtained by Harrison, Budoff and Greenberg (1975), who found that their MHC took longer to produce verbal associations to stimulus words than CA-matched NHC. These findings therefore suggest that although MHC can acquire and mentally represent a knowledge of superordinate–subordinate relationships in a similar manner to NHC, these children may not always be able to utilize this knowledge as efficiently as NHC. Another study which provides further evidence supporting this conclusion has been reported by Glidden and Mar (1978).

In the first of their experiments, Glidden and Mar tested a group of 40 mentally handicapped children (CA = 15.3 years, IQ = 60). These children were asked to retrieve as many instances of two superordinate categories (*sports* and *animals*) as they could. It was found that the MHC retrieved fewer instances of these two categories than a group of CA-matched NHC. The children were then given a list of 24 names of particular sports and animals; this list contained both high-frequency and low-frequency names. The children had to decide to which category each name belonged. Using this procedure, which entailed recognition rather than recall of the category instances, it was found that the MHC performed as well as the NHC on the high-frequency names (but apparently not as well as the NHC on the low-frequency names).

In their second experiment, Glidden and Mar tested a group of 21 educable mentally handicapped children (CA = 15.9 years, IQ = 64.6) in order to find out whether the provision of intermediate superordinate cues (e.g. *birds, insects, pets*, etc.) would help them to retrieve instances of the category *animals*. It was found that the external provision of such cues did indeed improve the children's retrieval performance. However, this improvement in performance was not subsequently carried over into another retrieval test in which the intermediate superordinate cues were no longer provided externally by the experimenter; this suggests that the MHC were unable to adopt this more efficient retrieval strategy spontaneously.

To summarize, then, it is clear that MHC sometimes acquire a knowledge of superordinate and subordinate words, although this knowledge is probably not as advanced as their knowledge of basic-level words (Winters and Brzoska, 1976; Harrison, Budoff and Greenberg, 1975). In all likelihood, the meanings of superordinate and subordinate words are mentally represented by MHC in the same way as by NHC (Tager-Flusberg, 1985, 1986); MHC who acquire superordinate words also appear to represent mentally the semantic relationships which exist between the meanings of these words and the meanings of basic-level words in the same way as NHC (Bender and Johnson, 1979; Davies, Sperber and McCauley 1981). There is no comparable evidence yet available concerning MHC's representations of the relationships between basic-level words and subordinate words. However, it appears that MHC are not as efficient in the utilization of their semantic knowledge as CA-matched NHC (Harrison, Budoff and Greenberg, 1975; Davies, Sperber and McCauley, 1981; Glidden and Mar, 1978); whether or not they can utilize their semantic knowledge as efficiently as younger MA-matched NHC has not yet been investigated. Some of the difficulties which MHC encounter in retrieving semantic information can be partially alleviated by giving these children recognition rather than recall tasks, and cued rather than uncued recall tasks (Glidden and Mar, 1978). However, some of the other difficulties which are experienced by MHC may be much more intractable, as these children seem to process semantic information far less efficiently than CA-matched NHC, particularly as indexed by their semantic processing times (Harrison, Budoff and Greenberg, 1975; Davies, Sperber and McCauley, 1981).

It should be noted, however, that all but one of the preceding conclusions have been derived from studies which have used only mildly handicapped children as subjects (the exception here is the conclusion drawn from the studies by Tager-Flusberg, 1985, 1986; these two studies tested moderately handicapped children instead). As a consequence, it must be borne in mind that these conclusions only apply to mildly handicapped children; we still have no knowledge on the majority of these issues as far as moderately and more severely handicapped children are concerned.

Thus further studies are still required to investigate the knowledge that more severely handicapped children may have of superordinate and subordinate lexical relations. Additional studies are also required to explore the acquisition of lexical relations other than hyponymy by all MHC. We currently have just a few tiny scraps of information concerning MHC's knowledge of synonymy and cohyponymy (e.g. the information reported by Harrison, Budoff and Greenberg, 1975, and Bender and Johnson, 1979), and no real information at all concerning their knowledge of antonymy. Thus MHC's knowledge of lexical relations is an area which clearly stands in need of a great deal of further research.

1.5 CONCLUSION

From the research reviewed in this chapter, we can now draw the following general conclusions. First, it appears to be the case that although MHC may begin to learn the meanings of words at the same MA as NHC, they soon start to fall behind MA-matched NHC in their lexical development. This lag in lexical development appears to continue throughout childhood. However, with the additional life experience that is acquired with increasing years, some mentally handicapped adults may eventually overtake MA-equivalent NHC in the size of their vocabularies. In addition, it appears that vocabulary growth in MHC is not just slower than in NHC; vocabulary growth in MHC is very uneven when compared against the non-handicapped norm. Consequently, at any given point in development the total lexical resources of a mentally handicapped child may differ from those of a younger non-handicapped child.

Secondly, there is no evidence yet available to suggest that MHC with different syndromes display qualitatively different patterns of lexical development. However, the available data-base on this issue is extremely weak, with only DS vs non-DS comparisons having been made. Additional research is still required to investigate this issue properly.

Thirdly, we are now beginning to obtain some idea of how MHC acquire and mentally represent the meanings of object names. These meanings appear to be acquired and mentally represented by these children in the form of prototypical referential exemplars; as a consequence, both the production and the comprehension of these words by MHC are subject to a variety of typicality effects. This conclusion implies that the optimal way in which to facilitate the acquisition of the meanings of object names by MHC is by reference to typical referents (which bear a high degree of resemblance to prototypical referential exemplars) rather than by reference to both typical and peripheral referents (as the latter are more likely to hinder the acquisition of the appropriate prototypes). However, this implication still needs to be tested with populations other than severely handicapped children. Also, we still have no real idea of how the meanings of any other types of words are acquired and mentally represented by MHC; this area therefore stands in need of a great deal of further research.

Finally, we have seen that the only lexical relation to have received any real attention in MHC is hyponymy. It appears that mildly MHC do acquire a knowledge of not just basic-level words, but also superordinate and subordinate words (although their knowledge of these latter words is probably not as advanced as their knowledge of basic-level words). In addition, these children do appear to represent mentally the semantic relationships which exist between the meanings of these different words. However, no research seems to have been conducted into how these MHC actually acquire their knowledge of superordinate–subordinate lexical relations, nor into how the acquisition of lexical relations by MHC can be facilitated. There is also virtually no research that has ben conducted into the acquisition of lexical relations by moderately and more severely handicapped children.

Consequently, if there is any single conclusion which should be drawn from this chapter, it is that the topic of lexical development in mentally handicapped children has been vastly underinvestigated to date. It is clear that until further research is conducted to rectify this situation, we will remain ignorant on several very fundamental issues concerning these children's language acquisition.

NOTE

1. Type-token ratios (TTRs) are essentially a measure of lexical diversity. Thus, the greater the number of different word types which are present in a speech sample consisting of a fixed number of word tokens, then the higher the TTR, and the more varied and diverse is the vocabulary which occurs in that sample. In addition, because one would normally expect a person with a large vocabulary to be capable of producing speech which is more lexically diverse than someone with a small vocabulary, TTRs are often interpreted (particularly in the literature on MHC) as indexing vocabulary size.

REFERENCES

Barrett, M.D. (1981) The communicative functions of early child language, *Linguistics, 19*, 273–305.

Barrett, M.D. (1982) Distinguishing between prototypes: the early acquisition of the meanings of object names in *Language Development. Volume 1, Syntax and Semantics* (ed. S.A. Kuczaj), Lawrence Erlbaum, Hillsdale, NJ, pp. 313–34.

Barrett, M.D. (1986) Early semantic representations and early word-usage in *The Development of Word Meaning* (eds S.A. Kuczaj and M.D. Barrett), Springer-Verlag, New York, pp. 39–67.

Barrett, M.D. (in press (a)) Early language development in *Infant Development* (eds A. Slater and J.G. Bremner), Lawrence Erlbaum, Hillsdale, NJ.

Barrett, M.D. (in press (b)) Lexical contrasts and the rescission of object name over-extensions, *J. Child Language.*

Bartel, N.R., Bryen, D. and Keehn, S. (1973) Language comprehension in the moderately retarded child, *Exceptional Children, 39*, 375–82.

Beier, E.G., Starkweather, J.A. and Lambert, M.J. (1969) Vocabulary usage of mentally retarded children, *Am. J. Ment. Defic., 73*, 927–34.

Bender, N.N. and Johnson, N.S. (1979) Hierarchical semantic organization in educable mentally retarded children, *J. Experimental Child Psychol., 27*, 277–85.

Benedict, H. (1979) Early lexical development: comprehension and production, *J. Child Language, 6*, 183–200.

Bless, D., Swift, E. and Rosen, M. (1985) Communication profiles of children with Down syndrome, unpublished paper; cited by Miller (in press).

Bowerman, M. (1978) The acquisition of word meaning: an investigation into some current conflicts in *The Development of Communication* (eds C. Snow and N. Waterson), Chichester, Wiley, pp. 263–87.

Cardoso-Martins, C. and Mervis, C.B. (1985) Maternal speech to prelinguistic children with Down syndrome, *Am. J. Ment. Defic., 89*, 451–8.

Cardoso-Martins, C., Mervis, C.B. and Mervis, C.A. (1985) Early vocabulary acquisition by children with Down syndrome, *Am. J. Ment. Defic., 90*, 177–84.

Carey, S. (1982) Semantic development: the start of the art in *Language Acquisition: The State of the Art* (eds E. Wanner and L.R. Gleitman), Cambridge University Press, Cambridge, pp. 347–89.

Clark, E.V. (1973) Non-linguistic strategies and the acquisition of word meanings, *Cognition, 2*, 161–82.

Clark, E.V. (1983) Meanings and concepts in *Cognitive Development* (eds J.H. Flavell and E.M. Markman); *Handbook of Child Psychology* (ed. P. Mussen), 4th edn, Wiley, Chichester, pp. 787–840.

Coggins, T.E. (1979) Relational meaning encoded in the two-word utterances of stage 1 Down's syndrome children, *J. Speech Hearing Res.*, *22*, 166–78.

Cook, N. (1977) Semantic development in children with Down's syndrome, paper presented at Eighty-fifth Annual Convention of the American Psychological Association, San Francisco, Calif., USA; cited by Rondal (1984).

Cunningham, C.C. and Sloper, P. (1984) The relationship between maternal ratings of first word vocabulary and Reynell language scores, *Br. J. Educational Psychol.*, *54*, 160–7.

Davies, D., Sperber, R.D. and McCauley, C. (1981) Intelligence-related differences in semantic processing speed, *J. Exp. Child Psychol.*, *31*, 387–402.

Dooley, J.F. (1976) Language acquisition and Down's syndrome: a study of early semantics and syntax, unpublished doctoral dissertation, Harvard University, Cambridge, Mass., USA.

Furth, H.G. and Milgram, N.A. (1965) The influence of language on classification: a theoretical model applied to normal, retarded, and deaf children, *Genet. Psychol. Monogr.*, *72*, 317–51.

Gillham, B. (1979) *The First Words Language Programme: A Basic Language Programme for Mentally Handicapped Children*, Allen and Unwin, London.

Glenn, S.M. and Cunningham, C.C. (1982) Recognition of the familiar words of nursery rhymes by handicapped and non-handicapped infants, *J. Child Psychol. and Psychiat.*, *23*, 319–27.

Glidden, L.M. and Mar, H.H. (1978) Availability and accessibility of information in the semantic memory of retarded and nonretarded adolescents, *J. Expl. Child Psychol.*, *25*, 33–40.

Gopnik, A. (1987) Language before stage 6, paper presented at Fourth International Congress for the Study of Child Language, Lund, Sweden, July.

Harrison, R.H., Budoff, M. and Greenberg, G. (1975) Differences between EMR and nonretarded children in fluency and quality of verbal associations, *Am. J. Ment. Defic.*, *79*, 583–91.

Hupp, S.C. and Mervis, C.B. (1982) Acquisition of basic object categories by severely handicapped children, *Child Dev.*, *53*, 760–7.

Hupp, S.C., Mervis, C.B., Able, H. and Conroy-Gunter, M. (1986) Effects of receptive and expressive training of category labels on generalized learning by severely mentally retarded children, *Am. J. Ment. Defic.*, *90*, 558–65.

Kamhi, A.G. and Johnston, J.R. (1982) Towards an understanding of retarded children's linguistic deficiencies, *J. Speech Hearing Res.*, *25*, 435–45.

Kay, D.A. and Anglin, J.M. (1982) Overextension and underextension in the child's expressive and receptive speech, *J. Child Language*, *9*, 83–98.

Kuczaj, S.A. (1982) Young children's overextensions of object words in comprehension and/or production: support for a prototype theory of early object word meaning, *First Language*, *3*, 93–105.

Lozar, B., Wepman, J.M. and Hass, W. (1972) Lexical usage of mentally retarded and nonretarded children, *Am. J. Ment. Defic.*, *76*, 534–9.

Lozar, B., Wepman, J.M. and Hass, W. (1973) Syntactic indices of language use of mentally retarded and normal children, *Language and Speech*, *16*, 22–33.

Lyle, J.G. (1960) The effect of an institution environment upon the verbal development of imbecile children: II, Speech and language, *J. Ment. Defic. Res.*, *4*, 1–13.

Lyle, J.G. (1961) Comparison of the language of normal and imbecile children, *J. Ment. Defic. Res.*, *5*, 40–51.

Lyons, J. (1977) *Semantics*, Cambridge University Press, Cambridge, Vol. 1.

Mein, R. (1961) A study of the oral vocabularies of severely subnormal patients: II, Grammatical analysis of speech samples, *J. Ment. Defic. Res.*, *5*, 52–9.

Mein, R. and O'Connor, N. (1960) A study of the oral vocabularies of severely subnormal patients, *J. Ment. Defic. Res.*, *4*, 130–43.

Mervis, C.B. (1984) Early lexical development: the contributions of mother and child in *Origins of Cognitive Skills* (ed. C. Sophian), Lawrence Erlbaum, Hillsdale, NJ, pp. 339–70.

Miller, J.F. (in press) Language and communication characteristics of children with Down syndrome in *Down Syndrome: State of the Art* (eds A. Crocker, S. Paschal, J. Rynders and C. Tinghey) Brooks, Baltimore, Md.

Miller, J.F., Chapman, R.S. and Mackenzie, H. (1981) Individual differences in the language acquisition of mentally retarded children, paper presented at Second International Congress for the Study of Child Language, Vancouver, Canada, July; cited by Miller (in press).

Nelson, K. (1973) Structure and strategy in learning to talk, *Monographs of the Soc. for Res. in Child Dev.*, *38*, 1–2 (serial no. 149).

Papania, N. (1954) A qualitative analysis of the vocabulary responses of institutionalized mentally retarded children, *J. Clin. Psychol.*, *10*, 361–5.

Rogers, M.G.H. (1975) A study of language skills in severely subnormal children, *Child: Care, Health and Dev.*, *1*, 113–26.

Rondal, J.A. (1978) Maternal speech to normal and Down's syndrome children matched for mean length of utterance in *Quality of Life in Severely and Profoundly Mentally Retarded People: Research Foundations for Improvement* (ed. E. Meyers), American Association on Mental Deficiency Monograph No. 3, Washington, DC, pp. 193–265.

Rondal, J.A. (1984) Linguistic and prelinguistic development in moderate and severe mental retardation in *Scient. Stud. in Ment. Retardation* (ed. J. Dobbing), Macmillan, London, pp. 323–45.

Rosch, E. (1977) Human categorization in *Adv. in Cross-Cultural Psychol.* (ed. N. Warren), Academic Press, London, Vol 1.

Rosch, E. (1978) Principles of categorization in *Cognition and Categorization* (eds, E. Rosch and B.B. Lloyd), Lawrence Erlbaum, Hillsdale, NJ, pp. 27–48.

Ryan, J. (1975) Mental subnormality and language development in *Foundations of Language Development: A Multidisciplinary Approach* (eds. E.H. Lenneberg and E. Lenneberg), Academic Press, New York, Vol. 2, pp. 269–77.

Ryan, J. (1977) The silence of stupidity in *Psycholinguistics: Developmental and Pathological* (eds J. Morton and J. Marshall), Cornell University Press, Ithaca, NY, pp. 101–24.

Steinberg, E.R. and Anderson, R.C. (1975) Hierarchical semantic organization in 6-year-olds, *J. Expl. Child Psychol.*, *19*, 544–53.

Tager-Flusberg, H. (1985) The conceptual basis for referential word meaning in children with autism, *Child Dev.*, *56*, 1167–78.

Tager-Flusberg, H. (1986) Constraints on the representation of word meaning: evidence from autistic and mentally retarded children in *The Development of Word Meaning* (eds. S.A. Kuczaj and M.D. Barrett), Springer-Verlag, New York, pp. 69–81.

Thompson, M.M. (1963) Psychological characteristics relevant to the education of the pre-school mongoloid child, *Ment. Retardation*, *1*, 148–151, 185–186.

Weil, C.M., McCauley, C. and Sperber, R.D. (1978) Category structure and semantic priming in retarded adolescents, *Am. J. Ment. Defic.*, *83*, 110–15.

Winters, J.J. and Brzoska, M.A. (1975) Development of lexicon in normal and retarded persons, *Psychol. Reps.*, *37*, 391–402.

Winters, J.J. and Brzoska, M.A. (1976) Development of the formation of categories by normal and retarded persons, *Developmental Psychol.*, *12*, 125–31.

2

Phonological Disorders and Mental Handicap

Barbara Dodd and Judy Leahy

Mentally handicapped children often suffer severe communication difficulties. They not only have problems in comprehending and generating
language, but they also frequently produce speech that is difficult to understand. This chapter is concerned with the phonological abilities of mentally
handicapped children: that is, with their ability to produce and sequence
the sounds of language. A clinical research study is presented which
measured the efficacy of a parent-centred intervention programme for
phonologically disordered Down's syndrome children. This showed that
unintelligible speech is not a corollary of that condition.

2.1 PHONOLOGY DEFINED

Speech is a code. The units of the code are phonemes (speech sounds).
Each language combines phonemes in particular sequences to make words
(symbols for concepts), and the words are combined in specific ways (syntax) to convey meaning. A phoneme is not an acoustic entity, since the way
a phoneme sounds depends upon where it occurs in a word ($/k/$ in *kill* is
spectrographically very different from $/k/$ in *dark*), and also according to
who is speaking (children compared to adults). Rather a phoneme is a
linguistic abstraction. It is defined as the smallest distinctive unit that distinguishes between words. For example, $/r/$ and $/l/$ are two phonemes in
English because they can be used to differentiate between the meanings
conveyed by *lip* and *rip*. However, in some languages $/l/$ and $/r/$ are
considered to be only one phoneme, leading to native Japanese speakers
making particular errors when they learn English, e.g. *rip-reading* for *lip-
reading*. They perceive $/l/$ and $/r/$ as one speech sound.

2.2 NORMAL PHONOLOGICAL DEVELOPMENT

When children learn to talk, they have to master the rules of the phonological system of their native language. They not only have to learn how to articulate the set of phonemes that constitute their language, but also the constraints that govern the ways in which phonemes may be combined. For example, in English certain consonant clusters, such as $/sv/$ and $/sb/$, do not occur, and $/\eta/$ cannot occur in a word-initial position. In Japanese the only word-final consonant is $/n/$. That is, all languages not only have their own set of phonemes, but also a set of rules that governs how these phonemes may be combined to structure words.

Until they are about 6 years old, most children make speech errors. Some of these errors can be attributed to motor difficulty in articulating specific sounds, e.g. even some adults substitute $/w/$ for $/r/$. Other errors may be due to children not perceiving a word adequately, and mentally representing its phonological form incorrectly. One child referred to a pet rabbit as $/fam/$ although its name was *Fang*, but at that time she usually realised $/\eta/$ as $/n/$ as in *ran* for *rang*, *sin* for *sing*, etc. (Dodd, 1975a). However, most errors cannot simply be explained in terms of these two factors. Studies have shown that the ability of children to discriminate perceptually between minimally paired words, like *pin* and *bin*, *ship* and *chip*, is excellent by 18 months of age (Svachkin, 1948; Barton, 1976). Further, whether a phoneme is pronounced correctly or in error depends on where it occurs within an utterance, so that while $/s/$ may be correct in *sun*, it may be deleted as in *poon* for *spoon*, and while $/d/$ may be realized as $/g/$ before syllabic $/l/$, it may be correct elsewhere.

Analyses of normal developmental errors (Smith, 1973; Dodd, 1975a; Ingram, 1976; Grunwell, 1981) reveal that they are systematic, and can be described in terms of rules or processes. For example, early in phonological acquisition all words have a CVCV canonical form, and consonant harmony (use of only one consonant per word as in *tat* for *cat*, *lellow* for *yellow*) is a dominant process. Consonant clusters are reduced in a consistent fashion, e.g. $/s/$ deletes preconsonantally; $/l, r, w/$ delete postconsonantally as in *tain* for *train*, *bu* for *blue*. It is as if children use a set of phonological constraints to govern word production. As their experience of language expands and they mature neurologically, they become more aware of the nature of the phonology of their native language, and come to use the accepted, correct set of constructions.

2.3 CLASSIFICATION OF PHONOLOGICAL DISORDERS

Not all childen learn phonology with ease. About 3% of the normal infant and primary school population are phonologically disordered (Kirkpatrick and Ward, 1984). For many years these children were considered to be a homogeneous group, although there are many labels that describe the disorder such as dyslalia, articulation disorder, verbal dyspraxia, dysphonology. Although some researchers suggest that speech-disordered children could be divided into delayed and disordered groups (Ingram, 1976; Leonard, 1979), there has been no investigation of the factors underlying the two types of disorder, nor of the efficacy of different therapeutic techniques. However, recent research indicates that it is possible to distinguish three subgroups of phonological disorder (Dodd, 1982).

(a) Delayed group

The phonological development of some children is delayed. That is, they follow the normal course of development, but at an inappropriate rate, so that 6-year-olds may be using phonological systems typical for 3-year-olds. While for most of these children there is spontaneous change along normal lines, some exhibit arrested development — i.e. their phonology becomes frozen at an immature level.

(b) Deviant consistent group

Another group of children have rule-governed phonology, but the rules used do not occur in normal development (Compton, 1970). They seem to have abstracted the wrong organizing principles, e.g. deletion of all word-initial consonants, use of a glottal stop to mark all word-medial consonants. These children have deviant development, but their errors are predictable and consistent.

(c) Deviant inconsistent group

A third, small group have inconsistent errors, many of which are deviant rather than developmental. Such children are likely to pronounce the same word in a variety of different ways, e.g. pronouncing *horse* as *shorsh, os, orsi* and *osh* in one assessment session. Inconsistent errors are characteristic of adult verbal dyspraxia (impaired programming of voluntary motor movements), which follows brain damage (Darley, Aronson and Brown, 1975). Thus the label developmental verbal dyspraxia is sometimes used to describe these children (Parsons, 1984). But the adult and developmental forms of the disorder have other, different characteristics. The children are fluent, speaking in sentences, and often unaware that they are unintel-

35

ligible. They do not grope for the correct articulation. They have no auditory discrimination difficulties. Typically, the adults are non-fluent, are aware of their errors, their articulatory movements show groping, and they may also have auditory discrimination problems. It is likely therefore that the developmental disorder is linguistic, rather than motor. This type of error pattern is typical of the speech of Down's syndrome children and adults.

There is now evidence that phonological disorders are the result of a cognitive impairment (Dodd and Cockerill, 1986). Further evidence that phonological errors arise at a central, rather than a peripheral, point in the speech-processing chain comes from studies showing that grammatical class and semantic complexity can affect errors (Camarata and Schwartz, 1985). That is, the difficulties rarely arise from problems in perceiving or articulating sounds. Rather the unintelligibility arises from an impaired or incomplete understanding of the constraints of the phonological system to be acquired. Mental handicap is likely therefore to be associated with disordered phonology.

2.4 INCIDENCE OF DISORDERS IN THE MENTALLY HANDICAPPED POPULATION

Most surveys indicate a markedly high incidence of speech defects in the mentally handicapped population. The estimates vary from 25% (Burt, 1937) to 95% (Schlanger and Gottsleben, 1957), according to the criteria used and the population tested. In one recent study (Leeming *et al.*, 1979) severely mentally handicapped children aged between 7 and 14 years were rated by their class teacher and by a stranger as producing speech that was unintelligible, mostly unintelligible, mostly intelligible and intelligible. Of those children who had spoken language, 19.5% were rated unintelligible or mostly unintelligible by their teachers, whereas strangers rated 27.7% of the children unintelligible or mostly unintelligible. This indicates that familiarity with the children's speech influences estimates of incidence. However, studies have rarely discriminated between phonological disorder on the one hand, and defective speech due to other factors such as hearing loss, peripheral motor deficits and anatomical abnormality on the other hand. Thus the real incidence of phonological disorders is as yet unknown. A variety of factors determines the degree of severity and type of phonological disorder associated with mental handicap. The most important of these are: cause of handicap, degree of cognitive impairment and type of care.

(a) Cause of mental handicap

Certain aetiological groups of mental handicap are reported to vary in their ability to produce intelligible speech. For example, the Down's syndrome population is particularly prone to disordered phonology (Schlanger and Gottsleben, 1957) and many of them exhibit deviant inconsistent errors (Dodd, 1976a). Goertzen (1957) suggested that children with acquired brain damage were likely to be more severely phonologically disordered than congenitally mentally handicapped children, although this was dependent upon the degree of speech development before injury.

(b) Degree of mental handicap

The incidence of speech disorder rises as the measured level of intelligence falls (Schiefelbusch, 1972). While children in the 50–70 IQ range have delayed onset of language development, their phonology often develops spontaneously, if slowly, and follows the normal course. Children with a greater degree of mental handicap are more likely to have disordered phonology.

(c) Type of care

The highest incidence figures for speech impairment are found among the institutionalized mentally handicapped. Although these children are likely to be the most severely handicapped, and therefore to have poorer language skills than home-reared children, there is evidence that the type of language learning experience available in institutions affects acquisition negatively (McNutt and Leri, 1979). There is also evidence that even children reared at home may be exposed to language interactions that do not maximize their language learning potential (Buim, Rynders and Turnure, 1974; Cross, 1981). These studies suggest that the language learning environment is a very important determinant of the type and rate of language acquisition.

2.5 FACTORS CONTRIBUTING TO UNINTELLIGIBLE SPEECH

Although unintelligible speech is associated with mental handicap, many researchers hold that the relationship is not directly causal (e.g. Kastein, 1956). Alternative explanations of the association are: that the communication disorder and the mental handicap may both be due to a common cause (Berry and Eisenson, 1962); that impaired language abilities may lead to a child being classified as mentally handicapped (Fawcus, 1965); and that factors commonly associated with mental handicap, such as hearing loss or behavioural disorders, may underly the communication impairment (Matthews, 1957). To examine the causes of phonological disorders among the mentally handicapped population, it is necessary to examine those factors associated with defective speech, distinguishing between phonological disorders that are cognitively based and speech unintelligibility because of difficulties in the articulation of speech sounds.

(a) Abnormal oral anatomy

It is a common lay assumption that speech impediments are due to malfunction of malformation of the speech-producing mechanism. For example, early treatments for stammering often involved oral surgery or prostheses. In fact research clearly shows that anatomical abnormalities have to be gross, e.g. cleft lip and palate, before the ability to articulate speech sounds is impaired (Fawcus, 1965). Nevertheless, oral surgery is currently being used as a way of treating the unintelligible speech of Down's syndrome children (Olbrisch, 1982). The justification put foward is that Down's children have large tongues that cannot be contained within the oral cavity, and that this precludes the normal articulatory movement necessary for speech. Surgery involves removing a section of the blade of the tongue, and post-operative complications include excessive bleeding, nerve damage and swelling of the tongue such that it impedes breathing (Lemperle and Radu, 1980).

The arguments against such an approach to the treatment of unintelligible speech are compelling. There is no evience that Down's syndrome people's tongues are larger than those of the normal population (Ardran, Harker and Kemp, 1973). The tongue may appear large because it sometimes protrudes, but this is due to low motor tone, not size. The type of speech errors made by Down's syndrome children, and the fact that they are better at imitation than in spontaneous speech production (Lenneberg, 1967; Dodd, 1976a) is consistent with a phonological disorder, and not with speech errors due to anatomical abnormality. Surgery should, then, have no effect on speech. Confirming this, a forthcoming study by Iacano, Parsons, and Rozner clearly demonstrates that children make the same number and type of speech errors after surgery as they do before.

(b) Chronic physiological disorders

There are two common physiological conditions that contribute to speech unintelligibility among the mentally handicapped. One is chronic upper respiratory tract infection (URTI) that leads to blockage of the nasal cavity with catarrh. In turn, this results in a lack of nasal resonance that distorts speech sound, and in mouth breathing. Since it is difficult to talk and breathe through the mouth simultaneously, speech phrasing and prosody are disrupted, contributing to unintelligibility. Another common problem is that of motor difficulties such as spasticity or flaccidity. Even very slight disturbances in muscle tone can affect clarity, since the movements required for speech articulation are rapid and precise and involve a large number of muscles. Both of these conditions can co-exist with phonological disorders, but by themselves are peripheral articulatory difficulties, not cognitive ones.

(c) Hearing loss

The mentally handicapped are more likely to suffer from hearing loss than the normal population (Webb and Kinde, 1967). However, early research may have overestimated the real incidence of hearing loss because the testing techniques employed did not take into account task difficulty (Fulton and Lloyd, 1969). A recent survey (Murphy, 1978) found that 6.1% of mentally handicapped children with an IQ in the 50–70 range suffered hearing loss, compared with 10.8% of more severely handicapped children. These figures are well above the average for schoolchildren with normal intelligence, where only 0.1% have been found to suffer a hearing loss (HMSO, 1976).

Deafness and mental handicap are conditions that are sometimes confused since both may be associated with an imperfect or inadequate use of heard speech (Waldon, 1968). If a child suffers from both conditions, even if the hearing loss is mild and variable, the effect on speech intelligibility is likely to be serious. One reason for this is that the child comes to rely more on vision for information about the world, and fails to develop adequate auditory attention. However, even profoundly deaf children can develop a phonological system, albeit slowly, and typically follow the normal course of acquisition (Dodd, 1976b). A detailed phonological analysis of the type of speech errors made can, then, provide clues about the extent to which a child's speech disorder is due to hearing loss. For example, a Down's syndrome child who has a recurrent mild loss and inconsistent and deviant speech errors has a phonological disorder that cannot be solely attributed to the hearing loss.

(d) The language learning environment

Current language acquisition theory holds that the most important aspect of that process is the interaction between mother and child (McLean and

Snyder-McLean, 1978). As primary caregivers, mothers are thought to adjust their language structure (syntax, vocabulary, topic, speech rate and prosody) to suit their child's linguistic competence (Gunn, Clark and Berry, 1980). There is some evidence, although it is controversial (e.g. Rondal, 1978), that mothers of developmentally delayed children may not provide their children with appropriate language experience.

Buim, Rynders and Turnure (1974) found that Down's syndrome children were exposed to a greater number of utterances that were shorter in length, and less likely to be grammatically complete, than were normal children. They were also exposed to more imperative sentences and single-word utterances, and fewer syntactic complexities such as indefinite pronouns, WH questions and conjunctions. Other studies have found that mothers of language-delayed children may contribute to that delay by restricting the amount of commenting, modelling and feedback (Price, 1983), and by failing to follow the child's conversational topic (Cross, 1981). However, Conti-Ramsden (1985) has pointed out that many such studies are methodologically flawed. In some studies the subject groups were heterogeneous in terms of aetiology and linguistic skill, and control groups were sometimes chronologically age matched rather than language or mental age matched. Further, the reciprocal nature of social interaction between mother and child means that if a child fails to develop language appropriately, the mother's language is affected. Although no one seems to have examined the amount and type of feedback given about word pronunciation, it seems likely that since most parents and teachers seek meaning in children's speech, they may be unaware of the pronunciation errors. Thus caregivers may not be providing the type of language learning experience that maximizes the phonological learning potential of mentally handicapped children.

Another aspect of the language learning environment that has been examined is the nature of current classroom-based intervention programmes for mentally handicapped children. In recent years the approach to teaching speech and language has focused on the acquisition of syntax, with consequent neglect of functional language use including phonology (see Wulz, Hall and Klein, 1983, for review). The programmes have reported success, in that measures of vocabulary, mean length of utterance and acquisition of syntactic forms of show steady improvement. Other studies have shown that this type of language teaching intervention produces better results than if children are left to acquire language spontaneously, or even provided with a generally stimulating environment (Mittler, 1974; Fenn, 1976).

However, recent research suggests that these programmes have severe limitations (Wulz, Hall and Klein, 1983). Although children can acquire certain language skills as responses after intensive training (Robson, 1984), they fail to use that language spontaneously to communicate their thoughts and needs (Lovaas *et al.*, 1973; Bloch, Gersten and Korblum, 1980). The training of speech responses was easier than teaching the spontaneous use of language in non-training situations (Guess, Keogh and Sailor, 1978). One reason why children may be unwilling to make use of the language they have been taught is that while their speech may be intelligible in context, they may have learnt that their speech is unintelligible functionally, and thus resort to gesture.

(e) Phonological development and cognition

Early studies of the phonological abilities of mentally handicapped children were reviewed by Matthews (1957). He concluded that the evidence indicated that the type of speech errors made were, in general, similar to those made by phonologically disordered children of normal intelligence. Most of these studies used a taxonomic approach, listing those speech sounds most prone to error irrespective of their phonetic context. Dever (1966) criticized the taxonomic approach to analysing phonological errors. He suggested that it would be better to describe the 'dialect' used since it would provide better data for evaluating differences between normal and handicapped children. More recent studies have described the phonological systems of mentally handicapped children in terms of rules or processes.

Dodd (1976a) compared groups of ten normal, ten Down's syndrome and ten non Down's syndrome, non-epileptic mentally handicapped children, matched for mental age (of 3.5 years) and social and educational background. The two mentally handicapped groups were also matched for chronological age of 10.5 years. All subjects who took part in the study had some spoken language while none had any hearing loss or gross motor impairment of the vocal apparatus. The subjects were shown pictures of familiar objects and asked to name them, and then to imitate the experimenter's naming of the same pictures. The tape recorded utterances were independently transcribed by two speech pathologists, and only those utterances transcribed identically in terms of consonants were used as data. The analyses showed that the non Down's syndrome group and the mental age matched normal group did not differ. They made the same number of errors, the errors were of the same type, and error types were used consistently. The Down's syndrome group performed poorly in comparison. They made more errors than the other two groups, and their errors were inconsistent. They also made significantly fewer errors in imitation than in spontaneous naming. Another factor which may influence intelligibility is the size of a child's vocabulary (Ingram, 1987). The more words used, the greater the need for marking the phonological contrast between words. A phonologically disordered child with a small vocabulary may be better understood than one with similar phonological competence but a larger

Table 2.1: Mean number of errors and error types, according to group

	Normal controls	Mental handicap	Down's syndrome
Spontaneous trial			
Errors	23.0	18.8	46.4
Error types	8.4	9.0	15.6
Imitation trial			
Errors	21.6	15.4	41.4
Error types	9.7	9.0	15.7

vocabulary. (See Table 2.1.) This study confirms Lenneberg's findings that Down's syndrome children are better at imitation than in spontaneous speech, and that their speech is poor in comparison to other mentally handicapped children and also in terms of their syntactic competence. Jarvis (1980) found that Down's syndrome adults showed a similar pattern of performance.

The results suggest that the phonological development of mentally handicapped children is slow, being linked to mental age, but that it follows the normal course of development in terms of number and type of errors. That is, the phonological disorder of most mentally handicapped children is one of delay rather than deviance. The major exception to this general pattern is the Down's syndrome population, whose phonological systems are often not appropriate for their mental age, and are characterized by inconsistent, deviant errors. This means that their speech is particularly difficult to understand, and also difficult to remediate. The remainder of this chapter is concerned with the phonological difficulties of Down's syndrome children.

2.6 CLINICAL RESEARCH STUDY: THE EFFICACY OF PARENT-CENTRED INTERVENTION

(a) The problem

Typically the speech of Down's syndrome children is characterized by inconsistent, deviant errors (Dodd, 1976a). That is, every time they say a word they are likely to pronounce it differently. They have poor functional language because their speech is unintelligible. Their phonological skills lag behind their syntactic and semantic skills (Lenneberg, 1967). A number of factors can exacerbate their phonological difficulty including chronic URTI, low motor tone, fluctuating hearing loss and mental handicap (above). One explanation of the inconsistency of their errors may be that they have a specific motor memory deficit.

In one study, Dodd (1975b) compared two groups of subjects, ten Down's syndrome children and ten non Down's syndrome mentally handicapped children matched for chronological age of 9 years, IQ (range 30–59) and educational experience. Each subject attended two testing sessions. In one session their ability to recognize real and nonsense words was tested, and in the other session their ability to imitate these words was measured. The effect of immediate response as compared with a delayed response of 15–30 s was also tested. The results indicated that Down's syndrome children were slightly better at recognizing real and nonsense words than the other mentally handicapped children. This finding indicated that the atypical phonology of Down's syndrome children's cannot be attributed to an inability to store and recognize auditory information.

However, the Down's group performed poorly on the word-reproduction task. Their imitative ability did not differ from the control group when the response was required immediately, but when a delay was introduced their ability to remember how to say words deteriorated (see Table 2.2). A comparison of the subjects' performance on real vs nonsense words showed that while the non Down's children made fewer changes in the way they pronounced real words than nonsense words over the three delays, the Down's subjects performed equally badly on both types of words, i.e. prior experience of words was of no advantage to them. It was as if each time they say a word it is for the first time. These findings suggested that the Down's syndrome subjects have a memory deficit for sequences of fine motor movements. This is in agreement with Frith and Frith (1974), who made similar findings using a pursuit rotor task. A remediation programme for phonology should therefore take into account the need to train motor memory.

Table 2.2: Mean correct scores for groups, accordng to response type, word type and length of delay

| | Delay: | | | | | |
| | Mentally handicapped | | | Down's syndrome | | |
	0 s	15 s	30 s	0 s	15 s	30 s
Recognition						
Real	7.8	7.9	6.0	8.8	7.8	7.9
Nonsense	7.2	7.1	6.0	8.2	7.6	6.8
Reproduction						
Real	10.0	9.6	6.9	9.8	6.0	4.2
Nonsense	9.6	8.7	6.1	9.4	4.7	2.9

(b) The intervention approach

Dissatisfaction with the language skills of children taught in highly structured classroom or clinical settings has grown in recent years. Orlansky
claimed that such teaching environments provide 'virtually no opportunity
for exploration of the environment, spontaneous communication or
independent play' (1979, p. 254). Spontaneous speech can be considered
disruptive (Winnett and Winkler, 1972). The language taught can be stilted
and used to elicit a specific response in a task setting that has no analogue
in the target environment, i.e. the home and community.

Current theory holds that language acquisition is the result of a process
of social interaction (e.g. Halliday, 1977; Snow, 1979). These interactions
occur around shared activities, the adult providing language appropriate
for the child's focus of attention and interest in a natural situation.
Language use is thus taught alongside form (grammar and vocabulary).
Wulz, Hall and Klein (1983) consider family-based teaching essential for
the acquisition of appropriate language by mentally handicapped children.
It seems obvious that successful intervention for disordered phonology
should also involve parents as agents of therapy.

However, parents of handicapped children do not necessarily provide
optimal speech and language experience for their children. For example,
Cheseldine and McConkey (1979) report that parents of Down's syndrome
children do not structure their interactions with their children to maximize
language learning. They concluded that parental expectations of language
progress were too limited. Further, parents do not often perceive themselves as being an active and essential part of their child's language learning, seeing their role as supplementary to that of professionals. They are
often asked to repeat tasks that have been devised for structured teaching
at home, to 'enhance generalisation' (Baker, 1976). Parents report that
these sessions are time-consuming and difficult to maintain (Baker, Heifetz
and Murphy, 1980). Also the formal nature of the home training restricts
rather than enhances generalization of language skills because, although
the sessions occur in the target environment, they are separate from the use
of language for social interaction.

An alternative approach is to teach parents to act as the agents of
therapy, by changing the nature of the adult–child interactions that are part
of daily routine. Wulz, Hall and Klein (1983) concluded that although the
natural interaction between parent and child as it exists before intervention
is not sufficient to enhance language acquisition, parents can effectively
change their child's linguistic behaviour once they are taught. Further,
parents generalize their training beyond what is specifically taught by
professionals, and continue training beyond the period of direct parent
training.

Hornby and Singh (1984) argue that training parents in groups is advantageous. Groups provide a mutually supportive atmosphere in which parents are more responsive, and more likely to change attitudes and learn new procedures. They provide a wider range of learning and management problems for discussion, providing a base for the handling of future difficulties. As the group teaching progresses artificial barriers between parents and professionals become less rigid, and parents become a source of ideas for management and thus develop greater self-esteem. Group training is also cost-effective (Tams and Eyeberg, 1976).

While parent-centred treatment programmes have been shown to be successful for the teaching of language (Wulz, Hall and Klein, 1983; Hornby and Singh (1984), no research so far has measured the efficacy of this approach for the remediation of disordered phonology. The study reported here evaluated that use of this approach, by teaching the parents of preschool Down's syndrome children to be the agents of therapy for their phonological disorder.

(c) Methodology

1. Subjects.

The subjects attended an early intervention programme for Down's syndrome children at the Macquarie University Special Education Unit. Initially a general meeting of all parents and teachers was held, and the aims and methods of the clinical research study were outlined. Parents of the eight older children (3.5 to 5 years) agreed that their children be assessed for possible inclusion in the study. These children were fully assessed (phonological, expressive and receptive language measures), and case histories were taken. One child had no functional language, although he could imitate some single words. Three made phonological errors that were delayed rather than deviant. Four made phonological errors that are typical of the Down's syndrome population. It is interesting that three of the children appeared to be following the normal course of phonological development. There is no clear-cut reason for this high level of delayed

Table 2.3: Clinical research study: subject information

Subjects	M.T.	B.H.	T.H.	T.S.
Age	4 yr 4 mth	3 yr 6 mth	3 yr 8 mth	4 yr 10 mth
Sex	F	F	M	M
Diagnosis	Trisomy 21	Trisomy 21	Trimsomy 21	Trisomy 21
Other problem	–	–	–	Visual

Note: All children had a history of recurring ear infections, but were under the management of ENT specialists.

rather than deviant acquisition. It may have been due to a combination of factors including the preschool intervention programme, parental concern over intelligibility and degree of handicap.

In a second interview parents were given an assessment report and asked to be part of the parent training group. They were told that only those four children with phonology typical of Down's syndrome would be included in the study proper, but all parents were welcome to attend the group sessions; the other four children's progress would also be monitored, though not in such detail. Six parents agreed to participate, the four mothers of the phonologically deviant children, the mother of the non-verbal child and one of the mothers of the delayed children. Table 2.3 sets out details of the experimental subjects.

The research design did not include a control group. The children acted as their own controls, in that despite having attended a preschool intervention programme for several years (children start attending before their first birthday), and in all four cases varying lengths of weekly speech therapy, their speech was unintelligible because of inconsistent deviant errors. Thus the success of the parent-centred approach to remediation had to be assessed in terms of change between baseline measures and status at the follow-up assessment.

2. The parent training group.

This consisted of the six mothers, two speech pathologists and one teacher from the intervention programme. A sociologist, the mother of a Down's syndrome child, whose research interest is concerned with the problems of parenting handicapped children, ran a discussion group once a fortnight for the mothers alone. She also attended some of the other sessions.

The group met weekly, except for the first week when two sessions were held, for $2\frac{1}{2}$ h. At least 1 h each week was set aside for discussion of parents' individual difficulties with their child. Although language acquisition, particularly phonology, was the focus of discussion, other problems such as the causes of Down's syndrome, management of hearing loss, opinion on surgical intervention for cosmetic reasons and behaviour were also raised by parents. After each child assessment (carried out at three-weekly intervals) a report was given to each parent, and each child's progress was discussed by the group. The group then planned home activities for each child that should be carried out over the following weeks.

Special teaching sessions occurred each week. Topics included: the speech-producing mechanism, phonetics, auditory training, management of hearing loss (by an audiologist), oral exercises for improving motor tone, teaching of techniques such as how to correct speech errors, how to provide positive feedback, how to cope with a child's failure to achieve a target, viewing and discussion of video tapes of teaching methods by special education teachers and speech pathologists, and discussion of videotapes of each parent interacting with her child. One equipment-making session was held to provide a basis for home equipment-making.

3. Therapeutic approach.

Since the greatest phonological problem was the inconsistency of the children's errors, it was decided to use a whole word approach to remediation. Ten words were selected as initial targets for each child. The ten words consisted of some words chosen by parents, usually names of family members and names for common foods and drinks, some powerful words included to stress the functional power of language (e.g. *more, yuk, no, can't*), and also some words to teach specific phonological regularities. For example, several children were not using a voice/voiceless distinction, voicing all sounds. These subjects were given word pairs such as *bee* and *pea, pat* and *bat, coat* and *goat, toe* and *dough*. One child who tended to omit word-initial consonants was given word pairs such as *egg* and *leg, egg* and *peg, eight* and *gate*.

Parents were told that only one pronunciation was allowed for each of these ten words; that is, the words did not have to be pronounced correctly, but if an error was made, it had always to be the same, developmental error. The words were to be elicited in game situations at home, as often as possible. Parents chose the activities, which included home-made picture lotto and snakes-and-ladders, hiding pictures around the room in an adaptation of treasure hunts, etc. Parents also only accepted the one pronunciation when the words occurred in spontaneous speech. Words of a high frequency of occurrence were selected whenever possible to increase the likelihood of spontaneous usage. As it became apparent that a child had mastered a word in the assessment sessions, new words were added to the list. The teacher representative who attended the group kept the early intervention programme staff informed about the target words and the children's progress. One meeting was held with the staff of the intervention programme during the parent training programme. They were concerned that mothers had been advised that the children needed to return to the one-word stage in the training activities in order to maximize phonological learning, and establish consistent production patterns. The teaching staff felt that such an approach ran counter to their policy of increasing mean length of utterance. The problem was solved by introducing sentence frames once words had been mastered in isolation, e.g. 'it's a ...', 'there's a ...', etc.

(d) Results

Parents were video taped and/or audio taped interacting with their child in a free play situation on seven occasions: once three weeks before the parent teaching programme began, five times during the running of the thirteen-week programme and once three months after the programme had ended. The data gained were transcribed by a speech pathologist, and five of the tapes were transcribed twice to check reliability of transcription by another speech pathologist or by a student trained in phonetics. Agreement was high, above 95%. For each session a minimum of 56 and a maximum of 152 intelligible utterances were analysed. In the early assessments several factors contributed to more of the utterances being classified as unintelligible than in the later assessments: the children's phonology was very inconsistent, making interpretation difficult; parents had not yet learnt to repeat what their child had just said to ensure correct perception, and provide a feedback model; and the transcribers were unfamiliar with some of the children's idiosyncratic productions, e.g. one child sometimes used jargon words in picture-naming tasks, producing / ɛsdeɪ/ as a response irrespective of the stimulus picture. However, this higher proportion of unintelligible utterances for the early sessions biased the results against finding an improvement in the children's phonology over time.

The transcriptions were analysed to find: the percentage of consonants produced correctly in spontaneous speech, and the percentage of errors that could be classed as acceptable developmental errors in spontaneous speech. Imitated utterances were excluded from the analysis because Down's syndrome children's imitation has been shown to be superior to their spontaneous production (above). The results are shown in Tables 2.4–2.6.

Statistical analysis was not carried out. The reults show that all four children made exceptional improvement in the number of consonants produced correctly over the thirteen weeks of the parent teaching programme. Further, the type of errors changed during the programme. At baseline, around 70% of the children's errors were classed as deviant, whereas by the final assessment less that 50% (mean 41%) of the errors were deviant. This indicates that the therapeutic approach used successfully encouraged the acquisition of developmentally normal phonological processes.

Table 2.4: Percentage correct consonants in spontaneous speech

Subject	Baseline	Assessments					Follow-up
		1st	2nd	3rd	4th	5th	
M.T.	27	36	40	54	66	62	63
B.H.	25	32	48	44	47	56	54
T.H.	33	35	51	50	60	69	64
T.S.	44	48	47	64	75	78	67

Table 2.5: Percentage of errors classed as normal developmental errors*

Subject	Baseline	Assessments					Follow-up
		1st	2nd	3rd	4th	5th	
M.T.	32	35	26	55	56	56	59
B.H.	26	32	37	32	52	57	58
T.H.	32	29	37	36	46	73	69
T.S.	17	39	48	59	38	50	59

*The following errors were classed as developmental (from Dodd, 1975a; Grunwell, 1981): 1, cluster reduction, e.g. *poon/spoon*, *bu/blue*, *tain/train*; 2, consonant harmony, e.g. *gog/dog*, *lellow/yellow*; 3, deletion processes: weak syllable deletion, e.g. *bella/umbrella*; *h* initially; 4, substitution processes: $f/v \rightarrow p/b$, $s/z \rightarrow t/d$, $r \rightarrow w$, $k/g \rightarrow t/d$, intervocalic t/k, glottal stop.

The analysis of data from the follow-up assessment session showed that the improvement made during the programme was not lost, but neither were further gains made. Other research using the parent-centred approach had indicated that parents continue home training with beneficial results (Hornby and Singh, 1984). The lack of continued improvement in phonological skills after the end of the parent teaching programme is disappointing. However, it does indicate that it was the programme itself that brought about the change measured during its thirteen-week trial. If the changes had been spontaneous, they would have continued.

(e) Discussion

The results indicate that the phonological disorder typical of Down's syndrome children can be successfully remediated, using parents who participate in a parent teaching programme as the agents of therapy. The success of the intervention programme gives rise to doubts about the cause of the typical phonological disorder of the Down's syndrome children. The

Table 2.6: Percentage consonants correct plus normal developmental errors

Subject	Baseline	Assessments					Follow-up
		1st	2nd	3rd	4th	5th	
M.T.	50	58	55	79	84	83	85
B.H.	44	54	67	62	80	80	81
T.H.	55	54	69	72	78	91	89
T.S.	48	68	72	85	84	88	86

disorder can be accounted for in terms of a motor memory deficit for sequences of fine motor movements (Dodd, 1976a). However, the relative ease with which the number and type of errors could be changed leads to the speculation that the environment may play an important role in the maintenance of the disorder.

The preschool intervention programme stressed syntactic and semantic learning, without attending to how words were pronounced. Consequently, parents and teachers were always seeking meaning, and accepted a variety of pronunciations for any particular word. It may seem reasonable to accept and try to interpret unintelligible verbalization in terms of the context in which it is uttered. However, such a strategy teaches children that pronunciation is unimportant. For example, at least one of the children in the study used a number of jargon words in naming tasks. These were accepted and reinforced, without listeners being aware that the child was not even attempting to produce a particular word. Functional communication is dependent upon intelligible speech. The development of intelligible speech is dependent on children grasping the concept that each lexical item consists of a specific string of phonemes. Listeners who accept a variety of phonological forms for any one word provide feedback that interferes with the development of this crucial concept.

However, if language experience were the primary cause of the disorder, then other mentally handicapped children should also be prone to inconsistent deviant phonology. Previous research indicates that their phonology is more likely to be delayed (Dodd, 1976b). It seems reasonable to conclude that some organic factor (e.g. cerebellar dysfunction; Frith and Frith, 1974) predisposes Down's syndrome children to inconsistent deviant phonology, but that the language environment can be structured to ameliorate the tendency. This may also explain why three of the children originally assessed showed delayed rather than deviant phonological development.

The design of the clinical trial does not allow its success to be attributed to any one factor. However, in discussion with those involved in the programme it seems likely that there were three crucial factors.

1. Parents as agents of therapy. Parents could provide daily practice, in a natural, functional setting. Their knowledge of their child's interests, behaviour and attention span allowed them to choose and time activities that allowed phonological learning to become fun rather than work. Their need to communicate verbally with their children maintained their high motivation. Further, their self-esteem was enhanced by being made responsible for their child's language learning.

2. Group parent teaching. In the study reported here all the mothers had known each other before the start of the programme. This had obvious advantages in the group discussions. The fact that they knew each other's children also meant that their suggestions for games and coping strategies were usually sound. The mutual support they provided was tempered by an unexpected spirit of competition for their child to achieve the targets set. The group situation was valuable because it broke down the usual inhibition between parent and professional, allowing the mothers to express doubts about aspects of the programme, and to ask for explanations and justifications of therapeutic strategies suggested.

3. *The therapeutic approach.* The choice of whole words as the phonological unit taught was important for children with inconsistent deviant errors. Research in progress suggests that other approaches (phoneme level, phonological process level) are less effective in remediating this type of phonological disorder. Targeting words, initially in isolation, then in sentence frames and spontaneous speech, allowed the integrated teaching of phonology, vocabulary and syntax. Setting a small number of targets, especially since mothers helped choose them, provided feasible and concrete goals. The choice of high-frequency, powerful words (e.g. *won't*, *yuk*) taught children the power of functional language.

Regular assessment of the children was extremely important for three reasons: the way in which the mothers were interacting with their children could be monitored; feedback to the mother could be provided; and when necessary demonstrations could be given. The changes occurring in each child's phonological system could be analysed and therapy carefully planned to be individually appropriate. Assessments of the children's spontaneous speech, in terms of the percentages of consonants correct and types of errors made, provided a concrete measure of progress for the mothers. These measures provided a spur regularly to carry out work at home.

During the course of the parent teaching programme the children showed considerable improvement in their phonological skills. However, the follow-up assessment showed that they achieved no further improvement. Phonology may be one aspect of language where ongoing assessment and planning of remediation requires a level of expertise that cannot be taught in a short teaching programme. That is, while the parents may have been taught how to act as the agents of therapy, the planning of therapy must by carried out by speech pathologists who regularly assess the children's phonological status. Parents were not taught the necessary skills for planning appropriate therapy because the level of expertise required was beyond the scope of a relatively short programme. Another likely contributing factor was that once the weekly parent teaching sessions were completed, parents did not work at home with the same degree of enthusiasm.

2.7 CONCLUSION

The clinical study reported here has treatment implications for other handicapped groups besides the Down's syndrome population. Although parts of the methodology would need to be changed according to the symptomology of the children's phonological disorder and the needs of parents, the general approach is likely to be beneficial. The widespread growth of preschool intervention programmes for children with developmental disabilities provides an opportunity to shape children's phonological systems during the acquisition phase rather than attempt to ameliorate a disorder that has become a set pattern. For this shaping to occur, it is essential that parents as primary caregivers and teachers of functional language have an understanding of the rationale as well as the techniques. However, the study indicated that speech pathologists play an important role in the assessment of disorders and in planning phonological remediation. The level of expertise required to perform these critical functions could not be taught in a parent teaching programme.

Unintelligible speech is often a major problem for parents and teachers of mentally handicapped children. This is not surprising since phonology appears to be a cognitive skill (Dodd and Cockerill, 1986). Mental handicap usually results in delayed phonological acquisition, although certain diagnostic subgroups have deviant development. Other factors that are influential in determining the development of intelligible speech include the language learning environment, hearing, physiology, motor skills and behaviour. Each mentally handicapped child with unintelligible speech is therefore in need of careful assessment, so that individually appropriate intervention can be planned.

Language is often conceived of as a set of related abilities — syntax, semantics and phonology. This has led to the assumption that it is possible to teach these aspects formally and separately and thus improve children's linguistic skills. Recent research has indicated that such an approach has not been successful in terms of functional communication (Wulz, Hall and Klein, 1983). Obviously the ideal would be to teach language use (function), form (syntax and phonology) and content (meaning) together (Bloom and Lehay, 1978). Such an approach is likely to be more successful than teaching subsets of linguistic skills in isolation.

Although the clinical trial that we have reported measured only phonological skill, it provides an example of how phonology, syntax and semantics can be taught together, to improve functional communication. By teaching parents to act as agents of therapy, professional skills were used effectively in the target environment, the home and community. Problems encountered in generalizing from a particular situation or teacher were therefore avoided. Pronunciation and vocabulary were taught together, initially at the single-word level, using carefully chosen target words that had a high functional communication value as well as illustrating phono-logical contrast. Once words were mastered phonologically and seman-tically, their use in sentence frames and then 'stories' encouraged syntactic development. The variety of interactive activities selected for teaching one set of target words emphasized the functional aspect of language, and faci-litated generalization across contexts.

Thus, while the focus of the study was phonological, its primary aim (and effect) was to improve functional communication. Teaching children to pronounce words correctly is not enough. They must also use that ability to communicate. Remediation of phonology is most effective when it is taught in a functional context, so that children become aware that *how* a word is pronounced is important for conveying meaning. This awareness, combined with an understanding of the power of language, provides a crucial base for expressive language growth.

ACKNOWLEDGEMENTS

The clinical research study could not have been carried out without the co-operation of Moira Peiterse and the staff of the Down's syndrome Preschool Intervention Programme; audiological testing and advice from Philip Newell; and a literature search by Rae Collins. We are indebted to the mothers and children for their help and friendship. Financial support was provided by NH and MRC, and Macquarie University research grants. This chapter is dedicated to Myffy Thomas.

REFERENCES

Ardran, G.M., Harker, P. and Kemp, F.H. (1973) Tongue size in Down's syndrome, *J. Ment. Defic. Res.*, *16*, 160–6.

Baker, B.L. (1976) Parent involvement in programming for developmentally disabled children in *Communication Assessment and Intervention Strategies* (ed. L.L. Lloyd), University Park Press, Baltimore, Md.

Baker, B.L., Heifetz, L.J. and Murphy, D.M. (1980) Behavioural training for parents of mentally retarded children: one year follow-up, *Am. J. Ment. Defic.*, *85*, 31–8.

Barton, D. (1976) Phonemic discrimination and the knowledge of words in children under three years in *Papers and Reports on Child Language Development*, Department of Linguistics, Stanford University, Stanford, Calif., USA, pp. 61–8.

Berry, M.F. and Eisenson, J. (1962) *Speech Disorders: Principles and Practices of Therapy*, Peter Owen, London.

Bloch, J., Gersten, E. and Kornblum, S. (1980) Evaluation of a language program for autistic children, *J. Speech Hearing Dis.*, *45*, 76–89.

Bloom, L. and Lehay, M. (1978) *Language Development and Language Disorders*, Wiley, New York.

Buim, N., Rynders, J. and Turnure, J. (1974) Early maternal linguistic environment of normal and Down's syndrome language learning children, *Am. J. Ment. Defic.*, *79*, 52–8.

Burt, C. (1937) *The Backward Child*, University of London Press, London.

Camarata, S.M. and Schwartz, R.G. (1985) Production of object words and action words: evidence for a relationship between phonology and semantics, *J. Speech Hearing Res.*, *28*, 323–30.

Cheseldine, S. and McConkey, R. (1979) Parental speech to young Down's syndrome children: an intervention study, *Am. J. Ment. Defic.*, *83*, 612–20.

Compton, A.J. (1970) Generative studies of children's phonological disorders, *J. Speech Hearing Dis.*, *35*, 315–40.

Conti-Ramsden, G. (1985) Mothers in dialogue with language-impaired children, *Topics in Language Disorders*, *5*, 58–68.

Cross, T. (1981) The linguistic experience of slow learners in *Adv. in Child Development* (ed. A.R. Nesdale), Cambridge University Press, Cambridge.

Darley, F.A. Aronson, A. and Brown, J. (1975) *Motor Speech Disorders*, W.B. Saunders, Philadelphia, Pa.

Dever, R.B. (1966) A new perspective for language research, *Ment. Retardation*, *4*, 20–3.

Dodd, B.J. (1975a) The acquisition of phonological skills in normal, severely subnormal and deaf children, unpublished PhD thesis, University of London.

Dodd, B.J. (1975b) Recognition and reproduction of words by Down's syndrome and non-Down's syndrome retarded children, *Am. J. Ment. Defic.*, *80*, 306–11.

Dodd, B.J. (1976a) A comparison of the phonological systems of mental age matched normal, severely subnormal and Down's syndrome children, *Brit. J. Dis. Commun.*, *11*, 27–42.

Dodd, B.J. (1976b) The phonological systems of deaf children, *J. Speech Hearing Dis.*, *41*, 185–98.

Dodd, B.J. (1982) Sub-groups of phonologically disordered children, paper presented at neurolinguistics and speech pathology conference, University of Newcastle upon Tyne, November.

Dodd, B.J. and Cockerill, H. (1986) Phonological coding deficit: a comparison of the spelling errors made by deaf, speech disordered and normal children in *The Cultivated Australian* (ed. J. Clarke), Vol. 48 of *Beitrage zur Phonetik und Linguistik*, Springer Verlag, Hamburg.

Fawcus, M. (1965) Speech disorders and therapy in mental deficiency in *Mental Deficiency: The Changing Outlook* (eds A.D.B. Clarke and A.M. Clarke), Methuen, London, pp. 447–81.

Fenn, G. (1976) Against verbal enrichment in *Language and Communication in the Mentally Handicapped* (ed. P.B. Berry), 3rd edn, Edward Arnold, London, pp. 84–94.

Frith, U. and Frith, C.D. (1974) Specific motor disabilities in Down's syndrome, *J. Child Psychol. Psychiat.*, *15*, 293–301.

Fulton, R. and Lloyd, L.L. (1969) *Audiometry for the Retarded*, Williams and Wilkins, Baltimore, Md.

Goertzen, S.M. (1957) Speech and the mentally retarded child, *Am. J. Ment. Defic.*, *62*, 244–53.

Grunwell, P. (1981) *The Nature of Phonological Disability in Children*, Academic Press, London.

Guess, D., Keogh, W. and Sailor, W. (1978) Generalization and language behaviour: measurement and training in *Bases of Language* (ed. R. Schiefelbusch), University Park Press, Baltimore, Md.

Gunn, P., Clark, D. and Berry, P. (1980) Maternal speech during play with a Down's syndrome infant, *Ment. Retardation, 18*, 15–18.

Halliday, M.A.K. (1977) *Learning How to Mean: Explorations in the Development of Language*, Dover, New York.

HMSO (1976) *Statistics of Education. Vol. 1, 'Schools' England and Wales,* HMSO, London.

Hornby, G. and Singh, L.N.N. (1984) Behavioural group training with parents of mentally retarded children, *J. Ment. Defic. Res., 28*, 43–52.

Ingram, D. (1976) *Phonological Disabilities in Children*, Elsevier, Amsterdam.

Ingram, D. (1987) *Proc. First Internat. Symp. Specific Speech and Language Dis. Children*, University of Reading, 29 March–3 April.

Jarvis, C. (1980) A comparison of the phonologies of young adult Down's syndrome and non-Down's syndrome subjects resident in an institution, unpublished B.Sc. thesis, University of Newcastle upon Tyne.

Kastein, S. (1956) Responsibility of the speech pathologist to the retarded child, *Am. J. Ment. Defic., 60*, 750–4.

Kirkpatrick, E. and Ward, J. (1984) Prevalence of articulation errors in NSW primary school pupils, *Austr. J. Human Commun. Dis., 12*, 55–62.

Leeming, K., Swan, W., Coupe, J. and Mittler, P. (1979) Teaching language and communication to the mentally handicapped, *Schools Council Curriculum Bulletin*, Evans/Methuen Educational, London, Vol. 8.

Lemperle, G. and Radu, D. (1980) Facial plastic surgery in children with Down's syndrome, *Plastic Reconstructive Surg., 66*, 3.

Lenneberg, E.H. (1967) *Biological Foundations of Language*, Wiley, New York.

Leonard, L.B. (1979) Language impairment in children, *Merrell-Palmer Quart., 25*, 205–30.

Lovaas, O.I., Koegel, R.L., Simmons, J.Q. and Long, J.S. (1973) Some generalisation and follow up measures on autistic children in behaviour therapy, *J. Appl. Behav. Anal., 6*, 131–66.

McLean, T.E. and Snyder-McLean, L.K. (1978) *A Transactional Approach to Early Language*, Charles E. Merrill, Columbus, Ohio.

McNutt, J.C. and Leri, S.M. (1979) Language differences between institutionalized and non-institutionalized retarded children, *Am. J. Ment. Defic., 83*, 339–45.

Matthews, J. (1957) Speech problems of the mentally retarded in *Handbook of Speech Pathology* (ed. L.E. Travis), Peter Owen, London, pp. 531–51.

Mittler, R.P. (1974) Language and communication in *Mental Deficiency: The Changing Outlook* (eds. A.D.B. Clark and A.M. Clark), 3rd edn, Methuen, London.

Murphy, K. (1978) Results of a survey to discover the percentage of ESN(S) and ESN(M) children who have some degree of hearing loss, *RNID Survey No. 3.*

Olbrisch, R.R. (1982) Plastic surgical management of children with Down's syndrome: indications and results, *Brit. J. Plastic Surg., 35*, 195–200.

Orlansky, M.D. (1979) "Sam's Day"; a simulated observation of a severely handicapped child's educational program, *AAESPH Review, 4*, 251–8.

Parsons, C.L. (1984) A comparison of phonological processes used by developmentally verbal dyspraxic children and non-dyspraxic phonologically impaired children, *Aust. J. Human Commun. Dis., 12*, 93–107.

Parsons, C.L., Iacono, T.A. and Rozner, L. (in press) Effects of tongue reduction on articulation in Down's syndrome children, *Amer. J. Ment. Defic.*

Price, P. (1983) A preliminary report on an investigation into mother–child verbal interaction strategies with mothers of young developmentally delayed children, *Aust. J. Human Commun. Dis., 11*, 17–24.

Robson, C. (1984) Issues in the development of language intervention programmes, *J. Ment. Defic. Res.*, *28*, 89–100.

Rondal, J. (1978) Maternal speech to normal and Down's syndrome children matched for mean length of utterance, *Monograph Am. Assoc. Ment. Defic.*, Washington, DC.

Schiefelebusch, R.L. (1972) Language disabilities of cognitively involved children in *Principles of Childhood Language Disabilities* (eds. J.V. Irwin and M. Marge), Appleton-Century-Crofts, New York, pp. 209–34.

Schlanger, B.B. and Gottsleben, R.H. (1957) Analysis of speech defects among the institutionalized mentally retarded, *J. Speech Hearing Dis.*, *22*, 98–103.

Shvachkin, N.K.L. (1948) The development of phenomic speech perception in early childhood, *Isvest. Akad. Pedagog. Hank RSFSR*, *13*, 101–32.

Smith, N.V. (1973) *The Acquisition of Phonology*, Cambridge University Press, Cambridge.

Snow, C. (1977) The development of conversation between mother and babies, *J. Child Language*, *4*, 1–22.

Tams, V. and Eyeberg, S. (1976) A group treatment program for parents in *Behaviour Modification Approaches to Parenting* (eds E.J. Mash, L.D. Hamerlynck and L.C. Handy), Brunner and Mazel, New York.

Waldon, Y. (1968) Deafness and the mental handicapped in *Studies on the Mentally Handicapped Child* (ed. A.B. Boom), Edward Arnold, London, pp. 32–48.

Webb, C.E. and Kinde, S. (1967) Speech, language and hearing of the mentally retarded in *Mental Retardation: Appraisal, Education and Rehabilitation* (ed. A.A. Bavmeister), Aldine, Chicago, pp. 96–119.

Winnet, R.A. and Winkler, R.C. (1972) Current behaviour modification in the classroom: be still, be quiet, be docile, *J. Appl. Behav. Anal.*, *5*, 499–504.

Wulz, S.V., Hall, M.K. and Klein, M.D. (1983) A home centered instructional communication strategy for severely handicapped children, *J. Speech Hearing Dis.*, *148*, 2–10.

3

Signs of Language?

Paul Light, Bob Remington, Sue Clarke and Julia Watson

3.1 INTRODUCTION

The past decade has seen a considerable expansion in the use of manual sign language with mentally handicapped children. In parallel with this, although lagging somewhat behind, there has been an increase in the research literature concerning the relative merits of speech and sign. A variety of strong claims have been made by practitioners and researchers in this field. Important among these are the suggestions that sign mastery has significant facilitatory effects upon the understanding and use of speech, and that not only single signs, but also syntactically complex sign combinations may be fairly readily acquired. Assertions of this kind create a sense of optimism and enthusiasm among practitioners which may well be valuable in the short term, but may prove to be damaging if ultimately they cannot be sustained. Our own experimental programme arose from our feeling that there was a need to question these claims and the evidence relating to them, primarily because we hoped that the effectiveness of sign teaching could be maximized on the basis of surer knowledge of the learning processes involved (Remington and Light, 1983). In this chapter we will present findings arising from our own experimental studies on the relation between signing and speech and on the issue of sign combinativity. We shall argue that this kind of detailed experimental work can be revealing not only about the best ways to approach sign language training, but also about the relationship between acquired signing proficiency and other aspects of the mentally handicapped child's communicative repertoire. Before reviewing our own research, however, we will briefly sketch the background to the current interest in signing.

In the late 1970s and early 1980s, at a time when the use of British Sign Language for the deaf was achieving a notably higher public profile (as witness the BBC's *Vision On,* and the use of sign language 'subtitling'), the use of signing with non-deaf mentally handicapped children blossomed dramatically. Surveys in England and Wales showed that by 1980 some

75% of ESN(S) schools reported the use of a sign system, mostly the Makaton vocabulary of BSL (Jones, Reid and Kiernan, 1982). The sheer speed with which the approach took hold in school settings underlines the fact that there was an enormous need for a rapid and effective method of communication training which had not been met by previous speech-based programmes. Signing had a number of obvious advantages over speech which gave the sign training packages (e.g. Makaton) a high level of 'face validity' even before any attempt was made at implementation.

The most obvious advantage of signing is the relative ease with which signs can be modelled and prompted during teaching. In speech the child has to be shown how to produce, and encouraged to make, correct sounds. It is extremely difficult to 'shape' verbal imitation in a child who is initially mute, and many language training programmes have broken down at this point (Goetz, Schuler and Sailor, 1979). By contrast, in teaching a sign the teacher can physically mould the child's hands into the correct shape. Also the child can actually see what the teacher is doing in making the sign, so that imitation is much easier.

In addition to these practical teaching considerations, there are empirical grounds for supposing that autistic and other mentally handicapped children may suffer modality-specific cognitive and perceptual processing deficits which make mastery of speech peculiarly difficult (Hermelin and O'Connor, 1970). However, the evidence on this score is by no means straightforward, and the heterogeneity of the groups involved is such as to make generalization difficult (see Light, Remington and Porter, 1982). Regardless of the merits of this argument, signing has a clear-cut advantage over speech in terms of the its 'teachability', as we have already noted, and it has other more clearly demonstrable benefits in terms of its reliance on pre-existing cognitive abilities. These stem from the non-arbitrary relationship between signs and their referents. A sign may be *iconic* (with the referent directly guessable on the basis of the sign) or at least *translucent* (where the relation of sign and referent is clear as soon as one knows the latter). On the other hand, spoken words typically relate to their referents only in an arbitrary way. Available evidence comparing the acquisition of different signs suggests that both iconicity (e.g. Griffith and Robinson, 1980) and translucency (Luftig, 1983) make a significant contribution to reducing the difficulty of sign learning.

Once a child has begun to acquire functional signing in the context of a specific teaching situation, several practical questions arise concerning the generalized effects of training. The most obvious of these involve the generalization of sign use to other novel situations (stimulus generalization) and the maintenance of signing over time. In the case of signing, however, many of the more interesting questions concern any changes in behaviour, other than the signing activities specifically taught, which may nevertheless be attributed to specific sign training experiences (response generalization).

We consider both of these issues briefly below.

Attempts to teach spoken words to initially non-verbal children through structured training programmes have been dogged by problems of lack of stimulus generalization. Even such words as are learned are often not used spontaneously or outside the context of training, and are not combined in novel ways (e.g. Carr, 1985; Howlin, 1981). The sign training literature has been somewhat more encouraging: in the context of stimulus generalization, in particular, there are many reports of spontaneous usage and generalization to new situations (e.g. Creedon, 1973; Schaeffer *et al.*, 1977). Although some of the evidence is quite convincing, either in terms of showing generalization (e.g. Carr and Kologinsky, 1983) or failing to show it (Faw *et al.*, 1981), there is more anecdotal than systematic research in this area. Because many of the available studies suffer from one or more of the methodological weaknesses and interpretative ambiguities discussed by Remington and Light (1983), only the most cautious conclusions may be drawn (Clarke, 1986).

One important issue that might be considered as a generalization question, albeit one of response rather than stimulus generalization, concerns changes in a child's social behaviour following sign training. Improvements in children's general conduct with decreases in disruptive and stereotyped behaviours have frequently been reported (e.g. Bonvillian and Nelson, 1982), and Carr and Durand (1985) have shown that the training of specific requests in sign language can reduce the likelihood of non-verbal (e.g. disruptive) behaviour which was previously being used by the child to achieve the same result. However, it is also the case that the frequently reported global improvements may, to a large extent, result from the introduction of organized teaching procedures and other associated non-specific factors rather than from sign learning, *per se* (Francis and Williams, 1983).

Another issue concerned with the topic of response generalization, this time relating more specifically to signing behaviour, focuses on the child's ability to incorporate learned signs into syntactically structured novel combinations. Behaviour of this kind is significant for important practical reasons since if it fails to occur every sign string would have to be trained individually. For just this reason, sign combinativity is also highly significant at the conceptual level. As with the chimpanzee signing literature (e.g. Gardner and Gardner, 1969), the issue of combinativity may be seen as central to any consideration of the linguistic status of the behaviours learned. We shall give further detailed consideration to this important topic, which has been the focus of one series of studies conducted at Southampton by Julia Watson, in section 3.3 of this chapter (see also Watson, 1986).

A final topic, which might for convenience be considered a form of response generalisation, concerns changes in natural language ability following sign training. The relationship between speech and sign has been a major focus of interest both for practitioners and researchers. As several British surveys (e.g. Jones *et al.*, 1982; Kiernan, 1983) have shown, speech is almost invariably used in sign language programmes alongside sign. One of the principal justifications for this so-called 'total communication' approach (and indeed one of the reasons often given for the introduction of signing) is that the joint use of speech and sign will facilitate the children's acquisition of speech. Such improvements may occur in either expressive and/or receptive speech skills.

As far as expressive speech is concerned, a number of studies have reported facilitation through total communication training (Casey, 1978; Cohen, 1981; Konstantareas, Webster and Oxman, 1979), although in all cases the participants were children who were at least able to imitate speech sounds at the outset. Because these children might be considered good candidates for speech-alone training, however, the real question is whether total communication (using sign and speech) is a more effective way of developing speech than straightforward speech training. Recent attempts to address this question have indicated that total communication often *does* have an advantage over speech-alone training in this respect (Barrera and Sulzer-Azaroff, 1983; Sisson and Barrett, 1984), although some studies have failed to show any significant difference (e.g. Reid, 1981).

At the lower end of the ability range there exists a group of children without vocal imitation skills. If imitative ability is thought of as a prerequisite for functional expressive speech, there is little reason to expect that total communication will lead to such an outcome with this population. Even so, there is the possibility that total communication may facilitate *receptive* speech development. While there is some evidence of improvement in the understanding of speech among more able children (e.g. Penner and Williams, 1982), there is in fact little in the literature to suggest that total communication will facilitate even receptive speech in initially mute children. One of the difficulties, as Remington and Clarke (1983) noted in a study with autistic children, is that such children frequently show overselectivity of attention, and may attend only to either the visual (sign) mode or auditory (speech) mode during total communication training. Clearly only those children who attend to the speech component can acquire receptive speech and, according to Carr and Dores (1981), such children are typically *not* mute, having pre-existing vocal imitation skills. Their study showed that only verbally imitative autistic children acquired receptive speech as a result of total communication training.

We shall be developing this theme in the following section, along with a complementary issue which has received a good deal less attention in the literature, but which formed the basis of a series of studies at Southampton by Sue Clarke (1986). This concerns the possibility that the *speech* component of 'total communication' facilitates *sign* acquisition (Remington and Light, 1983). More generally, we will focus on the following question: to what extent is the acquisition of signing by mentally handicapped children grounded upon their prior achievements in understanding spoken language? Here again we have an issue which is important not only practically, in terms of selecting efficient teaching procedures, but also conceptually. Is signing to be thought of as offering a *route into language* (and potentially a language in its own right) for these children — as it clearly can be for some deaf children? Or is it better thought of primarily as an *expressive* modality, the effectiveness of which is limited by linguistic achievements already made in comprehension of spoken language?

3.2 SIGNS AND WORDS

In studies of the effectiveness of sign language teaching — which, as we have noted, typically means 'total communication' teaching — researchers have rarely made any attempt to assess the children's prior comprehension abilities. Because an effort is generally made to use familiar or useful referents in sign teaching, it is very likely that in most of those studies the children knew the spoken names of the objects receptively from the outset, even if they could not articulate them expressively. Remington and Light (1983) suggested that the success of total communication in terms of sign learning might be dependent to a considerable extent upon the children's prior verbal comprehension.

Studies which have shown that 'total communication' is more effective in teaching *signing* than is sign-alone training (e.g. Barrera, Lobato-Barrera and Sulzer-Azaroff, 1980) have not included pretests to assess whether the children knew the names for the items beforehand. Penner and Williams (1982), however, included only items which were receptively *un*known to the children, and failed to find any superiority of 'total communication' over sign-alone teaching. The same result was obtained by Remington and Clarke (1983) using a within-subject design with two autistic children.

The studies reviewed above are concerned with the interaction of two independent variables — the method of sign training and a child's receptive knowledge of words corresponding to the to-be-trained signs. What seems to be needed at this point is a factorially designed experiment of the kind suggested in Table 3.1. This would allow a direct comparison of 'total communication' and sign-alone training using signs for both receptively 'known' and 'unknown' words. However, a number of difficulties stand in the way of such an endeavour. First, because of the great heterogeneity of the population concerned, a between-subject comparison of the kind suggested by the table would be hopelessly compromised if only small

Table 3.1: Methods of training signs for words which were receptively 'known' and 'unknown'. The pairwise comparisons investigated by experiment are shown by the arrowed lines

		Method of sign training	
		Total communication	Sign-alone training
	'known' words	A◄ - - - - - -►B	
Receptive speech	- -		
	'unknown' words	C◄ - - - - - -►D	

numbers of children participated, and to get large numbers of children in each teaching condition would be impossibly time-consuming. Thus such comparisons can only realistically be made on a within-subject basis, and given the individual differences involved, an approach in which each child experiences teaching in all the conditions seems to make more sense. But to alternate four different teaching regimes with an individual child, in practice, runs the risk of generating only confusion in both participant and teacher. A further practical problem arises in the choice of referents. If the 'known' words relate to familiar, commonplace items (as is likely to be the case) and the 'unknown' words to less familiar or unfamiliar items, then any differences in outcome might arise from familiarity or salience of the referents, *per se*, rather than the associated verbal comprehension. However, if one is interested in establishing the role of a child's pre-existing, naturally established verbal comprehension, then there is no way of entirely getting round this problem.

Given the difficulties, our approach was to make pairwise within-subject comparisons of the conditions, as shown in Table 3.1. In our first study (Clarke *et al.*, 1986) we carried out a within-subject comparison of signing acquisition for receptively known and unknown words using 'total communication' throughout. To avoid having a preponderance of highly functional words in the 'known' condition and obscure words in the 'unknown' condition, illustrations of people in various occupational categories (nurse, fisherman, policeman, etc.) were used as referents. Three children from schools for the educationally severely retarded took part in the study. One carried a diagnosis of phenylketonuria, the others no specific diagnosis. All had normal hearing and vision, and only one had had any sign training before the study. Their chronological ages (CAs) ranged from 6 to 11 years and their Merrill Palmer mental ages (MAs) from 2 years 10 months to 4 years 1 month. Receptive speech pretests were conducted to establish which of the 'people pictures' the children could pick out reliably on the basis of their spoken names alone. The performance difficulty and translucency of the corresponding signs (which were drawn from the British Sign Language and Makaton vocabularies) were assessed using a sample of non-handicapped children. For each of the three children in the study, two groups of five pictures were selected such that one consisted of items corresponding to words which were 'unknown' in receptive speech and the other of 'known' words. We ensured that the signs corresponding to these two groups of pictures were of comparable difficulty and translucency.

Prior to *functional* sign training, the children were taught simply to imitate the signs in order further to reduce any possible differences in sign difficulty that would have confounded the comparison. At this point, we began to teach expressive signing using total communication. On each trial the teacher presented a picture and simultaneously named the item shown; the sign was prompted, as necessary, and the child's attempts at expressive signing reinforced. Each child had two teaching sessions per day: on one day the morning session might be for the 'unknown' items, the afternoon for the 'known' items; and then on the next day the order would be reversed (an 'alternating treatments' design; see Hersen and Barlow, 1978). Video tapes were made of all sessions, which allowed scoring of successful unprompted sign responses and estimates of scoring reliability (these or similar procedures were used in all of the subsequent studies referred to in this chapter).

On average, the three children learned the signs in the 'known' condition in only about two-thirds of the time it took for them to learn the signs in the 'unknown' condition. The difference was statistically reliable for each of the three children. Moreover, at a two-month follow-up, all children showed better retention of signing for the 'known' items, this difference being statistically reliable in two of the three cases. At the end of the teaching programme the children could correctly produce the signs taught in the 'known' condition, both when pictures were presented without speech (visual stimulus control) and when pictured items were simply *named* by the teacher (vocal stimulus control). However, for the signs taught in the 'unknown' condition only one of the children appeared to have mastered both these connections between sign, picture and word. Taken together, these results suggest a very significant degree of facilitation of sign language learning by prior receptive language abilities. Was this facilitation dependent upon the use of the spoken word alongside sign (i.e. 'total communication') in training? To examine this point a second study was conducted, along much the same lines as the first, but using sign-alone teaching (for full details of this and other studies in this section see Clarke, 1986).

Three different children participated in this study (CAs 4 to 9 years, MAs 2 years 5 months to 3 years 8 months), all with normal vision and hearing, two with some previous experience of signing. The procedures

63

were exactly as before except that speech was *not* used alongside sign during the teaching. In contrast to the result of the earlier study, all three children showed very similar overall rates of learning in the 'known' and the 'unknown' conditions, and none of them learned the signs corresponding to known words significantly faster. These results suggest that the superior performance in the 'known' condition in the first study was indeed a function of prior familiarity with the spoken words used in the teaching rather than an artefact of the greater salience or familiarity of the pictures that the words stood for. Prior receptive speech seems to be a significant facilitatory feature only when (as in 'total communication') the words are actually used in teaching.

As noted at the beginning of this section, both Penner and Williams (1982) and Remington and Clarke (1983) found no advantage for 'total communication' over sign-alone training when the items taught did *not* correspond to known words. Further studies in the present series have included two direct assessments of the relative efficacy of 'total communication' and sign-alone teaching where all words were *known* receptively beforehand. In both studies, as predicted, signs taught by 'total communication' were acquired faster than those taught by sign-alone teaching.

This series of experiments, in conjunction with Remington and Clarke's (1983) study, complete the possible pairwise comparisons between conditions, as illustrated in Table 3.1. Although not conclusive, the studies suggest a single coherent interpretation: the primary advantage of 'total communication' for single-sign acquisition is specific to the situation where the child already knows the words for to-be-trained signs receptively. In remedial contexts 'total communication' is almost always used. Moveover, as was found in the pretests of the studies described here, the receptive vocabularies of even severely handicapped children are usually quite extensive. In the case of the two studies reported above, for example, the children's receptive language ages as measured by the Reynell Developmental Language Scales (RDLS) ranged from 2 years 4 months to 3 years, corresponding to considerable vocabularies. Given the natural tendency of teachers to focus their efforts on familiar and functionally significant elements in the child's environment, it seems likely that most signs taught to most children with a mental handicap correspond to words already within their receptive vocabulary. And as we have seen, where that is the case there is every reason to suppose that the children's understanding of the spoken word is mediating and facilitating their mastery of the corresponding expressive sign.

In fact we did find some evidence of expressive speech facilitation as a result of total communication training, but it was limited, as might have been expected, to those children with pre-existing vocal imitation skills (Clarke, Remington and Light, in preparation). This improvement represents one of a number of useful new relationships that emerged as a result

Table 3.2: The possible relationships between signs, words and referent pictures in studies of signing acquisition

Association	Name
Sign – sign	Sign imitation
Word – word	Verbal imitation
Picture – picture	Picture matching
Word – picture	Receptive speech
Picture – sign	Visual stimulus control
Word – sign	Vocal stimulus control
Picture – word	Expressive speech
Sign – word	Sign naming
Sign – picture	Receptive signing

of the training procedures but which were not themselves *explicitly* taught. We have already mentioned another, the improvement in receptive signing that occurred with signs for known words following total communication training. The idea that 'you get more than you teach' can be formalized slightly if we consider the possible relationships between signs, words and pictures which may be examined in studies of this kind. These are shown in Table 3.2, and represented graphically in Figure 3.1.

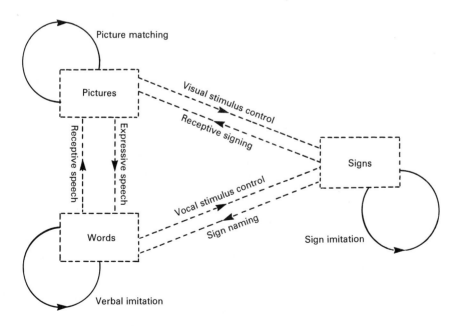

Figure 3.1: The sign, word and picture equivalence classes involved in the acquisition of single signs.

The possible associations represented in Table 3.2 can be divided into three categories: those that were present prior to sign training, those that were explicitly taught and those that could emerge as a result of training. In all of the studies we have reported we made certain that children could match pictures and imitate signs prior to functional sign training, and where known words were used, the associations involved in receptive speech were present by definition. Sign-alone training ensured the learning of associations between pictures and signs. In the case of total communication, an alternative or additional association between word stimuli and signing response could be formed, depending on whether or not a child attended to both visual and vocal aspects of the teacher's behaviour. Virtually all of the remaining relations between words, signs and pictures which we observed to emerge in posttests could be explained in terms of the concept of *functional stimulus equivalence*, developed by Sidman and Tailby (1982).

Two examples should make this clear. The first occurred in the study in which we compared the effects of word knowledge on speed of signing acquisition following teaching which used the sign-alone method (see p. 62). We found that despite the fact that spoken words were *never* used during training, all three children would make the correct sign when presented with the corresponding word — but only if the words were known prior to training. The explanation for this pattern of results is logical, if complex. Before training, the known words and corresponding pictures were functionally equivalent stimuli since both governed picture selection responses (receptive speech and picture-matching associations in Table 3.2). Sign-alone training ensured that picture stimuli governed signing responses (visual stimulus control in Table 3.2), and since known words were already equivalent to pictures, they also came to control signing. Because *un*known words did not control picture selection responses (by definition), unknown words and pictures were *not* equivalent prior to training, and vocal stimulus control could not thus occur as a mediated relationship.

For expressive speech to emerge spontaneously following sign training, the stimulus equivalence framework requires first that speech be available as a response; in other words, that the child can perform verbal imitation. Expressive speech will then emerge if words and signs become functionally equivalent stimuli. This occurs if a child is able to attend to both spoken words and pictures during total communication training such that both stimuli come to control signing responses. Under these circumstances, since words already control word responses (verbal imitation), pictures should also come to control words — emergent expressive speech. On the one occasion when we managed to arrange these conditions, we found a marked increase in expressive speech following total communication training, exactly as predicted by the stimulus equivalence model.

To some extent, the detailed consideration we have given in this section to the facilitative effects of receptive speech on sign learning can be seen as a corrective to an apparent bias in the literature. As we noted in the introduction, a great deal of attention has been given to the facilitative effects of sign learning upon speech acquisition. But little attention has been given to the question we have been addressing here. The fact that sign language *can* be acquired *de novo*, whether by the congenitally deaf child or even, perhaps, in very limited measure by the chimpanzee, should not lead us to suppose that all sign acquisition is of this type. Our results suggest that, for many mentally handicapped children, signing may be functioning largely as a secondary, expressive language representation, and the ease of sign learning may be very much dependent upon the existence of a solid basis of verbal comprehension. Such a conclusion has some implications for the development of fluent, recombinatory signing skills, a topic to which we now turn.

3.3 PRODUCTIVE SIGN COMBINATIONS

Most of the methodologically sound research on sign learning among mentally handicapped children has been focused on the acquisition of single signs. However, as we have noted earlier, interesting and important issues arise when we begin to consider the child's ability to combine signs with one another in ways which have not been specifically taught.

As Remington and Light (1983) noted, the term 'generalization' is often used to describe this flexible combination and recombination of learned signs in novel contexts, but the activity might more appropriately be described as 'productivity'. Reports of such productivity in sign use by mentally handicapped children are not infrequent, but many of the studies have been poorly controlled and there have been very few *experimental* investigations into the acquisition of productive signing. Rather the literature consists of case studies and programme reports which give very little information about how, if at all, sign combinations were taught. Some researchers appear to have trained only single signs, but observed subsequent multi-sign use (e.g. Benaroya *et al.*, 1979). Others have attempted to build up multi-sign use systematically, for example, beginning with nouns, followed by verb–noun combinations, etc. (e.g. Brady and Smouse, 1978). Overall, results seem to have been extremely variable. Miller and Miller (1973) reported that only one of 19 children learned to use two-sign combinations expressively. Bucher (1983), in an experimental study, showed only very limited transfer from single-sign training to posttests involving sign combinations. In contrast, Fenn and Rowe (1975) report a language programme using the Paget Gorman Signing System involving a group of children with mixed handicaps in which, through a procedure of gradually increasing difficulty, all of the children were eventually able to produce two- and three-sign combinations.

A small survey of three Southampton schools for children with severe learning difficulties (Watson, 1986) identified 30 children who were involved in sign programmes. Of these, nearly half (13) were described by their teacher as using multi-sign 'utterances'. On closer inspection, however, it seemed that the children used mainly single signs, and the combinations occurred in cases of well-learned strings such as 'biscuit-please'. Only 5 of the children were described as being able to recombine learned signs flexibly into novel multi-sign 'utterances'. All 5, though they had articulation problems, had recognizable expressive speech, and indeed when combining signs they typically accompanied each sign with the corresponding spoken word. It is, perhaps, worth noting in this context that of the 56 children across the three schools who were mute or had *no* recognizable speech, only 12 were involved in the signing programmes. This admittedly small survey suggests not only that signing programmes may be being aimed at the more verbally able among the severely mentally handicapped, but also that the relatively small proportion achieving productive sign combinations may already be capable of similar productivity in speech.

A significant development in research in this field occurred when Karlan *et al.* (1982) introduced a systematic approach to teaching sign combinations based upon a technique which we shall call 'matrix training'. Karlan *et al.* set out to teach moderately handicapped children to produce expressive signed verb–noun combinations using American Sign Language. The method, of which the origins date back to Esper (1925), involved constructing a matrix of all combinations of verbs and nouns of the kind shown in Table 3.3. Items selected for direct teaching fell stepwise along the diagonal of the matrix. Thus the first verb (V1) was taught in combination with the first noun (N1), followed by the combination V1–N2, followed by V2–N2, V2–N3, and so on. It was clear from Karlan *et al.*'s results that at least 2 of the 3 children not only produced the combinations which had been directly taught, but also responded correctly using combin-

Table 3.3: Training matrix for verb–noun combinations (items marked 'T' are trained; items labelled 'P' are probed to test for the presence of novel recombinations of training items)

		Noun				
		car	cup	paper	crayon	ball
	Push	T	T	P	P	P
	Turn	P	T	T	P	P
Verb	Cover	P	P	T	T	P
	Give	P	P	P	T	T
	Pick up	T	P	P	P	T

ations of nouns and verbs which had never been taught together.

A subsequent study by Romski and Ruder (1984), using a similar procedure with ten language-delayed Down's syndrome children was a good deal less successful, as was our own first attempt (for full details of this and subsequent studies see Watson, 1986). The participants in our first study were one Down's syndrome child and another severely retarded child (CAs, 5 and 9 years respectively; MAs, 2 years 7 months and 3 years 5 months). The task involved learning to use signs in combination to label pictures showing various uniformed people (nurse, policeman, etc.) with various emotional expressions (happy, sad, etc.). Using sign-alone training and a 3 × 4 training matrix, the children were quite successfully taught to label the 'stepwise-diagonal' items. In contrast, both children completely failed to produce appropriate sign combinations for those items which had *not* been directly taught.

One factor which distinguished our study from that of Karlan *et al.* (1982) was that they employed total communication, while we chose to use sign-alone training (the results of Sue Clarke's research programme were not available at that time). Moreover, as far as one can judge, the items included in Karlan *et al.*'s matrix were probably already within the children's receptive vocabulary. By contrast, in the present study pretests had established that very few of the individual items were known to the children either in speech or in sign. In Romski and Ruder's (1984) study, too, items had been *un*known, receptively and expressively, in speech as well as in sign. Given the role of receptive speech and total communication in sign learning (see section 3.2), with hindsight these differences in outcome are not too surprising.

Because we felt that receptive speech was likely to have been a significant factor, we conducted a second and larger study using 8 children. Of these, 4 were selected on the basis that they had at most single-word speech (two had none), and used at most single signs. A further 4 children, selected via the survey of local schools mentioned earlier, were *already* able to combine signs productively and spontaneously. Although they had articulation problems, all 4 of these children also produced multi-word speech; all 8 children, whose ages ranged from 6 to 16, and whose MAs ranged from 3 years 0 months to 7 years 6 months, were attending ESN(S) schools.

A 3 × 4, colour × object matrix formed the basis of this study. There were four line-drawing slides (fish, car, cup, house) and three coloured slides (red, green, yellow). Using a light-box, these could be combined to produce the two-dimensional stimuli (e.g. 'red fish'). We conducted pretests to establish that the individual elements (i.e. the object and colour names) were *within* the children's receptive vocabulary both in speech (i.e. 'known' words) and in sign. This was the case for all but a few elements, and here some preliminary teaching was given to fill in the gaps. In addition, most of the elements were within the expressive sign vocabulary of all the children, and within the expressive spoken vocabulary of 6 of the 8 children.

The matrix-training procedure involved the teacher presenting the 'stepwise' colour–object combinations, without labelling them in speech, and inviting the child to label them with the appropriate sign combinations. Of the 4 children who had been selected as being already able to combine signs in the classroom, 2 of them were able to label *all* the combinations in the matrix almost immediately and the remainder succeeded in doing so after only a few combinations had been taught. Of the 4 children who did *not* spontaneously combine signs, one had to be dropped because he could not learn to make successive red/green discriminations, but the other 3 children succeeded in learning all the 'stepwise-diagonal' combinations taught. When we posttested combinations *not* specifically taught, all 3 children were also able to produce appropriate sign combinations in almost all cases. Moreover, 2 of the 3 children could perform just as well with coloured pictures as with the slide–filter combinations used in the teaching programme, and using the light-box all three could handle combinations of colours and objects which had *not* been included in the original teaching matrix.

Since none of these 3 children was reported as ever combining signs productively, and since when we had begun teaching none had been able to label using two-sign combinations, these results were encouraging. But the status of the productive sign combinations achieved in such highly structured programmes is problematic: are the children merely learning a combinational 'trick' in the context of a specific kind of game played out between teacher and child? Or do the combinations have properties corresponding to two-word combinations in language? If we wish to pursue this question a little further, we need to consider the significance of sign order in structured communication. To do this we constructed a matrix using object–location combinations (e.g. 'brick (on) table'; 'key (on) plate'). Here, for the first time, the role of sign order is important: asking a child to put a letter on a book requires behaviour quite distinct from that necessary to comply with a request to put a book on a letter. Indeed this dependence of meaning on order is often held up, at least in the 'popular' literature, as a key criterion for 'true syntax' (e.g. Wilson, 1975).

In our third study we selected three new children, all 'single-signers', with CAs between 5 and 10 years and MAs 2 years 10 months to 3 years 6 months. Two were also capable of single-word speech. A 3 × 4 object (pencil, brick, key) × location (cup, table, bag, plate) matrix was used with each element corresponding to a scaled-down real object. Note that the matrix thus consisted of one set of items (pencil, etc.) which were always treated as 'objects', and another set (cup, etc.) always treated as 'locations'. Thus only combinations such as 'pencil (in) cup' and 'key (on) table' were generated during training. Pretests established that the children could *understand* between 50% and 100% of the sign combinations which they were to be taught to use expressively. Similar pretests conducted using speech rather than sign labels for the combinations produced between 60% and 100% correct responding. Because even the lowest of these percentages is well above chance, it was clear that there was a substantial level of comprehension of these combinations even before training began. However, none of the children succeeded in *expressively* labelling the combinations at pretest, either in speech or in sign. As before, children were taught to use signs to label particular combinations of objects and locations corresponding to the 'stepwise-diagonal' elements of the matrix using a sign-alone procedure.

One of the children (the one with the poorest pretest comprehension results for both speech and sign) failed to learn even to label the diagonal combinations which were directly taught. The remaining two succeeded and, as with the previous study, went on to show successful productive labelling of untaught object–location combinations. Sign order (object first, location second) was correctly used in these untaught combinations, but since reverse combinations (such as 'table (on) key') were never used and inherently implausible, it is not appropriate to assume that sign order was carrying meaning for the children. A posttest with similarly 'irreversible' combinations involving items which had not been included in the matrix, such as 'knife (on) box', showed over 80% correct receptive sign responses (i.e. matching the actions to the sign combinations given) and a similar level of success in generating expressive sign combinations. When the receptive task was presented using words instead of signs, the two children also performed very well, although successful expressive word combinations remained infrequent.

A further posttest with novel items was then conducted. In this case, however, the combinations were potentially 'reversible' because we selected items such as 'book' and 'letter' which could equally plausibly act as object or location. We used an arbitrary 2 × 2 matrix (rows: paper, letter vs columns: picture, book) and carried out both receptive and expressive posttests with one dimension of the matrix as 'object' and the other as 'location' (e.g. 'letter (on) book'), followed by the same tests with the dimensional categories reversed (e.g. 'book (on) letter').

In order to succeed on these tests the children would have to have grasped something of the syntactic significance of sign/word order. There was little evidence that they had done so. One child was above chance in his expressive signing for some reversible combinations, but performed poorly receptively, while the other child was wholly unsuccessful. Moreover, there were indications that the first child's partial success in the expressive mode arose on the basis of a tendency to make the first sign when the 'object' was still in the teacher's hand, and then to make the

71

second when the 'location' was selected. Such a strategy, unavailable in the receptive tests, clearly does not constitute evidence for an understanding of the significance of sign order (although it might plausibly form a basis on which its significance can be learned).

These results were thus distinctly discouraging. They prompted us to a further examination of the 4 children mentioned in connection with one of the earlier studies who were already known to be combining signs productively in the classroom. The earlier study established that they needed little or no structured teaching to achieve success on an 'irreversible' matrix, but would this be the case with a 'reversible' matrix?

Having established that the children knew all of the individual signs and words involved, they were presented with exactly the same tests (using 'irreversible' and 'reversible' combinations) which had been used as post-tests in the previous study. None of the children had any trouble with either the receptive or the expressive test involving 'irreversible' combinations. When it came to the 'reversible' items, 2 of the children sailed through the tests, showing no difficulty in expressing or comprehending reversible sign combinations in both orders of presentation. The other 2 children, equally convincingly, failed the 'reversible' tests. Almost all errors consisted of reversing the signs or the actions, and overall levels of success both on expressive and receptive tasks were little better than chance. The detailed error patterns were difficult to interpret, but forced the conclusion that these 2 children did not systematically attend to sign order cues.

It is clear that all 4 of these children, chosen on the strength of their ability to use signs in combination, were considerably more able in most respects than the children used in the previous studies. All 4 children could produce multi-word spoken utterances, though their articulation was very poor. The psychometric measures and clinical diagnoses (see Table 3.4) did not offer any obvious explanation for the fact that 2 of these children were sensitive to the information conveyed by sign order and 2 were not, although classroom observation suggested that the former showed higher levels of spontaneous communicative signing than the latter.

Table 3.4: Diagnostic and psychiatric information (given in years and months) for four children whose ability to respond to reversible sign sequences was assessed. The final column indicates the outcome of this assessment

Child	Aetiology	CA	MA	RDLS(C)	RDLS(E)	Outcome
A	Unknown	10	4–1	4–8	4–4	Unsuccessful
B	Unknown	12	4–7	4–2	2–10	Unsuccessful
C	Down's	12	3–4	3–8	3–7	Successful
D	Unknown	16	7–6	6–4	3–7	Successful

Next we made an attempt to improve the performance of the 2 children who had failed on the sign order test. This time we used a 3 × 4 matrix of reversible combinations in which the stepwise-diagonals were directly taught in *both* orders — for example, 'box (on) mirror' *and* 'mirror (on) box.' Despite considerable persistence and effort on everyone's part, this was also a complete failure. Neither child mastered even the initial discriminations between the different sign orderings required on the directly taught items. Virtually all errors consisted in using the right signs in the wrong order, and overall the responding was frequently at chance level because periodic increases in correct responding for one ordering were accompanied by decreases in correct responding for the opposite ordering. Preferred sign ordering would periodically switch, as if the children were trying vainly to find the 'right' solution.

What, then, has this series of studies shown? First, that where the individual items are already known to the children beforehand, in speech and/or in sign, the matrix teaching procedure can be very effective. Not only do the children learn to produce sign combinations which are directly taught, but they can also produce two-sign labels for combinations not encountered in teaching, both from within and beyond the original matrix. However, the studies with 'reversible' combinations suggest that single-signers who learn to combine signs using the matrix do not attach any particular significance to sign order. Some children who are already producing sign combinations spontaneously do (or at least can) use sign order 'syntactically', but others do not, and cannot apparently be taught to do so at all readily — certainly not merely by training both orders. It would indeed be useful to find a way in which to make sign order a salient cue, but in this series of studies we were not able to do so. If such a failure proved irredeemable with any training procedure, the linguistic status of signing in the severely mentally handicapped population would be highly questionable. In section 3.4 we consider this issue more generally.

3.4 DISCUSSION

Many aspects of the work reported in this chapter have revolved around the question of how mentally handicapped children's learning of manual sign relates to other aspects of their language competence. In section 3.2 we have examined the significance of pre-existing verbal comprehension for sign learning at the single-sign level. The studies showed that signs were learned more rapidly and retained better when they corresponded to words already within the child's receptive vocabulary, at least when 'total communication' was used in teaching. The fact that this difference was not apparent when sign-alone teaching was used suggests that, for these very handicapped children, their ability to use verbal mediation in learning depends upon a high degree of explicit verbal 'prompting' (cf. Constantine and Sidman, 1975). However, there is no reason, in principle, why a child's understanding of speech should not mediate acquisition of signing, even where speech is not used explicitly. Indeed the matrix-training studies showed that sign combinations never verbally labelled by the teacher were learned and productive recombination also occurred when, and only when, the corresponding words were in a child's prior receptive vocabulary. Perhaps the relevance of *overt* verbal labelling (as in total communication) declines as the children develop a greater range of linguistic skills. Similar kinds of changes have been reported in the literature on the development of verbally mediated self-control (e.g. Bem, 1967; Luria, 1961).

On the basis of our single-sign studies, however, it would seem that the advantage conferred by prior receptive knowledge is specific to 'total communication' teaching, and equally that the advantage of total communication is specific to teaching signs for which the child already understands the words. In practical terms, this suggests that at the start of a sign teaching programme it would be sensible to assess the child's receptive vocabulary and teach items from within it. To move beyond the child's existing receptive vocabulary, it might be worthwhile to establish understanding of the spoken words before using total communication to teach expressive signing. However, our investigations in this direction (see Clarke, 1986, experiments 5 and 6) suggest that, in practice, such an approach may have marked disadvantages (in terms of the time required) as well as some advantages (in terms of additional emergent associations).

These single-sign studies, reinforced by stimulus equivalence principles, support the view that, for severely mentally handicapped children, signing can often function as an expressive modality for pre-existing language skills. As such it can be extremely useful, both practically and socially. If our goals are realistic, we may expect valuable improvements in communication. The danger of neglecting the fact that signing achievements often stand on the shoulders of already existing abilities is precisely that practitioners may expect too much. If expectations of success and progress are untempered by consideration of the child's pre-existing language competences, they are likely to be frustrated, and potentially useful programmes may be abandoned. That would be a pity because the results of the matrix-training studies suggest that there are some grounds for believing that we can get well beyond the single-sign stage. Overall, we showed that if children were able to learn the series of overlapping combinations of elements which were directly taught, then they were very likely to show productivity (in the sense of being able to produce all other possible combinations of those elements). The main qualification to this again concerns prior verbal abilities.

Kiernan, Reid and Jones (1982) found that around one-third of children in ESN(S) schools had three or fewer words with which they could express needs or requests. Our limited survey of Southampton schools indicated that only a minority of children with *no* speech were involved in the signing programmes, the majority having a small expressive vocabulary of single-word speech, and an equally small expressive single-sign repertoire. In contrast, the pretest data from studies reported in section 3.3 suggested the existence of a relatively wide *receptive* vocabulary in both speech and sign. Here, as with the single-sign studies, attempts to teach children to combine signs productively can be seen in terms of developing expressive abilities on the basis of already established skills in linguistic comprehension. Without these prerequisite verbal abilities, children experienced great difficulties. For example, the first study in the series suggested that the productivity may not be readily obtained where the children lack prior comprehension of the individual element names. In contrast, it was apparent in the later studies that the 'successes' were almost all children who were able to produce at least a small number of recognizable spoken words.

Nevertheless, apart from the 4 specially selected 'multi-signers', the children who took part in these studies had not been observed to combine signs before, and were unable to label any of the matrix combinations at pretest. To this extent, the success of the matrix approach is impressive. From a practical point of view, the technique offers a potentially valuable way of getting the children over a major hurdle in their expressive language development. The value of such a procedure, though, obviously depends upon the extent to which the children's combinatorial ability can be extended beyond the immediate context and content of the teaching. The second and third studies described in section 3.3 showed that once productivity was established within the matrix, it could be extended to combinations of the same type which had not formed part of the training matrix.

The methods of teaching we adopted for these studies were highly structured, involving a series of discrete 'trials' in a preprogrammed sequence. Even if the matrix approach were being used 'for real', rather than in a research context, its reliance upon specific ordering and overlapping of the combinations would necessitate a structured rather than a more 'naturalistic' mode of teaching. Carr (1985) has suggested that in such circumstances structured 'discrete trial' teaching should be used to establish language *forms*, but that 'incidental' teaching procedures (Hart and Risley, 1974) in the classroom and elsewhere are required to establish *functional* use of language in the child's natural environment. It would be of some interest to see whether such a tactical separation of form and function would, in practice, prove successful.

The matrix studies we have described have involved two distinct types of combination, which may be glossed as adjective–noun and object–location. Karlan *et al.* (1982) used action–object combinations. All these represent types which have close parallels in the two-word utterances of normally developing young children. From an analysis of data gathered by Bloom

(1970), Brown (1973) and others, McLean and Snyder-McLean (1978) were able list the six most frequently occurring forms of two-word utterance. The three types of combinations which have been trained in sign were among those listed and most, if not all, of the remaining forms would also be amenable to a matrix-training approach. Whether productivity established in respect of one combination type could be generalized to another is at present unknown.

One approach to the question of how 'language-like' the two-sign combinations produced by matrix training actually are concerns sign order. Single-signers who successfully achieved productivity within an 'irreversible' matrix regularly signed in the conventionally appropriate order, but posttests with 'reversible' combinations indicated that sign order was not an effective controlling variable. Even among those few children who regularly combined signs were some for whom the significance of a two-sign combination remained resolutely independent of sign order. It would be particularly interesting to know both what distinguishes such children from those for whom sign order functions as a readily discriminable cue to meaning, and how to make sign order an effective cue during training.

If these findings caution against reading too much into the children's achievements, they also present some puzzles which may be well worth solving. We are tempted to suppose that the solution here, as elsewhere, may lie in the children's existing linguistic abilities. The recurrent theme of this chapter has been that the achievements of mentally handicapped children in manual sign language may be heavily dependent on the children's pre-established language skills. Indeed paradoxically, perhaps, such dependence may provide one of the strongest arguments for treating what the children are learning in studies like ours as truly language-like. Be this as it may, the observed interdependency strongly suggests that those who would devise more effective sign teaching programmes for mentally handicapped children should not ignore the development of speech and, more especially, of verbal comprehension. Conversely, it may be the case that in the structured techniques we have been discussing, students of normal language development could find some valuable tools for the furtherance of their own enterprises.

ACKNOWLEDGEMENT

All the research discussed in this chapter was funded by an ESRC Research Studentship awarded to Julia Watson, and by ESRC Linked Studentship No. L82/25621/PSY obtained by Bob Remington and Paul Light, and held by Sue Clarke. The work was made possible through the cooperation of the headteachers, staff and pupils of a number of schools in Hampshire and Dorset.

REFERENCES

Barrera R., Lobato-Barrera, D. and Sulzer-Azaroff, B. (1980) A simultaneous treatment comparison of three language training programs with a mute autistic child, *J. Autism and Developmental Disorders, 10,* 21–37.

Barrera, R., and Sulzer-Azaroff, B. (1983) An alternating treatment comparison of oral and total communication programs with echolalic autistic children, *J. Appl. Behavior Analysis, 16,* 379–94.

Bem, S.L. (1967) Verbal self-control: the establishment of effective self-instruction, *J. Exp. Psychol. 74,* 485–91.

Benaroya, S., Wesley, M., Ogilvie, L., Klein, L. and Clarke, E. (1979) Sign language and multisensor input training of children with communication and related disorders, *J. Autism and Childhood Schizophrenia, 9,* 219–20.

Bloom, L. (1970) *Language Development: Form and Function in Emerging Grammars,* MIT Press, Cambridge, Mass.

Bonvillian, J., and Nelson, K. (1982) Exceptional cases of language acquisition in *Children's Language* (ed. K. Nelson), Lawrence Erlbaum, Hillsdale, NJ, Vol. 3.

Brady, D. and Smouse, A. (1978) A simultaneous comparison of three methods of language training with an autistic child, *J. Autism and Childhood Schizophrenia, 8,* 271–9.

Brown, R. (1973) *A First Language,* Harvard University Press, Cambridge, Mass.

Bucher, B. (1983) Effects of sign language training on untrained sign use for single and multiple signing, *Analysis and Intervention in Developmental Disabilities, 3,* 261–77.

Carr, E.G. (1985) Behavioral approaches to language and communication in *Current Issues in Autism* (eds. E. Schopler and G. Mesibor), Plenum, New York, Vol. 3.

Carr, E.G. and Dores, P.A. (1981) Patterns of language acquisition following simultaneous communication with autistic children, *Analysis and Intervention in Developmental Disabilities, 1,* 347–61.

Carr, E.G. and Durand, M.V. (1985) The social–communicative basis of severe behavior problems in children in *Theoretical Issues and Behavior Therapy* (eds. S. Reiss and R. Bootzin), Academic Press, New York, pp. 219–54.

Carr, E.G. and Kologinsky, E. (1983) Acquisition of sign language by autistic children, II, *J. Appl. Behavior Analysis, 16,* 297–314.

Casey, L. (1978) Development of communicative behavior in autistic children, *J. Autism and Childhood Schizophrenia, 8,* 45–59.

Clarke, S. (1986) An evaluation of the relationship between receptive speech and manual sign language with mentally handicapped children, unpublished PhD thesis, University of Southampton.

Clarke, S., Remington, B., and Light, P. (1986) An evaluation of the relationship between receptive speech skills and expressive signing, *J. of Appl. Behavior Analysis, 19,* 231–9.

Clarke, S., Remington, B. and Light, P. The role of referential speech in sign learning by mentally retarded children: a comparison of total communication and sign-alone training, *J. of Appl. Behavior Analysis* (in press).

Cohen, M. (1981) Development of language behaviour in an autistic child using total communication, *Exceptional Children, 47,* 379–81.

Constantine, B. and Sidman, M. (1975) Role of naming in delayed matching to sample, *Am. J. Ment. Defic., 79,* 680–9.

Creedon, M.P. (1973) Language development in nonverbal autistic children using a simultaneous communication system, paper presented at the Society for Research in Child Development, Philadelphia, March.

Esper, E. (1925) A technique for the experimental investigation of associative inter-ference in artificial linguistic material, *Language Monographs No. 1*.

Faw, G.D., Reid, D.H., Schepis, M.M., Fitzgerald, J.R. and Welty, P.A. (1981) Involving institutional staff in the development and maintenance of sign language skills with profoundly retarded persons, *J. Appl. Behavior Analysis*, *14*, 411–23.

Fenn, G. and Rowe, J. (1975) An experiment in manual communication, *Br. J. Disorders of Communication*, *10*, 3–16.

Francis, V. and Williams, C. (1983) The effects of teaching British Sign Language to mentally handicapped, non-communicating children, *Br. J. of Mental Subnormality*, *29*, 18–28.

Gardner, R. and Gardner, B. (1969) Teaching sign language to a chimpanzee, *Sci.*, *165*, 664–72.

Goetz, L., Schuler, A. and Sailor, W. (1979) Teaching functional speech to the severely handicapped: current issues, *J. Autism and Developmental Disorders*, *9*, 325–43.

Griffith, P. and Robinson, J. (1980) Influence of iconicity and phonological similarity on sign learning by mentally retarded children, *Am. J. Ment. Defic.*, *85*, 291–8.

Hart, B. and Risley, T.R. (1974) Using preschool materials to modify the language of disadvantaged children, *J. Applied Behavior Analysis*, *7*, 243–56.

Hermelin, B. and O'Connor, N. (1970) *Psychological Experiments with Autistic Children*, Pergamon, Oxford.

Hersen, M. and Barlow, D.H. (1981) *Single Case Experimental Designs*, Pergamon, New York.

Howlin, P. (1981) The effectiveness of operant language training with autistic children, *J. Autism and Developmental Disorders*, *11*, 89–105.

Jones, L., Reid, B. and Kiernan, C. (1982) Signs and symbols: the 1980 survey in *Signs, Symbols and Schools* (eds. M. Peter and R. Barnes), NCSE, Stratford.

Karlan, G., Brenn-White, B., Lentz, A., Hodur, P., Egger, D. and Frankoff, D. (1982) Establishing generalized productive verb–noun phrase usage in a manual language system with moderately handicapped children, *J. Speech Hearing Dis.*, *47*, 31–42.

Kiernan, C. (1983) The exploration of sign and symbol effects in *Advances in Mental Handicap Research. Vol. II, Aspects of Competence in Mentally Handicapped People* (eds. J. Hogg and P. Mittler), Wiley, Chichester, pp. 27–68.

Kiernan, C., Reid, B. and Jones, L. (1982) Signs and symbols: a review of literature and survey of the use of non-vocal communication systems, *Studies in Education No. 11*, University of London Institute of Education.

Konstantareas, M., Webster, C. and Oxman, J. (1979) Manual sign language acquisition and its influence on other areas of functioning in four autistic-like children, *J. Child Psychol. and Psychiat.*, *20*, 337–50.

Light, P., Remington, B. and Porter, D. (1982) Substitutes for speech? Nonvocal approaches to communication in *Children Thinking through Language* (ed. M. Beveridge), Edward Arnold, London, pp. 216–38.

Luftig, R. (1983) Translucency of sign and concreteness of gloss in the manual sign learning of moderately/severely retarded students, *Am. J. Ment. Defic.*, *88*, 279–86.

Luria, A.R. (1961) *The Role of Speech in the Regulation of Normal and Abnormal Behavior*, Liveright, New York.

McLean, J. and Snyder-McLean, L. (1978) *A Transactional Approach to Early Language Training*, Charles E. Merrill, Columbus, Ohio.

78

Miller, A. and Miller, E. (1973) Cognitive-developmental training with elevated boards and sign language, *J. Autism and Childhood Schizophrenia*, *3*, 65–85.

Penner, K. and Williams, W. (1982) Comparison of sign versus verbal symbol training in retarded adults, *Perceptual and Motor Skills*, *55*, 395–401.

Reid, B. (1981) An investigation of the relationship between manual sign training and speech development for mentally handicapped children, *Final Report to the DHSS; Thomas Coram Research Unit.*

Remington, B. and Clarke, S. (1983) Acquisition of expressive signing by autistic children: an evaluation of the relative effects of simultaneous communication and sign-alone training, *J. Applied Behavior Analysis*, *16*, 315–28.

Remington, B. and Light, P. (1983) Some problems in the evaluation of research on non-oral communication systems in *Advances in Mental Handicap Research. Vol. II, Aspects of Competence in Mentally Handicapped People* (eds. J. Hogg and P. Mittler), Wiley, Chichester, pp. 69–94.

Romski, M. and Ruder, K. (1984) Effects of speech and sign instruction on oral language learning and generalisation of action + object combinations by Down's syndrome children, *J. Speech Hearing Dis.* *49*, 293–302.

Schaeffer, B., Kollinzas, G., Musil, A. and McDowell, P. (1977) Spontaneous verbal language for autistic children through signed speech, *Sign Language Studies*, *17*, 287–328.

Sidman, M. and Tailby, W. (1982) Conditional discrimination vs matching-to-sample: an expansion of the testing paradigm, *J. Experimental Analysis of Behavior*, *37*, 5–22.

Sisson, L. and Barrett, R. (1984) An alternating treatments comparison of oral and total communication training with minimally verbal retarded children, *J. Applied Behavior Analysis*, *17*, 559–66.

Stremel-Campbell, K., Cantrell, D. and Halle, J. (1977) Manual signing as a language system and a speech initiator for the non-verbal, severely handicapped student in *Educational Programming for the Severely and Profoundly Handicapped* (eds. E. Sontag, J. Smith and W. Certo), Council for Exceptional Children, Reston, Va.

Watson, J. (1986) Matrix training and sign language for the mentally handicapped, unpublished PhD thesis, University of Southampton.

Wilson, E. (1975) *Sociobiology*, Harvard University Press, Cambridge, Mass.

PART II

Language and Cognitive Processes in People with Mental Handicaps

Chapters 4–6 in this part consider three different aspects of the relationship between language, communication and cognition in mentally handicapped persons. Chapter 4, by Kamhi and Masterson, looks at whether the delay vs difference controversy is a conceptual artefact of the way the question is interpreted. Their careful analysis paves the way for an end to research into spurious phenomena and suggests a more productive way forward. In Chapter 5, Owens examines in detail the implications for both 'process' and 'developmental' approaches to cognition in people with mental handicaps. The chapter considers the ways that each approach can be used to derive theoretically sound intervention programmes. Chapter 6, by Beveridge, presents a link between cognition and the interactive environment of mentally handicapped people. He argues for the relevance of 'social cognition' to our understanding of the development of their ways of thinking. The author's work on the interactive environment is discussed from the social cognitive perspective.

4

Language and Cognition in Mentally Handicapped People: Last Rites for the Difference–Delay Controversy

Alan G. Kamhi and Julie J. Masterson

Mental retardation manifests itself in a variety of behavioral domains. Among the most serious and obvious deficits is delayed language development. Language and intelligence are so intimately related that some people have essentially defined mental retardation in terms of a language deficit (Bereiter and Engelmann, 1966; Stamm, 1974). Ingalls (1978, p. 219), in his book on mental retardation, states that a deficit in language skills is perhaps the single most important characteristic that distinguishes a retarded person from a non-retarded one. Drew, Logan and Hardman (1984) find that it is common for parents and teachers to attribute most, if not all, of the retarded child's learning problems to language deficiencies.

One of the fundamental issues in the literature on the language abilities of mentally handicapped people has been whether there are quantitative or qualitative differences between the language of mentally handicapped and non-handicapped children (Yoder and Miller, 1972). Is the language development process for retarded children just a slowed down version of the one for non-retarded children? Or are there some differences in the language of a mentally handicapped child and a younger normal child of the same cognitive level?

A similar controversy underlies questions about the cognitive abilities of mentally handicapped children. In this case, the issue is referred to as the developmental–difference controversy (Zigler and Balla, 1982). The issue concerns the similarity of the cognitive abilities of a mentally handicapped child and a younger non-handicapped child at the same level of cognitive development. Adherents of the developmental viewpoint argue that the cognitive abilities of retarded and non-retarded children equated for cognitive level are essentially similar (e.g. Zigler, 1969). In contrast, proponents of the difference view (e.g. Das, 1972, 1984; Milgram, 1973) argue that retarded children's cognitive processes are in some way different than those of normal children.

In this chapter we will argue that it is time to move beyond the delay–difference controversy and ask different and more appropriate questions about the language and cognitive abilities of retarded individuals. The chapter is divided into three major parts. In the first part we review the literature that has dealt with the nature of the mental handicap in retarded individuals. In the second part we discuss the nature of the linguistic impairment in people with mental handicaps. In the final part of the chapter we attempt to put to rest the delay–difference controversy by turning it into a non-issue.

4.1 COGNITIVE ABILITIES IN MENTALLY HANDICAPPED PEOPLE

The cognitive abilities of mentally handicapped people have been examined within every conceivable theoretical orientation to intelligence and cognition, including the psychometric approach, Piagetian approach and a variety of information processing approaches. As we have suggested, the data on retarded children's cognitive abilities have been interpreted to support either the developmental view or the difference view. Before discussing some of the actual studies, the two positions are now elaborated.

On one side of the controversy is the developmental position advocated by Zigler (1969) and elaborated by Weisz, Yeates and Zigler (1982). This position, which applies only to individuals who do not suffer from organic impairment, holds that mentally handicapped and non-handicapped individuals pass through cognitive developmental stages (e.g. the stages described by Piaget, 1970) in an identical order, but differ in rate and the upper limit of development. Retarded children move through the various stages more slowly and attain a lower developmental level than non-retarded children. In Zigler's (1969) own words:

> According to this model, the cognitive performance of individuals of differing IQs who are at the same cognitive level and, therefore, at different chronological ages, should [be] exactly the same on cognitive tasks. Cognitive performance is thus viewed as totally a function of the cognitive level of the individual, irrespective of the amount of time it took that individual to reach that cognitive level. (p. 540)

On the other side of the controversy is the difference position. According to this position, retarded and non-retarded children, even when equated for level of development, will differ in the cognitive processes they use in reasoning. Spitz (1976), for example, argues that retarded individuals show a marked deficiency on tests requiring foresight and logical analysis, and to a lesser extent on tests requiring verbal abstraction and conceptual ability.

Weisz and Yeates (1981) have pointed out that the developmental vs difference controversy involves two separate hypotheses. One hypothesis is that retarded and non-retarded children pass through cognitive developmental stages in the same order. This has been referred to as the 'similar sequence hypothesis'. Most of the evidence, derived from Piagetian research (e.g. Weisz and Zigler, 1979), supports this hypothesis.

The second hypothesis concerns the similarity of the cognitive structures in retarded and non-retarded children at a particular cognitive level. This hypothesis has been labelled the 'similar structure hypothesis' (Weisz and Yeates, 1981). The term 'cognitive structure' represents the organization of thinking and learning processes that underlie human understanding, reasoning and the acquisition of information. As Weiss, Weisz and Bromfield (1986) point out, however, cognitive structure must be inferred from observable measures such as effectiveness of problem-solving and speed of learning. The similar structure hypothesis holds that retarded and non-retarded children of similar mental age (MA) will not differ reliably on such measures.

Differences theorists, such as Milgram (1973), argue that retarded children are inferior to their non-retarded MA peers in a number of reasoning processes. Supporting this claim, several researchers (e.g. Das, 1972, 1984; Das, Kirby and Jarman, 1975; Detterman, 1979; Greenspan, 1979; Inhelder, 1966; Stephens and McLaughlin, 1974; Spitz, 1976) have found discrepancies in the cognitive abilities of retarded and non-retarded children unaccounted for by MA. Inhelder (1966), for example, reported that retarded children showed fixations in operational activities at different stages of development. In addition, retarded children had considerable difficulty moving from one stage to the next.

Stephens and McLaughlin (1974) administered a large battery of Piagetian tasks to retarded and non-retarded individuals between the ages of 6 and 20 years. They reported significant differences between the two groups that could not be explained by differences in MA. These differences involved the categorization, flexibility and reversibility required in conservation and classification tasks.

Das and his colleagues (Das, 1972; Das, Kirby and Jarman, 1975) found significant differences between retarded and non-retarded groups on a series of memory and reasoning tasks. They explained these differences in terms of Luria's (1966) dimensions of simultaneous and successive synthesis. Simultaneous synthesis involves the arrangement of stimuli into simultaneous spatial groups, whereas successive synthesis requires that stimuli be arranged into temporally organized sequences. Das, Kirby and Jarman found evidence that retarded children have deficient simultaneous integration skills. They further suggested that these deficits were caused by the use of less efficient problem-solving strategies.

Support for the difference view also comes from a series of studies by Semmel and his associates on the development of paradigmatic functioning (e.g. Semmel, Barritt and Bennett, 1970). At around the age of 6 years (see

Nelson, 1977), a developmental shift occurs in children's word associations from predominantly syntagmatic (e.g. *chair–sit*) to predominantly paradigmatic responding (e.g. *chair–table*). Semmel, Barritt and Bennett found that retarded children had inferior paradigmatic abilities in comparison to MA-matched controls.

The studies discussed thus far support what has been called the conventional difference position. The unconventional position is taken by Kohlberg (1968); his position is that 'general experience' plays an important role in the development of reasoning skills. Consequently, retarded children should be cognitively more advanced than their MA-matched peers, because they have lived longer and experienced more. There is some support for this position. In one study Kamhi (1981) found that school-age (mean MA = 62.4 months) retarded children performed significantly better than MA-matched non-retarded children on a mental displacement task. This was a task for which children had to mentally combine two adjacent simple geometric forms (e.g. a horizontal line and a square) such that one of the forms was superimposed on the other. Consistent with Kohlberg's claim, the superior performance of the retarded children was attributed to the influence of their additional age- and school-related experiences. The question was raised, however, of the effect these additional experiences had on the retarded children's performance on the other five tasks for which no group differences were found. Kamhi suggested that these experiences might reduce the potential gap between performance levels and cognitive capabilities, thus making performance levels a more accurate reflection of the retarded children's cognitive capabilities.

In another study, Eaton and Burdz (1984) found that retarded children (mean MA = 48.2 months) displayed significantly better gender constancy performance than their non-retarded counterparts. These authors found that the better constancy performance of the retarded children was the result of their correct responses to the two most difficult items. They attribute this finding to CA-related knowledge superiority or to guessing behaviour on these items.

The most systematic attempts to address the developmental–difference controversy involves two recent studies by Weisz and Yeates (1981) and Weiss, Weisz and Bromfield (1986). In these studies, Weisz and his colleagues review the findings from a wide range of studies that compared the performance of retarded and MA-matched non-retarded children on Piagetian and non-Piagetian cognitive measures. The findings from these studies will be discussed in some detail below.

(a) Piagetian measures

In their first study, Weisz and Yeates (1981) reviewed the findings from thirty

86

studies that compared the performance of MA-matched retarded and non-retarded children on Piagetian tasks. A total of 104 comparisons were made in these studies. The overall analysis revealed that in 4% of the comparisons retarded subjects performed at higher levels than non-retarded MA peers. In 24% of the comparisons the retarded children performed more poorly than the non-retarded. Thus 72% of the comparisons supported the developmental hypothesis that there were no differences between the performance of retarded and non-retarded subjects.

Although the majority of studies supported the development hypothesis, Weisz and Yeates argued that there was no definitive support for it. They noted that the developmental hypothesis was essentially a null-hypothesis, that is across a range of studies significant results (differences) will be found only at a chance level. Hence, for the hypothesis to be supported, the number of comparisons showing significant group differences should be less than or equal to the total number of comparisons reviewed times the alpha-level (Weiss, Weisz and Bromfield, 1986, p. 158). When studies not explicitly controlling for organicity were included in the analysis, results favoured rejection of the developmental hypothesis. However, when the studies that excluded organically impaired subjects were considered, only 3 (9%) of 33 comparisons contradicted the hypothesis.

Weisz and Yeates (1981) concluded that the support for the developmental position appeared strong but was limited in scope since it was derived entirely from studies using Piagetian resoning tasks. They suggested the need for an examination of the literature using non-Piagetian measures of the cognitive performance of retarded and non-retarded individuals.

(b) Information processing measures

Weiss, Weisz, and Bromfield (1986) report the results of a selected review of studies from 1960 to 1983 that compared retarded and non-retarded individuals on non-Piagetian tasks. To be included in the review, studies had to meet three criteria. The retarded subjects had to be (i) matched for MA with a non-retarded group, (ii) screened to exclude organically impaired individuals and (iii) non-institutionalized.

Similar development level has generally been operationalized by matched retarded and non-retarded groups for MA, as measured by a standardized intelligence test that taps a relatively broad array of cognitive functions. Studies in which it was assumed that MA = CA for non-retarded subjects were excluded from the analysis.

The organicity criterion was more problematic. The developmental position as posited by Zigler and Balla (1982) specifically excludes retarded individuals with organic aetiologies because these individuals with known brain damage are clearly different relative to non-retarded individuals.

Unfortunately it is not possible to exclude organically impaired individuals with absolute certainty because the available methods of diagnosing organicity are relatively crude. With this caveat in mind, studies that were included in the analysis had to state that the subjects showed no indication of neurological involvement and/or that the subjects were 'familial' retarded.

Although the developmental view does not specifically exclude institutionalized individuals, factors such as motivation and expectancy of failure that might be associated with institutionalization can have an important impact on performance (Zigler and Balla, 1982). These kinds of non-cognitive factors can also influence the performance of non-institutionalized individuals. However, few investigators have attempted to control such factors. It is thus not possible to evaluate studies on the basis of their control over non-cognitive factors. Excluding studies that limited comparisons to institutionalized retarded individuals was the most conservative approach feasible.

Twenty-four studies involving 59 comparisons met the criteria for inclusion in the review. The studies were arranged into broad categories of information processing abilities. Weiss, Weisz and Bromfield (1986) were concerned that organizing the studies around a particular theoretical model of information processing might bias the data analysis. The categories examined were memory, paired-associated learning, input organization, selective attention, discrimination learning, incidental learning, concept usage and matching, and hypothesis-testing behavior. The studies were analysed from a categorical standpoint using a chi-square analysis. A meta-analysis was also performed in which the data were pooled in a way designed to maximize use of information and statistical power.

A summary of the findings indicated that 52% of the comparisons resulted in no significant retarded–non-retarded group differences. Significant differences in favour of the retarded children were found in 45% of the comparisons. Only 3% (2 comparisons) supported the unconventional difference view in which retarded subjects performed better than the non-retarded. The performance of the retarded subjects was most deficient in the area of discrimination (e.g. Harter, Brown and Zigler, 1971; Libkuman, 1972; Richman *et al.*, 1978). Deficits were found in printed word discrimination, picture discrimination and three-dimensional object discrimination. A pronounced deficit was also found in the area of memory (e.g. Brown, 1974; Fagan, 1968; Mosley, 1980, 1981). Retarded individuals performed significantly poorer than non-retarded in serial and non-serial auditory short-term memory (STM), visual iconic memory, visual STM, cross-modal STM and visual paired-associate learning. The non-retarded subjects were also consistently superior in their ability to explain the strategies they used in the various experiments. Finally, a significant interaction between CA and MA of the retarded was found. The higher the MA level of a retarded child, the higher the probability that performance was inferior to that of the non-retarded subjects.

The performance of the retarded and non-retarded subjects was comparable in several areas, including measures of incidental learning, concept usage and matching, and hypothesis-testing behaviour. There was some indication that in the area of distractability and selective attention, the performance of the retarded subjects was superior to that of the non-retarded.

The findings from these two studies clearly present a dilemma: the developmental position seems to hold for Piagetian tasks but not for information processing tasks. Weiss, Weisz and Bromfield (1986) consider several possible reasons for the conflicting findings. Artefactual explanations were considered first. For example, it might be that Piagetian tasks are more susceptible to ceiling and floor effects than information processing tasks, or that the information processing studies used inferior procedures for screening organicity. Although these explanations are plausible, they do not account for the strong consistency of the Piagetian findings and the clear variability in the information processing tasks. The alternative is that the different pattern of results was caused by factors inherent in the tasks themselves.

One task-based explanation is that Piagetian tasks (e.g. making moral judgements) are more 'lifelike' or 'ecologically valid' than information processing tasks (e.g. discrimination learning of coloured shapes). This may be true of the skills themselves, or of the manner in which the skills were assessed. However, a problem with this view is that many Piagetian tasks, such as conservation tasks and anticipatory imagery tasks, have little ecological validity.

Another explanation is that retarded and non-retarded children differ significantly on some extracognitive variable such as motivation or expectancy for success. Although it seems unlikely, retarded individuals might be more motivated to perform Piagetian tasks as opposed to information processing tasks. The significant interaction discovered between IQ and MA has bearing on this explanation. Weiss, Weisz and Bromfield (1986) cite a personal communication from J.P. Das (1984), who predicted this interaction based on the fact that school is often a primary site of failure for retarded children. As retarded children get older, their performance on information processing tasks (on which school performance is primarily based) may deteriorate relative to that of non-retarded persons. In support of this claim, Weisz (1979) found that retarded children were more helpless, relative to MA-matched non-retarded groups, at higher MA levels than at lower levels.

This is not the only explanation for the interaction between CA and MA. The interaction might be the result of the increases in cognitive complexity of the tasks used with older children. Spitz (1976) has suggested that retarded individuals show deficits in complex cognitive processes involved in solving more abstract problems with which older children are confronted. One might therefore expect that at low MA levels retarded and non-retarded children will perform similarly because the complex abilities on which they will ultimately differ are equally undeveloped in both groups. As the non-retarded children begin to develop more sophisticated cognitive abilities they will begin to outperform their retarded MA peers.

Kamhi (1981) suggested that differences between retarded and non-retarded children might be expected to emerge at an MA level of 6 years, when non-retarded children enter the transitional period between pre-operational and operational thought. Children's thinking undergoes several important changes during this period. Paradigmatic responses become preferred over syntagmatic ones, symbolic codes (namely, language) play a more central role in thought and simultaneous synthesis becomes preferred over successive synthesis. The changes that mark children's entry into the formal operational period at around the age of 11 would be expected to create even more pronounced differences between retarded and non-retarded peers.

There is little doubt that non-cognitive factors, such as motivation and learned helplessness, influence the cognitive performance of retarded children. However, the data suggest that even if all of artefactual effects and non-cognitive variables were controlled, one would find still that the development of retarded children within certain cognitive domains is inferior to that of their non-retarded MA peers. As Weiss, Weisz and Bromfield (1986) state, 'Our findings may merely reflect what they appear to reflect: retarded persons suffer from various cognitive deficits that are more than a simple developmental delay' (p. 172).

Indeed it is possible to argue, independently of the evidence from the study by Weiss, Weisz and Bromfield, that the cognitive domains most likely to reveal differences are those within the information processing tradition. Piagetian tasks are sensitive to developmental changes in transitional periods during which children move from one stage to another. These tasks are less sensitive to within-stage differences. In contrast, information processing tasks were originally developed to uncover individual and group differences. The measures obtained from these tasks thus are more discrete and sensitive to developmental changes within and across major developmental periods.

(c) The structure vs process debate

For many psychologists (e.g. Borkowski and Turner, 1986; Ellis, 1963; Sperber and McCauley, 1984), the developmental–difference controversy is part of a more basic structure–process debate. The question underlying this debate is whether deficient structures or processes define retardation.

Those who adhere to the structural position attempt to find innate, defining features or states that characterize retarded children's cognitive systems and claim that these features are relatively intractable. In contrast, those who support a process position believe that mental skills are acquired, relatively easy to modify, and interact with higher- and lower-order components. The structural view is consistent with the difference position, while the process view is consistent with the developmental position.

The research used to support the structural position is essentially the same as that used to support the difference view. Most of the structuralist explanations have looked for deficiencies in early stages of information processes. Ellis (1963), for example, proposed that the learning and memory deficiencies in the retarded could be attributed to the decreased intensity and duration of the short-term memory trace. Information in short-term memory faded more quickly for retarded individuals, and thus was less likely to be transferred to a more permanent memory store. Zeaman and House (1979) proposed that retarded individuals attended to fewer dimensions of a stimulus than non-retarded subjects, and therefore were less likely to focus on the relevant dimensions of a problem. Sperber and McCauley (1984) found that retarded individuals encoded information more slowly than non-retarded individuals. The pattern of these findings is consistent with Weiss, Weisz and Bromfield's (1986) conclusion that retarded and non-retarded differ significantly in the area of memory.

Other psychologists (e.g. Belmont and Butterfield, 1971; Brown, 1974) have focused on the role that processes and strategies play in retarded individual's learning difficulties. These investigators have found that retarded individuals often do not use rehearsal strategies to increase recall. Deficient strategies have also been found in paired-associate learning (Taylor and Turnure, 1979), categorization (Gerjouy et al., 1969) and organization (Spitz and Borys, 1977). Many investigators have reported success in training strategies to enhance performance on these tasks. Butterfield, Wambold and Belmont (1973), for example, improved the performance of retarded individuals to the level of untrained college students following extensive training of rehearsal and retrieval strategies. However, generalization of these skills has proven to be more difficult. Difficulties in executive functions (e.g. Butterfield and Belmont, 1977) and meta-memory (Borkowski, Reid and Kurtz, 1984) have been posited as potential sources for the generalization problem.

(d) An integrated model of cognition

In a recent paper, Borkowski and Turner (1986) recount the intensity of the structure–process debate in a 1980 conference on 'Learning and Cognition in the Mentally Retarded' at Vanderbilt University. They relate

91

the story of how David Zeaman walked slowly to the podium, paused and dramatically proclaimed that he had renamed and redirected his planned paper, which was to be about primary and secondary generalization. The new talk was titled, 'Retardation is more than just a bad habit'.

Borkowski and Turner (1986) agree that retardation is more than a bad cognitive habit. They also believe that structural deficiencies likely constitute a more basic and fundamental source of cognitive problems than do failures in the development of learning skills and processes. However, with equal vigour, they also assert that the social side of retardation also breeds many bad cognitive habits. It is thus possible to acknowledge that differences can exist in some basic cognitive processes while, at the same time, recognizing that these differences can lead to motivational deficiencies and negative, self-limiting attributional beliefs about learning potential.

The structural–deficit position and the process–developmental position are thus not theoretically incompatible. Several attempts have been made to develop integrated models of learning that attempt to combine components from these two positions. Detterman (1979) proposed a model that included structural and process-oriented constructs, but not motivational ones. As Zigler has argued, however, complex cognitive acts, such as reading, are inseparably linked to motivational states and personal dispositions, such as self-esteem. Motivational deficits in retarded individuals often become linked to poor learning histories, cognitive deficits and negative attributional states.

Borkowski and Turner (1986) outline a model of meta-cognition that includes a component of attributional beliefs, motivation and self-esteem. However, this model does not include basic cognitive structures and processes. A fully integated model needs to include all three components: (i) basic cognitive structure/processes such as attentional, memory and conceptual processes; (ii) executive and meta-cognitive functions and strategies; and (iii) motivational states and personal dispositions.

4.2 LANGUAGE ABILITIES IN MENTALLY HANDICAPPED PEOPLE

The developmental–difference controversy also permeates the literature concerned with the language abilities of retarded individuals. In this case, the controversy is referred to as the quantitative-qualitative debate or the difference–delay issue. Lenneberg (1967) provided the initial stimulus for research in this area by arguing that the language of retarded children differed quantitatively from that of non-retarded children. The quality of retarded children's language was claimed to be consistent with MA. Lenneberg further argued that the entire developmental process is slowed down during childhood and stops sometime during early adolescence.

The alternative view is that language development is not consistent with cognitive level. Given the heterogeneity of the retarded population with respect to aetiology, severity of the mental deficiency, motivational factors and age, one should not expect to find a single systematic pattern of language and cognitive development in retarded individuals (e.g. Miller, Chapman and MacKenzie, 1981). In other words, language development might not be commensurate with cognitive level in all retarded individuals.

Two general approaches have been used to address the relationship between language and cognitive skills in the retarded: (i) a correlational approach, and (ii) a descriptive linguistic approach. In the correlational approach, measures of cognitive and language performance are obtained from retarded subjects and compared. Correspondences between language and cognitive abilities support the quantitative delay position, whereas asynchronies support the difference view. With the descriptive linguistic approach, a particular aspect of retarded children's language is analysed and compared to that of non-retarded children matched for MA. If the retarded and non-retarded group exhibit comparable language abilities, the quantitative view is supported. Group differences support the qualitative difference view. Studies representing each of these approaches will now be discussed.

(a) Correlational studies

Several early studies examined the relationship between sensorimotor abilities and early language development in severely retarded individuals. Woodward and Stern (1963) found that only 4 out of 29 children, in stage 5, exhibited verbal comprehension. All of the stage-6 children, however, demonstrated evidence of comprehension. With respect to language production, some children in stage 5 produced meaningful words. Only stage-6 children produced word combinations.

Hulme and Lunzer (1966) studied the quality of free play, reasoning skills and the level of language behaviour in severely retarded children. No significant differences were found between the levels of organization of play. The retarded children, however, produced fewer words and less sophisticated language than the MA-matched non-retarded children.

In a more recent study, Casby and Ruder (1983) studied the relationship between symbolic play and language development in 20 moderate-to-severely retarded children (IQ 25–50). Half of the children had mean length of utterance (MLU) values of less than 1.5, and half had MLU values between 1.5 and 2.0. No significant differences were found in the symbolic play behaviours of the retarded and non-retarded children. Children at the higher language stage obtained higher symbolic play scores than children in the lower stage. The authors concluded that non-verbal symbolic abilities in the retarded were commensurate with their language skills.

Greenwald and Leonard (1979) studied the relationship between imperative and declarative performatives and levels of sensorimotor development in normal and Down's syndrome children. Stage-5 children produced more performatives than stage-4 children. The normal children at stage 5 used more words and vocalizations in the declarative task than the retarded children. Greenwald and Leonard concluded that early communicative and sensorimotor skills showed a similar sequence in development for both normal and retarded children. However, the retarded children appeared to have some difficulty in using more sophisticated levels of declarative performatives.

Mahoney, Glover and Finger (1981) studied the relationship between sensorimotor skills and language skills in Down's syndrome and normal children. The retarded children performed comparably to the non-retarded on the Uzgiris and Hunt (1975) scales, but obtained significantly lower scores on the receptive language measures.

The results of the studies discussed thus far have been inconclusive. The few studies cited above all involved severely retarded or organically impaired children and focused on the relationship between language and cognitive development only in the sensorimotor period. In addition, global stage measures of language development were often used rather than more sensitive linguistic measures.

The Wisconsin study.

The most comprehensive attempt to compare language and cognitive abilities in retarded children took place at the University of Wisconsin under the direction of Jon Miller. In 1976 a computerized clinical data-base was initiated which included 22 categories of developmental and non-developmental information. These categories involved measures of cognitive development, speech, language, hearing, aetiology and psychological characteristics. Subjects included in the data-base were children referred for a variety of developmental problems. In 1981 when the report was made (Miller, Chapman and Mackenzie, 1981), the data-base included 266 subjects. Within this group there were 130 subjects whose cognitive abilities were between 7 months and 7 years, and who had at least one comprehension measure. The majority of the children were functioning in the moderate to severe range of disability and were multiply handicapped.

Cognitive functioning was assessed by the Uzgiris and Hunt sensorimotor scales, observation of play behaviour, figure drawing, copying of forms, haptic perception and seriation tasks. From performance on these tasks children were classified as functioning in the age ranges associated with sensorimotor stages 4, 5 and 6, or early, middle and late preoperational periods.

Syntactic comprehension was assessed through tasks requiring compliance with commands, locative, instructions and answers to Wh-questions or the Miller–Yoder Test of Grammatical Comprehension. Receptive vocabulary was assessed with the Peabody Picture Vocabulary Test (Dunn, 1965). Spontaneous speech samples were also obtained. Children were assigned to Brown's language stages according to MLU or structures present.

The initial analysis considered the data on the 130 subjects for whom at least cognitive level and one measure of comprehension were obtained. Each of three language characteristics, comprehension of syntax, comprehension of vocabulary and syntactic production, was judged to be advanced, commensurate or delayed relative to a subject's cognitive level. The results are summarized below:

1. Delays in vocabulary comprehension existed at almost every cognitive level; 17% of the subjects showed delays in vocabulary comprehension, whereas 20% had delays in the comprehension of syntax;
2. 41% of the children had delays in productive syntax; production was never advanced relative to cognitive level;
3. Advances in vocabulary and syntax comprehension occurred at almost every level of cognitive development.

These data suggested that there were individual differences among the retarded in language performance relative to cognitive level. To further evaluate the nature of these differences a group of 42 subjects with complete language data was identified from the pool of 130 subjects. Within this subset of children nine patterns of language performance relative to cognitive level were identified. The three most frequent patterns were as follows.

Type 1: Delayed production. Comprehension was within the expected range but production was delayed relative to cognitive level; 24% of the subjects were in this category.
Type 2: Delayed comprehension and production. All language measures were delayed relative to cognitive level; 17% of the subjects fell into this category.
Type 3: No language delay. Language comprehension and production were within the expected range for cognitive level; 36% of the children were in this category.

The patterns of the remaining children differed from the three frequent profiles only in that one of the comprehension measures was within the expected range or advanced. When these children were included in the three frequent profile types, 50% of the children were functioning at or

95

beyond the language levels expected by cognitive level; 25% of the children demonstrated delays in both comprehension and production, while the remaining 25% showed delays only in productive syntax, but not comprehension of either syntax or vocabulary.

It should be apparent that the major finding of this study was that retarded children at equivalent cognitive levels demonstrated different patterns of language performance. This finding is not totally surprising, given the diversity of the retarded children in the data-base with respect to aetiology, severity of the cognitive deficiency, degree of physical handicap, and speech and hearing status. One is left with questions about how factors, such as severity of retardation and developmental age, influenced the patterns of language and cognitive performance uncovered. For example, were the mildly retarded younger children more likely to exhibit equivalent cognitive and language skills? Miller *et al.* (1980) do note that speech motor control and hearing status were not sufficient to explain the three major profile types.

(b) Descriptive linguistic studies

There is a rich body of literature that has attempted to describe the nature of the language deficiencies in the mentally handicapped (e.g. Lackner, 1968; Naremore and Dever, 1975; Newfield and Schlanger, 1968). This literature has been interpreted to support either the quantitative delay or qualitative difference view. Our discussion of this literature will begin with some early studies that examined syntactic and semantic abilities. Some problems with these studies will be discussed. Then some more recent studies that have examined linguistic and communicative abilities of the retarded will be presented.

The early studies (pre-1975).

Several studies have found evidence for qualitative differences in retarded children's language. Representative of this position is Jordan's (1967) conclusion, from a review of the literature, that retarded children produced shorter and structurally less complex utterances than their non-retarded peers. Jordan also found evidence that abstraction was less common in the language of the retarded.

Direct evidence for the qualitative view comes from studies by Newfield and Schlanger (1968) and the work of Semmel and his colleagues (e.g. Semmel, Barritt and Bennett, 1970). Newfield and Schlanger examined the acquisition of morphological markers in normal and institutionalized mildly retarded children. The mean age of the retarded children was 10 years 4 months. Subjects were given two sets of stimuli: Berko's Test of English Morphology, and a set of lexical items testing the same inflectional forms as the Berko Test. The order of acquisition of inflectional forms was the same for the two groups. The retarded children, however, performed significantly better with the real words than the nonsense words. Newfield and Schlanger attribute this difference to the institutionalized environment of the retarded. However, Yoder and Miller (1972) suggest that there may have been a qualitative difference in the learning strategies used by the two groups. The retarded children's ability to apply knowledge to novel situations may be deficient rather than their linguistic knowledge per se.

Semmel, Barritt and Bennett (1970) administered a close procedure to mildly retarded and non-retarded children. In this task the children had to supply words deleted from sentence contexts. The retarded children performed significantly poorer than MA-matched peers on this task. These findings led Semmel, Barritt and Bennett to conclude that 'the generative rules which are obviously present and utilized in their recoding of grammatical sentences do not appear to be as efficiently invoked toward efficient decoding performance by EMR children' (p. 688).

In summarizing the results from the studies, Yoder and Miller (1972, p. 98) noted that retarded children are not rule-oriented in their language behaviour. They seem to use a sequential strategy to string words together and do not have functional use of form/class categories. Although these studies appear to indicate qualitative differences in the application of linguistic knowledge to language-dependent tasks, a general conclusion that there is a qualitative difference may be a simplification. A study by Lackner (1968) is often cited in support of the quantitative view.

Lackner wrote grammars for 5 retarded children with MAs ranging from 2:8 to 5:9. He used both comprehension and production data in developing a grammar for each child. Rather than following each child over a period of time, he took the single grammar he had written for each child and viewed the development of grammar from child to child as MA increased. He found that the grammars of the retarded children were subsets of the adult grammar. For the children at lower MA levels, the grammars were very general, in that they lacked context-sensitivity at the phrase–structure and transformational levels. As MA increased the grammars became more characteristic of adult grammar. Lackner concluded that the language behaviours of the retarded were not qualitatively different because the retarded children and non-retarded children followed similar developmental trends.

A study by Graham and Graham (1971) supported Lackner's findings. They investigated the syntactic abilities of institutionalized males between the age of 10 and 20. Like Lackner, these authors found that increases in syntactic complexity were related to increases in mental age.

There is the possibiity that the relationship between language and cognitive abilities is not static throughout the developmental period. Recall that Weiss, Weisz and Bromfield (1986) found more support for the difference position as MA increased. Naremore and Dever's (1975) data support this possibility. In this study language samples of mildly retarded and non-retarded children were compared on a set of syntactic and fluency measures. Retarded children from five MA levels (6–10 years) were matched to non-retarded children whose CA ranged from 6 to 10 years. Discriminant analyses revealed that up until a mental age of 10, there were few if any qualitative differences in the language behaviour of the two groups. The oldest retarded children, however, produced significantly fewer utterances containing predicate elaboration, subordinate clauses and relative clauses. These findings indicate that at younger mental age levels, there may be few qualitative differences in the language of mildly retarded children. At higher MA levels, especially beyond an MA of 10 years, more qualitative differences might be expected.

Limitations of the early studies.

The conclusions made relative to the difference–delay issue in the early studies were limited by some of the same factors that influenced the developmental–difference debate. These factors include: (i) the heterogeneity of the retarded subjects, (ii) the types of language measures used and (iii) the way in which language performance was compared to cognitive level.

Just as the cognitive deficiencies exhibited by retarded individuals are affected by factors such as aetiology, institutionalization, severity of the retardation and age, so are the language deficiencies exhibited by retarded individuals. One should expect to find more qualitative language differences in individuals who are organically impaired, institutionalized and severely retarded. The extent of these differences also should increase with increases in age. Any attempt to address the quantitative-qualitative issue must take these variables into account.

With respect to the language measures used, it is often assumed that comparable language performance in one language domain signifies comparable language performance across other language domains as well. As Miller, Chapman and MacKenzie (1981) found, however, at least 50% of the retarded children they tested showed uneven language performance relative to cognitive level. For example, some retarded children demonstrated comprehension skills consistent with cognitive level while exhibiting delayed expressive language abilities. Another possibility is that the overall language patterns of retarded children are unlike those of any younger normal child.

A final concern is the way cognitive level is assessed. In most studies retarded and non-retarded children are matched according to MA, as measured by a standardized test of intelligence. However, it should be apparent from our earlier discussion of retarded children's cognitive abilities that MA is not an accurate reflection of cognitive level. In fact both difference and developmental theorists acknowledge that MA is not an accurate reflection of cognitive level. Recall that the disagreement concerns the cause of the cognitive deficit. Difference theorists attribute MA-inconsistent cognitive performance to structural deficiencies, whereas developmental theorists attribute poor cognitive performance to strategy (meta-cognitive) or motivational deficits.

If MA does not provide an accurate reflection of cognitive level, then studies that report qualitative language differences need to be interpreted cautiously. Language development might be consistent with general cognitive level or aspects of cognition that are more severely delayed (e.g. memory functions) but not be consistent with MA.

The later studies (post-1975).

The studies conducted after 1975 were more sensitive to the limitations discussed above. To a large extent, an understanding of the issues leads one to expect to find differences in the language of the retarded, especially if the retarded subjects are heterogeneous with regard to aetiology, educational placement, age and cognitive level. As with the developmental-difference controversy, perhaps the only way to resolve the delay–difference debate is to study non-organically impaired, mildly retarded individuals. Representative of these later studies is the one conducted by Kamhi and Johnston (1982); this study will be now discussed in detail.

Kamhi and Johnston addressed each of the three areas of concern in their study of retarded children's language. The retarded children studied were all taken from educable mentally retarded (EMR) public school classrooms, and none showed evidence of a genetically based syndrome. In contrast to most previous studies, descriptive linguistic procedures that measured the development of both syntactic and semantic systems were used. The semantic measures assessed developing propositional complexity, whereas the syntactic procedures (e.g. Developmental Sentence Scoring; see Lee, 1974) assessed knowledge of both base syntactic rules and grammatical morphology. Finally, in addition to a standardized measure of MA (the Leiter International Performance Scale), data from six non-standardized Piagetian tasks were available. These data, discussed earlier (Kamhi, 1981) indicated that the retarded and non-retarded children exhibited similar cognitive abilities in number, order, classification, haptic perception and mental rotation. Recall that the retarded children actually performed better than the non-retarded on the mental rotation task.

Subjects in the study were 10 retarded, 10 non-retarded and 10 children with a specific language impairment. The inclusion of the language-impaired (LI) children enabled us to compare the language abilities of the retarded to those of a group with known language deficiencies. The mean

MA of the three groups ranged from 60.6 months to 62.4 months. Spontaneous language samples of approximately 100 utterances were obtained from each child.

The results of the syntactic and semantic analyses suggested that the naïve observer would probably not notice any differences between the language of the retarded and non-retarded children. This observer would, however, notice differences between the retarded and language-impaired children. The LI children evidenced particular difficulty encoding grammatical morphemes correctly and produced structurally simple utterances that were shorter in length and propositionally less complex than those produced by the retarded children. In contrast, the retarded and non-retarded children used similar syntactic constructions, expressed the same propositional relations and evidenced little difficulty encoding grammatical morphemes.

Although the language of the retarded and non-retarded children was essentially comparable, three significant differences were found in the language of the retarded and non-retarded children. The retarded childen posed significantly fewer questions; produced significantly more sentences conjoined by *and*; and produced significantly more sentences in the progressive aspect (e.g. *He's running*). In interpreting these findings the possibility that these differences were the result of discrepancies in sampling conditions was first considered.

The LI children were tested in speech and hearing centres, an environment as formal — if not more formal — than the classroom setting in which retarded children were tested. However, the LI children asked twice as many questions as the retarded children, suggesting that the testing environment was at best only partially responsible for the few questions asked.

The language samples themselves were obtained in three conditions: story-telling, play and during the cognitive tasks. The retarded children produced a higher proportion of utterances in the story-telling condition than did the other two groups. The stories were clearly conducive to the production of sentences in the progressive aspect linked by the conjunction *and*. The frequent production of these kinds of sentence probably accounted for most of the language differences between the retarded and non-retarded children. The question, then, is why the language samples of the retarded children contained such a high proportion of utterances from the story-telling condition?

One reason was that the non-retarded children usually digressed while telling a story. They often spent as much time talking about related personal experiences as they did telling the story. The non-retarded children also took full advantage of the other two sampling conditions. The relatively continuous stream of speech produced by the non-retarded children, irrespective of the stimuli presented, reduced the proportion of language obtained from the story-telling condition. In addition, the non-retarded children used many more diversified language constructions than the retarded children in relating the stories.

We next considered the factors that might have caused the sampling discrepancies and the resultant MA-inconsistent language. One possibility was that these differences were the result of specific deficits in linguistic abilities. The data did not support this possibility. Retarded children's language was not only essentially comparable to that of the non-retarded children, but was also clearly superior to that of the LI children. The difficulties encountered by the LI children, particularly in encoding grammatical morphemes, were not present in the retarded children.

A second possibility was that the language deficits were the result of cognitive deficiencies. It is possible to argue, for example, that the retarded children used the conjunction *and* frequently because they did not understand conceptually more advanced conjunctions such as *when, because* and *if*. But the individual subject data indicated that seven of the ten retarded children produced more advanced conjunctions. Also all of the retarded children had instances of past tense sentences, indicating that their frequent use of progressive aspect sentences did not reflect a limited temporal focus on the here and now.

Having ruled out the possible influence of linguistic and cognitive factors, we suggested that deficient social and motivational behaviours were primarily responsible for the different language behaviors observed in the retarded and non-retarded children (see Kamhi and Johnston, 1982, p. 444). This explanation led to the more general claim that the overall cognitive level of mildly retarded individuals influences the qualitative aspects of language (i.e. the highest level of structural complexity possible), whereas non-cognitive factors, such as social-motivational behaviours, influence the quantitative aspects of language (i.e. the frequency with which various structures and forms are produced).

This interpretation of retarded children's language behaviours is not meant to explain the relationship between language and cognitive abilities in the larger population of retarded individuals. The interpretation is probably most accurate with young (MA < 7 years), mildly retarded, non-organically involved individuals whose cognitive and language abilities are relatively equivalent.

In conclusion, we suggested that the language performance of retarded children was influenced by the same kinds of linguistic, cognitive and social-motivational factors that influence normal children's language development. This conclusion suggests that models that place too much emphasis on the cognitive bases of language might be inaccurate. Before discussing some alternative models of language and cognition, studies that have evaluated pragmatic and general communicative abilities of retarded individuals will be discussed.

Communicative abilities.

In recent years the communicative or pragmatic abilities of retarded individuals have received considerable attention. A wide range of communicative abilities have been studied in retarded children and adults, including use of communicative functions (Greenwald and Leonard, 1979), presuppositional skills (Leonard, Cole and Steckol, 1979), perspective-taking (Bender and Carlson, 1982), role-taking (Affleck, 1976), conversational dominance (Selph and Kamhi, 1984; Bedrosian and Prutting, 1978), and discourse skills (Guralnick and Paul-Brown, 1986). Not unexpectedly, this research has been inconclusive with respect to the difference–delay issue. It is clear that individuals with organic impairments are at greater risk for communicative delays (Owens, 1985). But communicative differences have also been found in mildly retarded individuals. (Because Owens reviews much of this literature in Chapter 5 on communicative development in this book, we limit our discussion to two representative studies in this area.)

Guralnick and Paul-Brown (1986) analysed the communicative interaction of a group of mildly retarded children as they interacted with moderately and severely delayed companions as well as with non-handicapped and other mildly delayed children in a mainstreamed programme. The children ranged in age from 4 to 6 years. Communicative interactions were recorded over a five-month period during free play periods. Appoximately 200 utterances were obtained from the mildly retarded and non-retarded children. The communicative interactions were analysed in terms of syntactic complexity, semantic diversity, functional aspects of speech, the use of selected discourse devices (attentionals, such as *Hey!*, and self-repetitions of a speaker's preceding utterance), and the effectiveness of information and behaviour requests in relation to the developmental level of the listener.

The results indicated that the communicative interactions of the mildly delayed children were responsive to the cognitive and linguistic levels of their companions. Utterances with shorter mean lengths and a smaller proportion of long utterances were addressed to less developmentally advanced children. The function of the communicative interactions also varied with the developmental level of the listener. A greater proportion of behaviour statements with a correspondingly smaller proportion of information requests were directed to the more severely delayed children.

Guralnick and Paul-Brown (1986) cautioned that the similarities between the mildly handicapped and non-handicapped children should not be overstated. In related research, Guralnick and Weinhouse (1984) found that the social abilities of mildly handicapped children in interaction with their peers lagged considerably behind those of normally developing children matched for MA. They attributed the effectiveness of children in the current study to the fact that only immediate responses to behaviour and information requests were recorded. They go on to suggest that if utterances were tracked for longer periods, especially when initial failure occurred, a difference in the effectiveness and use of communicative strategies might be found. In a previous study, Guralnick and Paul-Brown (1984) found that non-handicapped children had lower perceptions of the social status of mildly handicapped children as reflected in the types of communicative strategies used to make behaviour requests. For example, the non-handicapped students rarely asked questions to the handicapped students. From these findings Guralnick and Paul-Brown (1984) concluded that differences in perceived social status have a considerable impact on communicative interactions.

In support of Guralnick and Paul-Brown's conclusions, there are several studies indicating that retarded persons play a non-dominant role in conversations. Bedrosian and Prutting (1978) found that retarded adults rarely exerted dominance in a conversation even when the communication partner was a child. A recent study by Selph and Kamhi (1984) explored the conversational roles of retarded children interacting with younger non-retarded children and the adult experimenter. Subjects were six retarded children ranging in age from 8 years 5 months to 12 years 1 month, with a mean MA of 6 years 5 months. The retarded children were matched for MA to six non-retarded children. The specific communicative abilities analysed included the use of requests and responses, topic maintenance and communicative sensitivity. Overall, the results indicated that the retarded and non-retarded children showed comparable abilities in the various communicative measures analysed. However, the retarded children talked less with the adult than MA-matched non-retarded peers and played a less dominant role with the younger children, as reflected by the use of fewer action requests.

Taken together, these studies indicate that mildly retarded children generally are competent communicators with respect to the use of appropriate communicative intentions, turn-taking skills, topic maintenance and listener sensitivity. As Guralnick and Paul-Brown (1986) have argued, however, one should not expect that the communicative interactions between retarded and non-retarded peers will remain unaffected by perceived differences in social status that exist in non-handicapped children. Retarded individuals have been found to play less dominant roles in conversation than non-retarded individuals.

4.3 LANGUAGE AND COGNITION IN MENTALLY HANDICAPPED PEOPLE

We began this chapter by noting that one of the fundamental issues involving retarded individuals was whether the language development process was just a slowed-down version of the one for non-retarded children. The alternative is that there are qualitative differences between the language behaviours of retarded and non-retarded children of the same cognitive level. In this final section of the chapter we attempt to show that the language delay–difference debate is essentially a non-issue. The question that underlies this debate concerns the effect the mental handicap has on language performance. Although this seems a reasonable question to ask, the way it is posed has led to several incorrect assumptions about cognition, language and the relationship between language and cognition.

One incorrect assumption is that cognitive level is a simple construct accurately reflected by MA. Recall that in the first part of this chapter we argued that cognitive performance was influenced by three factors: (i) basic cognitive structures and processes, (ii) executive and meta-cognitive functions and strategies and (iii) motivational states and attributional beliefs. Mental age, as reflected by a standardized intelligence test, cannot begin to sort out the influence these factors have on a particular child's cognitive performance. In the last few years researchers (e.g. Borkowski and Turner, 1986; Sperber and McCauley, 1984) have begun to examine how these three factors function independently and together to influence the cognitive performance of retarded individuals. Some cognitive acts, such as performance on decontextualized memory tasks, might best reflect basic structural deficits, whereas other cognitive acts, such as reading, are significantly influenced by meta-cognitive and motivational abilities.

A second incorrect assumption is that language development is synchronous across different linguistic domains. In section 4.2 we have reviewed studies that examined the linguistic and communicative abilities of retarded individuals. Several studies were discussed (e.g. Kamhi and Johnston, 1982; Miller, Chapman and MacKenzie, 1981) that showed that it was common for some aspects of language to be consistent with cognitive level, while other aspects of language were delayed or in advance of cognitive level. Language development in the retarded was thus no different than language development in non-retarded children, where asynchronies in development are more the rule than the exception.

A third assumption is that language and cognition are separable and distinct measurable entities. There can be no confounding of language in measures of cognition and vice versa if the nature of the language deficit is going to be defined in terms of cognitive functioning. In actuality, however, measures of language and cognition are often not uniquely 'cognitive' or 'linguistic'. The inevitable result is that whether one supports the difference or delay view depends, to a large extent, on the measures used to evaluate language and cognition.

A fourth assumption, and perhaps the most serious one, is that developments in language are contingent upon developments in cognition. This assumption reflects a particular view of the relationship between language and cognition, variously referred to as the Piagetian view or the 'strong cognition hypothesis' (see Rice and Kemper, 1984). During the past ten to fifteen years considerable evidence has accumulated that this view does not accurately reflect the relationship between language and cognitive development (e.g. Bates *et al.*, 1979; Miller *et al.*, 1980). Several views have emerged in response to this evidence, including (i) the weak cognitive view (Cromer, 1976), (ii) the correlational (homologue) view (Bates *et al.*, 1979) and (iii) the interactionist view (Schlesinger, 1977). Each of these views acknowledges that developments in language are not always preceded by developments in cognition. Proponents of these views also recognize that the relationship between language and cognition undergoes changes with development. The interactionist view is probably the most flexible by acknowledging not only the influence of non-cognitive factors on language development, but also the bi-directional relationship between language and cognition. In contrast to these views, which all attribute some role to cognition in language development, the view espoused by Chomsky (1965) posits the existence of innate language-specific mental structures.

It is not necessary here to debate the accuracy of the various alternatives to the strong cognitive hypothesis. The interested reader is referred to Rice and Kemper's (1984) excellent review and discussion of the various theoretical positions. What is important for our discussion of the difference–delay issue is the recognition that (i) factors other than cognitive ones (e.g. social and language specific processes) can influence language development, and (ii) developments in language can influence developments in cognition. Acknowledging the viability of these alternative views of language and cognition changes the way one interprets the data on retarded children's language. Under the theoretical umbrella of the strong cognition hypothesis a language delay relative to cognitive level was interpreted to reflect a qualititative difference in language behavior (e.g. Yoder and Miller, 1972). This qualitative difference, however, represents the discrepancy between language and cognitive level. It does not necessarily indicate that the retarded individual is following a different course of language development. There are at least two reasons why a discrepancy between language and cognitive level might occur.

First, as pointed out earlier, MA might not be an accurate reflection of the retarded child's cognitive level. A retarded child's language abilities might correspond to an aspect of cognition (e.g. short-term memory) that is also delayed relative to MA. This aspect of cognition might be commensurate with or, perhaps, in advance of MA in the matched non-retarded child. The differences in language behaviours between the retarded and non-retarded children are thus explained by differences in cognitive abilities not reflected by MA.

Secondly, asynchronies between cognitive development and language development are evidence against the strong cognition hypothesis. Because asynchronies between language and cognitive development occur frequently in non-retarded children, the occurrence of asyncronies in retarded children cannot be taken as evidence that such children are following a qualitatively different course of language development. As suggested earlier, asynchronies between language and MA reflect the influence of either cognitive abilities not measured by MA or non-cognitive factors. For example, expressive language abilities are particularly susceptible to the influence of social and motivational factors, whereas the acquisition of formal linguistic devices, such as grammatical morphemes, have been suggested to depend in part on specific linguistic processes (Cromer, 1981).

4.4 CONCLUSION

Considerable time and energies have been spent during the last twenty years attempting to determine whether retarded children show language delays or differences relative to cognitive level. Erroneous assumptions about language and cognition have proven difficult to overcome. Nevertheless, as models of language and cognition have become more complex and integrative it has become clear that different questions need to be asked about the relationship between retarded individuals' language and cognitive abilities. With respect to cognition, it is more appropriate to ask how cognitive structures, meta-cognitive functions and motivational states influence cognitive performance. With respect to language, researchers need to ask questions about how cognitive, linguistic, social-motivational and environmental forces influence the language behaviour of retarded individuals. The influence of social-motivational deficits on language behaviour is of particular concern, given the likelihood that many retarded individuals will experience deficits in this area.

By asking these kinds of questions about retarded individuals' language and cognitive performance, one not only affects the kinds of research performed, but also the educational and clinical programming of these children. Consider, for example, the effect that adherence to the strong cognitive hypothesis has had on eligibility decisions for speech–language services. In most states in the USA retarded individuals do not receive speech–language services unless there is a significant discrepancy between language performance and cognitive level. Oftentimes retarded children with significant communication deficits will not receive services because measures of syntactic or semantic abilities will be consistent with MA. Recognizing the validity of alternative views of language and cognition and the influence of non-cognitive factors on language performance enables one to justify speech–language services, even when certain aspects of language and cognitive development are at equivalent levels.

Perhaps the most appropriate conclusion for this chapter is to hope that it is the last one written on this topic. This is not because we wish to have the final word of the subject, nor is it because there is nothing more to be said about language and cognition in people with mental handicaps. Our concern is that by asking questions about the relationship between language and cognition in mentally handicapped people, and by devoting a separate chapter to this subject, one is encouraging and perpetuating the view that there is something unique about a mental handicap that somehow changes the nature of the relationship between language and cognition. We have attempted in this chapter to point out the problems with this view by showing that current conceptualizations of language and cognition lead to different questions about the language and cognitive abilities of mentally handicapped people. It is our hope that future efforts are devoted to addressing these questions.

REFERENCES

Affleck, G. (1976) Role-taking ability and the interpersonal tactics of retarded children, *Am. J. Ment. Defic.*, *80*, 667–70.

Bates, E., Benigni, L., Bretherton, I., Camaioni, L. and Volterra, V. (1979) *The emergence of symbols: cognition and communication in infancy*, Academic Press, New York.

Bedrosian, J. and Prutting, C. (1978) Communicative performance of mentally retarded adults in four conversational settings, *J. Speech Hearing. Res.*, *21*, 79–95.

Belmont, J. and Butterfield, E. (1971) Learning strategies as determinants of memory deficiencies, *Cog. Psych.*, *2*, 411–20.

Bender, N. and Carlson, J. (1982) Prosocial behavior and perspective-taking of mentally retarded and nonretarded children, *Amer. J. Ment. Defic.*, *86*, 361–6.

Bereiter, C. and Englemann, S. (1966) *Teaching Disadvantaged Children in the Preschool*, Prentice-Hall, Englewood Cliffs, NJ.

Borkowski, J. and Turner, L. (1986) Cognitive development, paper presented at the NIH Conference on Mental Retardation, Bethesda, Md., October.

Borkowski, J., Reid, M. and Kurtz, B. (1984) Metacognition and retardation: paradigmatic, theoretical, and applied perspectives in *Learning and Cognition in the Mentally Retarded* (eds. P. Brooks, R. Sperber and J. McCauley), Lawrence Erlbaum, Hillsdale, NJ, pp. 55–76.

Brown, A. (1974) The role of strategic behavior in retardate memory in *International Review of Research in Mental Retardation* (ed. N. Ellis), Academic Press, New York, Vol. 7, pp. 55–111.

Butterfield, E. and Belmont, J. (1977) Assessing and improving the executive cognitive functions of mentally retarded people in *Psychological Issues in Mental Retardation* (eds. I. Bialer and M. Sternlicht), Psychological Dimensions, New York, pp. 123–54.

Butterfield, E., Wambold, C. and Belmont, J. (1973) On the theory and practice of improving short-term memory, *Amer. J. Ment. Defic.*, *77*, 654–69.

Casby, M. and Ruder, K. (1983) Symbolic play and early language development in normal and mentally retarded children, *J. Speech Hearing Res.*, *26*, 404–11.

Chomsky, N. (1965) *Aspects of the Theory of Syntax*, MIT Press, Cambridge, Mass.

Cromer, R. (1976) The cognitive hypothesis of language acquisition and its implications for child language deficiency, in *Normal and Deficient Child Language* (eds. D. Morehead and A. Morehead), University Park Press, Baltimore, Md., pp. 283–333.

Cromer, R. (1981) Reconceptualizing language acquisition and cognitive development in *Early Language: Acquisition and Intervention* (eds. R. Schiefelbusch and D. Bricker), University Park Press, Baltimore, Md., pp. 51–139.

Das, J. (1972) Patterns of cognitive ability in nonretarded and retarded children, *Am. J. Ment. Defic.*, *77*, 6–12.

Das, J. (1984) Cognitive deficits in mental retardation: a process approach, in *Learning and Cognition in the Mentally Retarded* (eds. P. Brooks, R. Sperber and C. McCauley), Lawrence Erlbaum, Hillsdale, NJ, pp. 115–29.

Das, J., Kirby, J. and Jarman, R. (1975) Simultaneous and successive synthesis: an alternative model for cognitive abilities, *Psych. Bull.*, *80*, 97–113.

Detterman, D. (1979) Memory in the mentally retarded in *Handbook of Mental Deficiency, Psychologist Theory, and Research* (ed. N. Ellis), 2nd edn, Lawrence Erlbaum, Hillsdale, NJ, pp. 85–113.

Drew, C., Logan, D. and Hardman, M. (1984) *Mental Retardation: A Life Cycle Approach* (3rd edn), Times Mirror/Mosby, St Louis, Mo.

Dunn, L. (1965) *Peabody Picture Vocabulary Test*, American Guidance Service, Circle Pines, Minn.

Eaton, W. and Burdz, M. (1984) Gender understanding and the similar sequence hypothesis, *Am. J. Ment. Defic.*, *89*, 23–8.

Ellis, N. (1963) The stimulus trace and behavioral inadequacy in *International Review of Research in Mental Retardation* (ed. N. Ellis), McGraw-Hill, New York, pp. 213–54.

Ellis, N. and Meador, I. (1985) Forgetting in retarded and nonretarded persons under conditions of minimal strategy use, *Intel.*, *9*, 87–96.

Fagan, J. (1968) Short-term memory processes on normal and retarded children, *J. Exp. Child. Psych.*, *6*, 279–96.

Gerjouy, I., Winters, J., Pullen, M. and Spitz, H. (1969) Subjective organization by retardates and normals during free recall of visual stimuli, *Am. J. Ment. Defic.*, *73*, 791–7.

Graham, J. and Graham, L. (1971) Language behavior of the mentally retarded: syntactic characteristics, *Am. J. Ment. Defic.*, *75*, 623–29.

Greenspan, S. (1979) Social intelligence in the retarded in *Handbook of Mental Deficiency, Psychological Theory and Research* (ed. N. Ellis), 2nd edn, Lawrence Erlbaum, Hillsdale, NJ, pp. 54–93.

Greenwald, C. and Leonard, L. (1979) Communicative and sensorimotor development of Down's syndrome children, *Am. J. Ment. Defic.*, *84*, 296–303.

Guralnick, M. and Paul-Brown, D. (1984) Communicative adjustments during behavior-request episodes among children at different developmental levels, *Child Development*, *55*, 911–19.

Guralnick, M. and Paul-Brown, D. (1986) Communicative interactions of mildly delayed and normally developing preschool children: effects of listener's developmental age, *J. Speech Hearing Res.*, *29*, 2–11.

Guralnick, M. and Weinhouse, E. (1984) Peer-related social interactions of developmentally delayed young children: development and characteristics, *Dev. Psych.*, *20*, 815–27.

Harter, S., Brown, L. and Zigler, E. (1971) Discrimination learning in retarded and nonretarded children as a function of task difficulty and social reinforcement, *Am. J. Ment. Defic.*, *76*, 275–83.

108

Hulme, I. and Lunzer, E. (1966) Play, language, and reasoning in subnormal children, *J. Child Psych. Psychiat.*, *7*, 107–23.

Ingalls, R. (1978) *Mental Retardation: The Changing Outlook*, Wiley, New York.

Inhelder, B. (1966) Cognitive development and its contribution to the diagnosis of some phenomena of mental deficiency, *Merrill-Palmer Quart.*, *12*, 299–319.

Jordan, T. (1967) Language and mental retardation: a review of the literature in *Language and Mental Retardation* (eds. R. Schiefelbusch, R. Copeland and J. Smith), Holt, Rinehart and Winston, New York, pp. 20–38.

Kamhi, A. (1981) Development vs difference theories of mental retardation: a new look, *Am. J. Ment. Defic.*, *86*, 1–7.

Kamhi, A. and Johnston, J. (1982) Toward an understanding of retarded children's linguistic deficiencies, *J. Speech Hearing Res.*, *25*, 435–45.

Kohlberg, L. (1968) Early education: a cognitive-developmental view, *Child Devel.*, *39*, 1013–62.

Lackner, J. (1968) A developmental study of language behavior in retarded children, *Neuropsych.*, *6*, 301–20.

Lenneberg, E. (1967) *Biological Foundations of Language*, Wiley, New York.

Leonard, L., Cole, B. and Steckol, K. (1979) Lexical usage of retarded children: an examination of informativeness, *Am. J. Ment. Defic.*, *84*, 49–54.

Libkuman, T. (1972) Word frequency and pronunciation and the verbal-discrimination learning of nonretarded and retarded children, *Am. J. Ment. Defic.*, *77*, 322–37.

Luria, A. (1966) *Higher Cortical Functions in Man*, Basic Books, New York.

Mahoney, G., Glover, A. and Finger, I. (1981) Relationship between language and sensorimotor development of Down syndrome and nonretarded children, *Am. J. Ment. Defic.*, *86*, 21–27.

Milgram, N. (1973) Cognition and language in mental retardation: distinctions and implications in *The Experimental Psychology of Mental Retardation* (ed. D. Routh), Adline, Chicago, pp. 157–230.

Miller, J., Chapman, R., Branston, M. and Reichle, J. (1980) Language comprehension in sensorimotor stages V and VI, *J. Speech Hearing Res.*, *23*, 284–311.

Miller, J., Chapman, R. and MacKenzie, H. (1981) Individual differences in the language acquisition of mentally retarded children, *Proceedings from the Second Wisconsin Symposium on Research in Child Language Disorders*, University of Wisconsin, pp. 130–47.

Mosley, J. (1980) Selective attention of mildly mentally retarded and nonretarded individuals, *Am. J. Ment. Defic.*, *84*, 568–76.

Mosley, J. (1981) Iconic store readout of mildly mentally retarded and nonretarded individuals, *Am. J. Ment. Defic.*, *86*, 60–6.

Naremore, R. and Dever, R. (1975) Language performance of educable mentally retarded and normal children at five age levels, *J. Speech Hearing Res.*, *18*, 82–96.

Nelson, K. (1977) The syntagmatic-paradigmatic shift revisited: a review of research and theory, *Psych. Bull.*, *84*, 93–116.

Newfield, M. and Schlanger, B. (1968) The acquisition of English morphology by normals and educable mentally retarded children, *J. Speech Hearing Res.*, *11*, 693–706.

Owens, R. (1985) Mental retardation: difference or delay? in *Language and Communication Disorders in Children* (eds. D. Bernstein and E. Tiegerman), Charles E. Merrill, Columbus, Ohio, pp. 172–233.

Piaget, J. (1970) Piaget's theory in *Carmichaels' Manual of Child psychology* (ed. P. Mussen), 3rd edn, Wiley, New York, pp. 703–32.

Rice, M. and Kemper, S. (1984) *Child Language and Cognition*, University Park Press, Baltimore, Md.

Richman, C., Adams, K., Nida, S. and Richman, J. (1978) Performance of MA-matched nonretarded and retarded children on discrimination learning and transfer-shift tasks, *Am. J. Ment. Defic.*, *83*, 262–9.

Schlesinger, I. (1977) The role of cognitive development and linguistic input in language acquisition, *J. Child. Language.*, *4*, 153–69.

Selph, S. and Kamhi, A. (1984) Communication abilities of retarded children, paper presented at Annual Meeting of the American Speech–Language–Hearing Association, San Francisco, Calif., USA, November.

Semmel, M., Barritt, L. and Bennett, S. (1970) Performance of EMR and non-retarded children on a modified close task, *Am. J. Ment. Defic.*, *74*, 681–8.

Sperber, R. and McCauley, C. (1984) Semantic processing efficiency in the mentally retarded in *Learning and Cognition in the Mentally Retarded* (eds. P. Brooks, R. Sperber and C. McCauley) Lawrence Erlbaum, Hillsdale, NJ, pp. 141–64.

Spitz, H. (1976) Toward a relative psychology of mental retardation, with a special emphasis on evolution in *International Review of Research in Mental Retardation* (ed. N. Ellis), Academic Press, New York, Vol. 8, pp. 35–56.

Spitz, H. and Borys, S. (1977) Performance of retarded and nonretarded adolescents on one- and two-bit logical problems, *J. Exp. Child Psych.*, *23*, 415–29.

Spitz, H. and Borys, S. (1984) Depth of search: how far can the retarded search through an internally represented problem space? in *Learning and Cognition in the Mentally Retarded* (eds. P. Brooks, R. Sperber and C. McCauley), Lawrence Erlbaum, Hillsdale, NJ, pp. 333–58.

Stamm, J. (1974) Behavioral counseling with the mentally retarded in *Mental Retardation: Rehabilitation and Counseling* (ed. P. Browning), Charles C. Thomas, Springfield, Ill., pp. 186–211.

Stephens, B. and McLaughlin, J. (1974) Two-year gains in reasoning by retarded and nonretarded persons, *Am. J. Ment. Defic.*, *79*, 116–26.

Taylor, A. and Turnure, J. (1979) Imagery and verbal elaboration with retarded children: effects on learning and memory in *Handbook of Mental Deficiency, Psychological Theory and Research* (ed. N. Ellis), 2nd edn, Lawrence Erlbaum, Hillsdale, NJ, pp. 659–97.

Uzgiris, I. and Hunt, J. (1975) *Assessment in Infancy: Ordinal Scales of Psychological Development*, University of Illinois Press, Chicago.

Weiss, B., Weisz, J. and Bromfield, R. (1986) Performance of retarded and non-retarded persons on information-processing tasks: further tests of the similar structure hypothesis, *Psych. Bull.*, *100*, 157–75.

Weisz, J. (1979) Perceived control and learned helplessness among mentally retarded and nonretarded children: a developmental analysis, *Dev. Psych.*, *15*, 311–19.

Weisz, J. and Yeates, K. (1981) Cognitive development in retarded and nonretarded persons: Piagetian tests of the similar structure hypothesis, *Psych. Bull.*, *90*, 153–78.

Weisz, J., Yeates, K. and Zigler, E. (1982) Piagetian evidence and the developmental-difference controversy in *Mental Retardation: The Developmental–Difference Controversy* (eds. E. Zigler and D. Balla), Lawrence Erlbaum, Hillsdale, NJ, pp. 213–76.

Weiss, J. and Zigler, E. (1979) Cognitive development in retarded and nonretarded persons: Piagetian tests of the similar sequence hypothesis, *Psych. Bull.*, *86*, 831–51.

Woodward, M. and Stern, D. (1963) Developmental patterns of severely subnormal children, *Brit. J. Ed. Psych.*, *59*, 10–21.

Yoder, D. and Miller, J. (1972) What we may know and what we can do: input toward a system in *Language Intervention with the Retarded: Developing Strategies* (eds. J. McLean, D. Yoder and R. Schiefelbusch), University Park Press, Baltimore, Md, pp. 89–111.

Zeaman, D. and House, B. (1979) A review of attention theory in *Handbook of Mental Deficiency: Psychological Theory and Research* (ed. N. Ellis), 2nd edn, Lawrence Erlbaum, Hillsdale, NJ, pp. 63–120.

Zigler, E. (1969) Developmental versus difference theories of mental retardation and the problem of motivation, *Am. J. Ment. Defic.*, *73*, 536–56.

Zigler, E. and Balla, D. (1982) *Mental Retardation: The Developmental–Difference Controversy*, Lawrence Erlbaum, Hillsdale, NJ.

Cognition and Language in the Mentally Retarded Population

Robert Owens

Possibly we can find some explanation for the language difficulties of the retarded population in an examination of the cognitive development and functioning of that population. Here we shall explore the latest research in both areas.

5.1 COGNITION AND LANGUAGE DEVELOPMENT

In general, mentally retarded and non-retarded individuals go through the same stages of cognitive development. Obviously the retarded individual develops more slowly. Mental development continues well into the third and fourth decades of life for retarded adults although at a decreasing rate (Berry *et al.*, 1984).

Piaget views cognitive development as a series of qualitative changes involving reorganization and restructuring of mental structures or concepts, called schema. This series of changes describes a hierarchy of development, which can be referred to by stages of development. Each stage can be characterized in terms of sets of behaviour that reflect the underlying system or pattern of cognitive concepts and strategies. In other words, each stage can be characterized by the acquisition of specific cognitive skills that reflect environmental events and the strategies developed by the individual for responding to these events. Piaget refers to these stages as sensorimotor, preoperational, concrete operational and formal operational.

During the first two years of life the non-retarded child experiences tremendous cognitive growth and the basic structures of intelligence begin to evolve. Throughout most of this sensorimotor stage the child's schema are organized according to sensory input and motor responses. Piaget has divided this period into six stages. By stage 6, at the end of the sensorimotor period, the child is capable of symbolic or representational thought. Morehead and Morehead (1974) have described sensorimotor development as a progression from signal to sign. By about 6 months of age, near the end of stage 3, the non-retarded child responds to signals or to familiar objects that he associates with activities. Many adult behaviours, such as adult–child games, become the signal for certain child behaviours in response. By 8–12 months the signal has become decontextualized and the child can interpret the signal without the immediate contextual cues. The child is also learning to use signals expressively through gestures and vocalizations. During stage 5, from 12 to 18 months, symbols appear in which the non-retarded child will represent one object with another such as a shoe to represent a telephone or a word to represent an object which is present. Finally, in stage 6, as the child approaches age 2 years, he or she is capable of using true 'signs' with which to discuss concepts rather than the specific objects and actions in the immediate context. Not all sensorimotor developmental change is of equal importance for symbolization. The most pertinent include object concept, physical imitation, means–ends and play.

Object concept consists of object permanence, object constancy and object function. Object permanence is knowing that an object exists, even though it has been removed from one's immediate perception. Although considered by some to be a strong prerequisite to symbol use in non-retarded children, others have found that object permanence is not as strongly correlated with language development as are other sensorimotor behaviours (Bates *et al.*, 1979; Miller *et al.*, 1980; Moore and Meltzoff, 1978; Siegel, 1979). Object constancy — knowing that an object's shape and size are relatively fixed — and object function knowledge may be even more important in the formation of early concept meanings which are usually based on static perceptual attributes and/or functions.

A number of studies have labelled physical imitation as a prerequisite to speech, language and communication development (Moore and Meltzoff, 1978; Rees, 1975; Snyder, 1978). In general, imitation is important for symbolic development because of the child's ability to construct internal representations of the behaviour of others. At first, the child imitates the entire behaviour, but this lessens until a portion of the behaviour represents the whole as a word will later represent the whole. Vocal imitation and gestures are significantly correlated at about 9 months of age (Bates *et al.*, 1979). Truly symbolic functioning is associated with deferred imitation. As with the true 'sign', deferred imitation can be emitted without the presence of a referent. The child has a mental image of the event or referent.

Means–ends behaviours, or the use of an item or person to attain a desired end, is significantly correlated with the development of gestures at 9 months of age (Bates *et al.*, 1979). Thus the development of means–ends appears to be closely related to the development of intentionality. This relationship might be assumed since gestures are a means of fulfilling some ends. It is within the intentions initially expressed in these gestures that first words later appear.

Finally, play has been demonstrated to be highly important for the development of language, especially at 10–13 months (James, 1980; Miller *et al.*, 1980; McCune-Nicolich and Carroll, 1981; Snyder, 1978). Although play is highly correlated with language, the level of play required for symbol use is in question. Although important for the development of true signs, symbolic play is not necessary prior to the appearance of single-word referential speech.

Piaget theorized that only in the last six months of the sensorimotor stage is the child capable of truly symbolic behaviour in which he or she can represent absent referents. To begin to use words referentially, the child need only have a notion of object permanence and of means–ends, although he/she need not be able to solve complicated problems using either or both of these skills. Deferred imitation and symbolic play develop later and may contribute more to vocabulary growth, word combinations and true signs.

Most studies of the sensorimotor period have found similar developmental sequences for retarded and non-retarded persons (Kahn, 1975, 1976; Rogers, 1977; Westby, 1980; Wohlhueter and Sindberg, 1975). This data should not be taken as an indication that all areas of development are similar at a given stage. For example, severely retarded children do not exhibit the same levels of play as their mental age-matched non-retarded peers (Hulme and Lunzer, 1966). Although Whitaker (1980) reports a similar progression in the development of symbolic play for profoundly retarded and non-retarded subjects, Wing *et al.* (1977) could find no symbolic play in 108 retarded subjects below a cognitive level of 20 months, well after it has developed in non-retarded toddlers.

For the retarded population, in general, language development lags behind overall cognitive development. Although much of the data is complicated by the motoric problems of the retarded population, the deficit still exists, even when this factor is minimized. This data is summarized in Table 5.1.

Although Snyder (1978) found development of non-verbal declarative and imperative gestures for both retarded and non-retarded children at the one-word stage to be related to means–ends, she also found the retarded children to be deficient in their production of verbal responses. Greenwald and Leonard (1979) report a similar finding for Down's syndrome preschoolers. Both their retarded and non-retarded subjects used imperative performatives at stages 4 and 5 and declarative performatives somewhat later, but the retarded preschoolers performed at a lower level than their non-retarded peers.

This language lag has been noticed particularly in the Down's syndrome population. Mahoney, Glover and Finger (1981) concluded that 'Down syndrome children are more delayed in their rate of language acquisition than might be predicted from general indices of their level of intellectual functioning' (p. 25). At a cognitive age of approximately 17 months the

Table 5.1: Presymbolic cognitive and communicative development by non-retarded and retarded individuals

| Cognitive development | Communicative development | | References |
	non-retarded	retarded	
Sensorimotor stage 4			
	Comprehension of names of entities present; few proto-declaratives and proto-imperatives, no words	No comprehension; few proto-declaratives, no words	Greenwald and Leonard (1979); Snyder (1978); Woodward and Stern (1963)
Sensorimotor stage 5			
	Comprehension in context of absent entities and action words; proto-declaratives and proto-imperatives non-referential speech	Comprehension in context by a few individuals; gestural proto-declaratives and proto-imperatives; jargon with some meaningful words	Greenwald and Leonard (1979); Woodward and Stern (1963)
Sensorimotor stage 6			
	Comprehension out of context and of agent + action constructions; semantic relations expressed in word combinations	Comprehension of words and phrases in concrete situations; ten or more word vocabulary with a few combinations; more immature and fewer verbal responses	Cardoso-Martins, Mervis and Mervis (1985); Jones (1975); Kahn (1975); Leifer and Lewis (1984); Terdal, Jackson and Garner (1976)

Down's syndrome children were just beginning to use single words, while their non-retarded peers were combining words and increasing their vocabularies rapidly. Cardoso-Martins, Mervis and Mervis (1985) report a similar lag in vocabulary growth behind cognitive development, although the words acquired were similar for the Down's and non-retarded children (Gillham, 1979).

As a group, according to Woodward and Stern (1963), severely retarded individuals in sensorimotor stage 5 exhibit only scattered comprehension skills. By stage 6 all individuals can comprehend words and simple phrases. Although stage 5 non-retarded children use non-referential speech, retarded children tend still to rely on gestural communication. Only those severely retarded individuals who have attained stage 6 are able to produce meaningful words and word combinations albeit at a very concrete level (Woodward and Stern, 1963). Attainment of stage 6 sensorimotor skills may not be sufficient for the acquisition of language by all individuals (Kahn, 1975), although some less severely retarded individuals do exhibit language at lower levels of cognitive development.

The preoperational child gains knowledge through direct experience. Through the use of his symbolic abilities he or she can represent reality and experience and store this information for future use. He/she is capable of performing some mental operations on these symbols, such as classification, which is initially based on physical attributes and only gradually on more abstract bases; one-to-one correspondence; and seriation or ordering based on some attribute.

The young preoperational child is very dependent on his senses and makes judgements based on the way things look. The child operates by the rule, 'If it looks different, it must be ...' Usually by age 6 or 7, the child is able to solve these types of problems.

The young preoperational child performs mental operations in one-directional linear fashion. Events are related sequentially, and it is difficult for the child to reverse this order. Generally by age 5 the child is able to reverse the sequence in order to explain physical events. The preoperational child is quite egocentric and tends to interpret information from his/her own point of view. They have difficulty understanding the perspectives of others.

These cognitive developments are reflected in the child's language. Many of the child's descriptors and relational terms are based on the physical environment. The child has difficulty with temporal and familial terms and with complicated explanations. The child relies on sequential order for interpretation. He/she has difficulty taking the perspective of others, and this is reflected in the initial confusion with deictic terms such as 'here' and 'there'.

The concrete operational child is able to think in many different ways. He/she can mentally manipulate symbols and understand relationships such as time. Able to construct hierarchies or classes of objects, he/she can classify easily on the basis of a number of abstract relationships. The child is able to reverse thought sequence and does not rely strictly on sensory information. In addition, he/she is able to perform seriation on the basis of two characteristics at once.

During this period the child learns many of the relational terms used in his/her language. Word definitions become more conventional and include categorical assignment. Less egocentric than the preoperational child, he/she is able to take the perspective of the conversational partner and has no difficulty with most deictic terms.

After age 11, the non-retarded child is capable of abstract thought and does not rely solely on sensory input for information. His or her thinking is flexible and he/she can test hypotheses mentally without reliance on physical problem-solving. Language takes on the quality of adult discourse.

Unfortunately there is little research with retarded individuals in the preoperational period. In the concrete operational period a number of studies have reported that non-retarded and retarded subjects performed similarly when matched for cognitive levels (Gruen and Vore, 1972; McManis, 1970; Woodward and Hunt, 1972).

Summary

In his study of non-retarded children, Piaget has suggested qualitatively different stages of cognitive development that impact upon language. In general, retarded and non-retarded individuals demonstrate similar stages of development, although the language skills of the retarded population may lag behind that of MA-matched peers. Piaget's model suggests a number of developments that are relevant to intervention services for the mentally retarded population.

5.2 COGNITIVE PROCESSES

Other factors must be considered in order to explain the lag in some areas of cognitive and language development. The human brain can be described in terms of its structures and control processes. Structures are the fixed anatomical features of the central nervous system and probably vary little from person to person. Processes are the voluntary problem-solving strategies of each person, the way that each responds to, organizes, analyses and synthesizes incoming information. Information processing can be divided into the processes of attention, organization, memory and transfer. Possibly, there are differences in the structures or processing mechanisms of the retarded population as a whole.

As a group, retarded individuals are less efficient in the manner in which they process information (Brooks and McCauley, 1984). There is a relationship between measured intelligence and the speed of information processing (Sperber and McCauley, 1984). For example, as a group mentally retarded individuals have slower short-term memory and slower retrieval of overlearned information from long-term memory (Maisto and Jerome, 1977; Sperber *et al.*, 1983). This memory deficit not only affects 'accessibility', or what can be retrieved, but also 'availability' of information for retrieval (Winters and Semchuk, 1986).

Basic anatomical structures are assumed to be similar for most retarded and non-retarded individuals. It has been suggested, however, that more severely involved persons may have organic structural deficits that result in qualitatively different neurological functioning (Robinson and Robinson, 1976; Snart, O'Grady and Das, 1982; Zigler, 1967). Most researchers attribute observed qualitative differences to operational or processing deficits. For example, there appear to be differences between the automatic and effortful processing abilities of the retarded and non-retarded populations (Meador and Ellis, 1987). Automatic processes are those that are unintentional or that have become routinized and thus require very little of the available cognitive capacity. Individual differences in automatic processing are minimized, and such processing neither interferes with other tasks nor becomes more efficient with practice (Hasher and Zacks, 1979). Effortful processing, on the other hand, requires concentration and attention by the brain. When retarded and non-retarded subjects are matched for mental age, there is little difference in their automatic processing abilities (Nigro and Roak, 1987). However, in the retarded population effortful processing is slower to develop and requires greater effort.

Despite these differences and the resultant difficulties with problem-solving (Butterfield and Belmont, 1977), mentally retarded individuals do exhibit problem-solving behaviours in their everyday life (Friedman *et al.*, 1977; Levine and Langness, 1985; Levine, Zetlin and Langness, 1980). Although most of the data has been collected from the mildly and moderately retarded, it generally supports the notion that there are information processing differences between the retarded and non-retarded populations.

(a) Attention

Attention includes both awareness of a learning situation and active cognitive processing. The individual does not attend to all stimuli. Attending can be divided into orientation, reaction and discrimination. Orientation is the ability to sustain attention over time. In part, this is related to the individual's ability to determine the uniqueness of the stimulus. Reaction refers to the amount of time required for an individual to respond to a stimulus. In part, reaction time is a function of the individual's ability to select the relevant dimensions of a task to which he or she is to respond. Discrimination is the ability to identify stimuli differing along some dimension. If an individual cannot identify the relevant characteristics, he/she will have difficulty comparing the new input with stored information.

In general, less developmentally mature populations are less efficient at attention allocation and have a more limited attentional capacity (Nugent and Mosley, 1987). These processes are relatively automatic for older or non-retarded individuals and require only minimal allocation of the available resources of the brain. In contrast, these processes do not seem to be automatic for the retarded population and thus require the allocation of the limited resources of the brain at this level. Thus fewer resources are available for higher-level processes (Sperber and McCauley, 1984).

In general, mildly retarded individuals react more slowly than CA-matched peers (Baumeister and Kellas, 1968). Studies with MA-matched subjects are not as definitive (Krupski, 1977; Liebert and Baumeister, 1973). In part, slower reaction time, especially for more severely involved individuals, may reflect the poorer scanning and selective attending abilities of the mentally retarded. Nettelbeck and McLean (1984) report that mildly mentally retarded adults require a longer inspection time compared to non-retarded peers in order to recognize items to which they are attending. This delay may be the result of slower initial sensory registration or, more likely, of a higher process which is responsible for directing attention. This difficulty can also be seen in the discrimination abilities of the retarded population.

In general, the mentally retarded individual experiences difficulties identifying and maintaining attention to the relevant stimulus dimensions that aid discrimination (Mercer and Snell, 1977; Zeaman and House, 1979). Mildly and moderately retarded persons attend to fewer dimensions of a task than do their non-retarded peers, and by projection, we can assume that the more severely retarded attend even less. This inability reduces an individual's opportunities to compare new information with previously learned information. This, in turn, increases the amount of time and practice needed by the retarded individual in order to understand the dimensions of a learning task. Once a task is understood or trained, however, mildly mentally retarded individuals can perform as well as their non-retarded MA-matched peers (Ross and Ross, 1979). It should not come as a surprise that, as a group, mildly retarded individuals can learn discrimination tasks more rapidly than their more retarded CA-matched peers (Ellis *et al.*, 1982). Still, there are substantial individual differences.

After studying the visual recognition behaviours of mildly retarded individuals, Mosley (1985) concluded that the slower recognition time of the subjects suggested a difference in memory scanning rather than in the mechanics of encoding, deciding and responding to the stimulus.

Discrimination can be enhanced and generalized even by severely retarded individuals if they are taught to identify verbally the salient dimensions of the item observed (Wacker and Greenbaum, 1984). Colour coding of the distinctive features of shapes can aid the visual discrimination learning of severely and profoundly retarded individuals (Meador, 1984). In other words, highlighting the distinctive features can enhance discrimination learning.

(b) Organization

The organization of incoming sensory information is important for later retrieval. Information is organized or 'chunked' by category. Poor organization will quickly overload the storage capacity of the brain and hinder memory. Case (1978) has theorized that memory capacity is fixed, thus better memory results from better organization; in other words, better organization results in more efficient use of the limited capacity.

In general, mentally retarded individuals exhibit difficulty in developing categorizing strategies for new information that are easily remembered (Spitz, 1966). The lack of 'chunking' hinders later recall and quickly over-loads the individual's memory capacity because it is more difficult to recall unrelated bits of information. Mildly and moderately retarded individuals do not appear to rely on mediational or associative strategies to the extent evident in their non-retarded peers. In mediational strategies a symbol forms a link to some information. For example, an image might facilitate recall of an event. In associative strategies a symbol is linked to another as in such common linkages as *men and* — or *pins and* —. Mildly retarded individuals can learn to use associative strategies if the two symbols are easily associated and concrete in nature.

Retarded individuals are able to retain information more easily if it is pre-organized. For example, mildly retarded individuals have better recall if material is grouped spatially (Harris, 1982; MacMillan, 1972; Spitz, 1966). Therefore, it is easier for a mildly retarded person to recall a string of digits if they are grouped spatially in pairs prior to learning.

Language information may be coded for organization by two parallel processes. These are sequential or successive synthesis and simultaneous synthesis (Das, Kirby and Jarman, 1979). Successive coding, located in the frontal–temporal region of the brain, is linear and processes linguistic infor-mation sequentially as it enters. Each discrete bit of information is analysed and then passed on for higher processing. In contrast, simultaneous syn-thesis, located in the occipital–parietal region, processes information all at once as several levels of analysis are activated. Simultaneous synthesis is more closely related to conceptual thought than to language, although this type of processing must relieve the successive processing system when it becomes overburdened. Although successive processing is more precise, it takes more of the brain's processing potential and is relatively slow. Occa-sionally language input enters so rapidly that successive processing over-loads. At this point, simultaneous processing intervenes and processes for the overall meaning rather than for symbol-by-symbol interpretation.

Although mildly retarded individuals exhibit both simultaneous and successive processes, there appears to be some difference in the manner in which these are employed in complex tasks, resulting in less efficient use (Jarman, 1978; Jarman and Das, 1977). For example, mildly mentally retarded adolescents have greater difficulty than non-retarded MA-matched peers in auditory sentence processing. The difficulty appears to centre on higher semantic-analytic or conceptual processing rather than phonological coding (Merrill and Mar, 1987).

Auditory processing problems are most evident in the Down's syndrome population who perform more poorly than either brain-damaged or other MA-matched retarded individuals on successive processing tasks. This deficiency may provide a partial explanation of the auditory memory and expressive language difficulties of the Down's syndrome population (Burr and Rohr, 1978; Evans, 1977; Sommers and Starkey, 1977).

Although Down's syndrome individuals are able to detect and categorize simple auditory stimuli, they exhibit difficulties related to the processing of this information (Dustman and Callner, 1979; Lincoln *et al.*, 1985; Schafer and Peeke, 1982). In both auditory and visual stimulus tasks, Down's syndrome subjects process slower than MA-matched non-retarded peers (Squires, Galbraith and Aine, 1979; Yellin, Ludvig and Jerison, 1980). Down's syndrome individuals tend to treat each reoccurrence of a stimulus as a novel one. The site of brain-wave activity suggests defective memory storage and retrieval mechanisms relative to classification of incoming information. Autopsies have demonstrated structural abnormalities in the hippocampus, an area of the brain important for interpretation of the meaningfulness of incoming auditory stimuli (Ball and Nuttall, 1980; Suetsugu, 1979).

As a group, mildly retarded and non-retarded individuals exhibit similar developmental trends in the grouping of information (Stephens, 1972). There is a developmental shift with some data from grouping on the basis of physical similarities to grouping by function. At an MA of approximately 9 years there is a shift to more categorical classification based on semantics.

(c) Memory

Recall or memory is the ability to recall information that has been learned previously. Short-term memory is limited and most adults can hold fewer than ten items simultaneously. Information is retained in long-term memory by rehearsal or repetition and organization.

Studies have demonstrated the generally inefficient use of memory strategies by the retarded population (Engle and Nagle, 1979). Mildly and moderately retarded individuals seem to be able to retain information within long-term memory as well as non-retarded individuals, especially if this information is pre-organized (Belmont, 1967; Ellis, 1963; Winters and Semchuk, 1986). Organizational deficits, however, may result in an over-reliance on rote memory (Spitz, 1966). In contrast, profoundly retarded individuals exhibit significant forgetting of learned behaviour within only a short interval (Ellis *et al.*, 1982).

Short-term memory deficiencies are more evident in the retarded population, especially within the first 10s after a stimulus is presented (Ellis and Wooldridge, 1985). In turn, such deficiencies may affect discrimination abilities (Lobb, 1974; Ullman, 1974). In general, retarded persons do not seem to rehearse information spontaneously, a process necessary for retention and/or transfer to long-term memory (Borkowski and Cavanaugh, 1979; Brown, 1974; Butterfield, Wambold and Belmont, 1973; Campione and Brown, 1977; Detterman, 1979; Frank and Rabinovitch, 1974; Glidden, 1979; Kellas, Ashcroft and Johnson, 1973; Reid, 1980). This reported 'rehearsal deficit' (Bray, 1979) may be a function of the recall task studied. For example, Turner and Bray (1985) report that mildly retarded children and adolescents use rehearsal when they are free to select their own learning strategy unconstrained by the task. The efficacy of this behaviour has not been assessed. However, even when rehearsal time is eliminated mildly and moderately retarded adults still forget more than MA-matched non-retarded peers. This suggests to some that there may be structural differences between the two populations (Clark and Detterman, 1981; Ellis, Deacon and Wooldridge, 1985). Mildly and moderately retarded individuals can improve their memory abilities through the training of rehearsal strategies (Brown, 1974; Burger, Blackman and Tan, 1980; Butterfield, Wambold and Belmont, 1973; Engle and Nagle, 1979; Kellas, Ashcroft and Johnson, 1973; Reid, 1980; Taylor and Turnure, 1979; Turnbull, 1974).

Every stimulus event has both a sensory impression or signal, which is inherent in the event, and an abstract or symbolic representation for that event (Dance, 1967; Whatmough, 1956). The signal is meaningful but non-linguistic. For example, the sound of an engine may signal an automobile. In contrast, the abstract representation or word is linguistic in nature. In early presymbolic development non-retarded children use sensory images in their cognitive processing. After the acquisition of language, these children have two available memory codes. In other words, the early meaning of *doggie* is based on the perceptual attributes of the examples of *dog* that are encountered; the symbol or word *doggie* is superimposed later. The ability to infer an entity from an auditory signal is part of the early linguistic knowledge base (Ervin-Tripp, 1973; Macnamara, 1972).

Retarded and non-retarded MA-matched children have similar recall for signal information, but retarded children have significantly poorer recognition and recall of symbolic representations (Lamberts, 1981). Pictures are also retained better and recalled more quickly than words by mildly and moderately retarded adults, a difference missing among-non-retarded adults (Ellis and Wooldridge, 1985; Owings *et al.*, 1980; Silverman, 1974). It is possible that the retarded population never gains facility with the more abstract language system and continues to depend on a more 'imaginal' code. Thus there appears to be a link between the reported language deficits of the mentally retarded population and auditory memory deficits (Brown, 1974; Ellis, 1970; Mittler, 1974; Reid and Kiernan, 1979).

The recall of semantic information from long-term memory is also slower overall for the retarded population (Merrill, 1985). The deficit in both short- and long-term semantic memory may reflect inefficiency of some central processing mechanism. Meaningful and integrated stories can facilitate recall of contained words immediately following and even several months after the stories are related (Glidden *et al.*, 1983; Glidden and Warner, 1983). This strategy does not appear, however, to affect serial recall performance (Glidden and Warner, 1985).

Sentence recall involves both reproduction of the memory episode and editing of the text (Kintsch and van Dijk, 1979). Since retarded individuals make frequent word substitution errors in sentence repetition, their performance may be breaking down in the second stage (Bilsky, Walker and Sakales, 1983). Poor sentence recall may reflect poor editing skills.

Poor reading recall, on the other hand, may be related to failure to use important textual information for organization (Borkowski and Wanschura, 1974; Brown, Campione and Murphy, 1974). However, retarded individuals can be trained to attend selectively to important portions of reading passages with resultant recall improvement (Luftig and Johnson, 1982).

Auditory memory deficits are particularly evident in the Down's syndrome population. Down's syndrome individuals are especially poor at long-term memory access for lexical items and short-term storage and processing of auditory information (Varnhagen, Das and Varnhagen, 1987), especially verbal-auditory material (McDade and Adler, 1980; Marcell and Armstrong, 1982; Schafer and Peeke, 1982; Snart, O'Grady and Das, 1982). This difficulty may be related to *echoic memory* which is 'the ability to hear a sound for some time after physical stimulation has ceased' (Watkins and Watkins, 1980, p. 252). In other words, echoic memory is the ability to remember what is heard when it is no longer present. It is a passive retention strategy related to immediate recall of linguistic stimuli, especially during the relatively rapid rates of presentation found in conversation (Hockey, 1973). This echo may decay more rapidly or at a rate too rapid for the slower processing of the Down's syndrome population when compared to the non-retarded population. Another possibility is that the Down's syndrome population does not use such passive strategies effectively.

In addition, as reported previously, Snart, O'Grady and Das (1982) found Down's syndrome individuals to have poorer successive cognitive processing than other retarded individuals. No doubt, this deficit in auditory sequential memory contributes to the lower language performance of the Down's syndrome population compared with other retarded populations (O'Connor and Hermelin, 1978).

(d) Transfer

Transfer or generalization is the ability to apply previously learned material to the solving of similar but novel problems. The greater the similarity between the two, the greater the transfer. When the two are very similar, generalization is called 'near transfer'. When very dissimilar, it is called 'far transfer'.

Although mildly retarded individuals can be taught some cognitive processing strategies, attempts to generalize these strategies generally have met with poor results (Brown, 1978; Campione and Brown, 1977; Evans and Bilsky, 1979). The transfer of more severely retarded individuals is even weaker (Bricker et al., 1969; Ellis et al., 1982; Reid, 1980).

In general, mildly retarded individuals demonstrate an ability to acquire learning strategies which enhance performance but not generalization (Burger et al., 1982). Generalization, whether near or far, does not appear for retarded persons to be a function of the similarity of tasks, but of the level of awareness required to detect such similarity. In part, generalization deficits may reflect the selection and organization problems of the retarded population noted previously. Generalization can be facilitated if the individual is aided with analysis of the similarities between old and new tasks. Strategy components required for generalization must be trained and individuals alerted to the ready applicability of the trained strategy to a new task.

Some studies have reported success in recall strategy generalization (Brown, Campione and Barclay, 1979; Kendall, Borkowski and Cavanaugh, 1980). Butterfield and Belmont (1975) theorize that transfer can only occur in the presence of task analysis and identification by the retarded individual of the strategies required. Burger, Blackman and Clark (1981) trained mildly retarded individuals to identify the relevant attributes of a task and either to observe the task or to learn it through self-instruction including verbal recall. Both groups of subjects generalized to novel situations better than control subjects who did not learn to analyse the task or to identify strategies. While explicit training does not seem necessary for better transfer, understanding of the task by the retarded individual seems essential. Although the exact nature of these cognitive processes is unknown, this model can help us to examine the cognitive functioning of the mentally retarded population and to relate this functioning to language intervention services.

Conclusion.

In general, the mentally retarded population develops cognitively in a manner similar to the non-retarded population but at a delayed rate. Both populations plan, monitor, check, test and evaluate their cognitive task-oriented strategies (DeLoache and Brown, 1979; Levine and Langness, 1985). However, some cognitive processing differences do exist, especially in the areas of organization and memory (Das, 1972; Das et al., 1979; Semmel, Barritt and Bennett, 1970; Stephens and McLaughlin, 1974). The major deficit seems to be the access of available information rather than the availability of information in the system for accessing (Glidden and Mar, 1978). Therefore, Merrill (1985) concludes, 'the relative inefficiency of cognitive processing by retarded persons may well represent a fundamental deficiency that does not differ markedly as a function of the specific stimulus materials used or the type of processing required' (p. 78). In other words, cognitive processing differences may represent a deficit in higher cognitive processing rather than in organization or memory. As the level of severity increases, the efficacy of cognitive functioning decreases, complicated by accompanying organic disorders.

Kamhi (1981) administered a number of cognitive tasks to retarded and non-retarded individuals at varying developmental levels. Mental age-matched subjects performed similarly on most cognitive tasks, except for those tasks involving symbolic skills. In other words, the skill area most related to language and communication lags behind other cognitive areas. For the speech–language pathologist, then, the intervention goal becomes one of enhancing cognitive skills that are relevant for symbolic processing.

5.3 LANGUAGE INTERVENTION

The developmental patterns and processing abilities of both the retarded and non-retarded populations suggest intervention strategies for retarded, language delayed and disordered individuals. At the very least, our discussion so far suggests that the cognitive abilities and deficits of the retarded population must be considered when training certain skills. A stronger sentiment might suggest that the training of certain prerequisite cognitive skills is absolutely essential and all that is necessary for the learning of certain language skills. In our discussion, I shall try to present a moderate position that considers other factors in language development and offers dissenting comments as necessary. Again, we shall discuss both the developmental and cognitive process approaches.

(a) Cognitive development and language intervention

There are several cognitively based language programmes available for use with retarded or multiply handicapped individuals (Bricker and Bricker, 1974; Dunst, 1980; Horstmeier and MacDonald, 1978a; McLean and Snyder-McLean, 1978; Manolson, 1983; O'Regan-Kleinert, 1980; Owens, 1982; Reichle and Yoder, 1979; Robinson and Robinson, 1983; Strong, 1983; Swope and Libergott, 1980). Most of the cognitively based intervention materials available have been designed for that portion of the retarded population functioning at the presymbolic level. These intervention materials and programmes subscribe, at least in part, to the premiss that in order for an individual to use symbols to communicate, that individual must possess a certain level of cognitive functioning. Although some of the older intervention materials, such as Bricker and Bricker (1974), are almost totally cognitive in nature, many of the newer programmes, such as Owens (1982), also include the more recent research on the social and communicative bases of language use. Early presymbolic training usually includes, but is not limited to, auditory, visual and/or tactile attending; motor imitation, especially deferred imitation; object permanence and function; means–ends; receptive understanding; and vocal imitation. At the vocal imitation stage expressive use of signs or printed symbols, such as photographs or pictures, might be used with those individuals with oral motor difficulties. A summary of each level of training is presented in Table 5.2. Once the retarded child or adult has completed all levels of training, it is assumed that he has the cognitive skills necessary for symbol use. In general, the cognitive approach has been most successful with young children or with the mildly to moderately retarded population.

Behavioural approaches and communication-oriented approaches generally look askance at cognitive-only intervention methods for presymbolic retarded individuals. Cognitive approaches are considered unfairly by these others to be 'wait-and-see' strategies that delay language and communication intervention until the retarded client is 'ready' for language. In part, this prejudice reflects the frustration of many speech–language practitioners with the slow progress of cognitive prerequisite training, especially with the severely/profoundly retarded population. Several recent communication-first approaches have emphasized establishing an initial communication system, followed by expansion of this system towards symbol use (Keogh and Reichle, 1985; Sternberg, McNerney and Pegnatore, 1987; Yoder, 1985). Focusing on prelanguage communication goals, these communication approaches reason that many severely and profoundly retarded individuals may never function within a symbolic communication system. In the meantime a basic presymbolic communication system can be trained. Nevertheless, Sternberg, McNerney and Pegnatore (1987) caution that a 'subject's present cognitive and communication competence must be considered as a crucial variable in one's ability to acquire prelanguage communication skills' (p. 18).

Sailor, Guess and Baer (1973) reviewed many of the older behavioural studies of language intervention with severely and profoundly mentally retarded persons. Most studies, they found, resulted in speech but failed to demonstrate generalization beyond the training setting. Kahn (1984) suggests that the reason for this failure may be that the subjects were taught to respond on cue but were not cognitively ready for referential speech. In other words, both mentally retarded and non-retarded individuals need to have acquired sensorimotor stage 6 in order to use symbols meaningfully (Bates *et al.*, 1979; Kahn, 1975). Kahn (1984) concludes:

Table 5.2: Levels of presymbolic training

Level	Explanation
Identifying input and output Modalities (auditory/verbal, visual/manual, tactile) Notice Search Recognition	Train client to notice stimuli in various sensory modalities and to respond via some initial signal system. From level of response, train search for interesting stimuli and recognition of familiar stimuli
Responding/turn-taking	Train a sequence of stimulus–response behaviours to approximate caregiver–infant turn-taking games
Motor imitation Visible physical imitation Partially visible physical imitation Invisible physical imitation Deferred imitation Memory (repetitive actions) Memory (sequential motor imitation)	Train motor imitation as a presymbolic cognitive skill leading to deferred imitation, and as a sequential and fine motor skill for later production of symbols through the modalities identified earlier
Object permanence Visible displacement Problem-solving	Train client to recognize that objects exist through mental representation even when he can't see them. Symbols are a form of representation
Turn-taking Motor imitation Gaze coupling	Reintroduce trained behaviours as turn-taking behaviours to increase the strength of this type of response for communication
Functional use of objects	Train functions as a basis for early definitions. Also used to increase client awareness and knowledge about the world
Means Object retrieval Personal assist	Train client to use other objects or persons in order to gain entities, much as language will be used later
Communicative gestures Requesting Pointing Showing Giving	Train standard gestures for expression of early intentions. Requesting seems to be the easiest to train. Client idiosyncratic gestures can be modified or incorporated into this gestural complex
Receptive language Auditory memory Symbol recognition	Train recognition of conventional gestures, first, through non-symbolic memory training, then with symbol-referent pairing
Sound imitation Vocal response Vocal turn-taking Vocal shaping Sequencing vocal imitation	Train sound imitation with those clients for whom a verbal mode of expression is appropriate. Initial training concentrates on responding and is only gradually modified to require the correct imitation

Source: Adapted from Owens (1982).

children who function below Stage 6 cannot be expected to develop productive oral language ability, even if they can learn to produce sound patterns in response to specific stimuli. These children would probably benefit more from activities directed toward accelerating their rate of cognitive development. After they reach Stage 6, they can reasonably be expected to benefit from language intervention.

Kahn (1978, 1984) demonstrated that severely and profoundly retarded individuals generalize cognitive training across cognitive domains and that those individuals trained to presymbolic cognitive skills learn oral language better than those individuals trained to oral language alone. In general, the language-only group made little language progress, generalized poorly, retained less and used fewer spontaneous utterances than the cognitive group. As in the non-retarded population, means–ends appears to be the most significant presymbolic behaviour.

In a like manner, Hupp *et al.* (1986) report that receptive language training with severely retarded children results in more accurate generalization to novel examples than does expressive language training. In other words, expressive training alone does not automatically generalize to labelling of novel items. It has been suggested that receptive language use may be easier to learn and to apply in communication (Huttenlocher, 1974; Snyder, 1978).

A more moderate position would suggest an integrated approach which combines cognitive and communication training (Owens, 1987). First, input and output modalities for communication are determined. An initial communication system using the existent modalities and incorporating the client's current idiosyncratic communication system is then established. Donnellan *et al.* (1984) use an assessment protocol that attempts to determine the communicative function of aberrant behaviours. A similar evaluation could be accomplished with the client's idiosyncratic behaviours. Once the client's communicative functions have been determined, the clinician can aid the client to use more appropriate ways of expressing these functions. For the seemingly non-communicative client, an initial signalling system can be established using 'resonance' training (Sternberg, McNerney and Pegnatore, 1987) or a behaviour chain interruption strategy (Goetz, Gee and Sailor, 1985). In resonance training the clinician establishes close physical contact by cradling the client and begins rocking. Initial stages of training are interested in the client's notice that something is happening. The client is then trained to signal when he wishes for the activity to continue. Behaviour-chain interruption is similar, in that any pleasurable activity is interrupted in order to have the client signal for continuation.

While the client's communication system is enhanced and broadened through training, he is also trained in presymbolic cognitive skills, mentioned earlier. Robinson and Robinson (1983) offer the following guidance for selection of training objectives.

> The primary question to be answered when identifying instructional objectives for any child concerns the functional utility of a particular behaviour for that child.... Time spent teaching behaviors that may not be physically possible for a child and that are questionable prerequisites to later tasks is wasted. Any activity chosen for instruction should lead toward a skill that gives the child additional control over either the physical environment or the social environment. (p. 235)

It is important that these skills be trained within the context of ongoing activities within the client's daily communicative context (Garcia, 1974; Looney, 1980; Owens, 1987; Robinson and Robinson, 1983). This and the inclusion of the client's communicative partners as language facilitators will increase the possibility of generalization to the communication context.

Many assessment tools are available that attempt to assess the retarded individual's cognitive readiness for symbol use (Horstmeier and MacDonald, 1978b; Owens, 1982; Uzgiris and Hunt, 1975). The Ordinal Scales of Psychological Development (Uzgiris and Hunt, 1975), based on Piaget's sensorimotor stages, is one of the most thorough. Not all subtests need to be administered, and the clinician can limit herself to those areas of cognitive development that are particularly important for the development of symbols. The Ordinal Scales can be reliably administered to the severely handicapped since they demonstrate the same ordinality as non-handicapped infants (Kahn, 1976; Silverstein et al., 1975; Wohlheuter and Sindberg, 1975). Often the physical problems of the severely and pro-foundly retarded individual make it difficult for that individual to perform the behaviour criteria specified within the scales. This does not present a problem for the creative clinician because tasks can be adapted to each individual's physical abilities. Piaget did not specify behaviours or skills, rather he addressed a sequence of conceptual development. For most indi-viduals, Ordinal Scale tasks can be incorporated into play or administered within pleasurable activities.

Play and the level of play can also be valuable intervention tools and indicators of the individual's cognitive development. Play provides a context for both assessment and intervention centring on the skills and interests of the child. Several assessment tools are available for determining the level of an individual's play (Hill and McCune-Nicolich, 1981; Lowe and Costello, 1976). Corresponding levels of play and development are listed in Table 5.3. In general, play begins at the lowest level with non-symbolic manipulative behaviour prior to six months and moves through object-related behaviour and play with a scene and a theme to play with a story (Li, 1985). Play intervention is usually child- or client-centred with

129

Table 5.3: Levels of play and development

Piagetian levels	Characteristics
Pre-stage VI	Child demonstrates presymbolic understanding of object use by brief recognitory gestures
Stage VI	Child pretends in self-related activities involving his own body, such as simulating eating from an empty bowl
Symbolic stage I	Child extends symbolism beyond his own actions by including other people or objects or pretending activities, such as vacuuming the floor or using environmental noises with toys. Later, the child may exhibit (i) a pretend action relating to several people or objects, such as giving himself, mother and a doll to drink from an empty cup; (ii) a sequence of pretend actions; and (iii) planned symbolic actions indicated by announcing this to his audience or by searching for several objects to use in one activity
Symbolic stage II	Symbolic identification of one object with another, such as calling a sheet of paper 'blanket' and then covering a doll with it, or identifying a part of his body with another person.
Symbolic stage III	Sequence of planned actions used to create a real or near-real activity, such as pretending to prepare and serve dinner to some puppets

Source: adapted from Nicolich (1977) and Piaget (1962).

caregivers taking a supportive role (Johnson, Dowling and Wesner, 1980; Mahler, Levinson and Fine, 1976; McCune-Nicolich and Carroll, 1981).

Only a few intervention materials exist that integrate both cognition and language for higher functioning individuals (Strong, 1983). It is good practice, however, for the speech–language clinician to consider the cognitive underpinnings of any language structure to be trained, such as relational terms for location (Johnson, 1981) and time (Harner, 1981), numerical terms (Saxe, 1981) and causality (Ammon, 1981). The language training is more meaningful if taught within the everyday context of an ongoing meaningful activity which includes the concept (Keith, 1977). For example, locational term might be taught within the context of hide-and-seek or descriptive terms within a 'twenty-questions' guessing game format. This type of training will enhance the possibility of generalization to the ultimate use environment (Owens, in press).

(b) Cognitive processes and language intervention

The cognitive processing problems of the retarded population suggest a number of possible targets for training within a language intervention paradigm. Two general approaches have been utilized, the deficit approach and the prescriptive approach (Brooks and McCauley, 1984). The deficit approach assumes that there is a cognitive processing deficit common to all mentally retarded persons, and that this process should be identified and trained. In contrast, the prescriptive approach emphasizes the cognitive abilities of the individual and the processes needed in order to attain the desired response. The second approach seems to be more relevant to language intervention and can be adapted to the language concept being trained. Speech–language clinicians can determine the cognitive processes to address by carefully analysing the learning task.

It is not possible within the confines of a single chapter to provide a task analysis of all the possible language training objectives. I therefore offer a few intervention tips that the group data on the cognitive processes of the retarded population suggest. Facilitative techniques to aid the cognitive processing of retarded individuals are presented in Table 5.4; this table should not be interpreted as implying that all retarded persons are similar or that this information is relevant to every retarded language-impaired client. Nor will every suggestion apply to every language teaching situation.

Readers will recall that as a group the retarded population demonstrates limited attention as a result of poorer scanning and selection. In addition, the retarded population experiences difficulty identifying relevant stimulus dimensions of sensory input, thus decreasing discrimination abilities. Retarded individuals can be trained to identify the relevant dimensions by increasing the perceptual salience of these stimuli, and tasks can be modified as suggested by Table 5.4 in order to enhance performance (Soraci *et al.*, 1983). For example, clients can be trained to identify the relevant social and contextual cues that are the signals for certain language and communication responses such as requests and greetings.

Retarded clients can also be trained to develop organizational strategies, aided by clinicians who preorganize training content for easy recall. For example, Scruggs, Mastropieri and Levin (1985) report 50% better performance by mildly retarded clients taught vocabulary words using an associational strategy of key words than by clients receiving a direct teaching approach. Likewise, Borys (1978) used sentence elaborations as mediational devices with mildly retarded adolescents in order to enhance integration of pictures into organized 'chunks'. Finally, Burger *et al.* (1978) report increased learning and recall of pictures following a categorization task. While these studies are most relevant to the learning of vocabulary, the chunking of word classes and sentence types could also be employed. Categorization learning is best when many examples of the category are provided, so that the client can clearly identify the organizing principle (Haywood and Switzky, 1974). Naturally this organization will aid later recall of information.

Finally, generalization can be enhanced by ensuring that the retarded client understands the similarities between two sentences or two communication situations. The controlling stimuli need to be identified and highlighted. The method of instruction can also facilitate transfer. In general, clients who understand the language rules they are learning and the

Table 5.4: Facilitative techniques to aid cognitive processing with retarded individuals

---

Attention

1 Highlight visually or auditorily those stimulus cues to which clients are to attend. In conversation, turn-change points and utterances that signal that a response is required should be emphasized. Decrease cues as attention becomes more automatic

2. Train scanning techniques to enable clients to identify and attend to relevant cues against a background of competing stimuli. Train clients to attend to facial expressions and to para-linguistic cues as well as linguistic information

3 I lighlight and explain the differences between or distinctive features of stimuli used in discrimination. For example, the semantic content of different Wh- or constituent question words must be noted in order to determine the correct type of response. Clients must realize what is being asked before they can identify the correct response

Organization

1 'Pre-organize' information for easier storage. Spatial and visual stimuli may aid this process. The visual image of the concepts of various nouns and verbs, for example, might aid simple sentence formation and aid learning of these categories

2 Train associative strategies for storage and recall of information. Tactile, visual and auditory similarities, and later, semantic categories can be explained, demonstrated and trained

3 Use short-term memory tasks to aid clients with simultaneous and successive processing of linguistic information. Clients can be trained to repeat verbal information and also to interpret what they hear

Memory

1 Train rehearsal strategies for short- and long-term memory. Initially, these strategies may be physical, but they can gradually shift to more symbolic and linguistic tasks

2 Use overlearning and plentiful examples of underlying language rules

3 Train both signal and symbol recall of an event. Since signal recall seems to be easier for the retarded individual, pairing of the two should aid or trigger symbol memory

4 New words and concepts should be trained with a number of associations to improve recall. Sentential or story formats may aid recall of individual words

5 Highlight important items or concepts to be remembered, thus enhancing selective attending

6 Use visual memory to enhance auditory memory

Transfer

1 Ensure that training situations are initially very similar or nearly identical to the intended generalization context. For example, use actual menus and telephone directories when training restaurant ordering or telephone use

2 Highlight similarities between situations and between new and old information and tasks. When the client is ready to use his/her new language skill in the everyday context, help the client to recall the similarities with the training context

3 Aid clients to discover strategies for approaching new tasks by recalling previous learning and problem-solving

4 Use those in the client's everyday environment as language trainers

---

language variables they are manipulating are better able to generalize to novel content and situations (Burger, Blackman and Clark, 1981). Examples of the concept being taught should be clear and easily identifiable and plentiful. According to Hupp and Mervis (1982), 'systematic selection of good examples to represent the categories to be trained is essential in order to obtain an appropriately generalized response'(p. 767).

The teaching strategies suggested in this section do not directly address cognitive skills instruction. This task is somewhat outside the bounds of typical speech–language intervention. Rather I have suggested strategies that can enhance the teaching of language concepts, given the particular cognitive abilities of the retarded population.

CONCLUSION

Both the developmental and the process models of cognition offer targets and techniques for language intervention with the retarded population. The knowledgeable speech–language clinician should be able to design and implement language intervention programmes based on these special cognitive and language abilities and on the needs of the retarded individual.

REFERENCES

Ammon, M. (1981) The understanding of causality in preschool children: from action to explanation, *Topics in Language Disorders*, 2, 33–50.
Ball, M. and Nuttall, K. (1980) Neurofibrillary tangles, granulovacuolar degeneration and neuron loss in Down syndrome: qualitative comparison with Alzheimer dementia, *Annals of Neurol.*, 7, 462–7.
Bates, E., Benigni, L., Bretherton, I., Camaioni, L. and Volterra, V. (1979) *The Emergence of Symbols: Cognition and Communication in Infancy*, Academic Press, New York.
Baumeister, A. and Kellas, G. (1968) Distribution of reaction times of retardates and normals, *Am. J. Ment. Defic.*, 72, 712–18.
Belmont, J. (1967) Long-term memory in mental retardation in *International Review of Research in Mental Retardation* (ed. N. Ellis), Academic Press, New York, 219–55.
Berry, P., Groeneweg, G., Gibson, D. and Brown, R. (1984) Mental development of adults with Down syndrome, *Am. J. Ment. Defic.*, 89, 252–6.
Bilsky, L., Walker, N. and Sakales, S. (1983) Comprehension and recall of sentences by mentally retarded and nonretarded individuals, *Am. J. Ment. Defic.*, 87, 558–65.
Borkowski, J. and Cavanaugh, J. (1979) Maintenance and generalization of skills and strategies by the retarded in *Handbook on Mental Deficiency* (ed. N. Ellis), 2nd edn, Lawrence Erlbaum, Hillsdale, NJ., pp. 569–617.
Borkowski, J. and Wanschura, P. (1974) Mediational processes in the retarded, in *International Review of Research in Mental Retardation* (ed. N. Ellis), Academic Press, New York, Vol. 7.
Borys, S. (1978) Effect of imposed vs self-generated imagery and sentence mediation on the free recall of retarded adolescents, *Am. J. Ment. Defic.*, 83, 307–10.
Bray, N. (1979) Strategy production in the retarded, in *Handbook of Mental Deficiency* (ed. N. Ellis), 2nd edn, Lawrence Erlbaum, Hillsdale, NJ, pp. 699–726.
Bricker, W. and Bricker, D. (1974) An early language training strategy in *Language*

Acquisition — Assessment, Retardation, and Intervention (eds. R. Schiefelbusch and L. Lloyd), University Park Press, Baltimore, Md., pp. 431–68.

Bricker, W., Heal, L., Bricker, D., Hayes, W. and Larsen, L. (1969) Discrimination learning and learning set with institutionalized retarded children, *Am. J. Ment. Defic.*, *74*, 242–8.

Brooks, P. and McCauley, C. (1984) Cognitive research in mental retardation, *Am. J. Ment. Defic.*, *88*, 479–86.

Brown, A. (1974) The role of strategic behavior in retardate memory in *International Review of Research in Mental Retardation* (ed. N. Ellis), Academic Press, New York, Vol. 7.

Brown, A. (1978) Knowing when, where, and how to remember. A problem of metacognition in *Advances in Instrumental Psychology* (ed. R. Glasser), Lawrence Erlbaum, Hillsdale, NJ, Vol. 1.

Brown, A., Campione, J. and Barclay, C. (1979) Training self-checking routines for estimating test readiness: generalization from list learning to prose recall, *Child Development, 50*, 501–12.

Brown, A., Campione, J. and Murphy, M. (1974) Keeping track of changing variables: long-term retention of a trained rehearsal strategy by retarded adolescents, *Am. J. Ment. Defic.*, *78*, 446–53.

Burger, A., Blackman, L. and Clark, H. (1981) Generalization of verbal abstraction strategies by EMR children and adolescents, *Am. J. Ment. Defic.*, *85*, 611–18.

Burger, A., Blackman, L., Clark, H. and Reis, E. (1982) Effects of hypothesis testing and variable format training on generalization of a verbal abstraction strategy by EMR learners, *Am. J. Ment. Defic.*, *86*, 405–13.

Burger, A., Blackman, L. and Tan, N. (1980) Maintenance and generalization of a sorting and retrieval strategy by EMR and nonretarded individuals, *Am. J. Ment. Defic.*, *84*, 373–80.

Burger, A., Holmes, M., Blackman, L. and Zetlin, A. (1978) Use of active sorting and retrieval strategies as a facilitator of recall, clustering, and sorting by EMR and nonretarded children, *Am. J. Ment. Defic.*, *83*, 253–61.

Burr, D. and Rohr, A. (1978) Patterns of psycholinguistic development in the severely mentally retarded: a hypothesis, *Soc. Biol.*, *25*, 15–22.

Butterfield, E. and Belmont, J. (1975) Assessing and improving the executive cognitive functions of mentally retarded people in *The Psychology of Mental Retardation: Issues and Approaches* (eds. I. Bialer and M. Sternlicht), Psychological Dimensions, New York, pp. 277–318.

Butterfield, E., Wambold, C. and Belmont, J. (1973) On the theory and practice of improving short-term memory, *Am. J. Ment. Defic.*, *77*, 654–69.

Campione, J. and Brown, A. (1977) Memory and metamemory development in educable retarded children in *Perspectives on the Development of Memory and Cognition* (eds. R. Kail and J. Hagen), Lawrence Erlbaum, Hillsdale, NJ, pp. 367–406.

Cardoso-Martins, C., Mervis, C. and Mervis, C. (1985) Early vocabulary acquisition by children with Down's syndrome, *Am. J. Ment. Defic.*, *90*, 177–84.

Case, R. (1978) Intellectual development from birth to adulthood: A neo-Piagetian interpretation in *Children's Thinking: What Develops?* (ed. R. Siegler), Lawrence Erlbaum, Hillsdale, NJ, pp. 37–71.

Clark, P. and Detterman, D. (1981) Performance of mentally retarded and nonretarded persons on a lifted-weight task with strategies reduced or eliminated, *Am. J. Ment. Defic.*, *85*, 530–8.

Cromer, R. (1976) The cognitive hypothesis of language acquisition and its implications for child language deficiency in *Normal and Deficient Child Language* (eds. D. Morehead and A. Morehead), University Park Press, Baltimore, Md, pp. 283–333.

Dance, F. (1967) Toward a theory of human communication in *Human Communication Theory: Original Essays* (ed. F. Dance), Holt, Rinehart and Winston, New York, pp. 288–309.

Das, J. (1972) Patterns of cognitive ability in nonretarded and retarded children, *Am. J. Ment. Defic.*, 77, 6–12.

Das, J., Kirby, J. and Jarman, R. (1979) *Simultaneous and Successive Cognitive Processes*, Academic Press, New York.

DeLoache, J. and Brown, A. (1979) Looking for Big Bird: studies of memory in very young children, *Quarterly Newsl. Lab. Comp. Hum. Cognition*, 1, 53–7.

Detterman, D. (1979) Memory in the mentally retarded in *Handbook of Mental Deficiency* (ed. N. Ellis), 2nd edn, Lawrence Erlbaum, Hillsdale, NJ, pp. 726–60.

Donnellan, A., Mirenda, P., Mesaros, R. and Fassbender, L. (1984) Analyzing the communicative functions of aberrant behavior, *J. Ass. for Persons with Severe Handicaps*, 9, 201–12.

Dunst, C. (1980) *A Clinical and Educational Manual for Use with the Uzgiris and Hunt Scales of Infant Psychological Development*, University Park Press, Baltimore, Md.

Dustman, R. and Callner, D. (1979) Cortical evoked responses and response decrement in nonretarded and Down's syndrome individuals, *Am. J. Ment. Defic.*, 83, 391–7.

Ellis, N. (1963) Stimulus trace and behavioral inadequacy in *Handbook of Mental Deficiency* (ed. N. Ellis), 2nd edn, Lawrence Erlbaum, Hillsdale, NJ, pp. 134–58.

Ellis, N. (1970) Memory processes in retardates and normals in *International Review of Research in Mental Retardation* (ed. N. Ellis), Academic Press, New York, Vol. 4.

Ellis, N., Deacon, J., Harris, L., Poor, A., Angers, D., Diorio, M., Watkins, R., Boyd, B. and Cavanaugh, A. (1982) Learning, memory, and transfer in profoundly, severely, and moderately mentally retarded persons, *Am. J. Ment. Defic.*, 87, 186–96.

Ellis, N., Deacon, J. and Wooldridge, P. (1985) Structural memory deficits of mentally retarded persons, *Am. J. Ment. Defic.*, 89, 393–402.

Ellis, N. and Wooldridge, P. (1985) Short-term memory for pictures and words by mentally retarded and nonretarded persons, *Am. J. Ment. Defic.*, 89, 622–6.

Engle, R. and Nagle, R. (1979) Strategy training and semantic encoding in mildly retarded children, *Intel.*, 3, 17–30.

Ervin-Tripp, S. (1973) Some strategies for the first two years in *Cognitive Development and the Acquisition of Language* (ed. T. Moore), Academic Press, New York, pp. 261–86.

Evans, D. (1977) The development of language abilities in Mongols: A correlational study, *J. Ment. Defic. Res.*, 21, 103–17.

Evans, R. and Bilsky, L. (1979) Clustering and categorical list retention in the mentally retarded in *Handbook of Mental Deficiency: Psychological Theory and Research* (ed. N. Ellis), Lawrence Erlbaum, Hillsdale, NJ, pp. 533–67.

Frank, H. and Rabinovitch, M. (1974) Auditory short-term memory: Developmental changes in rehearsal, *Child Development*, 45, 397–407.

Friedman, M., Krupski, A., Dawson, E. and Rosenberg, P. (1977) Metamemory and mental retardation: implications for research and practice in *Research to Practice in Mental Retardation* (ed. P. Mittler), University Park Press, Baltimore, Md., Vol. 2.

Garcia, E. (1974) The training generalization of conversational speech form in nonverbal retardates, *J. Appl. Behavioral Analysis*, 7, 137–49.

Gillham, B. (1979) *The First Words Language Programme: A Basic Language Programme for Mentally Handicapped Children*, Allen and Unwin, London.

Glidden, L. (1979) Training of learning and memory in retarded persons: Strategies, techniques, and teaching tools in *Handbook on Mental Deficiency* (ed. N. Ellis), 2nd edn, Lawrence Erlbaum, Hillsdale, NJ, pp. 619–57.

Glidden, L., Bilsky, L., Mar, H., Judd, T. and Warner, D. (1983) Semantic processing can facilitate free recall in mildly retarded adolescents, *J. Exp. Child Psychol.*, 36, 510–32.

Glidden, L. and Mar, H. (1978) Availability and accessibility of information in the semantic memory of retarded and nonretarded adolescents, *J. Exp. Child Psychol.*, 25, 33–40.

Glidden, L. and Warner, D. (1983) Semantic processing and recall improvement of EMR adolescents, *Am. J. Ment. Defic.*, 88, 96–105.

Glidden, L. and Warner, D. (1985) Semantic processing and serial learning by EMR adolescents, *Am. J. Ment. Defic.*, 89, 635–641.

Goetz, L., Gee, K. and Sailor, W. (1985) Using a behavior chain interruption strategy to teach communication skills to students with severe disabilities, *J. Ass. for Persons with Severe Handicaps*, 10, 21–30.

Greenwald, C. and Leonard, L. (1979) Communicative and sensorimotor development in Down's syndrome children, *Am. J. Ment. Defic.*, 84, 296–303.

Gruen, G. and Vore, D. (1972) Development of conservation in normal and retarded children, *Developmental Psychol.*, 6, 146–57.

Harner, L. (1981) Children's understanding of time, *Topics in Language Disorders*, 2, 51–66.

Harris, D. (1982) Communicative interaction processes involving nonvocal physically handicapped children, *Topics in Language Disorders*, 2, 21–38.

Hasher, L. and Zacks, R. (1979) Automatic and effortful processes in memory, *J. of Exp. Psychol: Gen.*, 108, 356–80.

Haywood, H. and Switzky, H. (1974) Children's verbal abstracting: effects of enriched input, age, and IQ, *Am. J. Ment. Defic.*, 78, 556–65.

Hill, P. and McCune-Nicolich, L. (1981) Pretend play and patterns of cognition in Down's syndrome children, *Child Development*, 52, 611–17.

Hockey, R. (1973) Rate of presentation in running memory and direct manipulation of input processing strategies, *Quarterly J. Exp. Psychol.*, 25, 104–11.

Horstmeier, D. and MacDonald, J. (1978a) *Ready, Set, Go — Talk to me*, Psychological Corporation, San Antonio, Tex.

Horstmeier, D. and MacDonald, J. (1978b) *Environmental Prelanguage Battery*, Psychological Corporation, San Antonio, Tex.

Hulme, I. and Lunzer, E. (1966) Play, language, and reasoning in subnormal children, *J. Child Psychol. and Psychiat.*, 7, 107–23.

Hupp, S. and Mervis, C. (1982) Acquisition of basic object categories by severely handicapped children, *Child Development*, 53, 760–7.

Hupp, S., Mervis, C., Able, H. and Conroy-Gunther, M. (1986) Effects of receptive and expressive training on category labels on generalized learning by severely mentally retarded children, *Am. J. Ment. Defic.*, 90, 558–65.

Huttenlocher, J. (1974) The origins of language comprehension in *Theories in Cognitive Psychology: The Loyola Symposium* (ed. R. Solso), Wiley, New York, pp. 331–68.

James, S. (1980) Language and sensorimotor cognitive development in the young child, paper presented at New York Speech–Language–Hearing Association Annual Convention, April.

Jarman, R. (1978) Patterns of cognitive ability in retarded children: a reexamination, *Am. J. Ment. Defic.*, *82*, 344–8.

Jarman, R. and Das, J. (1977) Simultaneous and successive synthesis and intelligence, *Intel.*, *1*, 151–69.

Jeffree, D. and McConkey, R. (1976) An observation scheme for recording children's imaginative doll play, *J. Child Psychol. and Psychiat.*, *17*, 189–97.

Johnson, F.K., Dowling, J. and Wesner, D. (1980) Notes on infant psychotherapy, *Infant Ment. Health J.*, *1* (1), 19–33.

Johnson, F., Levinson, J. and Fine, S. (1976) Notes on infant psychotherapy, *Infant Ment. Health J.*, *1*, 19–33.

Johnson, J. (1981) On location: thinking and talking about space, *Topics in Language Disorders*, 2, 17–32.

Jones, O. (1975) A comparative study of early mother–child communication with young, normal children and young Down's syndrome children, paper presented at the Loch Lomond Symposium on Communicative Development, University of Strathclyde.

Kahn, J. (1975) Relationship of Piaget's sensorimotor period to language acquisition of profoundly retarded children, *Am. J. Ment. Defic.*, *79*, 640–3.

Kahn, J. (1976) Utility of Uzgiris and Hunt scales of sensorimotor development with severely and profoundly retarded children, *Am. J. Ment. Defic.*, *80*, 663–5.

Kahn, J. (1978) Acceleration of object permanence with severely and profoundly retarded children, *Am. Ass. for the Severely/Profoundly Handicapped Rev.*, *3*, 15–22.

Kahn, J. (1984) Cognitive training and initial use of referential speech, *Topics in Language Disorders*, 5, 14–23.

Kamhi, A. (1981) Developmental vs different theories of mental retardation: a new look, *Am. J. Ment. Defic.*, *86*, 1–7.

Keith, J. (1977) Cognitive development in the preoperational, concrete operational, and formal periods in *Cognition and the Deaf–Blind Child* (eds. C. Ficociello and L. Ludwig), South Central Regional Center for Services to Deaf–Blind Children and Callier Center for Communication Disorders, University of Texas, Austin, Texas, USA.

Kellas, G., Ashcroft, M. and Johnson, N. (1973) Rehearsal processes in the short-term memory performance of mildly retarded adolescents, *Am. J. Ment. Defic.*, *77*, 670–9.

Kendall, C., Borkowski, J. and Cavanaugh, J. (1980) Maintenance and generalization of an interrogative strategy by EMR children, *Intel.*, *4*, 255–70.

Keogh, W. and Reichle, J. (1985) Communication intervention for the difficult-to-teach severely handicapped in *Teaching Functional Language* (eds. S. Warren and A. Rogers-Warren), University Park Press, Baltimore, pp. 157–96.

Kintsch, W. and van Dijk, T. (1979) Toward a model of text comprehension and production, *Psychol. Rev.*, *85*, 363–94.

Krupski, A. (1977) Role of attention in the reaction-time performance of mentally retarded adolescents, *Am. J. Ment. Defic.*, *82*, 79–83.

Lamberts, F. (1981) Sign and symbol in children's processing of familiar auditory stimuli, *Am. J. Ment. Defic.*, *86*, 300–8.

Leifer, J. and Lewis, M. (1984) Acquisition of conversational response skills by young Down's syndrome and nonretarded young children, *Am. J. Ment. Defic.*, *88*, 610–18.

Levine, H. and Langness, L. (1985) Everyday cognition among mildly mentally retarded adults: An ethnographic approach, *Am. J. Ment. Defic.*, *90*, 18–26.

Levine, H., Zetlin, A. and Langness, L. (1980) Everyday memory tasks in classrooms for TMR learners, *Quarterly Newsl. of the Lab. of Comparative Human Cognition, 2*, 1–6.

Li, A. (1985) Toward more elaborate pretend play, *Ment. Retardation, 23*, 132–6.

Liebert, A. and Baumeister, A. (1973) Behavioral variability among retardates, children, and college students, *J. Psychol., 83*, 57–65.

Lincoln, A., Courchesne, E., Kilman, B. and Galambos, R. (1985) Neuropsychological correlates of information-processing by children with Down syndrome, *Am. J. Ment. Defic., 89*, 403–14.

Lobb, H. (1974) Effects of verbal rehearsal on discrimination learning in moderately retarded nursery-school children, *Am. J. Ment. Defic., 79*, 449–54.

Looney, P. (1980) Instructional intervention with language-disordered learners, *Directive Teacher, 2*, 30–1.

Lowe, M. and Costello, A. (1976) *Manual for the Symbolic Play Test*, NFER, London.

Luftig, R. and Johnson, R. (1982) Identification and recall of structurally important units in prose of mentally retarded learners, *Am. J. Ment. Defic., 86*, 495–502.

McCune-Nicolich, L. and Carroll, S. (1981) Development of symbolic play: Implications for the language specialist, *Topics in Language Disorders, 2*, 1–15.

McDade, H. and Adler, S. (1980) Down's syndrome and short-term memory impairment: A storage or retrieval deficit?, *Am. J. Ment. Defic., 84*, 561–7.

McLean, J. and Snyder-McLean, L. (1978) *A Transactional Approach to Early Language Training*, Charles E. Merrill, Columbus, Ohio.

McManis, D. (1970) Conservation and transitivity of weight and length by normals and retardates, *Developmental Psychol., 1*, 373–82.

MacMillan, D. (1972) Paired-associate learning as a function of explicitness of mediational set by EMR and nonretarded children, *Am. J. Ment. Defic., 76*, 686–91.

Macnamara, J. (1972) Cognitive basis of language learning in infants, *Psychol. Rev., 79*, 1–13.

Mahler, A., Levinson, J. and Fine, S. (1976) Infant psychotherapy: theory, research, and practice, *Psychotherapy: Theory, Res. and Pract., 13*, 131–40.

Mahoney, G., Glover, A. and Finger, I. (1981) Relationship between language and sensorimotor development of Down Syndrome and nonretarded children, *Am. J. Ment. Defic., 86*, 21–7.

Maisto, A. and Jerome, M. (1977) Encoding and high-speed memory scanning of retarded and nonretarded adolescents, *Am. J. Ment. Defic., 82*, 282–6.

Manolson, A. (1983) *It Takes Two to Talk*, Hanen Early Language Resource Center, Toronto.

Marcell, M. and Armstrong, V. (1982) Auditory and visual sequential memory of Down syndrome and nonretarded children, *Am. J. Ment. Defic., 87*, 86–95.

Meador, D. (1984) Effects of color on visual discrimination of geometric symbols with severely and profoundly mentally retarded individuals, *Am. J. Ment. Defic., 89*, 275–86.

Meador, D. and Ellis, N. (1987) Automatic and effortful processing by mentally retarded and nonretarded persons, *Am. J. Ment. Defic., 91*, 613–19.

Mercer, C. and Snell, M. (1977) *Learning Theory Research in Mental Retardation*, Charles E. Merrill, Columbus, Ohio.

Merrill, E. (1985) Differences in semantic processing speed of mentally retarded and nonretarded persons, *Am. J. Ment. Defic., 90*, 71–80.

Merrill, E. and Mar, H. (1987) Differences between mentally retarded and nonretarded persons efficiency of auditory sentence processing, *Am. J. Ment. Defic., 91*, 406–14.

Miller, J., Chapman, R., Branston, M., and Reichle, J. (1980) Language comprehension in sensorimotor stages 5 and 6, *J. Speech Hearing Res.*, *4*, 1–12.

Mittler, P. (1974) Language and communication in *Mental Deficiency: The Changing Outlook* (eds. A.D.B. Clarke and A.M. Clarke), Methuen, London.

Moore, K. and Meltzoff, A. (1978) Object permanence, imitation, and language development in infancy: toward a neo-Piagetian perspective on communication development in *Communicative and Cognitive Abilities — Early Behavioral Assessment* (eds. F. Minifio and L. Lloyd), University Park Press, Baltimore, Md., pp. 151–84.

Morehead, D. and Morehead, A. (1974) A Piagetian view of thought and language during the first two years in *Language Perspectives — Acquisition, Retardation, and Intervention* (eds. R. Schiefelbusch and L. Lloyd), University Park Press, Baltimore, Md., pp. 154–90.

Mosley, J. (1985) High-speed memory-scanning task performance of mildly mentally retarded and nonretarded individuals, *Am. J. Ment. Defic.*, *90*, 81–9.

Nettelbeck, T. and McLean, J. (1984) Mental retardation and inspection time: a two-stage model for sensory registration and central processing, *Am. J. Ment. Defic.*, *89*, 83–90.

Nicolich, L.M. (1977) Beyond sensorimotor intelligence: Assessment of symbolic maturity through analysis of pretend play, *Merrill-Palmer Quarterly*, *23* (2), 89–101.

Nigro, G. and Roak, R. (1987) Mentally retarded and nonretarded adults' memory for spatial location, *Am. J. Ment. Defic.*, *91*, 392–7.

Nugent, P. and Mosley, J. (1987) Mentally retarded and nonretarded individuals' attention allocation and capacity, *Am. J. Ment. Defic.*, *91*, 598–605.

O'Connor, N. and Hermelin, B. (1978) *Seeing and Hearing in Space and Time*, Academic Press, New York.

O'Regan-Kleinert, J. (1980) Pre-speech/language therapeutic techniques for the handicapped infant, paper presented at American Speech–Language–Hearing Association Annual Convention, November

Owens, R. (1982) *Program for the Acquisition of Language with the Severely Impaired (PALS)*, Psychological Corporation, San Antonio, Tex.

Owens, R. (1987) The use of language facilitators with residential retarded populations, *Topics in Language Disorders*, *7*, 47–63.

Owens, R. (in press) *Functional Language Intervention*, Charles E. Merrill, Columbus, Ohio.

Owings, R., Baumeister, A., Laine, R. and Lewis, M. (1980) Memory scanning of shapes, colors, and compounds: a comparison of retarded and nonretarded adults, *Intell.*, *4*, 243–54.

Piaget, J. (1962) *Play, Dreams and Imitation*, Norton, New York.

Rees, N. (1975) Imitation and language development: issues and clinical implications, *J. Speech Hearing Dis.*, *40*, 339–50.

Reichle, J. and Yoder, D. (1979) Communication behavior of the severely and profoundly mentally retarded: assessment and early stimulation strategies in *Teaching the Severely Handicapped* (eds. R. York and E. Edgar), American Association for the Education of the Severely/Profoundly Handicapped, Seattle, Wash., USA, Vol. 4.

Reid, B. and Kiernan, C. (1979) Spoken words and manual signs as encoding categories in short-term memory for mentally retarded children, *Am. J. Ment. Defic.*, *84*, 200–3.

Reid, G. (1980) Overt and covert rehearsal in short-term motor memory of mentally retarded and non-retarded persons, *Am. J. Ment. Defic.*, *85*, 69–77.

Robinson, C. and Robinson, J. (1983) Sensorimotor functions and cognitive development in *Systematic Instruction of the Moderately and Severely Handicapped* (ed. M. Snell), Charles E. Merrill, Columbus, Ohio, pp. 102–53.

Robinson, N. and Robinson, H. (1976) *The Mentally Retarded Child: A Psychological Approach* (2nd edn), McGraw-Hill, New York.

Rogers, S. (1977) Characteristics of the cognitive development of profoundly retarded children, *Child Development, 48*, 837–43.

Ross, D. and Ross, S. (1979) Cognitive training for the EMR child: language skills prerequisite to relevant–irrelevant discrimination tasks, *Ment. Retardation, 17*, 3–7.

Sailor, W., Guess, D. and Baer, D. (1973) Functional language for verbally deficient children, *Ment. Retardation, 11*, 27–35.

Saxe, G. (1981) Number symbols and number operations: their development and interrelation, *Topics in Language Disorders, 2*, 67–76.

Schafer, E. and Peeke, H. (1982) Down syndrome individuals fail to habituate cortical evoked potentials, *Am. J. Ment. Defic., 87*, 332–7.

Scruggs, T., Mastropieri, M. and Levin, J. (1985) Vocabulary acquisition by mentally retarded students under direct and mnemonic instruction, *Am. J. Ment. Defic., 89*, 546–51.

Semmel, M., Barritt, L. and Bennett, S. (1970) Performance of EMR and non-retarded children on a modified cloze task, *Am. J. Ment. Defic., 74*, 681–8.

Siegel, L. (1979) Infant perception, cognitive, and motor behaviors as predictors of subsequent cognitive and language development, *Can. J. Psychol./Rev. Can. Psychol., 33*, 382–95.

Silverman, W. (1974) High speed scanning of normal phanumeric symbols in coutural-familially retarded and nonretarded children, *Am. J. Ment. Defic., 79*, 44–51.

Silverstein, A., Brownlee, L., Hubbell, M. and McLain, R. (1975) Comparison of two sets of Piagetian scales with severely and profoundly retarded children, *Am. J. Ment. Defic., 80*, 292–7.

Snart, F., O'Grady, M. and Das, J. (1982) Cognitive processing by subgroups of moderately mentally retarded children, *Am. J. Ment. Defic., 86*, 465–72.

Snyder, L. (1978) Communicative and cognitive abilities in the sensorimotor period, *Merrill-Palmer Quarterly, 24*, 161–80.

Sommers, R. and Starkey, K. (1977) Dichotic verbal processing in Down's syndrome children having qualitatively different speech and language skills, *Am. J. Ment. Defic., 82*, 44–53.

Soraci, S., Alpher, V., Deckner, C. and Blanton, R. (1983) Oddity performance and the perception of relational information, *Psychologia, 26*, 162–71.

Sperber, R. and McCauley, C. (1984) Semantic processing efficiency in the mentally retarded in *Learning and Cognition in the Mentally Retarded* (eds. P. Brooks, R. Sperber and C. McCauley), Lawrence Erlbaum, Hillsdale, NJ, pp. 141–63.

Sperber, R., Merrill, E., McCauley, C. and Shapiro, D. (1983) Intelligence-related differences in the efficiency of semantic coding, paper presented at Meeting of Society for Research in Child Development, Detroit.

Spitz, H. (1966) The role of input organization in the learning and memory of mental retardates in *International Review of Research in Mental Retardation* (ed. N. Ellis) Academic Press, New York, Vol. 2.

Squires, N., Galbraith, G. and Aine, C. (1979) Event related potential assessment of sensory and cognitive defects in the mentally retarded in *Human Evoked Potentials* (eds. D. Lehmann and E. Gallaway), Plenum, New York, pp. 397–413.

Stephens, B. and McLaughlin, J. (1974) Two-year gains in reasoning by retarded and nonretarded persons, *Am. J. Ment. Defic.*, *79*, 116–26.

Stephens, W. (1972) Equivalence formation by retarded and nonretarded children at different mental ages, *Am. J. Ment. Defic.*, *77*, 311–13.

Sternberg, L., McNerney, C. and Pegnatore, L. (1987) Developing primitive signalling behavior of students with profound mental retardation, *Ment. Retardation*, *25*, 13–20.

Strong, J. (1983) *Language Facilitation, a Complete Cognitive Therapy Program*, University Park Press, Baltimore, Md.

Suetsugu, M. (1979) Dendritic spine distribution along spinal dendrites of the pyramidal neurons in Down syndrome, *Fukujka Igaku Zasshi*, *70*, 23–40.

Swope, S. and Liebergott, J. (1980) What is the use of talking: the preschool language impaired child, paper presented at the Al Sigl Center, Rochester, NY, USA, April.

Taylor, A. and Turnure, J. (1979) Imagery and verbal elaboration with retarded children: effects on learning and memory in *Handbook of Mental Deficiency: Psychological Theory and Research* (ed. N. Ellis), Lawrence Erlbaum, Hillsdale, NJ, pp. 659–97.

Terdal, L., Jackson, R. and Garner, A. (1976) Mother–child interactions: A comparison between normal and developmentally delayed groups in *Behavior Modification and Families* (eds. E. Mash, L. Hamerlynck and L. Hardy), Brunner/Mazel, New York, pp. 243–64.

Turnbull, A. (1974) Teaching retarded persons to rehearse through cumulative overt labeling, *Am. J. Ment. Defic.*, *79*, 331–7.

Turner, L. and Bray, N. (1985) Spontaneous reheaual by mildly retarded children and adolescents, *Am. J. Ment. Defic.*, *90*, 57–83.

Ullman, D. (1974) Breadth of attention and retention in mentally retarded and intellectually average children, *Am. J. Ment. Defic.*, *78*, 640–8.

Uzgiris, I. and Hunt, McV. (1975) *Assessment in Infancy: Ordinal Scales of Psychological Development*, University of Illinois Press, Urbana, Ill.

Varnhagen, C., Das, J. and Varnhagen, S. (1987) Auditory and visual memory span: cognitive processing by TMR individuals with Down syndrome or other etiologies, *Am. J. Ment. Defic.*, *91*, 398–405.

Wacker, D. and Greenbaum, F. (1984) Efficacy of a verbal training sequence on the sorting performance of moderately and severely retarded adolescents, *Am. J. Ment. Defic.*, *88*, 653–60.

Watkins, O. and Watkins, M. (1980) The modality effect and echoic persistence, *J. Exp. Psychol.: Gen.*, *109*, 251–78.

Westby, C. (1980) Assessment of cognitive and language abilities through play, *Language, Speech, and Hearing Services in Schools*, *11*, 154–68.

Whatmough, J. (1956) *Language: A Modern Synthesis*, American Library, New York.

Whitaker, C. (1980) A note on developmental trends in the symbolic play of hospitalized profoundly retarded children, *J. Child Psychol. Psychiat.*, *21*, 253–61.

Wing, L., Gould, J., Yeates, S. and Brierly, L. (1977) Symbolic play in severely mentally retarded and in autistic children, *J. Child Psychol. Psychiat.*, *18*, 167–78.

Winters, J. and Semchuk, M. (1986) Retrieval from long-term store as a function of mental age and intelligence, *Am. J. Ment. Defic.*, *90*, 440–8.

Wohlheuter, M. and Sindberg, R. (1975) Longitudinal development of object permanence in mentally retarded children: an exploratory study, *Am. J. Ment. Defic.*, *79*, 513–18.

Woodward, M. and Hunt, M. (1972) Exploratory studies of early cognitive development, *Br. J. Educational Psychol.*, *42*, 248–59.

Woodward, M. and Stern, D. (1963) Developmental patterns of severely subnormal children, *Br. J. Educational Psychol.*, 59, 10–21.

Yellin, A., Lodwig, A. and Jerison, H. (1980) Effects of rate of repetition stimulus presentation on the visual evoked-brain potentials of young adults with Down's syndrome, *Biol. Psychiat.*, *14*, 913–25.

Yoder, D. (1985) Communication and the severely/profoundly retarded, paper presented at Conference on the State of the Art in Communication and the Developmentally Disabled, Buffalo State University, Buffalo, NY, USA, June.

Zeaman, D. and House, B. (1963) The role of attention in retardate discrimination learning in *Handbook of Mental Deficiency* (ed. N. Ellis), McGraw-Hill, New York, pp. 159–223.

Zeaman, D. and House, B. (1979) A review of attention theory in *Handbook of Mental Deficiency: Psychological Theory and Research* (ed. N. Ellis), Lawrence Erlbaum, Hillsdale, NJ, pp. 63–120.

Zigler, E. (1967) Mental retardation technical comment, *Sci.*, *157*, 578.

6

Social Cognition and
the Communicative Environment
of Mentally Handicapped
People

Michael Beveridge

The chapters in this volume show the advances in our understanding of the language of mentally handicapped people and communication processes between them and others. Research has helped to alter our perspective on their use of language, and mental handicap is no longer seen as a condition which prevents communication. Many mentally handicapped people are vibrant and highly motivated communicators; and as this volume demonstrates, researchers are now turning to the study of how they communicate, not why they cannot. This change of emphasis has led us to investigate the important influences on the use of language, by mentally handicapped people. Consequently, as this volume also shows, it has become important to study the different environments in which their language is put to communicative use. Considerable attention is now given to the different purposes served by their communicative acts.

Despite this change of emphasis, little attention has so far been given to the role of communication in their mental development (Beveridge and Conti-Ramsden, 1987). This is an important omission in the research agenda; and section 6.1 in this chapter suggests that some of the ways in which the language and thought processes of normal children are being studied might lead to better ways of understanding the educational difficulties experienced by the mentally handicapped. I will suggest, in particular, that approaches to learning based on the 'social cognition' of Vygotsky (1978) can help our understanding of the cognitive processes of handicapped people.

I also discuss in this chapter, from a socio-cognitive perspective, some of the work carried out by the research group with whom I have investigated the 'ecological' aspects of language function, including the role of language in solving everyday problems.

6.1 COMMUNICATION, SOCIAL COGNITION AND MENTAL HANDICAP

The term 'social cognition' has a number of interpretations, but essentially it captures the point that many thought processes have an inherently social origin. Its importance for the study of mental handicap is that this approach makes the course of cognitive development amenable to detailed study via analysis of social interactions. Intellectually handicapping processes can be identified and described during their development.

Social cognitivists argue that the rules of social interaction and discourse which are used for reasoning between people also underpin the logic of individual thinking (Vygotsky, 1978). For example, it has been argued that thinking occurs initially in the language of social contexts and we then internalize the procedures we have successfully acquired socially (Hickman, 1987). These procedures form the basis of thought. From this point of view, even logic and mathematics have their roots in social experience (Rotman, 1977). They are, in Donaldson's (1978) terminology, 'embedded' in real social contexts which have cultural meaning for the participants. This view has also been explored in the cross-cultural work of Michael Cole (1985) in which naturally occurring social transactions are shown to have complex cognitive structures in societies where formal education plays little part.

Some authors even take the view that language and logic are essentially the same. For example, Walkerdine (1982) writes:

In formal reasoning, truth is determined in terms of the internal relations of the statement itself ... the basis of formal reasoning need not be sought as an essential quality inside the mind, the result of the internalisation of structures of action. Rather we can see that the linguistic system itself provides the tools necessary to formal reasoning. (p. 138)

Walkerdine illustrates her argument with detailed descriptions of young children learning mathematical concepts. She shows that this process involves being guided into ways of talking while performing practical actions. Similar analyses by Edwards and Mercer (1987) have shown how adults also 'scaffold' (Bruner, 1985) children into such cognitive skills as rhetorical argument, scientific method and narrative forms of representation. However, as the chapters in this volume on the development of communication show, mentally handicapped children are not scaffolded in the same way.

The importance of this approach for the mentally handicapped cannot be overestimated. It presents us with a way of conceptualizing their development which places social and communicative experience at its centre. The implication is that the route to overcoming intellectual impairment is through the communicative exchanges that are, or can be, built into their lives. The following example from Beveridge (1981) shows how cognitive impairment can be embedded in children's social experience.

Two mentally handicapped children were sitting opposite each other with a draught-board between them and the pieces were set out as for the beginning of a game. One child begins the game with a correct move, and the other child also appropriately follows. This alternating pattern continues with the pieces being taken according to the rules of draughts. Although the particular strategies used by the children may not be the best possible from the point of view of winning the game, they do at this stage appear to be obeying the rules. However, as the game progresses we see that the children are increasingly planning their own moves ahead without taking account of the intervening moves of the other child, despite the fact that such moves radically alter the state of the board. As the game nears the end we see more evidence that they are paying little attention to each other's moves. Instead of moving alternately, on some occasions one child will make two moves to the other's one. Both children increasingly do this, until at the end of the game it becomes a race in which the winner is the child who can make his moves faster. When the game finishes in this way, the winner is acknowledged as such by both children.

In Beveridge's paper this example was used to illustrate several different aspects of communication by mentally handicapped children. The most important of which were, first, that knowing the rules of language does not guarantee successful interaction, and secondly, that complex interactions are often allowed to 'spiral' away from what was originally appropriate interplay.

However the draughts-game analogy also illustrates how inappropriate experience of conversational exchanges in which, for example, replies were not made relevant to previous utterances, are likely to make language ineffective for cognitive activity. Procedures like focusing on the right question, generating possible solutions and seeing contradictions require that the principles of relevance in discourse (Sperber and Wilson, 1986) are understood. Take, for example, the process of remembering. In a recent paper on remembering, Edwards and Middleton (in press) showed how the process of recalling events uses dialogue, both with others and ourselves, about the event which we are trying to reconstruct. If we are interested in functional activities like 'remembering' and not spurious faculties like 'memory', then separating the linguistic from the cognitive is not possible.

More crucially from the point of view of those many mentally handicapped persons whose communications are modelled by the draughts situation (above), the interactional procedures will not be well enough controlled to function as tools for cognition. The process of successful remembering is likely to be difficult to carry out; and as a consequence, memory will be limited to simpler tasks which require less active reconstruction. Recognition of common objects and familiar faces would not be as impaired as the kind of memory required for eye-witness testimony or recalling events from childhood. Both the latter activities rely on the stream of internal dialogue that allows us to talk ourselves into a frame of mind which cues a solution to a problem.

Furthermore, recent work on the way children come to understand scientific concepts has shown that they develop their own intuitive theories about the events that they see around them (Driver, 1983). However, it seems clear that these 'mini-theories' both emerge and change through dialogue with other persons. Concepts like 'energy' and 'evaporation' evolve over lengthy periods in which explanations come to be understood through socio-cognitive interchanges (Beveridge, 1985; Soloman, 1983). Moreover, the ways in which science borrows and changes ordinary language has a good deal in common with the role of metaphor in thought (Ortony, 1979).

The interrelation between linguistic skills, dialogic skills and scientific knowledge acquisition by normal children is now recognized, if not fully understood. The conclusion must be that with respect to populations with difficulties in knowledge acquisition, such as the mentally handicapped, it will be by understanding the way the above interrelationship operates for them that we will come to see how their minds develop. For this reason, much of the interactional data discussed in this volume provides important evidence on the emergence of knowledge structures as well as on communication skills in their own right. And detailed analysis of these social-cognitive processes is much required by educators and parents. We must begin to take another look at the role of communication in the cognitive development of mentally handicapped people.

As we have already indicated, the chapters on communicative development in this volume suggest that the early social-cognitive experiences of the mentally handicapped are not entirely typical of those experienced by normal children. In the remainder of this chapter, I will look at some of our own work on the interactions of school-age mentally handicapped children to see whether this typicality persists.

6.2 THE ECOLOGY OF MENTALLY HANDICAPPED CHILDREN'S COMMUNICATION

This section of the chapter briefly reviews some of the work we have carried out which looks at the general communicative ecology of the mentally handicapped, against which detailed analyses of socio-cognitive processes must be set.

Ryan (1975) and Leudar (1981) have argued that it was the search for what is wrong with retarded children that prevented us from understanding their behaviour in environmental and social terms. The tendency was to compare the performance of retarded people to non-retarded people on a variety of experimental tasks. These tasks generally were quite arbitrary and idiosyncratic to the laboratory environment and did not derive information about social factors which influence the daily lives of retarded people. A full understanding of the behaviour of retarded individuals can only be obtained by studying the interactions between such persons and key people in their lives. Some of our own studies began to address questions about how retarded children interact with their teachers, and also how retarded children communicate in a shared context.

Beveridge, Spencer and Mittler (1978) sought to gather basic information on the nature and development of social interaction in schools for mentally handicapped children. Initiations of interaction were noted in all the classrooms in schools using a scan sample technique which noted all interaction either ongoing or initiated during the period of each 5 s scan. The categories of interaction used were teacher to child, child to teacher, child to child and verbal or non-verbal interaction. The results indicated that the total number of child-initiated interactions increased with age, and increase was restricted to those interactions which were initiated verbally. Non-verbal initiations remained at the same level but it was not until the age of 10 years that the majority of interactions were initiated verbally. It has been noted elsewhere, not surprisingly, that the social relationship between children also affects the likelihood of conversations beginning (Leudar, Fraser and Jeeves, 1981).

Other work (Beveridge and Berry, 1977) noted that some children give the impression of social competence, but when listened to more closely, their language is at a very low level. Other children have superior language capacity but rarely engaged in verbal communication with others. It has even been suggested (Beveridge and Brinker, 1980) that structured language programmes may well be effective for children whose communicative problems are more linguistic than social. However, those children whose central problem is using their language competence in socially appropriate ways may benefit little from these approaches.

Another factor which might influence the occurrence of social interaction is children's views of themselves as communicators. In particular, there is evidence that children may differ in their tendency to blame themselves for any failures in communication (Robinson, 1986). One of our studies (Beveridge, Spencer and Mittler, 1979) identified a group of mentally handicapped adolescents who made little use of their relatively high linguistic ability to initiate social interactions. This group was then compared on their tendency to blame themselves for communication failure to a similar group who initiated interactions more frequently.

However, no differences were found between the two groups in respect of the frequency with which they blamed themselves; interestingly, the low interaction group did improve the clarity of their communicative messages after they failed. This study does not in itself prove that sensitivity to failure is not important in accounting for low frequencies of interaction. This work is difficult to carry out without methodological difficulty, and further studies in this area would be of value. We do not yet know enough about the influence of belief systems in the mentally handicapped on their social behaviour.

There is also evidence that aspects of children's classroom behaviour can be related to performance in discrimination learning tasks (Beveridge and Evans, 1978). This study related the observed frequency of initiation of interaction and amount of speech with teachers' rating of children as 'excitable'. This result would be trivial except that the same scale used for teacher rating has previously indicated that excitable children are more reward-seeking than inhibitable children in experimental learning tasks. The suggestion is that the tendency to seek reward is related to some of the differences between individual patterns of interaction observed in the classroom. There are clearly conceptual problems involved in this kind of explanation, but it does suggest that some individual differences in communicative behaviour are related to personality.

Of course, it is possible that any tendency to seek out particular aspects of the environment may be matched by a tendency for the environment to respond differently to individual children. Furthermore, there may well be an interaction between these two tendencies. Beveridge and Hurrell (1980) investigated this possibility with respect to teachers' views of mentally handicapped children's personality, and the responses of those teachers to child-initiated interaction. The aim was to identify differences between teachers' responses to children identified either as excitable or inhibitable, and to determine whether any variation in these teachers' responses was associated with the personality of the teachers themselves.

It was found that teachers' responses to child-initiated interaction were related both to the personality of the child and the personality of the teacher. While the majority of child-initiated interactions were not extended in any meaningful way by the teacher, they were more likely to do this with those children classified as inhibitable. This may represent an attempt on the teachers' part to encourage interactive behaviour among a group of children who interact less. However, the frequency of interaction among excitable children was hardly great enough to require its reduction by non-responding on the part of the teacher. It was also found that the more neurotic teachers were significantly more likely to respond in a negative way to excitable children. The more neurotic teachers were also more likely to respond non-verbally and to change the content of the child's initiation. There was also an indication that extrovert teachers were more likely

8. *Shoe polish* The teacher asks a class member to clean a pair of shoes, but the polish is empty.
9. *A felt pen* Everyone is asked to complete his hygiene chart, but pen and chart are missing for one pupil.

The importance of language to all these situations is that each task can be solved by communicating either with the teacher or another pupil: either by asking how to solve a problem or asking for a specific, already identified solution to be activated, e.g. asking for a new pair of shoe-laces.

Newton compared the performance of mentally handicapped children with non-handicapped children of similar mental age. This very interesting study reveals that the chance of handicapped persons solving problems collaboratively with others by using language depends on the particular problems presented. It was also found that there are some situations in which the handicapped population differs significantly from the non-handicapped in the likelihood of language being used, also that there were some situations in which there appeared to be no difference.

When contrasted to the non-handicapped children, the handicapped population were more reluctant to make social contact in order to solve the problems: for example, in the above situations they tended not to ask for a new shoe-lace or a sharpened pencil, or to ask the teacher why they had not been allocated a task. When this result is considered alongside that of Beveridge and Hurrell (1980), who found that more than 50% of the initiations made by mentally handicapped pupils to teachers were not responded to, it is perhaps not surprising that when a problem is presented handicapped children do not seek the teacher's help. Getting help from the teacher can itself be a problem.

Situations which predict effective use of language in the non-handicapped population will not necessarily have the same effect on the handicapped. As with the tendency to initiate interactions discussed earlier, contexts which encourage language in the handicapped will not necessarily have this effect on non-handicapped children. The ecology is important but we must take account of the reactions and perceptions of the individuals within it. Furthermore, if we try to generate language by manipulating the school environment, we should not regard schools especially for the handicapped as if they were the same as other schools.

Newton's (1981) study also showed that teachers of handicapped children are not particularly good at predicting whether particular children will be able to solve the problems presented to them, and are even less able to say whether a child will communicate his difficulty. Furthermore, the predictions that they do make tend to be non-specific as to situation. Children who are believed to be able to solve one problem will be seen as solving all problems; however, the data suggest that problem-solving ability is not of this kind. Many of these children were able to solve some of the problems but not others, and teachers were surprisingly unable to predict which would be successfully solved.

The study by Newton also supported the findings of Bolstad and Johnson (1977), who detected variations between teachers in the accuracy of their predictions about pupils' problem-solving ability. As with most aspects of education, not all teachers are equally good. Within the handicapped population those adolescents with higher verbal ages, IQ and social quotients tended to communicate with adults as a problem-solving strategy, whereas those with lower scores used this strategy rather less. However, this was a group tendency and masks variation within the groups. Hence, IQ and verbal age are not clearly predictive of the use of language to solve problems. The difficult issue for teaching and understanding the language of handicapped children is to relate performance in problem situations to an educational programme which gives children useful language skills and also teaches them to use these skills effectively in socio-cognitive contexts.

The daunting but important task for those of us involved in providing the language skills for handicapped children is to study the pragmatics of the language for individual children in different situations. They will be more successful in some situations than others and we need to understand why. Only when we make some progress in this direction can we begin to teach communication on a principled basis. And the cognitive uses of interactional rules will remain elusive to mentally handicapped persons.

REFERENCES

Beveridge, M.C. (1981) Communicative competence in mentally handicapped children, *First Language*, 2, 225–37.

Beveridge, M.C. (1985) The development of young children's understanding of the process of evaporation, *Br. J. Educational Psychol.*, 55, 84–90.

Beveridge, M.C. and Berry, P. (1977) Observing interactions in the mentally handicapped, *Res. in Education*, 17, 18–22.

Beveridge, M.C. and Brinker, R. (1980) An ecological–developmental approach to the study of communication in retarded children in *Language Disorders in Children* (ed. M. Jones) Medical and Technical Press, Lancaster, pp. 45–68.

Beveridge, M.C. and Conti-Ramsden, G. (1987) Social cognition and language development in the mentally handicapped, *Aus. and New Zealand J. Developmental Disabilities*, 13, 99–106.

Beveridge, M.C. and Evans, P. (1978) Classroom interaction: two studies of severely subnormal children, *Res. in Education*, 19, 39–48.

Beveridge, M.C. and Hurrell, P. (1980) Teachers' responses to the initiations of ESN(S) children, *J. Child Psychol. Psychiat.*, 21, 175–82.

Beveridge, M.C. and Mittler, P. (1977) Feedback, language and listener performance in severely retarded children, *Br. J. Disorders of Commun.*, 12, 149–57.

Beveridge, M.C., Newton, S. and Grantley, J. (1982) Referential communication as a technique in the teaching of work skills to severely subnormal adolescents, *Br. J. Disorders of Commun.*, 17, 68–77.

Beveridge, M.C., Spencer, J. and Mittler, P. (1978) Language and social behaviour in severely educationally subnormal children, *Br. J. Soc. Clin. Psychol.*, *17*, 75–83.

Beveridge, M.C., Spencer, J. and Mittler, P. (1979) Self-blame and communication failure in retarded adolescents, *J. Child Psychol. Psychiat.*, *17*, 75–83.

Beveridge, M.C. and Tatham, A. (1976) Communication in retarded adolescents: utilization of known language skills, *Am. J. Ment. Defic.*, *81*, 96–9.

Bolstad, O.D. and Johnson, S.M. (1977) The relationship between teachers' assessment of students and the student actual behaviour in the classroom, *Child Development*, *48*, 570–8.

Bruner, J. (1985) *Actual Minds: Possible Worlds*, Harvard University Press, Cambridge, Mass.

Cole, M. (1985) The zone of proximal development: where culture and cognition create each other in *Culture, Communication and Cognition: Vygotskian Perspectives* (ed. J.V. Wertsch), Cambridge University Press, Cambridge, pp. 146–61.

Donaldson, M. (1978) *Children's Minds*, Fontana, London.

Driver, R. (1983) Pupil alternative frameworks in science, *Eur. J. Sci. Education*, *3*, 93–101.

Edwards, D. and Mercer, N. (1987) *Common Knowledge*, Methuen, London.

Edwards, D. and Middleton, D. (in press) Joint remembering, *Discourse Processes*.

Hickman, M. (1987) (ed.) *Social and Functional Approaches to Language and Thought*, Academic Press, New York.

Leudar, I. (1981) Strategic communication in mental retardation in *Communication with Normal and Retarded Children* (eds. W.I. Frazer and R. Grieve), Wright, Bristol, pp. 113–29.

Leudar, I., Fraser, W. and Jeeves, M.A. (1981) Social familiarities and communication in Down's syndrome, *J. Ment. Defic. Res.*, *25*, 133–42.

Newton, S. (1981) Social aspects of communicative competence in mentally handicapped adolescents and non-handicapped children, unpublished PhD thesis, University of Manchester.

Ortony, A. (1979) (ed.) *Metaphor and Thought*, Cambridge University Press, Cambridge.

Robinson, W.P. (1986) Children's understanding of the difference between messages and meanings in *Children of Social Worlds* (eds. M. Richards and P. Light), Polity, Cambridge, pp. 213–32.

Rotman, B. (1977) *Jean Piaget: Psychologist of the Real*, Harvester Press, Hassocks.

Ryan, J. (1975) Mental subnormality and language development in *Foundations of Language Development* (eds. E.H. Lennebers and E. Lennebers), Academic Press, London, Vol. 2.

Soloman, J. (1983) Messy, contradictory and obstinately persistent: a study of children's out of school views about energy, *Sch. Sci. Rev.*, *65*, 225–9.

Sperber, D. and Wilson, D. (1986) *Relevance: Communication and Cognition*, Blackwell, Oxford.

Vygotsky, L.S. (1978) *Mind in Society*, Harvard University Press, Cambridge, Mass.

Walkerdine, V. (1982) From context to text: a psychosemiotic approach to abstract thought in *Children Thinking through Language* (ed. M. Beveridge), Edward Arnold, London, pp. 129–55.

PART III

Development of Communication in Mentally Handicapped Children

Chapters 7–9 in this part deal with the character of interactions between ordinary mentally handicapped children and their caretakers and with issues concerning intervention. It is recognized that the parents of mentally handicapped children may be less responsive and more directive. Anthony Wootton, in Chapter 7, uses conversation analysis creatively to investigate in detail why parents 'do not respond' to their children's communications. This involves him in a detailed study of mentally handicapped children's vocalizations, their functions and distinctions they encode as well as in the study of parental responses. Penny Price, in Chapter 8, critically reviews the results and the methodology of research on the development of communication of normal, language delayed and mentally retarded children with their caretakers. She focuses on pragmatic features such as initiating, eliciting and directing. She argues that, in general, caregivers provide a conversational framework which allows for the immature skills of the child, but she also notices context-dependent variations and a wide variation in the individual parental style as opposed to stable interactional patterns. In this light, she reviews language intervention programmes and discusses their effectiveness. Gina Conti-Ramsden, in Chapter 9, also deals with the problems in comparing communicative development and achievements of mentally handicapped and average children. Her focus is on research methodology and against the use of control groups which obscures unique variations within them. She argues that the transactional nature of communication dictates that individual differences are respected. She further argues that 'social-communicative skills are not a homogeneous interrelated set of skills' and points out that, depending on the basis for matching and on language indices compared, researchers may find mentally handicapped children to be backward, no different from or, in fact, to outperform average children. She criticizes the frequent assumption that the latter findings do not require explanation.

7

Speech to and from a Severely Retarded Young Down's Syndrome Child

Anthony Wootton

In recent years there have been several shifts of emphasis in the field of intervention programmes for handicapped young children. One of these has been towards making 'the most effective use of what is already available in ordinary everyday environments to encourage effective language and communication in retarded people' (Mittler and Berry, 1977, p. 246). For those children who live with parents or are adopted into normal homes this has usually meant that parents have been called upon to play a more prominent role in facilitating their children's development, even though in some cases perhaps all this has involved is some belated quasi-official recognition of the part that parents have been playing all along. Of course, this role can now take many forms, even if we restrict our attention to one facet of children's development, namely their language and communication skills. Several well-structured intervention programmes see parents as capable of playing a significant part in promoting these skills (e.g. Bochner, Price and Salamon, 1984; MacDonald, 1982; White and East, 1983), but numerous texts and guides appear to agree on certain things that parents should do. In the case of Down's syndrome children, parents should, for example, allow sufficient time for their children to respond to them, not use too many questions and directives, and so on. It is one such recommendation that I wish to discuss in this chapter, that is, the encouragement of parents to respond to their children's vocal communications.

Few experts would quibble with the advice given by Buckley *et al.* (1986) in their recent book on Down's syndrome when they suggest that parents 'Take the lead from him [the child] and respond to his communicative behaviour, as well as initiating your own' (p. 42). Indeed there are a number of reasons for thinking such advice especially pertinent to the young Down's syndrome children on whom my discussion focuses. Although in most ways the development of their communicative skills runs broadly parallel to those of normal children, albeit more slowly and with greater variability among them in speed of development, there are certain relevant respects in which differences have been found.[1] For example, studies which have looked at the overall rate of vocal initiation by Down's syndrome children suggest that they initiate less to their parents than normal children. In the most careful study of this, Fischer (1983) compared five Down's syndrome children with five normal children matched on a language age of about 13 months on the Gesell scale. About 24% of the Down's children's vocal signals were initiating as compared with 52% of those from normal children, a result which Fischer demonstrates not to be an artefact of the parents of Down's syndrome children producing a higher level of initiating/antecedent utterances to their children. If this finding is more generally valid, then it would seem to place a special premium on parents responding to those vocalizations that their children *do* initiate to them.

A second respect in which there is a suggestion of difference between Down's syndrome children and normal children in their course of development concerns gaze patterns. Although some studies suggest certain differences in this respect in the first year of life (Berger and Cunningham, 1981; Gunn *et al.*, 1982), that which concerns me here is the use of what Jones (1977) described as 'referential gaze' in her study of normal and Down's children with developmental ages between 8 and 19 months.[2] She describes this type of gaze as one where 'the child appeared to be making some reference to his, or her, activity by the glance up. It is typically described by a transfer of attention from the object of the activity between mother and child to the mother's face and then back to the object' (Jones, 1977, p. 394). This is reminiscent of the behaviour involved in accomplishing what Trevarthen and Hubley (1979) describe as 'secondary intersubjectivity', and which has been carefully discussed in the work of Bates (1979). At about 12 months of age, normal children coordinate such glances with their vocalizations, which are also frequently accompanied by hand gestures. If Down's syndrome children use such glances less frequently, or only coordinate them with vocal/gestural configurations at a later developmental point than normal, then that may well have consequences for parents' understanding of their children's vocalizations. For one part that such glances can play in the communication process is that they *display* to the child's recipient that they are indeed communicating to them, so that without that signal vocalizations intended by the child to be communicative may more frequently go unrecognized as such by the parent.

Research on the vocal initiation strategies of Down's syndrome children, and on their use of gaze, suggests therefore that these children may initiate vocalizations less frequently — and that even where they do so, there may be problems for parents in discerning the nature of these vocalizations. There may then be special grounds for sensitizing their parents to the importance of acting responsively to their children's vocalizations. Though having said that, it is probably important to recognize that such an argument need not necessarily be predicated on there being the differences between Down's syndrome and normal children to which the reader's attention has been drawn. Even if there were no differences, one might still argue, as have Cheseldine and McConkey (1979), that if a concomitant of a pattern of parent–child communication which is normal is radical language retardation for the child in question, then abnormal modes of involvement by parents may be more appropriate. If so, then surely one such involvement might take the form of engaging one's child in dialogue whenever the child appeared to initiate a bout of communication, perhaps to the extent of doing this more than would the parents of normal children.

In this chapter, I look in detail at the question of why parents may not respond to their children's vocalizations, and look more closely at various interactional contingencies which are associated with such outcomes. For it turns out to be the case that in not responding to their children's vocalizations, parents may be systematically attending both to the nature of the vocalizations that they hear and the accompanying non-verbal behaviour that they witness. And in doing this, they may be discriminating in important ways the signals that the child emits. Furthermore, parents have available to them various interactional strategies for handling different types of involvement with their children, some of these involving them in being more responsive to their children, some less so. However, examination of instances where parents are less responsive shows them nevertheless to be engaged in sophisticated interactional dealings with their children.

These issues will be explored here through an analysis of video recordings made in the home of one Down's syndrome child whom I shall call Adam. In effect, it is a fairly intensive case study undertaken in the context of a broader study[3] of such families which will examine these and other issues more generally. Adam was 3 years 7 months old when the 3-hour video recording was made in his home, the equipment being operated by his parents.[4] At the time of recording, he attended a school for the severely subnormal on each weekday. Very occasionally, he used a Makaton sign, but almost all his communication on the tapes was achieved via the same vocal/gestural means that normal children use; the only sign which his parents very occasionally used was that for *no*. Adam is an adopted Down's syndrome child with two sisters, both of whom are also mentally handicapped. Only his younger sister, aged 2 years 6 months, will play a significant part in the episodes that will be discussed, and she will be called Betty. Although there was no suggestion of abnormal hearing loss at the time of the recordings, Adam has a history of recurrent ear infections, like many Down's children (Cunningham and McArthur, 1981) and there seems little doubt that this has contributed to his level of retardation. Adam, even by the standards of Down's syndrome children, was relatively backward in communicative terms for his chronological age (CA), as the subsequent analysis will reveal. In fact it was this relative backwardness, and the possibility of detecting strategies for dealing with such backwardness, which led to Adam's family being approached in connection with the research.

When the recordings took place, Adam was not yet using conventional words. Nevertheless, it was possible to detect certain phonetically recurrent forms within his speech, and the first step was that of deciding what communicative significance to attach to these forms. The procedures for doing this are by no means clear-cut, even when we look at similar analyses carried out on normal children. Of course, it is not difficult to arrive at an interpretation of what these vocal forms might mean. The main problem, as several writers have pointed out (e.g. Francis, 1979; Grieve and Hoogenraad, 1979), is to know whether our interpretations of these forms represent distinctions made by the child within his own linguistic system, and to demonstrate our case for that in a way that is open to inspection and verification by others reading our analysis. To do this we potentially have access to two types of evidence in each instance where such sounds are used: first, the behaviour of the child that co-occurs with his production of the sound; and secondly, where the parent responds to what the child says we can examine that response to see what understanding it reveals the parent as making of the child's voke — though we cannot treat the second source of evidence as incorrigible, in that obviously the parent, like any partner in interaction, is vulnerable to misconstruing what the other person has said.

Indeed one of children's early interactional problems may be how to deal with such misconstruals, as well as those cases where the parent exhibits uncertainty as to what the child meant (Golinkoff, 1983). Within these two broad sources of evidence we cannot specify a priori which parameters will be crucial for identifying the communicative significance of vocalizations. Of course, it seems probable that such co-occurring gestures as reaching and pointing, used heavily by children in their preconventional speech phase, may be important clues as these play a significant part in the more compelling accounts of normal children's development (see e.g. Carter, 1979). But whether or not this is so in the case of our child, one who is severely handicapped, remains to be demonstrated through the analysis. So following a general conversation-analytic approach (Levinson, 1983, chapter 6; Heritage, 1984a, chapter 8; Wootton, in press), and bearing in mind these sources of evidence, I initially present such an inductive analysis, the procedure itself, of course, being one which could be equally well employed with the vokes of young normal children as well as with those of Down's syndrome children.

7.1 COMMUNICATIVE PROPERTIES OF THREE VOCALIZATIONS

The main reason for limiting the analysis to three of Adam's vokes was that those were the only ones which he produced in sufficient quantity to attempt a distributional analysis of the kind to be reported. He produced between 30 and 40 of what I shall take to be tokens of each of these three types of vocalizations, and only a handful of each of the small number of remaining types. The three types of vocalization in question were not recognizable versions of English words, though of course they may have originated in that way. They are vocal forms which appeared to have some phonetic consistency across a number of different interaction situations on the recordings. Phonetic transcriptions of these vocalizations in something like their canonical forms, and at a level of detail primarily intended to distinguish them from each other, would run something as follows:[5]

Type 1 [əba::]

Type 2 [↑ə̱:]

Type 3 [ʔəʔəʔəʔə] $\begin{bmatrix} ˤ & ˤ \end{bmatrix}$

where: ↑ = higher than normal pitch
− = stress
:: = sound extension
ˤ = voice quality consistent with being a product of friction in the pharyngeal region.

(A summary of the transcript conventions employed can be found at the end of this chapter.)

In practice, however, there were interesting variations in the phonetic realizations of these forms. Some of these will be addressed in what follows, but at this stage the following should be noted. Type-2 vokes most frequently approximated the canonical form, as described above, whereas types 1 and 3 frequently departed from it. At the segmental level type 1 could also be realized by a range of endings such as [əbad] and [əbat]; and they could be produced on different pitch contours with respect to supra-segmental features. Type 3 varied as to the number of 'beats' within any token; and there could be variations between them in detailed features of voice quality, and in supra-segmental features — though their variability was expressed 'horizontally' in terms of such features as sound sustension, rather than 'vertically' in terms of pitch movements. For examples of such variability, see extracts 3–5 and 8, below. Further discussion of these phonetic features is postponed until the analysis of the communicative properties of these three vokes has been completed.

This analysis is presented in summary form in Table 7.1. It consists of seven items which appear to discriminate one or more of the three types of vocalizations from each other; the first three items relating to ways in which these vocalizations are responded to by parents,[6] the next four to aspects of Adam's own behaviour associated with these sounds. In reading this table it is important to remember that (−) denotes that this feature is never associated with the sound in question; (+) denotes that this feature can be associated with the sound (but never always); and (∗) is used where a feature occurs with two vocalizations, and is used to indicate that type with which the feature is most frequently associated. One criterion for an adequate form of such an analysis might be that it provides for a unique combination of features for each vocal item, but the reader will note that Table 7.1 goes well beyond that. If there are further features which discriminate the set we are concerned with, then there seems little point in excluding them if our aim is to use these features to build up a picture of the distinctive communicative properties of items in the set. My next step then will be to decompose this table by illustrating for the reader each of the features shown by the analysis to have discriminating properties.

Table 7.1: Features associated with Adam's three types of vocalization

		Type 1 [əba::]	Type 2 [↑ɔ::]	Type 3 [ʔɔʔɔʔɔʔɔ]
1	Requires recipient confirmation alone	+	−	−
2	Treated as request for action	−	+	+
3	Treated as expressing distress	−	−	+
4	Co-occurrence with fretting/frustration signs	−	−	+
5	Co-occurring pointing	+∗	+ (1 case only)	−
6	Co-occurring reaching	−	+	−
7	Co-occurrence with each other	−	+	+

∗This feature is predominantly associated with this type of voke.

− never occurs; + this feature can occur, but does not always do so.

1. Only type-1 vokes could be responded to with confirmations, i.e. like the mother's [yes + nod] in extract 1, below. These confirmations are not constructed as preliminaries to some further action that the child is requiring of the parent: for example, as confirming that they recognize what the child wants them to do, prior to doing it. Rather they treat the child's voke as concerned simply and exclusively to bring something to their attention, for their appraisal.[7] This extract, in particular, has been selected partly because the type-1 voke does not here co-occur with a point, so making it less easy to argue that the parent's response is to the gesture accompanying the vocalization rather than the vocalization itself.

(1) V 26:07

Adam and his mother are sitting on the floor, and the mother is helping Adam to put different shapes through their appropriate holes in the lid of a container. Adam has a shape in his right hand and his mother, when she first speaks below, is holding this hand and attempting to re-orient it, so that the shape will fit into one of the apertures. A. and M.'s hands remain in this position throughout the following brief exchange:

M.: Turn it rou:::n:d

A.: [ɔ́ba::d] (+ gaze switch from container to M.'s face)

M.: Yes (+ nod + brief glance towards A.'s face) =

A.: = [?] (+ switches gaze back to container, *then* continues activity of putting shape into it)

2. Only types 2 and 3 were responded to by parents as if they required the parent to carry out some action in the child's immediate interests, as if they were requests for action. The actions in question could be diverse. They could involve, as in the extracts below, the parent passing food, drink or other objects to the child, or they could be interpreted as requests for the recipient to cease doing something, to give various forms of assistance to the child, and so on. Extracts 2 and 3 have been selected to illustrate this use of types 2 and 3 respectively. Again neither involves the child using a hand gesture, so the critical information available to the parent is the vocalization, and Adam's line of regard. In extract 2, though, the mother does not even have the latter information at her disposal when she displays her understanding of the child's voke. When Adam speaks, she is looking at Betty; she doesn't then turn to 'see' what Adam wants, but in the course of turning she simultaneously moves the spoon around so as to put it straight into Adam's mouth, presumably having arrived at her interpretation of the fact that he was wanting something on the basis of the vocalization above:

(2) VII 12:13

Adam and his mother are sitting side by side having a meal. A. is on M.'s right-hand side; on her left, also side by side, is Betty. M. is holding a bowl with food in it, and a spoon in her hands. She turns to Betty saying *D'you want some of this?* As she says this, A. makes his body as erect as his sitting position will allow, and gazes over his mother's arms at the food she is about to give to Betty. Then:

A.: [↑ʔə̲::] (+ gaze at bowl + no shifts in arm positions) =

M.: = (does 180° turn to A. and puts spoonful of food straight into his mouth) (For details of this turn see text)

(3) VII 10:33

Mother, Adam and Betty are sitting side by side at the meal table in the same positions as in extract 2. A.'s empty bowl has been moved by M. from in front of A. into the centre of the table. M. then changes the position of a cup on the table with her left hand (not A.'s cup). A. surveys the centre of the table, his left arm on the back of his chair, his right arm on the table, turned towards M. in a relaxed, sitting posture. After adjusting the cup's position, M. turns to gaze at A.; he is still gazing at the table:

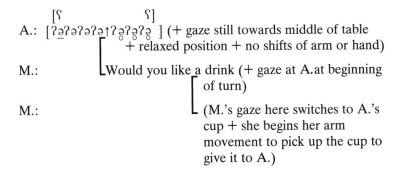

where:

↑ = perceptive pitch change (upwards)

° = voiceless

ʕ = pharyngeal friction.

Another reason for selecting extracts 2 and 3 was the apparent similarity between the two requests as regards what was being requested, where it was being requested and whom it was being requested of. In the light of such similarity, some investigators arrive at the view that different vocal forms can be treated as functionally parallel. But because it seems possible to employ a common descriptor, such as 'request', to two vocal acts does not imply that these vocalizations operate in equivalent ways as interactional devices (Wootton, 1981). When we go on to examine further features of the way in which these two vokes distribute, we will find it necessary to characterize them in different ways in this respect. In fact we can already find hints of such a differential characterization within extracts 2 and 3. In extract 2 we can notice the alert tenseness in the child's posture when making the voke, and his highly focused gaze on the object in question; in contrast, the type-3 voke (in extract 3) is accompanied by a more relaxed posture, and it is also more difficult to detect the focus of the gaze. In these ways, the type-2 voke, together with its accompanying behaviour in extract 2, makes the nature of Adam's concerns more transparent than is the case with the type-3 (in extract 3). In the latter the recipient is left more to interpret Adam's concerns from the context, these different configurations being nicely reflected here by the mother's opting to check what the child wants in extract 3 (with *Would you like a drink?*), whereas not feeling the need to do this in extract 2. Minimally there is a difference of design here in the clarity of the child's communication signals, a difference that will become more transparent in the course of the analysis.

3. One respect in which type-3 vokes were distinctive was that they could be treated by parents as evidence of the child being upset or unhappy, as evidence of distress. A typical example is contained in extract 4, below, where the mother's stroking of the head and her gentle encouraging words, *Come on*, display a recognition on her part that here Adam has a problem. As also do the father and mother's subsequent turns which more formally mark the existence of such a problem by proposing a possible solution, i.e. that they might help him. What help the child may require is not necessarily clear to parents as well as the analyst. Adam gives no gestural clues, and the problem might be bound up with the process of eating rather than toileting — Adam sometimes still required assistance with eating. Neither of the parents' turns, nor their accompanying actions, reveal a definite analysis of what Adam's problem was; and one consequence of responding in the way they do is to give themselves more time to scan him with a view to making some contextually based inference as to what this problem might be:

(4) X 4:12
     Adam is eating at the table with his mother sitting next to him on his left, his father at right angles on his right. A. stops eating, resting his eating utensils on the side of his plate. He gazes vacantly at the table in front of him and then gives a grunt, which sounds like a pushing noise associated with toileting (A. was still in nappies). Immediately after the grunt he says:

$$[ʕ \quad ʕ]$$
A.: [ʔəʰəːːʔəʔə] (.) [ʔəʰɝːː]
                          (+ gaze still towards table + no alteration of arm or hand positions)

M.: ᶠCome onᶠ (+ she strokes A.'s head with her right hand + gazes at A.)

$$(1.5)$$

F.: D'you want some help? (+ no shift of gaze from his own food)

$$(1.3)$$

M.: D'you want mummy to help? (+ still gazing at A.)

where:

　　　ᶠ = breathy voice
　　　~ = nasalization.

4. We might, of course, expect to find a symmetry between how the child's vocalizations are understood by parents and what the child may mean to convey through these same vocalizations. Some order of symmetry would seem to be a prerequisite for claiming that a child like Adam has a communicative system as his disposal at all, one which can be used to generate certain outcomes with some degree of assurance or predictability on the child's part. Examination of the details of Adam's own conduct in the context of these vocalizations does suggest that such a symmetry exists. Following point 3, where it was noted that Adam's type-3 voke could be understood as evidence of distress on his part, we can now note that independent evidence of distress and frustration can be found to co-occur with this same type of vocalization. The clearest examples of this occur in rather long sequences where Adam becomes increasingly irritated with his parents' behaviour. For this reason, producing the whole of such sequences even in the crude transcript form I am using is infeasible. Let me briefly describe therefore one instance by way of illustration. One breakfast-time Adam's father is preparing a second helping of cereal for Adam: this process takes quite some time as the cereal in question has to be fetched from the kitchen, broken down by the father with a spoon and then have various items added. At one stage the father turns the sequence into a dialogue with Adam by asking him if he wants milk with the cereal, but when he later asks, *How much milk?* (in the course of pouring it), Adam responds with a sharp type-3 voke, to which the father responds: *Didn't you eat yesterday?* In this, he recognizes a fairly pointed concern on Adam's part to get started on the food: the father continues mixing the food on the table throughout the following course of events:

(5) VII 4:52

　　　　　　[ˤ　　　　　ˤ]→
　(1) A.: [ʔë̃ʔë̃ʔë̃ʔë̃ʔeʔɐ:::]

(2)   [+ hands on table + gaze on mixing bowl) =

(3) F.: = That's a funny noise (+ continues stirring bowl)

(4) A.:   ⌐ (sharp tick-like turn of A.'s head to left and
then back to original position + no alteration
to hand positions)

        [ʕ ʕ] ~→~   →
(5) A.: [ʔəʔəʔə:: ə ə:::::ɸ] (latter part sounds like a whine)

(6) F.:   ⌐Aw : : : : :

(7)   (.)

(8) A.: (sharp flick of A.'s head to left, *then* slaps his own
forehead with left hand)

where:

        → = ingressive phonation
        ~ = nasalization
        ‾‾ = pitch contour
        ·· = vowel is more centralized than the vowel symbol
              suggests.

The sequence continues, but this is perhaps sufficient to give a sense of
the distress and frustration behaviour that can co-occur with Adam's
type-3 vokes: gestures of frustration here being evident in the head
movement referred to in line 4 and the head/hand movement in line 8;
distress in the quasi-crying of lines 1 and 5, the crying becoming more
overt shortly after this transcript is terminated. To speak of the co-
occurrence of these features with type-3 vokes is somewhat loose;
more accurately, these features are performed adjacent to the production of these vokes, but in close contiguity with them. And close
contiguity of such forms of behaviour was not found with either type-1
or type-2 vokes.[8]

5. Pointing was in the repertoire of manual gestures that Adam had at his
disposal, and whenever he pointed it always coincided with a vocalization. Where pointing did take place, it mainly co-occurred
with type-1 vokes, as in extract 6, though not all type-1 vokes were
accompanied by points (e.g. extract 1):

(6) III 2:55
    Mother is looking at a book with Adam, who is sitting on her knee,
    his arms on his lap. M. describes the content of a picture to A.:

M.: The mummy's sitting on the chai::r (+ pointing to a figure on the page)

(1.8)

M.: Listening to a story =

$$\left[[ə]–(.) \right] = [\overset{\frown}{ba} ::]^9 \text{ (+ left hand point to a}$$
different part of the same figure that M. is pointing to)

(.)

M.: That's mummy (.) mummy one

A very small number of points occurred with other forms of vocalization, but only one with either of the other two types that we are dealing with in this chapter. This occurs with a type-2 voke, and consists of a series of sharp up-and-down jabbing movements, the point not being held as it is in extract 6 above. But we would expect a child at Adam's stage of development to be extending his use of gestures from their canonical locations with particular types of vocalization into other vocal schemes. By 15 months of age a normal child would routinely use pointing in the context of requesting (e.g. see extract 9), so it is not surprising to find signs of such extension in use on the part of Adam, even though the primary locus at this time appears to be with type-1 vokes.[10]

6. Adam performed two types of reaching gestures on the recordings, both of which have been documented as occurring in the behaviour of all normal young children (e.g. Bates *et al.*, 1983). The first is a proffering gesture where the hand is held out to the recipient with an object in it, the child's objective being for recipient to either assist in doing something with the object (e.g. holding the child's hand and helping him to coordinate some action with the object, like helping him to manoeuvre a shape through a hole in the top of a shape bucket) or for recipient to take the object and do something with it that the child wishes (e.g. recipient to take shape and then put through a hole). In the latter case, the reach with the object held in the hand becomes a conventionalized signal for object transfer to the recipient. Both forms of this first reaching gesture, where the hand contains an object, could be employed by Adam without a vocalization, but of the three vokes with which we are concerned here, the type 2 were exclusively produced with this form of gesture.

The same holds true for the other main form of reach gesture that Adam employed, the open-handed reach, an instance of which is given below in extract 7:

(7) V 31:38

Mother is sitting on the floor by Adam's shape box: A. approaches and sits on his low chair, opposite M. As he approaches his gaze is on his box, and the moment he is seated he says:

A.: [↑ə:::] (+ non-effortful right arm reach towards the box
⌐ + gaze still on box)

M.: ⌐ (beginning to pass the box to A.)

Again, only the type-2 vokes were associated with such gestures. Furthermore, where the child produced other gestures which displayed a clear request like communicative intent (e.g. holding his arms up to be lifted down from a chair), then these also were exclusively associated with type-2 vokes.

7. My final observation about the differential distribution of these vocalizations is that two of them co-occur together, but neither co-occur with the third. The co-occurring vokes are the types 2 and 3, and one of the four instances in which this takes place is presented below:

(8) V 11:10

Adam has been watching TV in a low chair with a table on the front of it, one that makes it awkward for him to get out of himself, though he can manage it if necessary. A.'s elder sister is also watching TV when A.'s mother, at the other end of the room (out of camera shot), speaks to the elder sister. The latter turns towards M., as does A. A. looks in the direction of M. for about 2 s, putting his left-hand index finger to his mouth, then saying:

[ʕ   ʕ] [,   ,]

A.: [ʔəʔə(.)ʔɛ̆ʔɛ̆ʔəʔə () ə : : :]   (+
gaze towards M.) =

A.: = (*then* A. bangs on the arm of his chair with his left hand)

where:
' = creaky voice.

At this point, it is now possible on the basis of the above analysis to provide a rough characterization of the main distinctions between our three vocalizations. The type-1 are distinctive, in that they are heavily associated with pointing, and can be uniquely treated by recipients as being concerned simply to bring something to the recipient's attention; patently they are bound up with accomplishing acts of reference as such. And these features generate a sociolinguistic tendency for such sounds to occur in situations where referring is the primary form of speech act involvement, notably book-reading sessions — though they did not of course exclusively occur in such situations (see extract 1). Types 2 and 3 appear to be more similar, in that they both operate as requests, and can be jointly usable. But even when we compare their morphology in situations which seem to be very similar, as I did in relation to extracts 2 and 3, it is possible to discern contrasts which are borne out and supported by more extensive distributional analysis. In type-3 vokes the nature of the child's concern is made much less transparent in the design of the child's behaviour, the absence of any form of co-occurring gesture being especially important for this argument.[11] The only forms of gesture with which it does co-occur are the extreme fretting and frustration gestures illustrated in extract 5, and it can be treated, distinctively, by parents as expressing distress. The reader is also reminded of the variety of phonetic shapes in which it can appear. These suggest that it is a gradable signal, and the most obvious way of characterizing it might be as a gradable distress signal. The type-2 vokes are far less indexical requests than type-3 vokes. Through their frequently co-occurring gestures, and through sharply focused accompanying gaze, they make it possible for the recipient to have less recourse to context in order to attach sense to them. They are never used for some of the purposes that type-3 vokes are used for, such as expressing overt distress, and by virtue of the features that they do possess the type-2 are fitted to, and most frequently occur in the course of managing object transfer situations of various kinds; whereas type-3 vokes handle a much broader class of concerns. The type-3 can be taken by Adam's parents to reveal that he is not feeling well, that he wants one of them to come back into the room after having gone out, that he wants them to stop doing something, that he is upset about some specific thing that has happened, and so on. For reasons bound up with their indexicality there is often uncertainty as to the accuracy of these parental inferences, but they do suggest that type-3 vokes are interpreted as tools for expressing a wider set of concerns than type-2 vokes.

The picture of these vocalizations to emerge is one that places Adam squarely within the prespeech proto-word phase of linguistic development (Bates, 1976), one where the child uses phonetically consistent vocal forms but has yet to acquire a repertoire of conventional words. Adam uses these vocalizations in ways that largely run parallel to reports of their uses among normal children (Griffiths, 1985). Perhaps the most unusual feature that we have come across is the evidence that Adam can combine two of these vocalizations, as in extract 8; this might suggest that he is exercising skills well beyond those expected of his stage of development as there is no recognition within the literature on normal child language that children can combine sounds prior to their eventual combinations of conventional word-like forms. Of course, a moot-point is whether the four combinations like the one in extract 8 are to be considered as unanalysed wholes, chance concatenations of sounds or genuine productive combinations. Fortunately, Scollon (1976) has provided a useful discussion of all relevant considerations here, and he suggests four criteria for distinguishing productive combinations (pp. 153, 307). Our analysis suggests that Scollon's first criterion is met, in that the two vocalizations which make up for the pairs in question can be shown to have genuine independence from each other in as much as our analysis shows them capable of occurring separately as independent communicative devices; and the pause between the two vokes is short enough to meet Scollon's criterion of under 0.6 s. Our analysis may also suggest that Scollon's third criterion may be satisfied, that there be some semantically appropriate link between them (given that at some level of analysis they can share request-like concerns). But they do not meet his fourth criterion, which is that the two vokes are produced within a single intonation contour with initial primary stress (see extract 8). Nevertheless, it may be a feature of such combinations that they preserve the canonical intonation contours associated with their production as separate vokes, for I can find evidence of similarly produced combinations in my own (normal) daughter's vocalizations produced at 1 year 2 weeks of age, in instances such as:

(9)   Amy sits in her chair at table holding a peach in her right hand facing table, with her mother also at table at right angles to A. on her (Amy's) left. A. looks down table and says:

A.: [?əᴬ (.) ?əᴮ (.) ↑εᶜ]

where: A = here A.'s left hand is held slightly above her chair tray in a palm down, open position
         B = with this sound A's index finger is protruded from her left hand, though the hand stays in the same position
         C = left hand has moved into an arm-extended point to an object at the end of the table.

Here again, there is distributional evidence showing the independence of the [?ə] and [ε] sounds, so again we have a combination of sorts that partially meets Scollon's criteria and partially does not. But even if we accept that in these instances we have forms of early sound combination, then it seems that what we have come across in the case of Adam is not a child exercising skills beyond his developmental level, but one combining sounds in ways that normal children do, in ways which have yet to receive detailed attention from early child language specialists.

A final feature of note in Adam's behaviour is his use of gaze, as he does not coordinate brief glances to others with his vocalization/gesture complexes. He can, as is found in extract 1, gaze at his recipient while vocalizing, and afterwards his gaze may return to some relevant object; but there is no instance of a brief gaze from a relevant object, to a recipient, and back to the object being coordinated precisely with a voke. To this extent, he has yet to attain the stage of 'secondary intersubjectivity' that was described earlier in this chapter. Masur (1983) and Sugarman (1984), among others, have found that such coordinations predate the acquisition of more conventional words in normal children, and they have generally found such coordinations occurring by about 12 months of age. On these and other grounds therefore we would have to place Adam's communicative behaviour on something like the level of an 11-month-old normal child. Though following our earlier discussion, we have to bear in mind the possibility that Adam's use of gaze, in this respect, may not be as developed as his employment of the rest of his communicative apparatus.

7.2 SOME FEATURES OF PARENTAL RESPONSE

Having made a provisional analysis of the communicative significance of Adam's three main forms of vocalization, we can now turn to the question of how these vocalizations were treated by his parents. There are several grounds for caution, however, in looking at parental responses to these vokes, indeed parental responses to vocalizations of any children at this stage of development.[12] The main one is that, after a child vocalization, parents may respond as much to the child's accompanying action as to the vocalization (Harris, Jones and Grant, 1983). For example, in extract 10 the mother's *On there* (+ her finger gesture) follows up her identification of the *pink one* as the next block for stacking. In issuing this further guidance as to what to do next she treats Adam as either preoccupied with some other course of action than the one she is encouraging him to engage in, or has having some problem in knowing what the next step is:

(10) IX 2:08

Adam and his mother sit side by side at a table with building-blocks on it. A. has just tried to put one on top of another, but the top block then fell off. M. replaces it on top of the other, and then says *Now the pink one* = *This one* (+ point to pink brick) = *Pink one* (+ withdraws her point). Then:

A.: [ə:ba: :ᵏ] (+ A.'s left hand goes to the pink brick and holds it, not raising it off table + gaze on brick) =

A.: = (A. twists brick as if examining it + gaze on brick)

172

M.: On there (+ left hand points to top of upper brick, already stacked)

A.: (switches gaze to brick M. is pointing to — *then* begins to move brick in that direction)

M.: (withdraws her pointing finger)

where: k with , (k) = vestigial articulation.

In such a case, it clearly would be possible to argue that the mother's turn (*On there*) after the type-1 voke by Adam may be sensitive to the delay in his performing the action she wishes him to perform rather than to the voke *per se*. And there are many such instances where it would be difficult to make a case that parents were responding to the voke as such. This type of occurrence, by the way, also introduces an important complication to the recommendation that parents respond to what their children say, for in many cases it may be perfectly normal to respond to accompanying actions rather than the vokes. And for the same reasons, taking one's lead from the child may be quite a different matter to responding specifically to his vocalizations.

Nevertheless, there do seem to be a set of cases where parents, from the way in which they respond to the voke, appear to treat those vokes as conveying some distinct communicative intent. Extracts 1 and 2 provide examples of what I mean here; where the relevant parental actions which accomplished this are the *Yes* (+ nod) in extract 1, and the placing of the food in Adam's mouth in extract 2. Actions, rather than words, are often fitted responses to the type-2, given the frequency with which they are clearly designed to solicit some particular action by the parent — see also the mother's passing of the box to Adam in extract 7. If we go on to restrict our attention to such narrowly conceived responses, then the importance of distinguishing between the different types of vocalization is brought out fairly clearly. Only three of the type-2 vokes did not receive such responses, and in two of the three cases there seemed to be perfectly clear grounds on which a non-response would appear to be warranted and accountable. One of them, for example, is extract 8 where there is evidence that Adam's mother was engaged in a separate conversation with his elder sister at the time when he was trying to gain her attention. When we turn to type-1 vokes, however, a different pattern emerges. Here only a minority (8) of such child vokes have parental responses which overtly treat them as communicative (as in extract 1). It is important to stress that Adam's parents frequently speak or act in such a way as to fill the next sequential position after Adam's type-1 vokes, as the parent does in extract 10 with *On there*. But in cases such as this, these actions or words do not explicitly treat Adam's voke as having communicative intent, and the subsequent discussion is concerned with comparing the features of type-1 vokes which were given such explicit communicative significance (as in extract 1) with the remainder, as in extract 10, where this did not appear to be the case.

There are two aspects of the way in which Adam communicates which distinguish those type-1 vokes to which parents give such explicit responses; these are Adam's use of gaze and prosody. In this respect, gazing at the recipient in the course of vocalizing to them seems to be an especially powerful signalling device. Whenever this occurred in combination with this vocalization (as in extract 1), it was explicitly treated as communicative by the parent, the only exception being extract 11, where at the crucial moment that Adam's gaze goes to his mother, she is turned away attempting to curtail some object-in-the-mouth activity on the part of Betty:

(11) V 19:29

> Mother sits on floor opposite Adam, who is sitting on his low chair facing M., putting shapes into his shape container. Betty is on M.'s right, also on a low chair. M. guides A.'s hand, with a shape in it, to a particular aperture, saying *Now what shape is that one* (.) *It's that shape isn't it.* Her left hand holds A.'s wrist, but she then turns to face B. and takes an object from B.'s hand that she had near her mouth. In the course of this involvement, A. says:

> A.: [↑əba::d] (+ gaze switches from container to M.'s face) =

> A.: = (*then* his gaze follows M.'s arm to B., *then* monitors drop of M.'s arm *then* A. resumes his activity with the container)

Six of the eight cases where parents made explicit responses to type-1 vokes were accompanied by such gaze switches by Adam, and in the only other case where a type-1 is accompanied by such a gaze switch, extract 11, we know that this may not have been monitorable by the mother who was otherwise preoccupied. A prosodic feature of the type-1 vokes that accompany these gaze switches, and which itself may also play some part in eliciting overt parental responses, is rising pitch. Type-1 vokes could be produced on a variety of pitch contours: on a falling pitch, level pitch (extract 10) or on rising pitch (extracts 1 and 11). Overt parental responses were only constructed to those with rising pitch, though not to all those with rising pitch.

It has been argued, then, that parents may 'respond' to different aspects of what the child is doing at any given time, but that where they appear to give some explicit response to type-1 vokes they appear to take account of various aspects of the child's behaviour, namely gaze and possibly pitch. In effect, they are orienting more to vocal behaviour which *displays* that it is communicative, and from what we have said about Adam's level of development, it must be clear that such an orientation is well fitted to the skills that Adam is in the process of acquiring. He is, for example, on the verge of employing gaze referentially, so that in effect the selectivity of parents' responses based on his visual behaviour seems to acknowledge, perhaps even encourage, precisely those skills appropriate to his stage of development. Adam's use of pitch, and more especially gaze, also raises a possibility that will not be taken further here, namely that within his own communication system he may make a distinction between those type-1 vokes which are designed to elicit a response from recipient (marked perhaps by (+ gaze + rising pitch)) and those not so intended — a possibility which, it should be noted, would significantly complicate the kind of functional description that has been given of this type of voke in section 7.1 of this chapter.

7.3 BOOK READING AND FORMS OF DIALOGUE

In the earlier discussion it was noted that the distinctive referential properties of what have been called type-1 vokes generated a tendency for them to be used more frequently in some situations rather than others, the context of book-reading being their most favoured site. There were two occasions on the recordings when Adam had a book read to him, covering about 7 min in all; and it is to this interactional domain that the analysis now turns in order to investigate in more detail the nature of the interaction between parent and child, and to look more closely at the circumstances which appear to be associated with a low level of overt responsiveness by parents to Adam's type-1 vokes. It will become evident that such a form of responsiveness is an outcome of parents' choosing to construct their interactions with Adam, in the context of book-reading, in particular ways. However, in order to get a sense of the distinctiveness with which this is done, it may be useful initially to present another style of book-reading to children, as describd in the classic work of Ninio and Bruner (1978).

Their study investigated one child, focusing especially on the ages of 11 to 18 months; therefore, as far as possible, our account of their findings is drawn from the earlier phase of that child's development. The picture which emerges is one in which the mother frequently initiates talk about what is on a page with words like *look* or *what's that?* Either then, or at some later point in what Ninio and Bruner call the 'cycle', the child frequently takes a turn, which implies that a slot is often left by the mother in which the child could take up such an opportunity. Where the child did something or said something (not necessarily a conventional word) that was construable as a response, then the mother responded with labels (e.g. *it's an X*), or with what Ninio and Bruner term 'feedback' — e.g. *Yes* or *Yes, it's an X* — i.e. the sort of turns that I've described as overt and explicit responses. And where the child initiated shifts of focus, or

175

attempted to begin new cycles, then the mother was particularly likely to respond.

The reading sequences between Adam and his mother tended to take a different shape. Where Adam's mother used what Ninio and Bruner refer to as attentional vocatives (e.g. *Look*) or queries (e.g. *What's that?*), they were frequently followed immediately by a further description of what was on the page by the mother, no slot being left for the child to fill (e.g. mother turns page and says, *Look what are they doing here* = *Look they've got their clean mittens on*). Frequently, however, the mother moved straight into a description of what was on the page without doing prior attentional vocatives or queries. As a result, the most frequent pauses left by the mother are after her descriptions of what is on a page. Adam's own vocalizations are infrequently responded to; of nine type-1 vokes with accompanying points, only three are directly and explicitly acknowledged by his mother. Furthermore, his initiations of some transfer of focus from one page to another, or from one point on the page to another were also infrequently responded to, whereas Ninio and Bruner found them to be the subject of particular attention by the mother they studied. Finally, within the main book-reading sequence, about 4 min long, there were only two instances of what Ninio and Bruner refer to as 'feedback' responses, where the parent makes some overt acknowledgement of what the child says. In summary, whereas extract 12, reproduced from Ninio and Bruner, stands as an illustration of the characteristic shape of the sequences they studied, extract 13 is more typical of the sequences between Adam and his mother:

(12) From Ninio and Bruner (1978, pp. 6–7):
    Mother: Look
      Child: (*Touches picture*)
        M.: What are these?
       Ch.: (*Vocalizes a babble string and smiles*)
        M.: Yes, they are rabbits
       Ch.: (*Vocalizes, smiles and looks up at mother*)
        M.: (*laughs*) Yes rabbit
       Ch.: (*Vocalizes, smiles*)
        M.: Yes (*laughs*)

(13) III 1:54
    Mother after finishing looking through a book turns book over to look at the back cover, on which are pictures of three of the characters that have appeared in the main text of the book; Adam is on her lap:

    M.: Oh there they are again = They're putting their mittens on

[ˏˊˏ]

A.: [əba₍<::] (right hand points to one of the figures on the
            page)
            (.)

M.: (takes A.'s pointing hand by the wrist, and moves it to point at
    a different figure on the page; her hand stays on the wrist
    from here on) =

M.: = O:n:e

                (.)
            [ˏˏ]ˢ
A.: [ʔa::] =

M.: = Tw::o:: (+ moves pointing hand to second figure)

A.:   ⌊[ɐ: :ˡ]

M.: (starts moving pointing hand to third figure) (see text)

A.: [ʔa:: ʔə̥]

M.:   ⌊Three::::=

A.: = [ɐ::ˡ] (+ A. shifts pointing finger back to second figure)

            (.)

M.: Any more on the front (+ M. turns book over)

where:
            < = increased volume
            ɭ = velarized alveolar lateral (produced here as a vestigial
                articulation)
            ╱= pitch movements.

Before discussing what seems to me of interest in this comparison, let
me make clear what I am not concerned with. It is not my claim that the
style of reading adopted by the mother in Ninio and Bruner's study is typical of the way in which normal children are read to, or that this style plays
any particular role in the acquisition of language, or that the style adopted
by Adam's mother is in some way deficient as compared with the other
mother. Close examination of extract 13 between Adam and his mother
reveals the mother to be employing intricate and delicate techniques in her
handling of the interaction. Take, for instance, the way in which the counting is done, and the ways in which the mother makes that into a joint
activity between herself and Adam. The mother's long-sustained sounds on
the first two numbers themselves make it possible for Adam to come in and
produce a sound either closely adjacent (as in his response to mother's

One) or in overlap (in response to mother's *Two*). In the case of the slot where *Three* should go, the mother makes it possible for Adam to fill the slot prior to herself doing so. She does this partly by withholding her own production of *Three* ... until after Adam has begun his sound, but also by moving Adam's finger to the third figure slowly, and on an unnecessarily exaggerated upwards then downwards trajectory, so that he is both cued into and given every chance of producing his sound on or before the arrival of the finger at the third figure. The outcome that these delicate strategies make possible, then, is for Adam to initiate the third step in the sequence, the orderly nature of his contribution being confirmed by the mother's production of *Three* in overlap with Adam's [ʔaː].

Within both the Ninio and Bruner pattern and the patterns of Adam and his mother therefore it is possible to discern highly delicate and sophisticated interactional techniques in what the parents do. Nevertheless, having said that, there are clear differences between the techniques of the two mothers which are paralleled by different structures of participation by the children. Adam's mother takes the lead in discussion and overtly instructs Adam as to what can be seen on the page as well as using the occasion as an opportunity to teach routines like counting. She avoids opportunities to follow his lead and, in the main, any overt recognition (through 'feedback' responses) of what Adam says. In general terms we can, perhaps, describe it as an instructional style in which the role created for Adam places a premium on passive listening and looking skills, and on reproducing certain expectable sounds in particular positions — the counting sequence in extract 13, for example, is clearly a regular occurrence. This is a style perhaps symbolized, in the last analysis, by the hand on the wrist, a practice frequently adopted on such occasions by Adam's mother. The dialogic style of extract 12 still of course contains instruction; here the name *rabbit*, for example, is being taught. But it is embedded in other forms of speech involvement which patently place a premium on (and encourage) different interactional skills on the part of the child.

For me, two things emerge from this discussion. The first is that if we are considering a matter like the extent of parental responsiveness to the vocalizations of children like Adam, then such parental behaviour has to be seen as an outcome of them choosing to handle their interactions with the child in particular ways. The low level of response to Adam's type-1 vocalizations is partly an outcome of his parents taking into account his direction of gaze and the pitch pattern of the voke, but it is partly also an outcome of parents choosing to organize activities like book-reading in particular ways. These ways enable one to identify those sequences as having a more overt instructional quality than those analysed by Ninio and Bruner. In the latter the interactional tactics employed enabled the sequences to appear more child-led, one concomitant of this being a higher rate of overt response to the child's vocalizations. In fact the more instructional quality of Adam's book-reading sessions is consistent with the suggestions from a number of research studies that parents of the handicapped take on a more directive, teacher-like relationship with their children, so it is important to note that such a relationship can have as one of its possible by-products a low level of overt responsiveness to children. The second conclusion to be drawn from the discussion is that we need to be clear about what the properties are of these different ways of arranging any given experience such as book-reading. It has been emphasized, especially in connection with extract 13, that highly complex, delicate and coordinated interactional manoeuvres can take place just as much in more instructional sequences as they can in more child-led sequences. What we need therefore is careful analysis of both the range of interactional alternatives that appear usable in contexts like book-reading, and of the properties associated with each of these alternatives — and by 'properties' here I mean such things as the casts of roles thereby created, the skills that they make it possible for children to exhibit, the discourse options that each sets up, and so on. In this section I hope to have done enough to suggest that such variations may merit detailed attention. In the long run it seems most appropriate that those who give detailed guidance to parents about ways of interacting with their children should, at least, have knowledge of what is involved in such options. It would be useful then, in the end, rather than say to parents 'respond more to your child', to be able to say that if you handle a class of concrete situations in X ways, then the types of communication skill you will tap and foster will be Y.

7.4 CONCLUSION

My discussion in this chapter has centred around a $3^{1}/_{2}$-year-old child with Down's syndrome. Initially an analysis was made of three main types of vocalization that this child employed on the video recordings that constituted my immediate data-base. The analysis revealed that these vocalizations were used in systematic ways, and that they paralleled the kinds of communicative devices that other investigators report normal 11-month-old children as using. The parents were found to respond to the child's vocalizations in different ways and with different frequencies. Their responses to one of these types of vocalizations were examined in detail, and it was found that they appeared to take into account the pitch contour of the voke and the accompanying gaze pattern in selecting certain tokens of this type to be explicitly addressed. When we went on to examine the main speech use context in which this type of vocalization was produced, namely book-reading, we found that the mother's level of response to this type of vocalization was a by-product of a particular interactional style she adopted when handling this event. This style was contrasted with another way of organizing book-reading that researchers have identified and attention was drawn to the need for careful investigation of the interactional correlates of these different styles. As well as involving different degrees of overt responsiveness to the child, it was suggested that these different styles made it possible for the child to exercise different forms of interactional and communicative skills, and that the elucidation of such practices *in detail* was a significant practical objective for research.

A note on transcript conventions used in data extracts:

Speaker designations are indicated on the left: A, Adam; M, Adam's mother; F, Adam's father. All Adam's vocalizations are transcribed within square brackets, where IPA symbols are used, except for certain suprasegmental features which are transcribed using the conventions listed below. All adult vokes are shown in normal type.

Non-verbal information is contained in round brackets: (+ ...) indicates that the feature in question occurs coincident with the speaker's utterance which has been transcribed prior to the material in round brackets, thus [ʔə:] (+ reach) means that Adam *simultaneously* produced the sound and the reach; and (*then* ...) indicates that the feature in question occurs *after* what preceded it. Other conventions used are:

↑↓ ⌐ ⌐ ⁄ ＼	=	pitch patternings, the latter not to be confused with [~] which marks nasalization, or [→] which marks ingressive phonation.
◎	=	means that the utterance in question was said quietly and 'gently'.
[	=	marks points of overlap in speaker's talk, or where movements begin in relation to what is being said.
=	=	no audible gap between two words or between two utterances, or between some non-verbal action and talk.
-	=	a sound cut-off.
::	=	sound sustension.
(.)	=	pause of under ½s; longer pauses are timed, e.g. (1.7).
—	=	a dash under a word indicates stress.

NOTES

1. Relatively recent overviews of the communication and language skills of Down's syndrome children are contained in Gunn (1985) and Buckley *et al.* (1986): one relevant reference in this respect, cited by neither of these overviews, is Harris (1983). It should be stressed that the discussion of differences that follows in the text is not intended to be exhaustive.

2. A serious problem in interpreting Jones's study, and many other studies, is that the matching of normal and handicapped children is done on the basis of mental age (the Cattell Infant Intelligence Scale, in Jones's case) rather than on some measure of communicative development. This is a problem because there are several reasons for supposing the retardation in language of Down's syndrome children to be more pronounced than would be expected on the basis of their mental age. For example, Share (1975) found them to be most retarded in the domain of language development, and several writers (e.g. Ryan, 1975; Owens and Macdonald, 1982) have noted that in order to obtain matched samples on the basis of mean length of utterance, a measure of communicative development, Down's children with a higher mental age than normal children had to be selected.

3. I would like to acknowledge the financial support of the Economic and Social Research Council during the preparation of this chapter. The wider project, of which this report is but a preliminary part, will continue under their funding until October 1988. I would also like to acknowledge the helpful comments of the editors of this volume on an earlier draft.

4. For most of the time, the camera was left running on a tripod with a wide-angle lens setting rather than being operated manually by either the mother or the father. A variety of different activities were included in the recordings, such as meals, free play, structural play with parents, book-reading and scenes where there was no single predominant activity.

5. My phonetic transcriptions have been made possible through the patience, advice and encouragement of Dr John Local and other linguists at York; the short-comings of these transcriptions, however, should be credited to myself.

6. On the recordings there happens to be very little interaction directly between Adam and either of his sisters. Whether or not this was a typical pattern we are not in a position to say.

7. Our understanding of the part that little words like *yes, oh* and *uhuh* can play in interaction has been significantly advanced by recent work in conversation analysis. On these words see, in particular, Schegloff, 1982; Heritage, 1984b, Jefferson, 1984. These analyses begin to make it possible for more sophisticated treatments to be constructed of parents' talk to children, where similar words are employed. These analyses show that within particular types of interaction sequences such words can be demonstrated to do distinctive jobs. Armed with this knowledge, we can then discriminate more finely the different understandings of what their children have said which parents convey through their use of such words.

8. The closest approximation to such forms of behaviour with our other vokes occurs with a type-2 voke. In this case, the mother was reading a book to Adam, an activity that Adam clearly wished to terminate. He displayed this intention, first, by trying to shut the book, then when the mother opened the book again, by doing a type-2 voke + a shake of head + a shaking movement of the leg. These accompanying gestures are quite unlike the movements in extract 5, which appear to have an involuntary quality to them. Furthermore, there is no evidence of tears or overt distress in this instance, and the leg movements may simply mark the beginnings of Adam attempting to descend from his mother's knee. This is not clear mainly

because the video extract terminates immediately after the leg movement, which itself suggests an analysis by the camera operator (here, the father) of an intention by Adam to change his activity.

9. We have in this turn of Adam's a phenomenon that I have drawn attention to, and analysed elsewhere (Peskett and Wootton, 1985). Adam, on finding himself in overlap with his mother, here cuts off the initial [ə] sound, but resumes his production of this form when out of overlap.

10. The production of type-1 vokes by Adam was also associated with pointing actions on the part of his parents; for an example see extract 10 in the text.

11. The nearest we get to a co-occurring gesture with type-3 vokes is Adam's bang on the arm of his chair in extract 8, but this case is obviously complicated by the presence there also of the type-2 sound, the latter immediately preceding the gesture.

12. A further problem to the one I mention in the text is that of knowing whether or not to treat other forms of action in next position to a child voke as 'responses' to that voke. See, for example, the mother's movement of Adam's pointing hand to a different location after his type-1 voke in extract 13. One might say that it is responsive to the voke + gesture, but it is hardly a fitted response to this communicative act.

REFERENCES

Bates, E. (1976) *Language and Context: The Acquisition of Pragmatics*, Academic Press, New York.

Bates, E. (1979) *The Emergence of Symbols*, Academic Press, New York.

Bates, E., Bretherton, I., Shore, C. and McNew, S. (1983) Names, gestures, and objects: symbolization in infancy and aphasia in *Children's Language* (ed. K.E. Nelson), Lawrence Erlbaum, Hillsdale, NJ, Vol. 4, pp. 59–123.

Berger, J. and Cunningham, C.C. (1981) The development of eye contact, between mothers and normal versus Down's syndrome infants, *Dev. Psych.*, 17, 678.

Bochner, S., Price, P. and Salamon, L. (1984) *Learning to Talk*, Macquarie University Special Education Centre, Sydney.

Buckley, S., Emslie, M., Haslegrave, G. and Le Provost, P. (1986) *The Development of Language and Reading Skills in Children with Down's Syndrome*, Portsmouth Down's Syndrome Project.

Carter, A.L. (1979) Prespeech meaning relations: an outline of one infant's sensorimotor morpheme development in *Language Acquisition* (eds. P. Fletcher and M. Garman), 1st edn, Cambridge University Press, Cambridge, pp. 71–93.

Cheseldine, S. and McConkey, R. (1979) Parental speech to young Down's syndrome children: an intervention study, *Am. J. Ment. Defic.*, 83, 612.

Cunningham, C.C. and McArthur, K. (1981) Hearing loss and treatment in young Down's syndrome children, *Child: Care, Health and Dev.*, 7, 357.

Fischer, M.A. (1983) An analysis of preverbal communicative behaviour in Down's syndrome and non-retarded children, unpublished PhD thesis, University of Oregon.

Francis, H. (1979) What does the child mean? A critique of the functional approach to language acquisition, *J. Child Language*, 6, 201.

Golinkoff, R.M. (1983) The preverbal negotiation of failed messages: insights into the transition period in *The Transition from Prelinguistic to Linguistic Communication* (ed. R.M. Golinkoff), Lawrence Erlbaum, Hillsdale, NJ, pp. 57–78.

Grieve, R. and Hoogenraad, R. (1979) First words in *Language Acquisition* (eds. P. Fletcher and M. Garman), 1st edn, Cambridge University Press, Cambridge, pp. 93–105.

Griffiths, P. (1985) The communicative functions of children's single word speech, in *Children's Single-Word Speech* (ed. M.D. Barrett), Wiley, New York, pp. 87–112.

Gunn, P. (1985) Speech and language in *Current Approaches to Down's Syndrome* (eds. D. Lane and B. Stratford), Holt, Rinehart, New York, pp. 260–81.

Gunn, P., Berry, P. and Andrews, R.J. (1982) Looking behaviour of Down syndrome infants, *Am. J. Ment. Defic.*, *87*, 344.

Harris, J. (1983) What does mean length of utterance mean?, *Brit. J. Dis. Comm.*, *18*, 153.

Harris, M., Jones, D. and Grant, J. (1983) The nonverbal context of mother's speech to infants, *First Lang.*, *4*, 21.

Heritage, J. (1984a) *Garfinkel and Ethnomethodology*, Polity Press, Cambridge.

Heritage, J. (1984b) A change of state token and aspects of its sequential placement in *Structures of Social Action* (eds. J.M. Atkinson and J. Heritage) Cambridge University Press, Cambridge, pp. 299–346.

Jefferson, G. (1980) Notes on a systematic deployment of the acknowledgement tokens 'Yeah' and 'Mm hm', *Papers in Linguistics*, *17*, 197–206.

Jones, O.H.M. (1977) Mother child communication with pre-linguistic Down's syndrome and normal infants in *Studies in Mother–Infant Interaction* (ed. H. Schaffer), Academic Press, New York, pp. 379–401.

Levinson, S.C. (1983) *Pragmatics*, Cambridge University Press, Cambridge.

MacDonald, J.D. (1982) *Language through Conversation*, Ohio State University Parent Child Communication Project.

Masur, E.F. (1983) Gestural development, dual-directional signaling and the transition to words, *J. Psycholing. Res.*, *12*, 93.

Mittler, P. and Berry, P. (1977) Demanding language in *Research to Practice in Mental Retardation* (ed. P. Mittler), University Park Press, Baltimore, Md., Vol. 3, pp. 245–51.

Ninio, A. and Bruner, J. (1978) The achievement and antecedents of labelling, *J. Child Language*, *5*, 1.

Owens, R.E. and MacDonald, J.D. (1982) Communicative uses of the early speech of nondelayed and Down syndrome children, *Am J. ment. Defic.*, *86*, 503.

Peskett, R. and Wootton, A.J. (1985) Turn-taking and overlap in the speech of young Down's syndrome children, *J. Ment. Defic. Res.*, *29*, 263.

Ryan, J. (1975) Mental subnormality and language development in *Foundations of Language development* (eds. E.H. Lenneberg and E. Lenneberg), Academic Press, New York, pp. 269–77.

Schegloff, E.A. (1982) Discourse as an interactional achievement: some uses of 'uh huh' and other things that come between sentences in *Georgetown University Roundtable of Language and Linguistics* (ed. D. Tannen), Georgetown University Press, Washington, DC, pp. 71–93.

Scollon, R.T. (1976) *Conversations with a One-Year-Old*, University of Hawaii Press, Honolulu.

Share, J.B. (1975) Developmental progress in Down's syndrome in *Down's Syndrome (Mongolism): Research Prevention and Management* (eds. R. Koch and F.F. de la Cruz), Bruner/Mazel, New York.

Sugarman, S. (1984) The development of preverbal communication in *The Acquisition of Communicative Competence* (eds. R.L. Schiefelbusch and J. Pickar), University Park Press, Baltimore, Md., pp. 23–67.

Trevarthen, C. and Hubley, P. (1979) Secondary intersubjectivity in *Action, Gesture and Symbol* (ed. A. Lock), Academic Press, London, pp. 183–230.

White, M. and East, K. (1983) *The Wessex Revised Portage Language Checklist,* NFER-Nelson, Windsor.

Wootton, A.J. (1981) Two request forms of four year olds, *J. Pragmat.*, *5*, 511.

Wootton, A.J. (in press) Remarks on the methodology of conversation analysis in *Conversation: An Interdisciplinary Approach* (eds. D. Roger and P. Bull), Multi-lingual Matters, Bristol.

8

Language Intervention and Mother–Child Interaction

Penny Price

The search for effective language intervention procedures has become one of the major tasks for those involved with the provision of education and other services for people with mental retardation. Lack of adequate communication skills is perhaps one of the most limiting handicaps there is. Communication skills are crucial for all aspects of daily living, the basis for social interaction and the medium through which most learning takes place. Difficulty in developing adequate communication skills results in frustration for both the child and his or her family, can disrupt social relationships and cause high levels of anxiety.

Progress in the search for effective teaching procedures was hampered for many decades by failure to understand what was involved in the process of language acquisition. In normally developing children language skills are acquired so early and with such apparent ease that it did not attract the interest of pedagogical researchers in the same way that skills such as reading, writing and spelling did. Progress was hampered, too, by professional attitudes and values which saw the task in relation to the care of mentally handicapped people as being custodial rather than developmental and educational. Research effort and initiative is dependent on the prevailing value system.

Before attempting to facilitate language acquisition in children with communication problems, it is necessary to understand how language is acquired. In order for intervention procedures to be effective they must be derived from a sound theoretical basis. There is a need for flexibility to enable modification to intervention practice in line with new research findings and theoretical reformulations. Continuous evaluation of the effectiveness of the procedures is an essential part of the search for more effective measures, and this information should contribute to the confirmation or modification of current theoretical thinking.

Twenty-five years ago there was minimal concern with improving the communication skills of mentally handicapped people. It is now one of the major priorities of those concerned with the development of these children.

Theoretical thinking about the process of language acquisition has changed markedly during this period, from a conception of language as a genetically acquired, abstract structural system to a fundamental belief that language is essentially a social phenomenon, involving shared activity and taking place in specific social and physical contexts for an infinite variety of reasons, and acquired by the child in close interaction with a primary caregiver, usually the child's mother. These changes in theoretical orientation have been reflected in widely differing approaches to language intervention.

The purpose of this chapter is to review the developments which have influenced our current state of knowledge, to evaluate what we now know about the theory and practice of language intervention and to suggest future directions for research and practice.

This chapter reviews the following:

1. Changing theoretical approaches to language acquisition;
2. Research into mother–child interaction patterns with normally developing children;
3. Research into mother–child interaction patterns with developmentally and language delayed children;
4. Developments in language intervention;
5. Suggestions for future directions in research and intervention practice.

8.1 CHANGING THEORETICAL APPROACHES TO LANGUAGE ACQUISITION

Theory in the 1980s has been dominated by the key notion that language is social in origin, and Dale and Ingram (1981) have stated that explanations that ignore this aspect do little to enhance our understanding of the process of language acquisition. Lack of progress in developing successful strategies to facilitate early language development in developmentally delayed children — and adults — was due, in large measure, to a failure by early theorists and interventionists to understand this fact.

For many decades language deficiency was assumed to be part of the defining condition of mental retardation and therefore little effort was expended in trying to improve the language skills of mentally retarded people. This viewpoint was reinforced by the work of Chomsky (1957), who theorized that the ability to acquire language was genetically pre-determined, and that it occurred through the activation of a 'language acquisition device' in organically intact people. The outlook for those who were not organically intact was pessimistic and, not surprisingly, this theory did not generate any attempts at intervention. It was thought that the necessary condition for language learning was a stimulating environment, which Mittler (1975) described as a 'language bath' approach, stating that mere exposure to an environment rich in language usage was totally inadequate for improving the language skills of mentally handicapped people.

A much more optimistic period followed Skinner's (1957) behavioural theory of language acquisition. Skinner believed that language was a *learned* behaviour and could therefore be taught by means of controlling stimulus and response factors within the environment, and by the use of behavioural techniques such as initiation, modelling, shaping, chaining and fading. This approach gave rise to immense research and intervention activity. Skinner's behavioural methodology, implemented in clinical settings, was instrumental in teaching syntactic structures to populations varying widely in age, degree and type of retardation, in both institutional and school settings. This type of intervention was exemplified in the work of, among others, Lovaas *et al.*, (1966); Gray and Ryan (1971); Kent (1974); Stremel and Waryas (1974).

However, comprehensive reviews of language intervention research studies based on behavioural techniques used in the early 1970s reported limited success in the establishment of receptive and expressive behaviour using systematic instructional techniques and contingent reinforcement procedures. Methodological problems arose from the inflexible nature of the content and procedures, the use of reinforcement contingencies which were not in any way relevant to the communication behaviours elicited, the clinical setting and the use of personnel who were remote from the child's everyday life and natural environments. Snyder and McLean (1976), and Garcia and de Haven (1974), emphasized the failure to achieve maintenance and generalization of learned behaviours and called for an appraisal of findings based on developmental and psycholinguistic research to provide new insights into solving the problems of early language acquisition, the importance of interactions in language learning and in facilitating generalization through studies in natural settings, using natural personnel.

Research into the semantic and pragmatic aspects of language, into the relationship between cognitive development and language acquisition, and into the social, contextual base of language learning, led to radically different explanations of the process of language acquisition with strong implications for those concerned with the development of language intervention procedures. Research by psycholinguists such as Bloom (1973), Bowerman (1973) and Nelson (1973) studied semantic rather than syntactic aspects of language acquisition, suggesting that earliest utterances were based on the child's conceptual holdings about his or her environment and the relations within it; and furthermore, that the order in which these concepts were encoded in language was uniform across cultures, suggesting that language is dependent upon cognition for its earliest form and content. Research by Bates (1976) and Halliday (1976) investigated the pragmatic functions of language, emphasizing that language is embedded in social context and that communication will only take place if there is a purpose. Research into the earliest interactions between caregiver and child suggested that communicative behaviour has its origins in these early exchanges, where the adult is intent upon responding to the child's needs, and concerned with extending the child's capacity to take part in conversational exchanges, where meaning is shared, and ultimately to assist the child to achieve independent communicative functioning.

Research into the semantic, pragmatic and social bases of language has led to the formulation of a transactional model of early language acquisition which emphasizes the importance of interacting cognitive, linguistic and social factors, but stresses above all that unless children have a *reason* to communicate, and someone meaningful to communicate with, they will not learn to talk. Evidence from studies of children placed in institutions at an early age supports this view (Bochner, 1986). In analysing the process by which the specific linguistic code of a particular culture is transmitted to the prelinguistic infant, McLean and Snyder-McLean (1978, p. 112) stated that the infant enters into a language–learning partnership with the mature language users in his environment, and that both members of the partnership have an important role to play, that the mature language user typically facilitates the infants' task by marking the semantically relevant segments of an event and by providing appropriately modified language models. The infant must bring to the partnership his own mechanisms for establishing joint reference with his partner, selectively listening to the language input, and providing feedback.

The emphasis on the cognitive and social bases of language, on the active role of the child and the crucial nature of the interaction between child and caregiver has seen a shift in intervention programming from clinical to natural settings, from the use of clinicians as interveners to parents and preschool teachers being involved in the facilitation partnership, from a focus on syntactic structures to an emphasis on child-generated semantic and pragmatic content based on the activities and purposes relevant to the child's cognitive level and social environment. These developments will be reviewed in more detail in a later section.

The emphasis on the interactional process and the key role of the caregiver has generated an unprecedented quantity of research. Attempts to isolate the significant characteristics of adult input have given way to an attempt to understand how the language learning child acts on the linguistic environment within different interaction situations. This research will be reviewed in the following sections.

8.2 REVIEW OF MOTHER–CHILD INTERACTION RESEARCH WITH NORMALLY DEVELOPING CHILDREN

It may seem surprising that almost two decades of research has not provided more definitive answers to the questions surrounding the nature of the role played by the interaction between caregiver and child in the process of early language acquisition. Results of research studies have often provided conflicting information and the conclusions drawn from the findings have been confusing rather than elucidating. Clear guidelines sought by interventionists for incorporation into language intervention programmes have been elusive.

Two sets of factors have contributed to this state of affairs. The first is that although the basic primary data of the research, namely the interaction and conversations between a mature language user and a language learning child has remained the same, the aspects of the interaction which have been the focus of attention have changed over time. This has occurred as theoretical thinking has developed and changed, giving rise to a situation where a single body of data could be analysed and re-analysed, and give rise to different interpretations.

The second factor is that much of the early research was not carried out with the clear intent of investigating the effect of interaction on early language learning. The impetus was the unacceptability of Chomsky's (1957) innate theory of language acquisition, in which he played down the role of the environment stating that children couldn't learn from the language they heard addressed to them because this adult speech was 'disorganised, ungrammatical and confusing' (Wells and Robinson 1982, p. 14). Observational studies of young children, carried out by linguists and psycholinguists such as Snow (1972), Broen (1972), Nelson (1973) and many others did not confirm Chomsky's description. Their research, and that of others in this area, has been concerned with a number of questions:

1. What are the features which characterise the speech of caregivers to their young language learning children?
2. What purpose do these features serve in the early language learning process?
3. What have we learned from research?

The speech which adults addressed to young children was found to be markedly different from that addressed to adults and the term 'motherese' was adopted to describe the specific features of 'mother talk'. These have been very adequately summarized by Mahoney and Seely (1976).

Speech addressed to young children was observed to be slower, clearer and more fluent than that addressed to older children and adults. It was grammatical and intelligible, utterances were commonly shorter and syntactically simpler in terms of preverb length, complexity of verb phrase and percentage of complex sentences. Speech patterns tended to exhibit exaggerated pitch, duration and stress, and a greater than usual use of rising tones. Semantic simplicity was evident, in that utterances tended to be restricted to the small set of semantic relations that children themselves express in their earlier utterances. Repetition of words, phrases and whole utterances was frequent and topics tended to be restricted to present activities, or features of the environment which were immediately present, so that all conversation was embedded in the child's familiar, everyday environment and activities. In terms of function speech to very young children has been found to contain a relatively high proportion of imperatives and interrogatives and a low proportion of declaratives, but this pattern becomes more variable as the child progresses through different stages of language acquisition.

When Chomsky's work was stimulating early research into how mothers talk to their children, language was viewed as an abstract structural system and the primary interest was in how children acquired the syntactic system of their culture. Consequently, early explanations of the noticeably different patterns of mother talk were in terms of how the specific features observed facilitated the child's acquisition of syntax. Thus the findings that mother's speech is slower (Broen, 1972), with more pauses (Phillips, 1973), reduced in complexity (Baldwin and Baldwin, 1973), but that the complexity of mother and child speech is correlated (Snow, 1972), that the complexity increases with the age and stage of the child (Glanzer and Dodd, 1975), is lowest as the child is beginning to use his or her first words (Lord, 1975) and is inversely related to child participation, so that children who participate more are those who receive less complex syntax, were all interpreted in terms of the mother providing a clear, simple model of the syntactic structures which the child has to acquire.

As developments in semantics, pragmatics and discourse began to influence thinking about language acquisition, so the range of features investigated broadened and early assumptions about the effects of the adult contribution were thrown into question. The work of Bruner (1975) and Trevarthan (1974) clearly identified that communicative behaviour has its origins in the reciprocity developed between mother and child in infancy. In the early stages the mother takes both 'roles' in the conversation, imputes 'intent' for an infant too young to make intentional demands, and 'tunes in' to the child's movements and gestures, until the child gradually develops the skills of joint attention and turn-taking, and learns that his own sounds and actions cause predictable responses in the caregiver. Gradually his range of pragmatic functions is extended, as is his knowledge of semantic relations, as he explores his world jointly with the caregiver and learns the meanings which attach to the objects and actions with which he is involved. Finally, his sounds become modified into first words and then sentences as he acquires the syntactic skills of a mature language user. This perspective on how language is learned emphasizes the *interaction* between child and caregiver, and the effort made by the adult to involve the child in conversational exchanges. It provides the child with the conversational framework from within which he/she can learn the discourse, pragmatic, semantic and syntactic features of his language as he passes through the various stages of language development.

8.3 STUDIES WITH NORMALLY DEVELOPING CHILDREN: EXPERIMENTAL STUDIES

Many studies were carried out in the late 1970s and early 1980s. The majority of these were naturalistic observational studies but some experimental research was carried out. Nelson (1977), Nelson and Bonvillian (1978) and Wells (1980) demonstrated experimentally that the acquisition of tag questions and naming or labelling behaviour was facilitated by increased mother usage, and frequent use by mothers of simple recasting or rephrasing of the child's utterances was found to correlate with increased mean length of utterance (MLU) and auxiliary verb usage, and promoted linguistic growth. Nelson (1981) noted that positive effects were achieved when the experimenter was not the parent, and suggested that other adults and children could facilitate early language growth. He noted that the degree of individual variation in children's language growth and conversations was high, and that some children may only need a small amount of what he termed 'right' input. This input necessary to advance a child's syntax must be at a level which enables the child to make successful comparisons between the input constructions and those which are close to the ones already being used in the child's system. Nelson believed that the discrepancy in complexity between the language used by adult and child was a necessary condition for child progress, but stated that different input was crucial for different language skills and at different stages of the developmental process. He saw experimental methodology as ideal for studying discourse structure at different ages and stages but acknowledged the complexity of the interaction and called for a detailed analysis of possibly convergent data from a variety of experimental and observational paradigms in order to construct an adequate theory of language acquisition.

(a) Naturalistic studies

Naturalistic, observational studies differed from experimental studies, in that there were no constraints on the number and type of variables that could be investigated. The variables selected reflected the orientation of the researchers and studies in the mid to late 1970s which frequently investigated long lists of syntactic variables, to which were added isolated semantic and discourse features. More recent studies have tended to focus increasing attention on functional and conversational discourse features. Findings have tended to be inconsistent and contradictory, due partly to differences in methodology and partly to differences in interpretation.

(b) 'Fine-tuning' hypothesis

Cross (1981) made a significant contribution to what has been termed the 'fine-tuning hypothesis' of mother speech modifications, in a series of studies carried out in the late 1970s and early 1980s. This hypothesis suggests that the mother makes fine adjustments to the complexity of her speech, in line with the child's current stage of development, thus providing a continually adjusted optimal discrepancy between the language system of the child and the language system to which the child is exposed. In a study investigating changes in syntactic, semantic, pragmatic and discourse features in mothers' speech to two groups of children, one aged 3–7 months, the other 16–25 months, 46 out of 62 features studied showed significant changes with age of the child addressed. Cross noted that the child's actual behaviour in the conversational situation was the major determinant of maternal speech adjustments and that the adjustments were made in response to feedback that the mother received from the child during the interaction. The changes were related to changes in the child's comprehension and production skills, although Cross observed that individual differences in children at the same linguistic level affected mothers' speech styles. In another study, Cross (1977) looked at differences in maternal speech addressed to linguistically advanced and less advanced children and found that language addressed to more advanced children contained more semantically related utterances, frequent use of partial repetitions, expansions and elaborations, and involved the children in more turn-taking behaviour. Mothers of language-delayed children were found to be more directive, more unintelligible and more disfluent. The issue of directionality of influence was raised again with the strong suggestion that mothers were responding to characteristics in the child's behaviour. It may be that passive, non-initiating behaviour in the child provokes directive behaviour in the mother. She may initiate more in an attempt to involve the child in communicative behaviour and as the child's skill progresses and child initiations increase, the mother will reduce her initiation rate as she no longer has the sole responsibility for initiating conversations.

A third study by Cross (1980), using three groups of children, pre-linguistic and 1- and 2-year-olds, found that there were significant differences in the language used to prelinguistic children and to 2-year-olds. Contradictory results have been reported by Snow (1977), who found few changes in speech addressed to children between 3 and 18 months, and Gleitman, Newport and Gleitman (1984), who reported no major changes in mothers' language to children observed from 1 to 3 years of age. Gleitman *et al.* (1984), in a detailed review of their own earlier studies, and that of Furrow, Nelson and Benedict (1979), concluded that changes in correlations between certain features of mother speech and child language occurred as children moved from one stage of language to the next, indicating that the correlational findings were stage dependent. They noted, too, that most of the correlations they found were in younger children, 18–21 months of age, at an early stage of language development. Gleitman, Newport and Gleitman (1984) concluded that the changes over time were due to changes in the child's focus and the use that he or she made of the linguistic material provided by the mother. Bellinger (1980), while agreeing with Gleitman, Newport and Gleitman (1984) that most changes in maternal speech occur while the child is at an early stage, noted that there was considerable individual variation in maternal style and that this variation depended on the child's feedback and participation. In this study, Bellinger found that while discourse features of the mother's speech were well tuned, syntactic features were not. It may well be that the variation Bellinger found in maternal speech was due to maternal *responsiveness* to the changing capabilities of the child to engage in conversational discourse, to initiate and respond and engage in turn-taking exchanges. Gleitman, Newport and Gleitman's (1984) finding that mothers' language did not change over the period from 1 to 3 years is in keeping with Bellinger's finding that syntactic features of maternal speech were not well tuned. The studies Gleitman, Newport and Gleitman were reviewing focused predominantly on syntactic features, and they concluded that the changes observed were due to the child's changing focus and capacity to make use of the linguistic material provided by the mother. The combined findings would suggest that variation in mother speech is aimed at assisting the child to take part in conversational exchange and dialogue which provides the language learning environment which the child needs in order to select, process and integrate linguistic information at the rate suited to his/her individual learning capacity.

Criticism of the fine-tuning hypothesis has grown as researchers, operating from an interactionist rather than a formal structural perspective, have found that it failed to explain adequately many features of mother-child interaction patterns. Kavanagh and Jen (1981) stated that it had conceptual appeal but lacked empirical support, whereas Snow, Perlman and Nathan (1985) have criticized the approach in stronger terms, saying that the studies were predominantly atheoretical, consisting of a 'grab-bag' of factors in the search for correlations in which the causal relationships were far from clear. Gleitman, Newport and Gleitman (1984), commenting on Furrow, Nelson and Benedict's (1979) finding that mothers' use of verbs correlated negatively with the growth of child MLU and verb usage, emphasized the shortcomings of correlational studies with small numbers of subjects, and warned of their tendency to turn up nonsensical relationships. Snow, Perlman and Nathan (1985) concluded that the results overall were contradictory and irrelevant, that the inconsistencies may have been due to a failure to take context-specific adjustments into account, and that where there was evidence that relationships existed, there was little evidence to show that specific features of mother language facilitated or were necessary for child language learning. They supported their statements with cross-cultural evidence from Papua New Guinea and Samoa, where no reduction in complexity occurs in language addressed to young children, and they concluded their attack by noting that some features of speech to young children were also typical of speech to household pets and pot plants!

(c) 'Semantic contingency' or 'responsiveness' hypothesis

An increase in studies investigating pragmatic and discourse variables has reflected a shift in focus from form to function. Researchers with an inter-actionist perspective interpret the modifications in caregivers' speech to their young language learning children in terms of the adult involving the child in dialogue. This is learned from infancy by means of the inter-subjectivity which is developed through joint attention and joint action patterns by means of which the caregiver interprets the world to the child and provides the framework within which the child develops concepts and acquires the linguistic means to communicate his interpersonal and ideational understandings. Wells (1980) has stated that early communi-cation is concerned with pragmatic meaning, that the pragmatic function provides the child's entry intolinguistic communication, giving an essen-tial continuity in development from gesture to lexico-grammar. Only in conversation does the child learn all the other facets of language, and the mother provides the framework within which a smooth flow can be main-tained with immature language users, ensuring that 'what the child can do today in co-operation, tomorrow he will be able to do on his own' (Wells, 1981, p. 93). Snow, Perlmann and Nathan (1985) stated that the major function of speech to the child is to provide a *context* or meaning for the child's gestures and utterances. The task of the caregiver is to create discourse around the child's communications, which enables the child, gradually, to make increasingly complex linguistic utterances.

The notions of semantic contingency, and adult responsiveness, are commonly held in these viewpoints, as is the idea of the adult partner skilfully adapting the conversational roles to ensure the participation of the immature partners, thus providing a 'scaffolding' which assists the child to move from an immature level to that of a mature language user.

In their review of the area, Snow, Perlmann and Nathan (1985) have reported strong evidence that semantically contingent responses to the child's communicative attempts have a facilitative effect on language acquisition and cite the work of Nelson (1977), Cross (1978), Barnes *et al.*, (1983) and Goldfield (1985). Cross's (1978) finding that mothers of fast-developing children were more semantically responsive was confirmed by Wells (1981). He found that the characteristics of mothers' speech to fast as opposed to slow developing children included more utterances referring to the immediate situation in which mother and child were engaged in joint activity, and a higher proportion of utterances to children during routine household tasks, indicating that these mothers engage their children in conversation more than mothers of slow developing children. They used more directives, questions and commands, and corrected and acknowledged their children's utterances more frequently. Wells (1981) found no evidence that syntactic complxity was co-related. Wells's finding that directives have a facilitating effect is in contrast to Cross's (1978) result, and the issue of the role played by directives has given rise to a major controversy in recent years. Negative effects were reported by Hubbell (1977) and Newport, Gleitman and Gleitman (1977), whereas the reverse has been found by Ellis and Wells (1980), Kaye and Charney (1981) and Harris, Jones and Grant (1983). Several studies have reported that directives and mother initiations decrease with age and stage (Bellinger, 1979; Clarke-Stewart and Hevey, 1981). Conti-Ramsden and Friel-Patti (1984a), investigating language-delayed children and their mothers, have explained the high usage of both in terms of the mother's aim to keep the conversation going until the child has acquired initiating skills. Others have suggested that high usage of directives may represent a stable interaction style, characteristic of some mothers but not of others. McDonald and Pein (1982) and Olsen-Fulero (1982) have both suggested that mothers fall into one of two broad categories and are either predominantly controlling or conversationally eliciting. Failure to look at child behaviour or to vary the contexts in which data were collected over the two sessions, for children in only one age-group, lead to a necessary questioning of the validity and generalizability of Olsen-Fulero's results. This issue has important implications for development of intervention strategies for use with developmentally and language-delayed children. Research with these populations will be explored in section 8.4.

8.4 REVIEW OF MOTHER–CHILD INTERACTION RESEARCH WITH DEVELOPMENTALLY AND LANGUAGE–DELAYED CHILDREN

Research with populations of developmentally delayed and language-delayed children in interaction with their mothers has proved as contra-dictory and inconclusive as studies investigating their normal language learning counterparts. Initial concern was with determining whether maternal speech to developmentally delayed children is the same as or different from speech addressed to normal language learning children. Studies reporting differences have typically suggested that mothers spoke faster, with shorter utterances, and used more grammatically incomplete sentences and more demands and requests (Buium, Rynders and Turnure, 1974; Marshall, Hegrenes and Goldstein, 1973). Bricker (1981) noted that mothers tended to speak too often and too quickly, failing to give the child an opportunity to respond, or causing an overlap in the conversation which caused further confusion to the child. Cunningham *et al.* (1981) found that mothers of mentally retarded children initiated fewer interactions, and although more directive, they were less likely to respond positively to their child's compliance. These negative results were not supported, however, by Leonard (1977), Buckhalt, Rutherford and Goldberg (1978), and Rondal (1977, 1978) and Gutmann and Rondal (1979), who found no differences in maternal speech patterns when the children were matched for MLU rather than chronological age.

A further group of studies investigated whether there were differences in child characteristics, suggesting that differences observed in maternal speech patterns might be in response to characteristics in child behaviour that were associated with the handicapping condition. This line of investi-gation paralleled the concern in studies of normally developing children as to the direction of effect — whether from mother to child or child to mother, or, as seems most probable, bidirectional. Bricker and Carlson (1980), Jones (1980) and Schaffer (1977) have noted that developmentally delayed infants fail to initiate social interaction and to establish and sustain joint-action routines, that their vocalizations are longer and more repetitive with briefer pauses between breaths, making the mother's task in maintain-ing dialogue harder. Mahoney, Glover and Finger (1981) have suggested that Down's syndrome children were more delayed in the area of language skills than measures of their general intellectual functioning suggested. Dodd (1987) found that Down's syndrome children had particular phono-logical problems, and that mothers of Down's children accepted a wide range of poor approximations to the correct sounds, thus making the child's task harder through failing to provide appropriate, corrective feed-back. Both McConkey and Martin (1984) and Price (1984) found a wide range of individual variation in mothers' speech patterns. McConkey and Martin (1984) studied prelinguistic Down's syndrome children over a 12-

month period. They found no changes in mothers' speech in response to child vocalizations, but a steady increase in the percentage of mother utterances in response to child action. A decrease in initiations and imperatives, and an increase in feedback to the child, was interpreted as reflecting changes in the child's play behaviour. Price's (1984) study reflected changes in maternal speech patterns over a six-month period as children moved from the prelinguistic stage to one- and two-word utterances. At the preverbal stage all mothers exhibited high rates of directive behaviour, but as children reached the stage of one- and two-word utterances, two patterns became evident in mothers' speech. One group of mothers showed a decrease in directive behaviour and an increase in commenting, modelling, expansions and feedback, and children in this group showed steady language growth as measured by MLU. The second group of mothers was divided into two subgroups. Both showed a continued high usage of directives and an increase in the use of questions, but children who made fast as opposed to slow progress in this group received high rates of modelling, expansions and feedback. The numbers in the study were small, and detailed analysis of discourse features was not carried out, but the results suggest that a combination of strategies such as questioning, commenting, modelling, expansions and feedback reflect the mother's concern with semantic contingency, following the child's lead and keeping the conversation going. Detailed study of child behaviours, ability and willingness to initiate, and replication over settings and time is necessary before support can be lent to McDonald and Pein's (1981) suggestion that parents have stable interaction patterns which are predominantly either directive or conversation eliciting. Snyder and McLean (1976) have drawn attention to the severe deficits experienced by severely mentally retarded, autistic and brain-damaged children in their selective listening, information-gathering and joint referencing skills, all essential for language acquisition.

Studies of language delayed as opposed to developmentally delayed or mentally retarded children have produced similar patterns of results, some supporting the 'difference' thesis and others failing to find adequate evidence for it. Conti-Ramsden and Friel-Patti (1983, 1984a), in studies which focused on discourse features, noted that language-delayed children made fewer child initiations and more ambiguous responses, but that mothers' usage of requests and directives was no different from that of mothers of normal language learning children. They concluded that there was no clear relationship between the language environment and the child's language problem. Where Friel-Patti (1978) found mothers of delayed children initiated more and were more directive, it was because the children were initiating less and mothers' behaviour was aimed at keeping the interaction going. She achieved this within a framework of maternal regulation by taking both roles until the child developed the skills to participate more fully in the exchange. Dromi and Beny-Noked (1984), on the other hand, found that mothers of language-delayed children displayed a number of 'negative' features in a story-telling context including high usage of directives, failure to elaborate, short utterances, a tendency to dominate the conversation and making many consecutive utterances resulting in low turn-taking behaviour by the child. However, their interactive style was very different in a free play situation featuring more interaction and more utterances per turn — suggesting strongly that the context influences interaction style and highlighting the problem of making assumptions about maternal style from data collected in only one situation. Peterson and Sherrod (1982), in their comparison of speech to normal language learning children, developmentally delayed and language delayed, found that speech to the Down's syndrome children was less semantically contingent than to those with a high MLU, and found an even greater difference in the speech addressed to the language delayed, where one-third of all speech addressed to the child was not appropriate to the child's activity. No adequate explanation for these differences was presented, and it must be noted that the analysis was based on data collected by audio tape. The difficulty of transcribing adequate contextual information without the aid of video taped material cannot be underestimated; and without corroboration from further studies, findings such as these must be treated as equivocal. A study such as this raises the enormous issues of the part that methodological problems have played in achieving so many widely differing and conflicting results.

(a) Methodological problems

A major problem in reviewing the evidence from research into dyadic interaction is the lack of comparability of results from one study to the next. Different populations have been studied at various ages, and stages of development, and data have been collected in a variety of settings, using a variety of different procedures. The detailed analysis of samples of interactive dialogue between mother and child is both labour-intensive and time-consuming, although developments in computer technology are capable of reducing this burden and will, presumably, increasingly do so. However, population samples have tended to be small and non-representative, and largely middle class. Well's (1985) study of 128 children was an exception, in that it studied children's development longitudinally, over the period from 1 to 5 years, and his results disputed the notion that children from lower socioeconomic groups are necessarily exposed to an impoverished language environment. Heavy reliance on correlational statistical procedures has contributed to a tendency to include as many variables as possible, without reference to a coherent theoretical framework and, combined with the small numbers of children in the samples, has resulted in findings which sometimes lack logical plausibility. Effects of mothers' speech on child development have been claimed where causal relationships cannot be substantiated.

A further problem relating to the demonstration of effects on children's progress is the time period at which measures are taken. In some studies measures of mothers' speech and children's speech are taken concurrently, in others there is a time lapse of six to nine months, based on the assumption that there is a time lag between the mothers' behaviour and effect on child growth. The whole area of measurement of language skills in young children is problematic, and Wells (1985) has stated that one of the most urgent tasks in this area is the search for fine measures of receptive and expressive language, and discourse skills. The most commonly used measure, the MLU, is too gross and does not reflect the complexity of language behaviour — frequency of usage, the range of pragmatic functions, the variety of appropriate social contexts and the relative frequency of initiating and responding behaviours. This is a particular issue for mentally retarded children whose progress is slower and occurs in smaller steps (see, for example, Wootton, in Chapter 7 in this book), thus requiring finer measures to reflect, for instance, the increase from unintelligible to intelligible utterances, and usage of an increasing range of semantic-grammatical or syntactic rules, all of which can occur while the MLU remains unchanged.

Researchers have frequently failed to specify the characteristics of children in their samples, particularly when studying developmentally delayed and language-delayed children. Because of the ease with which they can be identified, Down's syndrome children frequently form the subject population in studies of the developmentally delayed, yet this condition represents only 10% of the mentally retarded population, and there is some evidence to suggest that they have some characteristics specific to their condition which affect their language growth (Mahoney, Glover and Finger, 1981). Specifying the level of mental retardation, from mild to severe, is equally necessary, and within any one level there are individual differences and uneven patterns of development which need to be noted. Recent studies of language-delayed children have attempted to limit the population studies to those children who show significant deficits in their linguistic functioning while exhibiting age-appropriate, non-verbal intelligence, and no evidence of physical or developmental abnormality (Dromi and Beny-Noked, 1984; Conti-Ramsden and Friel-Patti, 1983). Where the population is not specified, or heterogeneous populations are used, studies fail to provide the detailed information which is required to provide insights which can be used in intervention for specific populations. As Conti-Ramsden (1985) has said, subgroups of language-impaired children should be identified and their characteristics explicitly specified, and the conclusions drawn and recommendations made should be restricted to those groups of children who are comparable.

Studies making comparisons between mothers' speech to normal language learning and developmentally or language-delayed children have been confounded by the problem of adequate matching. Many early studies reporting differences in language used to the two groups matched children on CA, in spite of evidence suggesting that mother speech changes with the language stage of the child, thus comparisons were being made between groups of children at different stages of development. When children have been matched for MLU rather than CA, as in Rondal's (1977) study, no differences between the two groups were found, supporting the contention that language development in delayed children follows the same pattern as in normal children, but proceeds more slowly. Friel-Patti and Harris (1984) found that language-impaired children used their language skills less often, initiating and taking turns in dialogue significantly less frequently than their MLU counterparts. This finding reinforced Wells's (1985) call for finer-grained measures of all areas of language competence, and raises the issue of the relationship between language and social development.

The issue of setting and context is important when attempting to compare results across studies. Snow *et al.* (1985) and Dromi and Beny-Noked (1984) have provided evidence that features of mother language differ in a story-reading and free play situation. Different studies have used a wide variety of activities in home, laboratory and clinical settings; data have been collected by means of live observation and audio and video tape; and observers have been present in some cases, recording context information, and in other cases this has been collected by interview with the parent after the recording is over. Data are sometimes continuous and sometimes time-sampled, and at other times particular features are extracted and studied in isolation. Once again, there is a need for detailed description of the setting, activities and means of data collection. A further problem relates to the issue of direction of effect, where some studies have investigated changes in mother language and others have focused on the child; more recently, there has been an increasing tendency to focus on both. Current theoretical perspectives strongly suggest that looking at both members of the dyad, in interaction, is essential.

The current controversy surrounding the role of directives in facilitating or hindering language acquisition has its roots in many of these methodological problems. Studies have used different contexts and children at different ages and stages of development, where commonsense would suggest that mothers asked to interact with their young developmentally delayed children in a strange laboratory setting may be more inclined to display controlling behaviours than they would in a familiar play setting at home (Gunn, Clark and Berry, 1980). Few studies have related use of directives to other discourse variables, as Conti-Ramsden and Friel-Patti

(1984a) did, enabling them to provide an explanation in terms of the child's developing discourse skills. Studies suggesting that high directive usage reflects a stable mother interaction style have failed to collect their data in different contexts (Olsen-Fulero, 1982), and have failed to provide longitudinal data, and not succeeded in ruling out satisfactory explanations in terms of context or stage of development.

There is a need for longitudinal studies using dyadic methodology to investigate discourse in context. Detailed specification of child characteristics, context and variables under investigation is essential.

8.5 SUMMARY OF RESEARCH REVIEW

(a) What features characterize the speech of caregivers to their young language learning children?

The many features of 'motherese', described earlier, are undoubtedly evident in many samples of language collected when mothers were interacting with their normal language learning, developmentally or language-delayed children. Evidence suggests that syntactic features are not noticeably modified as children progress from one stage to the next, that parents tend to engage their children in conversations about here-and-now activities and to talk about things that interest and involve the child, thus displaying semantic responsiveness. Parents use a wide range of pragmatic functions when engaged in conversation, and these patterns may vary with the context or setting and the communicative purpose. The evidence to suggest that there is wide variation in individual parental style (Bellinger, 1980; McConkey and Martin, 1984) is stronger than the evidence suggesting that parents have a stable, interactional pattern, typified by either predominantly controlling or conversationally eliciting behaviours. There is some evidence to suggest that discourse features, such as initiating and responding, turn-taking and monologuing and correcting and acknowledging, do change in response to the child's increasing conversational competence. There is evidence, too, to suggest that child characteristics affect mother behaviour, as well as the reverse, and that children play an active role in the language learning process.

(b) What purpose do these features serve in the early language learning process?

The 'fine-tuning' hypothesis which states that mothers modify their speech for the specific purpose of 'teaching' their children language (Moerk, 1976), and that they achieve this by progressively modeling the language that the child needs to hear in order to acquire the increasingly complex syntactic structures of their native language, has not been supported by research evidence and is no longer widely held.

The semantic contingency or 'responsiveness' hypothesis states that the purpose of mother speech is to involve the child in conversation, as only in conversation does the child learn all the facets of the linguistic system. By providing the child with a conversational framework which allows for the immature skills of the child, the child is involved in meaningful interaction through which he/she gradually learns the discourse, pragmatic, semantic and syntactic skills of a mature language user. The child can attend to those features which are appropriate to his/her stage of conceptual, social and linguistic growth, and incorporate them into his/her system according to ability to do so, while the mother sustains the conversation. So the changes in maternal speech result from the development of the child's ability to take his/her turn in the conversation. Many studies have demonstrated the relationship between semantic contingency and mother responsiveness to child language acquisition, and the importance of involving the child in conversation about topics of shared interest and activity is now widely accepted.

(c) What have we learned from research?

We have learned from research that adjustments in maternal speech aimed at providing a simplified syntactic model for the child are not facilitatory, whereas semantic, pragmatic and discourse adjustments which ensure the child's participation in conversational exchange, irrespective of the immaturity of his or her skills, are facilitatory. We have learned that it is essential to look at the behaviour of both partners in the interaction, that the effects are bidirectional with the characteristics of the child affecting the mother's behaviour as much as the mother influences the child. Conti-Ramsden (1985) has emphasized the importance of this finding for the development of intervention procedures which have frequently focused on either the child or the mother. We have learned from Wells (1985) that engaging the child in conversation about the immediate situation, and the joint activity which occurs when mother and child are involved in routine, everyday tasks in their natural settings, results in rapid language development.

Variation in usage of pragmatic and discourse features in individual mother speech styles has been reported, as well as context-specific variation, and variation related to the language stage of the child. The controversial suggestion that different patterns of stable characteristics exist in mothers, some facilitating and some not facilitating language acquisition in the child, poses a problem for those concerned with developing language intervention procedures, as does the as yet unanswered question of the degree to which the language environment must be facilitating in order for the immature language learning child to learn from it. The extent to which these findings have been incorporated into language intervention procedures will be reviewed in section 8.6.

8.6 DEVELOPMENTS IN LANGUAGE INTERVENTION

Major changes have taken place in language intervention programmes since the early 1970s, and their implementation has had significant impact on the development of communication skills in developmentally delayed children. Programmes vary in their theoretical foundation and in their capacity to respond to changing ideas about language acquisition. Janko and Bricker (1987) refer to the huge investment in time and energy which is required to establish a programme and state that major changes to the structure and operation are both costly and disruptive and cannot be undertaken lightly. This problem accounts for the time lag which exists very often between the publication of research findings and their incorporation into language-intervention practice. A further problem, emphasized earlier in this chapter, is the frequently conflicting information forthcoming from various research enterprises. Trying to ascertain which findings warrant incorporation into intervention procedures is a major problem facing those involved in intervention. The dilemma lies on the one hand in resisting change and pursuing procedures which may not be as effective as would be modified practices based on current knowledge, and on the other hand adopting isolated findings without a full understanding of their implications in terms of the total theoretical framework. The controversy surrounding the role of directives in facilitating or impeding language growth is a case in point.

The dramatic developments which have occurred in language intervention procedures in the last decade are evidence of the fact that theoretical formulation and empirical evidence do have a continuing and desirable impact on practice. The programmes in operation in the early 1970s had their origins in behavioural theory and the experimental research generated by it, which demonstrated unequivocally that linguistic structures could be taught to populations of mentally retarded people previously thought incapable of learning language. The early behavioural programmes viewed the child as a passive learner who could be taught syntactic structures by means of a stimulus–response–reinforcement paradigm. Training was carried out in a clinical setting by a therapist or clinician. Failure of the language structures taught to generalize into everyday usage in the child's natural settings led to a serious questioning of this approach. The continued use of clinical settings by speech therapists and speech pathologists with language-delayed children is still a problem

(McConkey, 1981), although methods have changed and, in some instances, parents are more closely involved in intervention sessions.

Research findings in the area of semantics and pragmatics led to major changes in the content of language programmes, together with the settings in which they were implemented and the personnel used in implementation. Hart and Risley (1974, 1980) and Hart and Rogers-Warren (1978) accepted the necessity for teaching in natural settings in order to ensure generalization and developed what they termed 'incidental' teaching in pre-school settings, targeting functional language and making access to toys, teacher attention and other classroom activities contingent upon individually determined child verbalizations. Developments in their work have continued into the 1980s.

A programme which has had far-reaching effects in terms of further development of intervention procedures was the Environmental Language Intervention Program (ELIP), developed by MacDonald *et al.* (1974). The ELIP was a comprehensive package containing assessment procedures covering the child's use of language in the home, and the parents' attitude to the child's problem, the child's preverbal skills, verbal skills assessed in terms of semantic grammatical rules, and a handbook suggesting a format for weekly intervention sessions over a period of twelve weeks. The programme differed from its predecessors in the emphasis on ensuring the adequate development of preverbal skills before targeting verbal skills; and one- and two-word utterances were assessed in terms of semantic-relational categories, which were developed in structured and then semi-structured play routines with parents taking the role normally adopted by clinicians. Parents were viewed as real partners in the intervention process, selecting suitable goals for language targets in terms of the child's needs in his/her home environment. Instructions to parents on desirable modifications of their language when interacting with their child were limited to ensuring that the child was attending, that language used was clear and simple and restricted to classes of words that the child was learning, and encouraging expansions and comments — a mixture of suggestions stemming from both 'fine-tuning' and 'responsiveness' research. This work, developed at the Nisonger Centre, has been instrumental in stimulating intervention programmes in Canada and Australia. MacDonald's (1985) recent work has involved the development of a model for developing communication skills in severely delayed children. The model attempts to analyse the variables involved in the child, the significant adult with whom he/she is interacting, and the setting, with the primary goal of increasing the length of participation in turn-taking interactions — reflecting the current concern with facilitating language growth through participation in conversational discourse in the child's natural environment. Results of this approach are not yet available but the model may well prove to be a valuable addition to the predominantly, but not exclusively, behavioural procedures currently used with severely and profoundly retarded persons.

The Hanen Early Language Parent Program (Manolson, 1977) was developed to overcome the inadequacy of the speech pathologist's traditional, clinical role in providing services to the language-delayed child. Realization that normal patterns of communicative interaction frequently do not occur when a delayed child presents confusing cues and reduced responsiveness to parents (Laskey and Allen, 1977) led to the establishment of a programme which aimed at providing parents with the skills and experience to stimulate language growth at the prelinguistic and linguistic levels in the natural home environment. Informal teaching focused on facilitating interaction by responsiveness to the child, following his/her lead in play, encouraging child participation, ensuring the child has opportunity for turn-taking, and increasing semantically contingent strategies such as initiating, expanding, modelling, parallel talk and reducing the number of closed questions and demands, all well aligned with the 'responsiveness' theory of language facilitation. The formal part of the programme followed the structured and semi-structured procedures outlined in the ELIP (MacDonald, 1974). Parents were video taped in the home setting and feedback provided in group discussions on the facilitatory quality of the interaction. Efficacy data demonstrated improvement in children's communication skills and significant change in the teaching skills and attitudes of the parents (Manolson, 1977). More recent research from this programme has focused on the extent to which it has been effective in increasing conversational skills and, in particular, turn-taking behaviour. Turn-taking skills have been seen as a prerequisite to language development, a process which the child must learn, and the process through which learning is facilitated (Wells, 1980). Evidence that developmentally delayed children experience difficulty in turn-taking, topic-initiating and topic-continuing behaviours, and thus fail to receive feedback from mothers in the same manner as normal language learning children do, has been presented by Jones (1980) and Cunningham *et al.* (1981). The aim of this study was to investigate the structural aspects, such as length, size and quantity of turns, topical aspects such as the establishment of joint focus and the development of topic across speaking turns, and the children's communication skills. The twelve-week programme included suggestions to parents regarding reducing the number of topics they initiated, increasing their responsiveness to their children's communicative attempts, keeping the conversation going for longer sequences on a topic and increasing child initiations. Both experimental and control groups comprised a mixture of Down's syndrome and other developmentally delayed children. At post-test, experimental mothers demonstrated an increase in turn-taking, topic maintenance and overall responsiveness to the child, and children were initiating more topics, taking part in longer turn sequences and displayed a significant increase in turns containing words with a decrease in non-verbal turns. Parents were satisfactorily following the child's lead and providing feedback on the child's topic, and thus facilitated the use of words in conversational contexts as the children maintained their turn-taking in longer sequences. No change in child language level was evident when measured on the Sequenced Inventory of Communication Development (SICD) (Hedrick, Prather and Tobin, 1975). This reflects the problems in measuring change in language skills over relatively short periods of time for mentally retarded children. A further comment by Girolametta (1985) on the population in his study relates to the wide range of developmental levels, and he emphasized the necessity of separating effects for children at different levels, a problem faced by all researchers using populations of mixed developmental level.

The Early Environmental Language Intervention Program, developed at the Macquarie University Special Education Centre in Sydney, has much in common with the Hanen Program (Bochner, Price and Salamon, 1982). The programme was developed in response to a request to fill a gap in the early intervention services available to young developmentally delayed children. The major source of anxiety expressed by parents was the failure of their children to develop adequate communication skills. An initial parent training project was established based on the assessment and training procedures developed by Horstmeier and MacDonald (1975). Since 1980 the programme has been operating in community health centres as well as the University Special Education Centre, and has assisted several hundred children and their parents as well as providing training for students, preschool teachers and other professionals involved with the education of young developmentally delayed children. The programme has undergone considerable modification, with particular emphasis being placed on the skills required at the prelinguistic stage — looking together, turn-taking and appropriate play with objects and people — the building-blocks for language development. The section on how mothers talk to their children, emphasizing the necessity for responsiveness, extending the child's language and providing him or her with plenty of opportunity has been extended to include the importance of turn-taking, and extending the number of turns in a conversational sequence. In addition to suggesting games and activities appropriate to the home setting for skills ranging from preverbal to early sentences, the programme includes suggestions for group activities which allow for the participation of children at differing levels of language skill. A series of video tapes illustrates how to assess the child's level and demonstrates suitable strategies and activities for encouraging language growth.

Research reports have substantiated the overall effectiveness of the programme, with gains on the SICD (Sequenced Inventory of Communication Development) demonstrating growth over six months at a rate comparable to that of normal language learning children (Price and

Bochner, 1984; Bochner *et al.*, 1986), but global measures fail to provide information about which aspects of the programme are effective for which children at what stage of development. An early attempt to investigate changes in patterns of interaction between ten mothers and their developmentally delayed children over the six-month period of the language programme provided strong evidence of an increase in child turn-taking and a reduction in the amount that mothers talked, and very tentative evidence to suggest that a continued high usage of directives unaccompanied by commenting and feedback may be associated with slow language growth in children at the 2+ word level. The shortcomings of this study, which did not allow analysis within a discourse framework, led to the development of a longitudinal study which is attempting to look at changes in discourse patterns over an 18-month period. The study is particularly concerned with investigating how joint attention is negotiated between mother and child, what causes breakdown and how this is resolved. It is hoped that analysis of breakdown situations may lead to the development of suggestions and strategies which may be specifically, rather than generally, applicable to mothers who experience this problem, usually with children who are difficult to engage in joint activity and have very short attention spans. An analysis of correction strategies, ranging from direct to indirect, is being examined in relation to patterns of initiating and responding behaviour, and it is hoped to shed further light on the conversational-directive-style controversy and to obtain information about changing patterns of discourse features as they relate to different contexts and to stage of language development in children with different levels of retardation.

Another recent development is the establishment of a programme which combines parent training and home intervention with a classroom-based component which focuses on the child's use of language in social situations with other children and adults, and explores the effect of different contexts within the classroom on communicative behaviour (Bochner, 1987).

McConkey (1980) has long argued for implementation in the classroom of research findings on the early language development of mentally handicapped children, and has been actively involved in training teachers, preschool teachers, nurses, speech therapists and other para-professionals. At the same time, he has argued that the central role in facilitating early language in delayed children is that of the parent, and that the role of professionals is to increase the parents' knowledge about how this early learning takes place to enable them to help their child more effectively (McConkey, 1979a). McConkey's work and programmes have differed from others in his emphasis on the relationship between cognitive growth and linguistic development. He stresses the importance of play in child learning, and suggests that the different levels of play provide the experiences which the child needs in order to become familiar with the objects and actions and relations in his environment, and that until he or she reaches the representational stage of play, where a shoe-box can become a 'bed', the child is unable cognitively to deal with the idea of a particular set of sounds, namely a word, representing an object or action. The information provided to parents about the importance of involving children in play, and observing the *level* of play, allows the parent to understand the reason for the delay in vocal language. The emphasis on careful observation which, in his most recent programme (McConkey and Price, 1986), is extended to cover the child's earliest non-verbal communications provides the parent with an orientation to the child which is almost inevitably responsive, and which should facilitate interactions at all stages of language learning. An understanding of the *process* by which language is acquired allows the parent to accept the notion that he/she cannot *teach* the child language, but that she can provide the optimal language learning environment by observing and responding to every communicative attempt the child makes, by involving the child in increasingly complex joint play activities which enable him/her to learn about his world and, finally, to talk about it.

A more explicit programme which pays particular attention to the prerequisite social and cognitive or sensorimotor skills of the prelinguistic period has been developed by Bricker and Carlson (1980), who have developed a two-tiered lattice specifying in detail the social and cognitive skills essential for the development of referential behaviour, and verbal language. This represents an extension downwards in age of one of the earliest language intervention programmes developed (Bricker and Bricker, 1970) and reflects the capacity for modification which has been evident in most of the programmes reviewed. Bricker and Carlson's decision to programme for intervention from earliest infancy was in response to emphasis in the literature upon the crucial importance of the prelinguistic period for the development of communication.

A relatively recent programme, developed by Weistuch and Lewis (1985), focuses on the early cognitive stages, the relationship between representational and play behaviour and strategies which facilitate responsive interaction and extended discourse sequences. Using a strategy where mothers, first, observe staff integrate strategies into classroom activities, then interact with their own child in semi-structured and free play tasks, this programme has demonstrated a significant decrease in directive usage and increase in the use of contextual speech and topic extension. Data on child language growth have yet to be presented. A short-term study focusing on discourse variables, including strategies to resolve sequences and decrease breaks in dialogue was effective in increasing child initiations and mother attention and responsiveness to those initiations (Collins, 1986). A decrease in directive usage was, however, not maintained after the intervention period. The importance of this failure is difficult to determine, and raises the problem of attempting to modify specific behaviours without looking at the nature of the ongoing interaction between mother and child, and reinforces Bricker and Carlson's emphasis on the importance of intervention taking place within the framework of a global picture of language acquisition and the long-term goals of the child.

The demonstrated capacity of language intervention programmes to change and grow, in response to their own experiences, and developments in the literature, is cause for cautious optimism. The complexity of the issues raised and the contradictory nature of many research findings reported does nothing to simplify the task for those who are committed to improving the services provided to the many children who have difficulty learning to communicate.

8.7 FUTURE DIRECTIONS

Based on current theory and research evidence, it seems probable that modifications to current programmes, and programmes developed in the future, will be less structured rather than more so. Programmes will be organized such that the goals are meaningful to the child in his or her attempts to communicate and that they will be incorporated into the natural, everyday life of the child. Every opportunity for communication will be used rather than setting aside particular times and places for 'teaching' language. The general theoretical framework which has the caregiver's interactions with the child as its central tenet implies that 'intervention' takes place whenever the child is interacting in a meaningful, communicative manner with any significant person, child or adult, in his/her natural environment. The role of intervention will be to ensure that the significant people in the child's life understand the process by means of which the child acquires his/her language skills, and the crucial role that they can play in making the child's task easier. Parents and significant others may need to be taught to observe the child's earliest communicative attempts from infancy, to respond to them and to engage the child in meaningful, shared activity whenever possible in the course of the child's daily routines, in his/her natural environment. Individual variation in parental knowledge and receptivity, and the extent of the child's handicapping condition, will determine how much 'teaching' and demonstration are required to ensure that the interactions are positive and providing the child with the experiences and framework which he or she requires for growth. The detailed steps in an intervention programme must be flexible enough to cater for individual differences and a variety of settings.

(a) Research

Knowledge gained from research is cumulative and contradictory results serve to spur researchers on to shed further light on the issues. The present state of knowledge needs extending in many important directions.

1. We need to study child and adult behaviour, in interaction, in a variety of contexts, in order to determine what the child brings to the interaction and what effects different aspects of caregiver talk have on the child's capacity to learn.
2. We need to study the child in interaction with *different* partners, i.e. other children and adults, in order to focus on what the child does in different situations (Conti-Ramsden, 1985).
3. Further investigation is needed to determine whether parents and children have stable interactional styles which affect the way in which children learn to talk, or whether features of apparently stable style are really context or language–stage specific.
4. Research into the way in which normal children learn can be useful in extending our knowledge about the total process and key aspects of language acquisition, and may help to explain some of the difficulties experienced by developmentally and language-delayed children.
5. Studies comparing normally developing children with delayed children are frequently not productive because of the almost impossible task of matching children on any meaningful characteristics. Where these studies are carried out, they should specify the purpose and the populations used.
6. We need to study homogeneous subgroups of children to build up specific, rather than general, information about their characteristics and the effect that specific characteristics may have on their interactions and the language learning process. This would involve studying groups of children with differing degrees of developmental delay, different patterns of receptive and expressive language, different behaviour characteristics, at different stages of language acquisition, and should provide an information base to assist in the design of specific intervention procedures for specific groups of children.
7. The presentation of group results, even for more homogeneous subgroups of children, needs supplementing by analyses which attempt to account for wide individual differences in achievement. Cumulative information should assist in the appropriate individualization of intervention procedures.
8. There is a need for language-stage related research on pragmatic and discourse variables.
9. There is a need for specific research on specific aspects of social interaction: for example, strategies for resolving breakdowns in joint attention; and the effectiveness of different correction strategies on a direct–indirect dimension.
10. There is an urgent need to develop more adequate, fine-grained measures of language growth.
11. There is a need for validation of newer perspectives in language training, such as MacDonald's (1985) Ecological Communication (ECO) system

model, by means of rigorous research on its application to severely retarded populations.

12. Above all, there is a need for longitudinal research with large numbers of children. The evaluation of language-intervention efforts needs to be directed towards the accumulation of information that can be used to construct growth curves for subgroups of handicapped children. The curves might help determine which of the various approaches used in language intervention produce the greatest gains in specific groups of children. The advent of computer technology for the analysis of data from large groups of children may make this goal a reality in the foreseeable future.

(b) Intervention

1. Language can only be learned within the context of familiar and routine situations. Where the situation is unfamiliar, the child relies upon interaction with his or her caregiver to make the situation meaningful. It is important to ensure that the settings used for intervention provide the child with the necessary support to enable learning to take place.

2. Intervention requires a child-centred style of interaction, with a responsive adult providing whatever degree of conversational support is needed to allow the child to *use* his language at whatever level he has reached.

3. Handicapped children need dynamic, playful, spontaneously interactive parents and caregivers who are not deterred by unresponsive and difficult behaviour, although they may need help developing strategies to deal with this. They need an optimal social environment with constant access to caregivers able and willing to engage in contingent social interaction and the negotiation of real communicative intents.

4. Intervention may need to start earlier, as soon as a problem is identified. This may help circumvent many intractable problems faced in intervention when the child and parent have established a long-term confrontational interaction pattern. Few programmes have been specifically involved with infant interaction, although research has demonstrated the crucial nature of this period for later development. A noticeable exception to this is Bricker's prelinguistic programme (Bricker and Carlson, 1980). Many 'difficult' dyads would have benefited from assistance in establishing reciprocity in infancy, where the problem has its roots.

5. Intervention procedures must focus on both the mother and child in interaction, not on one or the other.

6. Intervention programmes cannot specify strategies which will be equally suitable for all dyads. Idiosyncratic patterns are determined by both partners and by environmental constraints. It is necessary to have a structure and a curricular approach which is infinitely modifiable in the hands of experienced interventionists.

7. The current state of knowledge is satisfactory for the development of general intervention procedures. Refinements will become possible as more detailed research is carried out on different subgroups of children, e.g. the stages involved in the development of discourse skills. What is needed is the development of specific procedures to overcome specific problems. A variety of strategies must be developed to help parents involve really difficult children in joint activities long enough for the child to learn turn-taking skills — the development of routine activities, nursery rhymes, action songs and finger plays and games which can be repeated over and over and involve the child physically. Lists of suitable activities are becoming more frequent in materials developed by various language programmes (Bochner, Price and Salamon, 1982; McConkey and Price, 1986).

8. People involved in language intervention programmes need to be wary of adopting particular research findings and implementing them in intervention before the real role played in the total communicative context and interaction is understood. Evidence that maternal usage of 'directives' has negative effects on child language growth is not conclusive, nor is the suggestion that parents have particular interaction patterns which are stable both across contexts and across time. There is a danger of 'categorizing' parents — and then 'seeing' the behaviour you expect. Pygmalion revisited!

Normally developing children have strategies which enable them to cope in an imperfect environment. They can learn by alternate pathways and can gain the attention they need to *demand* interaction. Developmentally and language-delayed children lack these skills. Failure to establish the close, reciprocal relationship which is necessary for language learning is a very real danger for many dyads. Those most at risk are very passive, non-responsive children, and the excessively difficult and hard to control. The result is frequently a total lack of synchrony and the development of confrontational interaction patterns, which leads to frustration for the adult and confusion for the language learning child. Early detection of these dyads, support for the parents and assistance in establishing early routines, can lead to effective intervention and the successful acquisition of language skills. Delayed children need optimal language learning environments and facilitation. The degree to which they need special help from caring and responsive adults is in direct relationship to the severity of their handicap.

REFERENCES

Baldwin, C.P. and Baldwin, A.L. (1973) Cognitive content of mother–child inter-action, unpublished ms., Cornell University, Ithaca, NY, USA.

Barnes, S., Gutfreund, M., Satterly, D. and Wells, G. (1983) Characteristics of adult speech which predict children's language development, *J. Child Language, 10,* 65–84.

Bates, E. (1976) *Language and Context: The Acquisition of Pragmatics,* Academic Press, New York.

Bellinger, D. (1979) Changes in the explicitness of mothers' directives as children age, *J. Child Language, 6,* 443–58.

Bellinger, D. (1980) Consistency in the pattern of change in mothers, *J. Child Language, 7,* 469–87.

Bloom, L. (1973) *One Word at a Time: The Use of Single Word Utterances before Syntax,* Mouton, The Hague.

Bochner, S. (1986) Development in the vocalisation of handicapped infants in a hospital setting, *Aust. and New Zealand J. Developmental Disabilities, 12,* 55–63.

Bochner, S. (1987) Preparation for preschool: report on a program for language-delayed 3 year olds, paper presented at Conference on Growing Up in Modern World, Centre for Child Research, University of Trondheim, Norway, June.

Bochner, S., Price, P. and Salamon, L. (1982) *Learning to Talk,* Special Education Centre, Macquarie University, Sydney.

Bochner, S., Price, P., Salamon, L. and Richardson, J. (1986) Language inter-vention in the pre-school using a parent group training model, *Aust. J. Human Communication Disorders, 14,* 55–64.

Bowerman, M. (1973) *Early Syntactic Development: A Cross-Linguistic Study with Special Reference to Finnish,* Cambridge University Press, Cambridge, Mass.

Bricker, D. (1981) Early communication: development and training, paper presented at Conference of the Australian Psychological Society, Macquarie University, Sydney, August 6–11.

Bricker, W.A. and Bricker, D.D. (1970) A program of language training for the severely language handicapped child, *Exceptional Children, 37,* 101–11.

Bricker, D. and Carlson, L. (1980) An intervention approach for communicatively handicapped infants and young children, *New Directions for Exceptional Children, 2,* pp. 33–48.

Broen, P. (1972) The verbal environment of the language learning child, *American Speech and Hearing Monographs, 17,* December (whole issue).

Bruner, J.S. (1975) The ontogenesis of speech acts, *J. Child Language, 1,* 1–19.

Buckhalt, J.A., Rutherford, R.B. and Goldberg, K.E. (1978) Verbal and non-verbal interaction of mothers with their Down's syndrome and non-retarded infants, *Am. J. Ment. Defic., 82,* 337–43.

Buium, N., Rynders, J. and Turnure, J. (1974) Early maternal linguistic environ-ment of normal and Down's syndrome language-learning children, *Am. J. Ment. Defic., 79,* 52–8.

Carlson, L. and Bricker, D. (1980) Dyadic and contingent aspects of early com-municative intervention in *Handicapped and At-risk Infants: Research and Application* (ed. D. Bricker), University Park Press, Baltimore, Md.

Chomsky, N. (1957) *Syntactic Structures,* Mouton, The Hague.

Clarke-Stewart, K. and Hevey, C. (1981) Longitudinal relations in repeated obser-vations in mother–child interaction from 1 to $2^{1}/_{2}$ years, *Developmental Psychol., 17,* 127–45.

213

Collins, R. (1986) Increasing spontaneous language through fluency in dialogue, unpublished thesis, Macquarie University, Sydney.

Conti-Ramsden, G. (1985) Mothers in dialogue with language-impaired children, *Topics in Language Disorders*, 5, 58–68.

Conti-Ramsden, G. and Friel-Patti, S. (1983) Mothers' discourse adjustments to language-impaired children and non-language-impaired children, *J. Speech Hearing Dis.*, 48, 360–7.

Conti-Ramsden, G. and Friel-Patti, S. (1984a) Mother–child dialogues and comparison of visual and language impaired children, *J. Commun. Dis.*, 17, 19–35.

Conti-Ramsden, G. and Friel-Patti, S. (1984b) Context and the characteristics of mother–child conversations, paper presented at Third International Congress for the Study of Child Language, Austin University, Austin, Texas, July 6–11.

Cross, T. (1977) Developmental aphasia, language delay, conversational derivation in *Proceedings of the 1976 Brain Impairment Conference, Neuropsychology Group*, Department of Psychology, University of Melbourne, Parkville, Victoria.

Cross, T. (1978) Mother's speech adjustments and child language learning: some methodological considerations, *Language Sciences*, 1, 1.

Cross, T. (1980) The linguistic experience of slow learners in *Advances in Child Development* (eds A.R. Nesdale *et al.*), National Conference on Child Development, University of Western Australia, Western Australia.

Cross, T. (1981) The linguistic experience of slow learners in *Advances in Child Development* (ed. A.R. Nesdale), Cambridge University Press, Cambridge, pp. 110–21.

Cunningham, C., Reuler, E., Blackwell, J. and Deck, J. (1981) Behavioural and linguistic developments in the interactions of normal and retarded children with their mothers, *Child Development*, 52, 62–70.

Dale, P. and Ingram, D. (1981) Parental influences on language development in *Child Language: An International Perspective* (eds. P. Dale and D. Ingram), University Park Press, Baltimore, Md.

Dodd, B. (1987) Development phonological disorders: processing of spoken language, ms.

Dromi, E. and Beny-Noked, S. (1984) Topic initiation and sustaining in conversations of language impaired children with their mothers, paper presented at Ninth Boston University Conference on Language Development, October.

Ellis, R. and Wells, C. (1980) Enabling factors in adult–child language discourse, *First Language*, I, 1–16.

Friel-Patti, S. (1978) Aspects of mother–child interaction as related to the remediation process in *Proceedings of a Scientific Dedication Conference Sponsored by the Boys Town Institute for Communication Disorders in Children*, Omaha, Nebr., 5–6 October.

Friel-Patti, S. and Harris, M. (1984) Language impaired children's use of play and socially directed behaviours, ms.

Furrow, D., Nelson, K. and Benedict, H. (1979) Mothers' speech to children and syntactic development: some simple relationships, *J. Child Language*, 6, 423–42.

Garcia, E. and de Haven, E. (1974) Use of operant techniques in the establishment and generalization of language: a review and analysis, *Am. J. Ment. Defic.*, 79, 169–78.

Girolametta, L. (1985) Hamen Early Language Parent Program, paper presented at Canadian Speech and Hearing Association Annual Convention, Ontario, Canada, May.

Glanzer, P.D. and Dodd, D.H. (1975) Developmental changes in the language spoken to children, paper presented at Biennial Meeting of the Society for Research in Child Development, Denver, March.

Gleitman, L.R., Newport, E.L. and Gleitman, H. (1984) The current status of the motherese hypothesis, *J. Child Language, 11*, 43–79.

Goldfield, B. (1985) The contribution of child and care-giver to individual differences in language acquisition, doctoral thesis, Harvard Graduate School of Education, Cambridge, Mass., USA.

Gunn, P., Clark, D. and Berry, P. (1980) Maternal speech during play with a Down's syndrome infant, *Mental Retardation*, February 15–18.

Gutmann, A. and Rondal, J. (1979) Verbal operants in mothers' speech to non-retarded and Down's syndrome children matched for linguistic level, *Am. J. Ment. Defic., 83*, 446–52.

Gray, B. and Ryan, B. (1971) *Programmed Conditioning for Language: Program Book*, Monterey Learning Systems, Monterey, Calif.

Halliday, M.A.K. (1976) *Learning How to Mean: Explorations in the Development of Language*, Edward Arnold, London.

Harris, M., Jones, D. and Grant, J. (1983) The non-verbal context of mothers' speech to infants, *First Language, 4*, 21–30.

Hart, B. and Risley, T. (1974) Using preschool materials to modify the language of disadvantaged children, *J. Applied Behavioural Analysis, 7*, 243–56.

Hart, B. and Risley, T.R. (1975) Incidental teaching of language in the pre-school, *J. Applied Behaviour Analysis, 8*, 411–20.

Hart, B. and Risley, T.R. (1980) In language intervention, *J. Applied Behaviour Analysis, 13*, 407–32.

Hart, B. and Rogers-Warren, A. (1978) A milieu approach to teaching language in *Language Intervention Strategies* (ed. R.L. Schiefelbusch), University Park Press, Baltimore, Md., pp. 193–236.

Hedrick, D.L., Prather, E.M. and Tobin, A.R. (1975) *Sequenced Inventory of Communication Development*, University of Seattle Press, Seattle, Wash.

Horstmeier, D.S. and MacDonald, J.D. (1975) *Ready, Set, Go: Talk to Me: Individualized Programs for Use in Therapy, Home and Classroom*, Charles E. Merrill, Columbus, Ohio.

Hubbell, R.D. (1977) On facilitating spontaneous talking in young children, *J. Speech and Learning Disorders, 42*, 216–31.

Janko, S. and Bricker, D. (1987) Language intervention with young children: current practice and future goals, *Aust. and New Zealand J. Developmental Disabilities* (forthcoming).

Jones, O. (1980) Prelinguistic communication skills in Down's syndrome and normal infants in *High-risk Infants and Children* (ed. T. Field), Academic Press, New York.

Kavanagh, R. and Jen, M. (1981) Some relationships between parental speech and children's object language development, *First Language, 2*, 103–15.

Kaye, K. and Charney, R. (1981) Conversational asymmetry between mothers and children, *J. Child Language, 8*, 35–49.

Kent, L.R. (1974) *Language Acquisition Program for the Severely Retarded*, Research Press, Champaign, Ill.

Laskey, E. and Allen, D. (1977) The effects of parent training programs on the mother's language patterns directed to her TMR child, paper presented at American Speech and Hearing Association, Chicago.

Leonard, L. (1975) Developmental considerations in the management of language disabled children, *J. Learning Disabilities, 8*, 232–7.

Lord, C. (1975) Is talking to baby more than baby talk? A longitudinal study of the modification of linguistic input to young children, paper presented at Meeting of the Society for Research in Child Development, Denver, March.

Lovaas, D.I., Berberich, J.P., Perloff, B.F. ad Schaeffer, B. (1966) Acquisition of imitative speech by schizophrenic children, *Sci.*, *151*, 705–7.

McConkey, R. (1979a) Reinstating parental involvement in the development of communication skills, *Child: Care, Health and Dev.*, *5*, 17–27.

McConkey, R. (1979b) *Putting Two Words Together*, St Michael's House, Goalstown.

McConkey, R. (1980) Implementation in the classroom of research findings on the early language development of mentally handicapped children, *First Language*, *1*, 63–77.

McConkey, R. (1981) Sharing knowledge of language with children and parents, *Br. J. Dis. Commun.*, *16*, 3–10.

McConkey, R. and Martin, H. (1984) A longitudinal study of mothers' speech to pre-verbal Down's syndrome infants, *First Language*, *5*, 41–55.

McConkey, R. and Price, P. (1986) *Let's Talk*, Souvenir Press, London.

McDonald, L. and Pein, D. (1982) Mother conversational behaviour as a function of interactional intent, *J. Child Language*, *9*, 337–58.

MacDonald, J.D. and Nickols, M. (1974) *Environmental Language Inventory Manual*, Columbus, Ohio.

MacDonald, J. (1985) Language through conversation: a model for interventions with language-delayed persons in *Teaching Functional Language* (eds. S.F. Warren and A.K. Rogers-Warren), Pro-Ed, Tex., pp. 89–122.

MacDonald, J., Blott, J., Gordon, K. Spiegel, B. and Hartmann, M. (1974) An experimental parent-assisted treatment program for pre-school language-delayed children, *J. Speech Hearing Disorders*, *39*, 395–415.

McLean, J.E. and Snyder-McLean, L.K. (1978) *A Transactional Approach to Early Language Training*, Charles E. Merrill, Columbus, Ohio.

Mahoney, G., Glover, A. and Finger, I. (1981) Relationship between language and sensorimotor development of Down syndrome and non-retarded children, *Am. J. Ment. Defic.*, *86*, 21–7.

Mahoney, G.J. and Seely, P.B. (1976) The role of the social agent in language acquisition: implications for language intervention in *International Review of Research in Mental Retardation* (ed. N.R. Ellis), Academic Press, New York, pp. 57–101.

Manolson, H. (1977) Parents as language teachers, paper presented at Annual Convention of the Canadian Speech and Hearing Association.

Marshall, N.R., Hegrenes, J.R. and Goldstein, S. (1973) Verbal interactions: mothers and their retarded children vs mothers and their non-retarded children, *Am. J. Ment. Defic.*, *77*, 415–19.

Mittler, P. (1975) Language development in the mentally handicapped: an overview in *Language Performance of Exceptional Children* (ed. R.J. Andrews), Fred and Eleanor and Schonell Educational Research Centre, University of Queensland, St Lucia.

Moerk, E.L. (1976) Processes of language teaching and training in the interactions of mother–child dyads, *Child Development*, *47*, 1064–78.

Nelson, K. (1973) Structure and strategy in learning to talk, *Monographs of the Society for Research into Child Development*, *38*, 1–2 (Serial no. 149).

Nelson, K. (1977) Facilitating children's syntax acquisition, *Developmental Psychol.*, *13*, 101–97.

Nelson, K. (1981) Individual differences in language development: implications for development and language, *Developmental Psychol.*, *17*, 170–87.

Nelson, K. and Bonvillian, J. (1978) Early language development in *Children's Language* (ed. K.E. Nelson), Gardener Press, New York, pp. 467–556.

Newport, E.L., Gleitman, L.R. and Gleitman, H. (1977) "Mother, I'd rather do it myself." Some effects and non-effects of maternal speech style in *Talking to*

Children: Language Input and Acquisition (eds. C.E. Snow and C.A. Ferguson), Cambridge University Press, Cambridge, pp. 109–19.

Olsen-Fulero, L. (1982) Style and stability in mother conversational behaviour: a study of individual differences, *J. Child Language*, 9, 543–64.

Petersen, G. and Sherrod, K. (1982) Relationship of maternal language to language development and language delay of children, *Am. J. Ment. Defic.*, 86, 391–8.

Phillips, J.R. (1973) Formal characteristics of speech which mothers address to their children, *Child Development*, 44, 182–5.

Price, P. (1984) A study of mother–child verbal interaction strategies with mothers of young developmentally delayed children in *Perspectives and Progress in Mental Retardation* (ed. J.M. Berg), University Park Press, Baltimore, Md., Vol. 1, pp. 189–200.

Price, P. and Bochner, S. (1984) Report of an early environmental language intervention program, *Aust. and New Zealand J. Developmental Disabilities*, 10, 217–28.

Rondal, J. (1977) Maternal speech in normal and Down's syndrome children in *Research into Practice in Mental Retardation. Vol. 2, Education and Training* (ed. P. Mittler), University Park Press, Baltimore, Md., pp. 239–44.

Rondal, J. (1978) Patterns of correlations for various language measures in mother–child interactions for normal and Down's syndrome children, *Language and Speech*, 21, 3.

Schaffer, H.R. (ed.) (1977) *Studies in Mother–Infant Interaction*, Academic Press, London.

Skinner, B.L. (1957) *Verbal Behaviour*, Appleton-Century-Crofts, New York.

Snow, C. (1972) Mothers' speech to children learning language, *Child Development*, 43, 549–65.

Snow, C.E. (1977) The development of conversation between mothers and babies, *J. Child Language*, 4, 1–22.

Snow, C., Perlman, R. and Nathan, D. (1985) *Why Routines are Different: Toward a Multiple-Factors Model of the Relation between Input and Language Acquisition*, Harvard University Press, Cambridge, Mass.

Snyder, L. and McLean, J. (1976) Deficient acquisition strategies: a proposed conceptual framework for analyzing severe language deficiency, *Am. J. Ment. Defic.*, 81, 338–49.

Stremel, K. and Waryas, C. (1974) A behavioural-psycholinguistic approach to language training in *Developing Systematic Procedures for Training Children's Language* (ed. L. McReynolds), ASHA Monograph No. 18.

Trevarthan, C. (1974) Conversations with a 2 month old baby, *Eng. New Sci.*

Weistuch, L. and Lewis, M. (1985a) The language interaction intervention project, *Analysis and Intervention in Developmental Disabilities*, 5, 97–106.

Weistuch, L. and Lewis, M. (1985b) The modifiability of maternal language use and its effects on delayed child language acquisition, Department of Pediatrics, Rutgers Medical School, New Brunswick.

Wells, G. (1980) Adjustments in adult–child conversation: some effects of interaction in *Language* (eds. H. Giles, P. Robinson and P. Smith), Pergamon, Oxford, pp. 41–8.

Wells, G. (1981) *Learning through Interaction*, Cambridge University Press, London.

Wells, G. (1985) *Language Development in the Pre-school Years*, Cambridge University Press, Cambridge.

Wells, C.G. and Robinson, W.P. (1982) The role of adult speech in language development in *Advances in the Social Psychology of Language* (eds. C. Fraser and K. Scherer), Cambridge University Press, Cambridge, pp. 11–76.

217

9

Parent–Child Interaction in Mental Handicap: An Evaluation

Gina Conti-Ramsden

This chapter aims to argue that a conceptual and methodological shift in the study of parent–child interaction with mentally handicapped children is necessary. The typical approach in this area of research in the last twenty years has been mainly descriptive, involving the elementary analyses of the characteristics of each of the partners involved in the dyad. This basic approach has provided a large data-base, which up to date has not been interpreted cohesively. As Price (in Chapter 8 in this volume) points out in her review, research in parent–child interaction with mentally handicapped children has proved contradictory and inconclusive. In this chapter it is suggested that the discrepancies in the literature can be, at least, partly resolved if we extend our conceptual and methodological perspective.

9.1 AN OVERVIEW OF THE ISSUES

Initial concern with the language learning process of mentally handicapped children led researchers to make comparisons between the language development of both mentally handicapped and non-handicapped individuals. Three major methodological matching methods were used in these studies. Some investigators have compared mentally handicapped children with non-handicapped children of the same chronological age (CA) (Kogan, Wimberg and Bobbitt, 1969; Marshall, Hegrenes and Goldstein, 1973; Stoneman, Brody and Abbott, 1983; Leifer and Lewis, 1984); some researchers have compared mentally handicapped children with non-handicapped children of the same mental age (MA) (Lyle, 1961; Terdal, Jackson and Garner, 1976; Jones, 1977; Mahoney, Glover and Finger, 1981; Eheart, 1982; Koenig and Mervis, 1984); and more recently, investigators have also compared mentally handicapped children to non-handicapped children of the same language level as measured by mean length of utterance (MLU) (Ryan, 1975; Rondal, 1977; Gutmann and Rondal, 1979; Petersen and Sherrod, 1982; Mervis, 1984).

Until recently, the interpretation on these three areas were as follows: studies in which children were matched for chronological age *always* indicated differences between mentally handicapped and non-handicapped children's language performance as well as that of their parents. Among the differences, researchers have found that mentally handicapped children are more unintelligible and initiate less (Kogan, Wimberg and Bobbitt, 1969; Marshall, Hegrenes and Goldstein, 1973), while their parents tend to speak faster, with shorter utterances and be more directive (Buium, Rynders and Turnure 1973; Marshall, Hegrenes and Goldstein, 1973). When children have been matched for MA, similar findings of difference in the language performance of the mentally handicapped children and their parents have been found as those described for the CA matches. Thus, Jones (1977, 1979, 1980) found mentally handicapped children initiated less and Terdal, Jackson and Garner (1976) found they responded less than non-handicapped children of the same mental age. Parents of mentally handicapped children matched for MA with non-handicapped children have also been found deficient. They are usually more dominant in conversation (Eheart, 1982) and provide less opportunities for language learning (Koenig and Mervis, 1984) than parents of non-handicapped children do. Finally, studies with language-stage matching have been interpreted differently. It has been suggested that when mentally handicapped children are matched to non-handicapped children of the same language stage, the differences mentioned above disappear. That is, mentally handicapped children's linguistic abilities are similar to those of non-handicapped children (Rondal, 1978) and parents of mentally handicapped children and non-handicapped children are no longer different (Rondal, 1977).

9.2 THE ISSUES REVISITED

A closer look at the literature in combination with more recent findings reveals that the picture is not as black and white as that painted above. Indeed it appears that there is little homogeneity of results in any of the three areas described: CA matching, MA matching and language-stage matching. Recall that it has been said that mentally handicapped children and their parents are different to their CA peers. A detailed look at such studies indicates that this interpretation may be being overgeneralized. Stoneman, Brody and Abbott (1983), for example, conclude in their study of 16 mothers, fathers and their 4- to 7-year-old mentally handicapped and non-handicapped children that parents of children with Down's syndrome interact differently. They suggest parents of handicapped children assume more dominant manager, teacher and helper roles. This conclusion is based on comparing these two sets of parents on 16 variables, six of which turn out to be significantly different while ten of them do not. That is, in ten variables parents of mentally handicapped children were *no different* than parents of their CA peers. This other side of the coin is never discussed in Stoneman, Brody and Abbott (1983), but it does need to be in order to begin to understand the complexity of the nature of the phenomenon we are observing.

Similarly, Leifer and Lewis (1984) rightly point out that investigations with MA-matching and MLU-matching have not been as clear-cut as previously thought. In these two areas conflicting findings have been reported. Unlike previous interpretations, MA-matching does not always lead to inferior performance in part of the mentally handicapped individuals and their parents. O'Connor and Hermlin (1963), for example, reported no differences in the verbal abilities (in terms of frequency of nouns, verbs and descriptive adjectives) of mentally handicapped children compared to those of their MA-matches. In the same vein, Kamhi and Johnston (1982) found that mentally handicapped children and MA-control children used similar syntactic constructions and expressed the same propositional relations, and both groups had little difficulty with grammatical morphemes. Furthermore, Spreen (1965) found that mentally handicapped children had *superior* performance on vocabulary measures than their MA controls. Similarly, Fischer (1987) found that mothers of Down's syndrome children responded more contingently than mothers of non-handicapped MA-matched children. Still on the same theme but not in the area of language, Kamhi and Johnston (1982) found superior abilities in mentally handicapped children vs MA controls in a mental-rotation Piagetian task.

The use of language stage as defined by MLU to compare mentally handicapped and non-handicapped individuals also has yielded discrepant results. Although Rondal (1977) argued strongly for similarities between parent–child dyads of mentally handicapped children and non-handicapped children of the same language stage, as early as 1978 he found two consistent differences between mentally handicapped children and their MLU matches (Rondal, 1978). First, mentally handicapped children had less advanced phonological skills, and secondly, mentally handicapped children had more advanced vocabulary skills than did non-handicapped children of the same linguistic level. In the same vein, Petersen and Sherrod (1982) found that mothers of Down's syndrome children used more irrelevant language than mothers of non-handicapped children of the same MLU. Much like CA matching and MA matching, we can find in MLU matching inferior performance, similar performance and superior performance by mentally handicapped children vs their controls.

9.3 THREE WAYS FORWARD

How can we make sense of the above data-base? Investigators have attempted to explain conflicting findings in terms of the methodologies used (Rondal, 1977) (see also Price, in Chapter 8 in this volume). Thus comparing mentally handicapped children to different sets of control children (MA, CA, MLU) naturally yields different results which are not comparable. This indeed is a methodological problem, but one that we would like to call a narrow methodological problem. It is narrow because it concerns itself with the specific tools used for comparison and not with the nature of the phenomenon under investigation. As argued above, the discrepant findings extend not just across methodologies, but within methodologies. That is, we find apparently contradictory results when we look only at studies which compare mentally handicapped children with MA matches. And we find the same within the CA matches and within the MLU matches literature. Once there are discrepancies in studies within similar methodologies as well as across methodologies, we need to evaluate the conceptual framework we are using in approaching the problem as well as its resulting methodology.

The first problem in our approach to parent–child communicative interaction with mentally handicapped children has been the erroneous assumption that the communicative abilities of mentally retarded individuals are a homogeneous, related set of skills and thus develop synchronously in each individual child. Much like Kamhi and Masterson (in Chapter 4 in this volume), we argue that asynchronies in communicative development are more the rule than the exception in non-handicapped children, so why should it be any different for the mentally retarded? Blank, Gessner and Esposito (1979) and Conti-Ramsden and Friel-Patti (1984) have found asynchronies in other atypical populations, so there is little basis for the assumption that mentally handicapped individuals should be different. Once we establish that social-communicative skills are *not* a homogeneous, interrelated set of skills in the mentally retarded, then we find that the discrepant findings of investigations may, at least in part, be explained by the highly diverse sets of linguistic variables used by different researchers. Thus, with this new assumption, it is not contradictory to say that mentally handicapped children are inferior, similar and superior to non-handicapped children of the same MA — if by inferior we are talking about their phonology, if by similar we are talking about their basic syntax and if by superior we are referring to their vocabulary skills. Methodologically, this reconceptualization has the effect of underlining the importance of the variables used in investigations and cautioning generalizations of the results beyond the scope of those variables.

A second problem in our approach to parent–child communicative interaction is our disregard for individual differences. Once again, research with non-handicapped children has revealed the individuality of children, the different interacting styles parents and children manage to mesh together as well as the enormous range of variables that may impinge on that interaction (Lieven, 1984) (see also Kamhi and Masterson in Chapter 4 of this volume). In the area of mental handicap we do not emphasize enough the range of behaviours our subjects exhibit, nor individual differences. We are much more interested in group behaviours and group results. In many of the studies described above some of the parent–child dyads with mentally handicapped children actually behaved similarly to the non-handicapped dyads and some were inferior, while others were superior. Once again, this reconceptualization does not make these findings contradictory. We accept there are vast individual differences and different types of interactive styles in parents and their children. Thus some parent–child dyads with certain characteristics may find an optimal 'match' between their interactive styles and so exhibit dyadic behaviours which are similar or superior to those of non-handicapped parent–child dyads. Other parent–child dyads with certain characteristics may find less optimal matches, thus there will be differing degrees of problems in the parent–child communicative interaction ranging from mild to complete non-interaction and rejection. Methodologically, then, we cannot generalize and talk about parent–child dyads with handicapped children. We need to begin to talk about *specific* parent–child dyads, with the parent having specific characteristics and the child having specific characteristics and us explaining how these characteristics interact in order to produce the observable behaviours under investigation (for a good example of such an attempt see Cardoso-Martins and Mervis, 1985; Fischer, 1987). Among the key child characteristics to consider are: aetiology, institutionalization, severity of retardation, age, language learning style, temperament and motivation, among others. And among the key parent characteristics to consider are: acceptance of handicap, the believed severity of retardation, believed child's linguistic ability, personality, motivation, family constitution and degree of support, among others. The transactional model, suggested in the late 1970s (Sameroff and Chandler, 1975; McLean and Snyder-McLean, 1978), that the communicative behaviours of any dyad result from the interactive process between the two members of that dyad needs to be taken to its fullest form. Historically we have been swayed from an emphasis on the problems within the child to an emphasis on what the environment does to the child. It is time that conceptually and methodologically we attempt to reach an equilibrium. Child and environment are equally involved in the developmental process of the mentally handicapped child.

Lastly, there is the problem of using the non-handicapped, normal population as the model parent–child dyads with mentally handicapped children should aim for. The three methodologies described above, CA matching, MA matching and MLU matching, all have as their main motivation to compare mentally handicapped individuals with some sort of norm. The fact that three methodologies arose in this attempt points to the complexity of this task. In fact comparability may be impossible in communicative interaction as the very reciprocal nature of this phenomenon (the mutual regulation of behaviours of the interactants) defines as different the interaction between mentally handicapped children and their parents and non-handicapped parent–child dyads (see Conti-Ramsden, 1985, for similar argument with language-impaired parent–child dyads). From this fact, some researchers have argued particularly with respect to intervention, that normal, adequate linguistic interaction may not be enough to help mentally retarded children learn language more successfully. That is, to apply the normal model may be insufficient, and indeed Cheseldine and McConkey (1979) and McConachie and Mitchell (1985) advocate non-normal modes of intervention with mentally handicapped parent–child dyads. This type of research should be less rare than it is now. Once we change our erroneous assumption that mentally handicapped children need to be compared with some sort of norm, we have a wider scope conceptually and methodologically. We cannot only have comparative studies, but investigations which remain within the population of mentally handicapped children, identifying and comparing different interactional styles in parent–child dyads, deriving histories of interaction after following a variety of mentally handicapped parent–child dyads over time, identifying successful vs non-successful dyads in terms of communicative interaction, planning intervention based on the information gathered from the handicapped population, and so on. Parents and their mentally handicapped children have long histories of shared successes and failures in communication, and we are yet to tap this source of information more fully.

REFERENCES

Blank, M., Gessner, M. and Esposito, A. (1979) Language without communication: a case study, *J. Ch. Lang.*, *6*, 329–52.

Buium, N., Rynders, J. and Turnure, J. (1973) Early maternal linguistic environment of normal and nonnormal language-learning children, *Proceedings of the Eighty-first Annual Convention of the American Psychological Association*, 79–80.

Cardoso-Martins, C. and Mervis, C.B. (1985) Maternal speech to prelinguistic children with Down syndrome, *Am. J. Ment. Defic.*, *89*, 451–8.

Cheseldine, S. and McConkey, R. (1979) Parental speech to young Down's syndrome children: an intervention study, *Am. J. Ment. Defic.*, *83*, 612–20.

Conti-Ramsden, G. (1985) Mothers in dialogue with language impaired children, *Topics Lang. Dis.*, *5*, 58–68.

Conti-Ramsden, G. and Friel-Patti, S. (1984) Mother–child dialogues: a comparison of normal and language impaired children, *J. Comm. Dis.*, *17*, 19–35.

Eheart, B.K. (1982) Mother–child interactions with nonretarded and mentally retarded preschoolers, *Am. J. Ment. Defic.*, *87*, 20–5.

Fischer, M.A. (1987) Mother–child interactions with preverbal children with Down syndrome, *J. Sp. Hr. Dis.*, *52*, 179–90.

Gutmann, A.J. and Rondal. J.A. (1979) Verbal operants in mothers' speech to nonretarded and Down's syndrome children matched for linguistic level, *Am. J. Ment. Defic.*, *83*, 446–52.

Jones, O.H.M. (1977) Mother–child communication with prelinguistic Down's syndrome and normal infants in *Studies in Mother–Infant Interaction* (ed. H.R. Schaffer), Academic Press, New York, pp. 379–401.

Jones, O.H.M. (1979) A comparative study of mother–child communication with Down's syndrome and normal infants in *The First Year of Life: Psychological and Medical Implications of Early Experience* (ed. H.R. Schaffer and J. Dunn), Wiley, New York, pp. 175–95.

Jones, O.H.M. (1980) Prelinguistic communication skills in Down's syndrome and normal infants in *High-Risk Infants and Children: Adult and Peer Interaction* (ed. T.M. Field), Academic Press, New York, pp. 205–25.

Kamhi, A. and Johnston, J. (1982) Toward an understanding of retarded children's linguistic deficiencies, *J. Sp. Hr. Res.*, *25*, 435–45.

Koenig, M.A. and Mervis, C.B. (1984) Interactive basis of severely handicapped and normal children's acquisition of referential language, *J. Sp. Hr. Res.*, *27*, 534–42.

Kogan, K., Wimberg, H. and Bobbitt, R. (1969) Analysis of mother–child interaction in young mentally retardates, *Child Devel.*, *40*, 799–812.

Leifer, J.S. and Lewis, M. (1984) Acquisition of conversational response skills by young Down syndrome and nonretarded young children, *Am. J. Ment. Defic.*, *88*, 610–18.

Lieven, E.V.M. (1984) Interaction style and children's language learning, *Topics Lang. Dis.*, *4*, 15–23.

Lyle, J.G. (1961) Comparison of the language of normal and imbecile children, *J. Ment. Defic. Res.*, *5*, 40–50.

McConachie, H. and Mitchell, D.R. (1985) Parents teaching their young mentally handicapped children, *J. Child Pychol. Psychiat.*, *26*, 389–405.

McLean, J. and Snyder-McLean, L. (1978) *A Transactional Approach to Early Language Training*, Charles E. Merrill, Columbus, Ohio.

Mahoney, G., Glover, A. and Finger, I. (1981) Relationship between language and sensorimotor development of Down syndrome and nonretarded children, *Am. J. Ment. Defic.*, *86*, 21–7.

Marshall, N., Hegrenes, J. and Goldstein, S. (1973) Verbal interactions: mothers and their retarded children versus mothers and their nonretarded children, *Am. J. Ment. Defic.*, *77*, 415–19.

Mervis, C.B. (1984) Early lexical development: the contributions of mother and child in *Origins of Cognitive Skills* (ed. C. Sophian), Lawrence Erlbaum, Hillsdale, NJ, pp. 339–70.

O'Connor, N. and Hermelin, B. (1963) *Speech and Thought in Severe Subnormality*, Macmillan, New York.

Petersen, G.A. and Sherrod, K.B. (1982) Relationship of maternal language to language development and language delay of children, *Am. J. Ment. Defic.*, *86*, 391–8.

Rondal, J.A. (1977) Maternal speech to normal and Down's syndrome children matched for mean length of utterance in *Quality of Life in Severely and*

Profoundly Mentally Retarded People: Research Foundations for Improvement (ed. E. Meyers), American Association of Mental Deficiency, Washington, DC. pp. 193–265.

Rondal, J.A. (1978) Developmental sentence procedure and the delay–difference question in language development of Down's syndrome children, *Ment. Retard.*, *16*, 169–171.

Ryan, J. (1975) Mental subnormality and language development in *Foundations of Language Development: A Multidisciplinary Approach* (eds. E.H. Lenneberg and E. Lenneberg), Academic Press, London. pp. 269–77.

Sameroff, A. and Chandler, M. (1975) Reproductive risk and the continuum of caretaking causality in *Review of Child Development Research* (eds. L. Horowitz, M. Hetherington, S. Scarr-Salapatek and G. Siegel), Academic Press, New York, pp. 269–77.

Spreen, O. (1965) Language functions in mental retardation: A review of language development, types of retardation and intelligence, *Am. J. Ment. Defic.*, *69*, 482–94.

Stoneman, Z., Brody, G.H. and Abbott, D. (1983) In-home observations of young Down syndrome children with their mothers and fathers, *Am. J. Ment. Defic.*, *87*, 591–600.

Terdal, L., Jackson, R. and Garner, A. (1976) Mother–child interactions: a comparison between normal and developmentally delayed groups in *Behavior Modification and Families* (eds. E. Mash, L. Hamerlynch and L. Handy), Brunner/Mazel, New York, pp. 243–64.

PART IV:

Communication in the Mentally Handicapped Adult Population

Chapters 10-12 in the last part of this book all deal with the characteristics of verbal interactions which involve adult mentally handicapped individuals. The chapters cover between them communications of mentally handicapped individuals who are well-adjusted or with behaviour problems, and of their non-handicapped partners. The focus is on documenting the problems which arise in interactions and on their analysis. All the chapters, however, provide conceptual bases and examples relevant to intervention and thus have implications for it. Keith Kernan and Sharon Sabsay, in Chapter 10, approach the communicative problems from the point of view of mildly mentally handicapped peoples' ability to design adequately their contributions to conversations, and to express their communicative aims effectively, so that they 'fit' into conversations. Using a broadly Gricean framework, they show that many mentally handicapped individuals have problems in abiding by maxims of conversation and producing coherent and relevant contributions to conversations, and that this may mark them as 'handicapped' in the eyes of the public. Paradoxically some communicative problems in fact seem to be a consequence of mentally handicapped individuals' attempts to present an impression of competence. Douglass Price-Williams, in Chapter 11, focuses on the communication of emotions and outlines some of the problems he as a clinician encounters when interviewing mentally handicapped people. Price-Williams's focus is on the problems with interpreting their imaginative contributions to interviews and he also outlines the deliberate use of imagination in clinical interviews, trying to reach withdrawn individuals. Ivan Leudar, in Chapter 12, complements Kernan and Sabsay's focus on individuals and argues that communicative problems stem not only from the lack of ability to design messages well, but also from the nature of communicative backgrounds available to mentally handicapped people and from the dialectics of the two. The chapter shows that the environments against which mentally handicapped people communicate do not provide the resource normally available to the average speakers and indicates systematic distortions especially for the mentally handicapped individuals with behaviour problems.

10

Communication in Social Interactions: Aspects of an Ethnography of Communication of Mildly Mentally Handicapped Adults

Keith T. Kernan and Sharon Sabsay

10.1 INTRODUCTION

For many decades mentally handicapped individuals in western culture were institutionalized and segregated from the rest of society. Today, as the result of changing social policies, the majority once again live in the community, attempting to manage the give-and-take of everyday inter-actions. In the course of their daily lives many mentally retarded individ-uals shop, pay bills, work, socialize with friends and chat with strangers, get their stereos repaired and try to untangle bureaucratic snarls. Yet, for the most part, they continue to be studied solely as clinical entities, not as persons immersed in the stream of social life. This approach has led not only to a lack of appreciation for the complexity of their lives and concerns, but also to an underestimation and incomplete understanding of their intel-lectual, social and communicative skills and the exact nature of their inter-actional difficulties.

In this chapter we report on research on the communicative behaviour of mildly mentally retarded people residing in the community, research we have conducted with members of this population for a number of years. Our primary approach is ethnographic, our principal methodology partici-pant observation. Participant observation calls for an investigator to enter as fully and naturally as possible into the lives of the people being studied, listening to what they say in the course of everyday life, observing what they do, asking questions if and when appropriate and participating in routine or special activities when that is acceptable. In conducting our research, then, we and our research assistants have observed the mentally retarded adults we study in all the settings and situations in which they normally find themselves in the course of their daily lives, visiting them in their homes and on their jobs, accompanying them on shopping trips and to the bowling-alley, eating with them in their homes and in restaurants and joining them on visits to parents, doctors and social workers. In short, we have attempted to observe their lives as they are lived in ordinary circumstances and, in particular, to observe how they manage communicative interactions.

Like 75–85% of those labelled mentally retarded, the adults with whom we work are relatively mildly handicapped, with IQs ranging from about 50 to 70. Like members of any other group defined solely by psychometric scores, mildly mentally retarded individuals comprise a heterogeneous group. Not all are intellectually or linguistically impaired to the same degree, nor in the same areas: cognitive and linguistic profiles vary as they would in a population defined by any other level of intelligence. So, too, do personalities and circumstances. Some of the members of the cohort we work with live with their parents or siblings, others in small family care or 'group' homes with a care-provider and six or seven other residents, and still others on their own — alone, with a roommate or with a spouse. Some have jobs in competitive employment situations and some work in sheltered workshops, and others are unemployed and depend on government assistance to the disabled. They interact to greater or lesser extent with the community at large and perform as best they can the communicative tasks required of the interactions in which they participate. In this chapter we illustrate the communicative impediments that are experienced by mildly mentally retarded people as they negotiate interactions, the ways in which they and their interlocutors perceive and deal with these difficulties, and the ways they deal with the risk or stigma of being perceived as incompetent. In so doing, we hope to capture and communicate something of the flavour of what the linguistic lives of mildly mentally retarded people are like.

10.2 COMMUNICATIVE PROBLEMS

Mentally handicapped individuals may be labelled as such by professionals on the basis of IQ scores or adaptive behaviour ratings, but many are recognized as 'retarded' or, at least, 'unusual' by the ordinary people they come into contact with because of the way they talk. In fact one of the first things one is likely to notice about a retarded person is something unusual about the way he or she speaks. The impression that there is something 'different' about the person one is talking to may be fostered by any number of linguistic problems or inappropriate communicative behaviours. It might be something in the quality of voice, a proclivity for malapropisms, incorrect grammar or inconsistent use of tenses. It might be the fact that someone speaks just a bit more loudly than is appropriate in a public place, makes irrelevant comments, gives intimate details of his or her life to a total stranger or tells a pointless story that is difficult to follow. Such problems may be slight and subtle, but they are usually evident and persistent. Many of the individuals with whom we have worked in fact have problems which are not subtle, but readily apparent and create distress in communicative interactions.

There are two broad areas which seem particularly problematic for mildly retarded individuals in their daily interactions: the communication of intended meaning, particularly in connected discourse, and the appropriate conduct of social interaction.

10.3 COMMUNICATING INTENDED MEANING

Mildly retarded speakers evince relatively few of the articulatory, grammatical and lexical deficits which are so frequently exhibited by individuals with more severe degrees of retardation. Much of their difficulty in communicative interactions stems rather from their inability to provide, organize and 'package' (Chafe, 1976) or 'design' (Sabsay and Kernan, 1983) information adequately in extended discourse. Many of the mildly retarded individuals we work with have a tendency to provide information piecemeal, to omit necessary information, to include irrelevant or unnecessary details, to voice incomplete thoughts and to run unconnected thoughts together in the same utterance, with the result that their interlocutors find their accounts, explanations and descriptions difficult to understand.

Meaning of course does not reside simply in the utterances that a speaker produces. Rather meaning results when hearers relate what a speaker says to information they already have and interpret it in terms of that information (e.g. Clark and Haviland, 1974; Grice, 1975; Halliday and Hasan, 1976; Sperber and Wilson, 1987). In order to communicate effectively, then, speakers must judge what information their hearers already have and what other information they need in order to be able to understand a particular utterance as intended, and then, by what they say and how they say it, provide their hearers with the needed information. In order for what they are saying to be understood, for example, speakers must indicate how what they are saying is related to the ongoing conversation (e.g. Labov and Waletzky, 1967; Kernan, 1977). When what they are saying is *not* related to the ongoing conversation, they must indicate that in some way as well. Speakers must make sure that, in so far as it is necessary to their understanding of what is being said, their listeners can identify the individuals, events and objects mentioned in the discourse, their relationships to one another, and the like (Labov and Waletzky, 1967). Speakers must also make sure that their listeners understand how the various pieces of information given in the discourse itself are related to one another and how they relate to information already available from other sources — shared background information, general cultural knowledge, the non-linguistic context of the discourse, and so on (Halliday and

Hasan, 1976). Finally, speakers must provide their hearers with only the information which is relevant to an understanding of their intended meaning and none which is irrelevant and therefore misleading (Grice, 1975). When, like many of the individuals with whom we work, speakers fail to give their hearers these types of information, or give their hearers more information than they need, their meaning, their communicative intention, is understood only with difficulty, if at all.

(a) Problems

Donald's speech epitomizes the communicative problems that can create distress in communicative interactions with retarded speakers. It is Donald's lack of ability to express himself that gives him away as being retarded, just about from the first sentence he utters. At first, listeners may think they don't understand what he is saying or that perhaps they didn't hear it right. But it is not long before they realize that he is simply not making sense. He changes topic in mid-sentence, says things that are not at all related and refers to people as 'he' or 'she' without identifying them. He has a tendency to give information that is irrelevant to his listeners' concerns or the immediate point of the conversation, and it is frustrating trying to get any information out of him because often his responses have very little to do with the questions asked of him. Donald is not aware of the confusion he causes, nor is he very much aware of other people at all.

Within the first few minutes of a researcher's initial visit, for example, Donald announced to her that he and his wife were being thrown out of their apartment. When she inquired as to the reason, Donald replied,

> Well, a couple reasons. They didn't — Number one, they didn't fumigate or anything the building. They go, 'That's a brand new door there'. And they say — the guy in one-oh-two smashed the other door.

Rather than telling her the grounds for the eviction, although that certainly seemed at first where he was heading, Donald began to relate pieces of two different stories. As the researcher later understood it, one apparently concerned one of several incidents leading up to the eviction on the grounds that Donald and his wife were causing trouble and creating too much noise in the buildings, an incident in which a neighbour had come to their apartment late at night to complain about the noise they were making and, according to Donald, broke the door. But he began by referring to his unsuccessful attempts to get his landlady to exterminate the cockroaches in their apartment, possibly as a countermeasure to fight the eviction.

Trying to make sense out of what Donald says can be exceedingly difficult because, as with other questions, he doesn't answer those aimed at eliciting necessary clarifying information. For example, confused by Donald's 'explanation' of why they were being evicted, the researcher asked, 'But why are they throwing *you* out then?' Donald replied,

Because a the *noise.* 'N — An' it's — first of all it's from ten to ten. It's like cooperation up here. So then I go to see a attorney yesterday. About it and ... the hassle that they be giving me ever since.

Often the only way to make sense out of what Donald says is to listen through all his various complaints, explanations and digressions and attempt to put all the pertinent information together into a coherent understanding. But that is like trying to put together a jigsaw puzzle with some of the pieces missing.

At the other end of the continuum from Donald is Carl, whose expressiveness, knowledge, confidence and success in the non-retarded world make him unique in our cohort. He has something to say on almost every subject. He is impressively articulate and speaks with a great deal of conviction, always trying to drive home his point. He has an interesting, argumentative style and uses numerous examples, metaphors and analogies to illustrate what he is saying. Superficially it is an effective style, but gradually one becomes aware that it is misleading. Although one doesn't necessarily notice while he is speaking, there are incomplete thoughts and contradictions in what Carl says: when one focuses on exactly what he is saying and tries to understand what his final point is, it becomes elusive and quite unclear.

For example, Carl often uses the rhetorical device of introducing statements with something like: 'There are two reasons why X. First of all because of A, and second of all because of B.' At first, this seems effective and organized, but when one listens closely, one realizes that the two different reasons have absolutely nothing to do with each other or that the second is a rewording of the first one. For instance, one day near Christmas Carl and his wife were discussing buying gifts and Carl said that he goes by the lesson he learned from his mother: 'There are two things not to do at Christmas time: not to spend too much and watch your spending.' Using the same formula, Carl attributed his inability to read to: 'One, it's my eyes. Two, my mind can't confersate.'

He likened the first election of Ronald Reagan to the US Presidency to the purchase of an automobile:

If you have an older car, you have to decide whether to put more money into it or to put the money into buying a new car. It's the same thing. Actually, people are buying Reagan to do a good job. If he screws up, you put a new guy in.

This argument makes reasonable sense and could be something one might hear in the neighbourhood bar. One has the feeling that Carl is repeating something he has heard from one of his non-retarded acquaintances but has left out a few phrases that would have given it a bit more coherence.

Carl hits his more usual stride in the following discussion of the campaign for the election, mentioned above. He said he didn't care who won, but he knew two weeks before the election that Reagan would win because:

> Just of the way Carter went along with what he was doing and the way Reagan came along and stood up in front of the people and told them he was going to do everything. I watched a bit of the 'bate with Carter. No, not Carter had it, but Reagan and George Bush had it. And you know that when Carter was standing there telling you something he was going to try his best to do it. But when Carter didn't want to compete with those two, then you know he's hiding something.

This explanation of how Carl knew that Reagan would win the election with its contradictions and inconsistencies is confusing — and indeed confused the researcher to whom it was told. In an attempt to make it clearer, Carl attempted to set up an analogous situation. 'If there was a whole line of white people, would you discriminate and let a black person take cuts?' he asked. The researcher said she wouldn't let anyone take cuts. 'No', Carl rejoined, 'if it was a 3-year-old kid and there was all adults, would you let a little kid at 3 years old get in line, black, take cuts?' The researcher hedged, 'It depends'. Unsatisfied, Carl insisted, 'Answer the question. Don't give me "It depends".' The researcher conceded, 'Well, if the person had a good reason to cut into the line, I'd let him in'. Exasperated, Carl asserted, 'You're not following my point' — the point apparently being that Carter discriminated against John Anderson (not George Bush) by not agreeing to debate with him, even though he is white.

At other times, however, when he uses examples and analogies to clarify a point, he does so quite well. For example, he likened the Argentine invasion of the Falkland Islands to a stranger coming into one's house and claiming it as his. Whether he invented this analogy or simply repeated something he had heard, he used it appropriately. On another occasion when he was talking about how his parents constantly pointed out any errors he made and criticized him for them, he equated the overall feeling to that feeling one might have when 'you're not sure if there's a cop behind a tree watching you jaywalking'. His point of feeling that his parents are always peering over his shoulder while he is being incompetent is well made. Carl works hard at being informative and in being thought right in his opinions, two attributes that help to define his worth and which, presumably, he considers to exhibit intellectual and communicative competence.

Kathy falls somewhere between Donald's incoherence and obliviousness and Carl's sometime eloquence. She has a tendency to make apparently unconnected leaps from one topic to another. While telling a researcher about her brother counselling her and her boyfriend about marriage, for example, Kathy said, 'These places would be too expensive for us'. It took a moment's reflection for the researcher to realize that Kathy had made a leap from the topic of getting married to the related topic of where they would live if they did, but she did not make the connection explicit. Similarly, Kathy will run thoughts together in the same sentences, failing to give her hearer enough information to make the connection between them obvious. For instance, when she was asked how her cold was, she replied, 'Fine, 'cause he sent me home a couple of weeks ago with a 101 temperature'. The researcher commented in her fieldnotes: 'I think she was telling me how bad the cold had been previously, causing her supervisor to send her home with a high temperature, and that now she was relatively "fine".' In these and many other instances, it was only the researcher's familiarity with Kathy, her circumstances, and the people in her life which enabled her tentatively to identify inadequately specified referents like 'these places' — the condominium complex where Kathy and her parents live — or 'he' — her supervisor at work — and to construct interpretations for Kathy's utterances.

On another occasion, asked about the possibility of layoffs at the school where she works part-time as a teacher's aide, a possibility she had been worrying about for some time, Kathy replied, 'They're doing it between an 8-hour and a 4-hour per- ... teacher though'. Asked for clarification, she did somewhat better: 'They were talking about either letting go an 8-hour or a 4-hour person, though, the other day.' In her latter response, Kathy clarified that what 'they' — presumably the administrators at the school — were doing was 'talking about letting go' either a part-time or a full-time teacher. However, the repeated 'though' suggests that there is even more she has not communicated. The occurrence of such a cohesive device, when used appropriately, indicates that the sentence stands in a particular semantic relationship — in this case an adversative conjunctive relationship — to some preceding part of the discourse and is to be interpreted in the light of that presupposed information (Halliday and Hasan, 1976). However, here there is no such presupposed information. Kathy may, as many others in the cohort are wont to do, simply have used the conjunction in disregard of its semantic function, or she may have actually intended to convey something like, 'They haven't decided anything definitely yet, *but* the other day they were talking about either letting go an 8-hour person or a 4-hour person', but again, she did not manage to do so adequately (see also Sabsay and Kernan, 1983).

Kathy is as likely to give too much information as too little. She has a roundabout way of answering questions which makes her seem at first not to be answering them at all. She gives extraneous information before eventually giving the desired answer and one cannot be sure until that point that she has understood the question and is actually answering it. For example, when she was explaining about having some ingrown toenails removed, the researcher asked her if the doctor cut the entire toenail off. Kathy responded, 'He gives you Novacaine like a dentist does in your mouth. They give you shots. That's a tender spot in the toes. And then he cuts the whole thing off.'

(b) Consequences

Discourse such as that we have been describing can be confusing even to interlocutors who can call on their intimate knowledge of speakers' lives to identify the events, individuals, and so forth, that are inadequately referred to or characterized and thus supply themselves the information that has not been given. But the real problems come when retarded individuals have to transact business with someone who is not familiar with them, and particularly when they are required to give complex accounts. For example, one day Jeff had to go to the Social Security office to ask to have a fine waived. He gave his name and the name of the social worker who had helped him the previous time to the receptionist. Then he tried to explain why he had come. In doing so, he drew on past incidents, many of which were irrelevant to the present problem and none of which he explained clearly. The receptionist was totally confused and the researcher, who had pieced together an understanding of the problem from repeated explanations, felt obliged to step in and clarify the situation. As they took their seats to wait to be called, Jeff thanked the researcher and said he was glad he had stepped in because he had been about to lose his cool. Later, in the social worker's office, Jeff again attempted unsuccessfully to explain why he had come, confusing the social worker, and once again the researcher stepped in. Ultimately the fine was waived and Jeff accomplished his intended goal, but not without intervention.

Jeff speaks and thinks quite slowly, and as exchanges in a conversation multiply, he gets further and further behind in his responses and understanding. In unfamiliar situations, especially those where understanding and being understood are of particular importance, he becomes nervous and insecure. Often, in anticipation of being confused or misunderstood, and possibly taken advantage of, he approaches such situations with a belligerent attitude, primed for conflict. As misunderstandings develop he becomes increasingly frustrated until eventually he blows up, hurling accusations and antagonizing everyone. Usually his wife, a social worker or a visiting researcher has to step in, smooth ruffled feathers, explain the problem and complete the transaction. Over and over again, the pattern is one of miscommunication, followed by confusion and anger and then followed by intervention.

For example, Jeff thought that he had given the cashier at the grocery store a $50 bill instead of a $20 bill and he expected more change than he received. Instead of calmly explaining what he thought was the problem, Jeff angrily insisted, 'You owe me more money!' He got angrier and angrier as the cashier did not understand what he was talking about. She asked, 'What did you say?', and instead of explaining, Jeff threw out the accusation, 'You are trying to cheat me'. The cashier was totally confused and called the store manager over to settle the problem. After reconstructing the story from information he laboriously elicited from Jeff, the manager looked through the till and determined that there was no $50 bill. Jeff tried to salvage his self-esteem by shouting at the manager that he wasn't going to shop there any more because they didn't treat him fairly. His wife, Carol, who had quietly pointed out to him in the midst of the confusion that the $50 bill was still at home, supported him during his argument with the others, but afterwards she told him he didn't need to yell and was in the wrong anyway. Jeff's response was, 'Maybe I did yell some, but they were not listening and were also yelling'.

If mildly retarded speakers are to be understood, then, their interlocutors must often undertake the frequently laborious, time-consuming and sometimes fruitless task of asking questions to achieve some clarification, offering hypotheses, and constructing interpretations, on occasions through giant leaps of faith or intuition. Too often, people in the community who interact with the mentally retarded individuals we have studied have neither the time nor the patience to undertake the effort, and much of what the mentally retarded speakers attempt to convey is either only partially understood or not understood at all. Parents impatient with their rambling, confusing or incomplete explanations or stories often step in and speak for them. Doctors and social workers frequently turn to whatever non-retarded person has accompanied their clients for explanations of the purpose of a visit or the presenting problem and sometimes treat their clients as non-persons altogether, speaking of them in their presence in the third person and never addressing them directly.

In many instances, however, non-retarded speakers' decision to pursue or abandon an attempt to understand is governed not by the effort required, but by an awareness of the discomfort of their interlocutors and the importance of understanding what is being said. Mentally retarded speakers are often quite sensitive to not being understood, and when what is not understood is not important, their interlocutors may try to avoid causing them embarrassment by not repeatedly attempting to get them to be clearer. As one researcher noted of a study participant's explanation of the work she did in her sheltered workshop, 'This wasn't at all clear to me and didn't really tell me anything, but I didn't pursue it any further as Hilary sometimes has such a hard time explaining things that it seems like an insensitive thing to do to keep asking the same things over and over again, especially when it doesn't seem very important'. Carl, like Jeff, is quite defensive if he feels that he is not being understood or believed. When he begins to feel frustrated or challenged, he will counter with a remark such as, 'You're not following my point!', again as Jeff does, placing the onus for the 'miscommunication' on the hearer rather than upon himself.

The difficulties mildly mentally retarded speakers have providing, organizing and marking information in their discourse result in a great deal of non-understanding and misunderstandings and affect their ability to participate smoothly and effectively in a variety of communicative interactions (Sabsay and Platt, 1985). They also seem to play a major role in the identification of such speakers as 'incompetent' or 'retarded' by their non-retarded interlocutors (Kernan, Sabsay and Rein, 1986; Kernan, Sabsay and Shinn, 1988). It is not only the incoherence of their discourse that causes problems in interaction, but also their conduct in the interactions in which the discourse occurs.

10.4 MANAGING SOCIAL INTERACTIONS

Mentally retarded individuals, like everyone, must not only make themselves understood, but must also participate in communicative interactions in socially appropriate ways: incoherent discourse itself is disruptive to the smooth working of social interaction, but even the most coherent, cogent discourse is inadequate if it is uttered in an inappropriate situation or an inappropriate manner. Many mildly retarded individuals, however, lack the communicative resources or the knowledge necessary to participate in interactions appropriately.

Probably the greatest problem that mildly retarded individuals face in communicative interactions is their limited repertoire of conversational topics. Few of the individuals in our cohort are capable of carrying on conversations on a wide variety of topics and many tend to perseverate on topics which are of immediate concern to them but which hold little interest for others and present little opportunity for general conversation. For example, Marilyn, at the age of 24 has an almost preadolescent fascination with television, movie and rock stars, and talk of them constitutes almost her entire conversational repertoire. While these media idols are the mainstay of conversations with her retarded friends and her detailed knowledge of them might be considered impressive, non-retarded interlocutors of her own age find her conversation limiting and her behaviour and concerns juvenile.

Kathy, too, has a very narrow range of topics. Talk of her many major and minor medical problems dominates her conversation and she presents them, as she does all her concerns, almost breathlessly, in run-on sentences and incomplete thoughts, introducing them with complete disregard for their relevance to the ongoing conversation. While she asks the routine questions which display polite interest in others' affairs and concerns, like many others she shows little interest in the answers and often interrupts them to return to her own preoccupations. In one-to-one conversations interlocutors quickly become accustomed to Kathy's ways of speaking and interacting and compensate for them rather automatically. But to observe her engaged in a multi-party conversation, interrupting, drawing attention to herself and causing awkward silences is to be struck once again by her self-involvement and the inappropriateness of her behaviour.

Unlike Kathy, John often has little to say, and drawing conversation out of him can sometimes be extremely difficult. When he does initiate conversation, it is frequently about such slightly bizarre and obsessive topics as boots or elevators. In addition, to compensate for his limited resources, he has developed a set of idiosyncratic techniques which allow him to hold up his end of a conversation, however inappropriately. John, for example, often repeats key words of another speaker's last utterance. During one visit, the researcher told John she had some questions to ask him about ideal relationships. 'Ideal relationships', echoed John. 'Okay'. 'Do you understand what "ideal" means?' the researcher asked. 'Somewhat, sort of means like perfect ones', she explained. 'The perfect ones', he repeated. 'Yeah, or like fantasy'. 'Fantasy', he echoed.

Another technique John uses to keep conversation going is to turn around questions asked of him, so that as soon as he gives his usual short, clipped answer, he asks the same question of his interlocutor. He does this even when the question could not possibly pertain to the person he's asking it of. He has also developed the irritating habit of asking questions to which he obviously knows the answer. After John had reported to the researcher that he had been to the dentist that day, for example, he asked her if she likes 'the dentist'. She said she doesn't, and John asked why. She said it was because dentistry hurts, and John said, 'Yeah. What hurts? That machine?' She concurred, and then John wanted to know, 'What type of machine does he use, that drill?'

One day John was getting dressed to go out to dinner with his mother. His mother was in conversation with a guest when he interrupted her as he was putting his shoe on to say, 'I won't tie this too tight?' She looked over and said, 'Not too tight. Just tie it loose'. John asked, 'How come?' His mother responded, 'So it won't hurt your foot'. John echoed, 'So it won't hurt my foot?', and his mother said, 'Yes'. John then announced, 'I picked up a lot of trash today. I was loaded.' His mother said, 'Were you?' and told him that it was time to go, at which point John asked her, referring to the shoe-lace, 'Is this too tight?'

During the course of a long evening with John, the researcher and a friend of hers, the topic of elevators came up repeatedly. John asked the friend, who managed an apartment building, a number of suspiciously informed questions about how elevators work — what do they use cables for? what do the cables wrap around? what's the pulley attached to? where's the main spring located? However, when the friend said they put the main spring in the basement, John said, 'They put the main springs at the top sometimes'. After John had told several stories about being stuck in different elevators, the researcher mentioned that she has always had a slight fear that a cable would break on an elevator and the whole thing would fall. John assured her that that would never happen as they have separate cables. Because of such comments, the researcher and her friend got the distinct impression that Jeff knew a great deal about elevators and was just asking questions to make conversation.

Mildly retarded individuals are not only limited in the topics they themselves are able to choose to discuss and the resources they can call upon to introduce and maintain conversation, they often fail to display reciprocal interest in the personal and general topics introduced by others. Like Kathy, some may ask polite questions of others but not attend to the answer, and others simply do not respond at all to topics others raise to broaden the conversation. For example, Hilary seems to interact well with the other residents of the small 'group home' where she lives and with her coworkers at the sheltered workshop. But conversations with Hilary are difficult for non-retarded interlocutors. She asks no personal questions of them and shows no interest in what they are saying. Her own contribution to a conversation is, for the most part, a litany of past and present sorrows. At lunch with two researchers, for instance, Hilary talked about being placed in a large institution for the mentally retarded by her stepmother when she was young, her bad feelings about her alcoholic father, her mistreatment by the operator of a family care home where she once lived, being teased at work for being overweight, the death of her twin, her problems with her teeth and the fact that her brother almost never visits or calls her. Although she answered questions directed to her, Hilary made no contribution to the conversation of the two researchers, despite their best efforts to raise topics which might have been of interest to her and to get her involved in them. The result of such conversation is not only embarrassment or awkward silences, but tedium. Hilary is simply an unrewarding and uninteresting conversational partner.

Some individuals, regardless of their ability to participate in conversations on a wide range of topics or their interest in others, are simply unable to join smoothly in ongoing conversation. For example, Pat, who can discuss a wide range of subjects in two-party conversations, seldom participates in general ones. In a room filled with people chatting she will remain, for the most part, divorced from the flow of conversation. While she is present, smiling and observing what is going on, she seems at times to be in a different world. The comments that she will occasionally make do not fit into the mainstream of the conversation, but rather are directed to one person, who is elected to be the recipient of the unrelated thought that has just popped into her head. Often such comments are made as the person to whom she is speaking is in the process of actively listening or even speaking with others. Her inability to handle social situations like this seems to be almost entirely a matter of lacking knowledge of the rules of social interaction. She simply has her own devices and her own ways of getting herself into conversation, many of which go against commonly understood ways of handling oneself in a social group.

Kathy's contributions to ongoing conversations are not only inappropriate in and of themselves, they are also inappropriately initiated. She will introduce a topic, for example, with 'Anyway, I . . .' 'Anyway' usually has a resumptive or dismissive function; it is used to indicate that a speaker is returning to the main point of a conversation after a digression (Halliday and Hasan, 1976), but Kathy uses it to introduce comments about things that neither she nor others have talked about before. It has the effect of causing the others to search their memories in vain for a previous discussion to which Kathy's comment is related, or of appearing to dismiss what others have been saying as unimportant or irrelevant, when in fact it is Kathy who is interrupting.

(a) Reactions

Interlocutors differ in their reactions to the inappropriate conversational behaviour of retarded individuals. John's roommate, who is also retarded, is sometimes driven to distraction by John's habit of asking questions to which he obviously knows the answer. However, most of John's non-retarded coworkers, like his mother, simply accept his questions and answer them with equanimity. The researcher who worked with John took a different tack, gently calling him on his behaviour. Instead of answering such questions, she began to turn them back on him, asking him, 'What do you think?' His sister, annoyed by John's most recent practice of repeatedly asking her what she and their mother had worn that day and what they intended to wear the next day, adopted a similar strategy but with a slightly sharper edge. Her response was to ask John what he planned to wear five years from then, or at 3 pm on 3 November. She told the researcher that he didn't like this response, but he got the message that she didn't want to answer his questions.

241

Those who interact regularly with mildly retarded individuals have basically two options available to them for managing inappropriate or bizarre behaviour. They may, like John's mother, act as if there were nothing wrong and attempt by their response to rectify any disruptions the inappropriateness may have caused in the interaction. Or they may, like John's sister, call attention to the behaviour and hold the retarded speaker accountable for violating the rules of social conduct. The presence of others may also affect how others react to the inappropriate behaviour of retarded individuals. When others are present, the inappropriate behaviour of retarded family members can be embarrassing for parents and siblings, but they will not scold or correct them as they might in private. For example, Pat is occasionally chided for her interruptions when company is present but, for the most part, they are simply tolerated, as a young child's might be, and someone turns to give her an attentive ear before rejoining the 'adult' conversation.

Strangers are often put off by the behaviour of retarded individuals. For example, David talks at the level of a jet-engine whine. It is impossible to have a conversation in a public place with him without all eyes turning to see what the disturbance is. His endless questions and his worries, voiced at booming volume, together with his bizarre appearance, cause him to be noticed and judged as strange. After a trip to the research offices, for instance, David was taken out to dinner by a researcher. David, who never took off his long black coat, fretted endlessly about what to order, asked the waiter innumerable questions and changed his order several times. The waiter quickly grew impatient with him and repeatedly gave the researcher conspiratorial looks, as if to say that it must be difficult to be associated with someone so strange. Roy, at an amusement park, repeatedly engaged strangers in conversation, speaking about inappropriate things and assuming that the people to whom he was speaking had a knowledge of him and his family background. Those he spoke to either made perfunctory acknowledgements of his comments and tried to disengage as quickly as possible or ignored him altogether.

Perhaps even more than their often confusing discourse, mildly retarded speakers' lack of interest in or ability to discuss a wide range of topics, their focus on their own concerns, their interruptions and inappropriate subjects, and their idiosyncratic techniques for managing conversation make them difficult conversational partners. Strangers are disturbed by their inept or intrusive attempts to engage in casual conversation, service personnel find them strange. Their inappropriate behaviour is a source of discomfort and embarrassment for their families. They themselves often are aware of the inappropriateness of their behaviour and take steps to avoid being judged as incompetent.

10.5 IMPRESSION MANAGEMENT AND THE MAINTENANCE OF SELF-ESTEEM

Like the rest of us, most mildly retarded persons are simply concerned with managing social interactions as appropriately as they can, despite limited resources and at the risk of embarrassing gaffes. John, who echoes what others say and asks inappropriate questions, and Marilyn, who speaks incessantly of her media idols, for example, do not seem to believe that there is anything embarrassing or shameful about being 'mentally retarded' or 'handicapped', nor to be aware that there is anything inadequate, inappropriate or stigmatizing about the way they speak or behave. Still, as Edgerton (1967) has so eloquently recorded, there are many mildly retarded individuals who are aware that they have limitations or deficits which discredit them in the eyes of others. While they may not believe that the limitations they have qualify them as 'mentally retarded', or be particularly concerned about being identified as 'retarded', they are none the less concerned about how such incompetencies might cause them to be perceived. In their interactions with others such individuals often have a hidden agenda. They are not only trying to convey information, ask a question or participate in a conversation, but they are trying to protect their self-esteem by demonstrating competence or disguising incompetence. They may do so by using any of a variety of strategies ranging from transparently false claims of accomplishments such as being a mathematician at UCLA (Turner, Kernan and Gelphman, 1984) to self-serving displays of knowledge (Platt, 1985), from disguising limitations (Edgerton, 1967) to avoiding situations in which they might be exposed.

(a) Avoiding negative impressions

Carl, for example, is constantly concerned with being seen as competent or even bright. While he is often aggressively defensive, self-righteous and self-aggrandizing in his efforts to establish his competence, he can be quite subtle and inventive in his efforts to conceal his limitations. Faced with a bewildering array of syrups in a restaurant, for instance, he may get around the fact that he cannot read by asking matter-of-factly, as anyone sifting through the various jars might, 'Which of these is regular?', or he might disguise the fact that he can't find his previously adamantly announced choice in the menu by declaring at the last minute that someone else's selection sounds more appealing. It is only if one knows that he cannot read that one even suspects that at such times he is engaged in impression management.

Despite the frequent success of such ruses, Carl is never free of fear of being seen as incompetent, and because he can't read and has a poor

243

command of numbers, business transactions are particularly fraught with danger. While negotiating a transaction at a bank, for example, Carl was anxious and nervous. He compensated by being loud and trying to be funny. In fact he only succeeded in being annoying and obnoxious, and while the teller was unfailingly polite, his expression made it clear that he thought he was dealing with someone strange. Given his discomfort in such situations, it is far more common for Carl to get his wife, Maureen, who reads and writes quite well, to deal with business transactions and anything else which requires literacy. However, to directly ask for assistance from a spouse who has been labelled mentally retarded, and whose abilities he constantly denigrates, would be too big a threat to his self-esteem. Instead he simply procrastinates until Maureen takes over. Urged to take care of something himself, he temporizes with such reasonable responses as 'I'll check into that some more' or 'I can't do that today, but I'll do it next week'. It is only after having urged him repeatedly and having received the same response that one realizes that he actually has no intention of taking care of the problem and is reluctant to deal with a situation in which his incompetence might be exposed.

Those business transactions he does undertake himself, rather than delegating to Maureen, Carl prefers to take care of in person instead of on the telephone, even though a call might save him a long bus ride to a distant part of the city. He may do so because he feels that his verbal skills are more effective in person. It is clear, at least, that by doing so he puts himself in a position to get visual clues to help him out if he doesn't understand something. For instance, he insisted on going in person to ask an insurance agent about insuring some of his figurines and plates. The agent recommended breakage insurance and, to make his point, pulled out his own policy and showed Carl how his own plates and figures were listed separately with their appraised value and cost of coverage. It was clear that this bit of visual demonstration made more sense to Carl than the agent's verbal explanation.

For Joe, as for Carl, the sole criterion upon which a man is judged is the extent of his knowledge. Sadly the most crucial aspect of a person in his mind is the one area in which he perceives himself as being deficient, and he devotes a great deal of ingenuity to covering up his lack of knowledge. He frequently tells off-colour jokes he himself doesn't understand and makes lascivious comments about passing girls, although he is totally naïve about sex and sexual relationships. So effective is his performance that it was only after 18 months of intensive fieldwork with Joe that the field-worker learned how innocent he was. The jokes Joe repeats and the comments he makes are part of an effort to say the right thing at the right time, elements in a front designed to satisfy whoever he is with that he does indeed know what he is talking about.

One evening, for example, the family had gathered to watch Mel Brooks on the television show, *Hollywood Squares.* It was put to Brooks that we all know the meaning of the word 'gynaecologist', but what was the meaning of the word 'gynephobia'? At Mel Brooks's pause and his sincerely offered, 'It's a fear of dark places', everyone laughed hysterically, with Joe leading the group in volume. But a few minutes later he asked, 'What was the question they asked Mel Brooks? Was it "diaphobia"?', clearly trying to get the line down pat, so that he could share it with others. While Joe laughed hysterically and appropriately exactly on cue, with no hesitation to see what others' reaction was, his later question revealed that he could not have understood the joke. But he knew that a line offered by Mel Brooks would be funny, that he would be expected to laugh, and so he did.

Craig, too, is very sensitive about anything that betrays a handicap, and some of it has to do with his speech. When he speaks, he often chooses the wrong word or uses a neologism, but he has worked out a unique way of getting around his lapses. Usually he tries to get by by not saying much, but when he does make a mistake and it is noticed, he acts as if he were intentionally making up a new word or phrase for what he was trying to say, or tries to pass it off as some of the slang used by the members of an amateur rock band with whom he spends a great deal of his time. This may in fact be how much of the slang originated. When Craig was telling his (non-retarded) friend, Kent, for example, that he had seen a lot of punk rockers in Westwood Village, he said 'punk arock' instead of punk rockers. Kent caught this error immediately and repeated back the 'punk arock'. Craig acted as if he had simply come up with a good new name to call them.

To avoid the embarrassment of having to admit that they have not understood something that has been said to them or that they have been asked to explain, an admission that might reveal them as incompetent, mildly retarded individuals will sometimes feign understanding. They may agree to something that they have not understood, just because they sense that agreement is expected. Cary, for instance, another member of the cohort we work with, will often agree to a scenario or an explanation that an interlocutor has pieced together out of the inconsistent and incomplete information he has given and presented to him for verification, but one gets the feeling that it is an empty 'yes', mere agreement for the sake of agreement. If one asks him the same question on another occasion, one is likely to get a different explanation. Cary, like many others, also tends to give the answer or opinion that he thinks an interlocutor expects rather than give what might be a 'wrong' response.

Most of the people we have worked with depend on someone, some benefactor (Edgerton, 1967), at some point or another to handle situations they themselves are incapable of dealing with. In many instances they do so to avoid the embarrassment of revealing themselves as incompetent as well as simply to get business taken care of. While some avoid such situations altogether, most of them, when they cannot avail themselves of assistance,

COMMUNICATION IN SOCIAL INTERACTIONS

muddle through situations as best they can, often eventually accomplishing their goals, even if sometimes they do so at the cost of their self-esteem.

For example, Jeff is unwilling to admit to any kind of handicap, but he is none the less aware that he has problems understanding and being understood in certain situations. In order to avoid such frustrating and ineffective encounters as those described above, which are damaging to his self-esteem, Jeff prefers to enlist the aid of non-retarded friends. In order to do so, however, he is sometimes forced to admit his inability to deal with such situations. Urging a researcher to accompany him to a garage to enquire about repairs on his car, for instance, Jeff at first maintained that he saw it as a chance to spend time with someone he didn't get to see as often as he would like. But when the researcher asked if that was the only reason, Jeff was forced to concede that, 'Sometimes I have trouble understanding what people say to me ... when they talk fast I get nervous. I know this doesn't happen to you.' In the event, he asked the mechanic the appropriate questions — could they do the job? how much would it cost? how long would it take? — but repeatedly tried to get the researcher involved by asking him, 'Does that sound right to you, Dave?' But, again, Jeff is reluctant to make such admissions and does so only in the face of necessity. More usually, he will try to bluff and shout his way through.

(b) Creating positive impressions

Mildly retarded individuals not only seek to avoid creating negative impressions by disguising incompetence, they also strive to create positive ones by demonstrating competence. They do so by displays of knowledge, real or feigned, by boasts about their accomplishments, by conscious attempts to project a desirable persona or by contrasting their knowledge and accomplishments with those of their peers.

As with sexual jokes and comments, Joe gleans facts and opinions from others' conversation, adopting them as his own in an effort to present himself as an expert or a man of the world. Joe listened carefully, for instance, as his father and brother, both professional musicians, discussed a new tape by Jerry Reed. Not long afterwards, the tape was played for guests and Joe was quick to offer as his own the comments he had overheard.

While Joe borrows others' expertise, there are those who use their own very real knowledge in some area to impress others and demonstrate their competence. Having ascertained that the researcher knew little about the latest trends in rock music, for example, Craig used his undeniable familiarity with bands and music to try to impress her. Carl, though he will hold forth at length on anything, especially enjoys talking about model trains, a hobby in which he is totally absorbed, and often does so endlessly. It is his undeniable expertise in this area that has gained him acceptance among non-retarded hobbyists. Bill, who is obsessed with aircraft and aviation and has memorized the flight schedules of all the major airlines in the Los Angeles area, cannot allow a plane to fly overhead without announcing its destination, schedule, airline and type. It doesn't matter that such information is totally unrelated to the ongoing conversation, that no one is interested and that there is no way of knowing whether he is correct or not; in Bill's view, this information establishes him as an expert on an important topic.

Others attempt to create impressions of competence not by displaying their knowledge, but by telling proudly of their accomplishments. Some of the accomplishments reported with such pride are real but embarrassingly ordinary, things no non-retarded person would think to mention such as being able to do one's own laundry. Other claims of accomplishments are exaggerated if not altogether false. For example, Bruce had recently moved out of his parents' home into an apartment and he related to a researcher with great pride how he had initiated the move and managed to locate the apartment on his own. The researcher soon discovered by talking to Bruce's parents, however, that Bruce had actually played a very small role in the move. It was his father who advocated Bruce's moving out, gained his reluctant agreement and handled nearly all the business of finding and securing the apartment.

Cary, too, is likely to overstate his accomplishments. Speaking on one occasion about his various skills, Cary professed to being able to sew. Does he ever have to exercise the skill, he was asked. 'Oh yeah.' 'Like what kinds of things?' 'Like my buttons on my shirts. I sew my own buttons on my shirts. I sew my own buttons on my shirts.' Asked, however, if that meant he didn't take them to his housemother, Cary admitted, 'Well, now, I let Fran do it because I can't, you know, sew a button on a shirt, you know, too good because if the hole's over in here I put it all the way over here. I get too nervous when I do it so I let Fran do it.' Similarly, in another discussion, Cary maintained that he makes most of the major decisions in his life. Keeping his room clean, he volunteered, was his decision. When the researcher asked him what Fran would do if he stopped vacuuming, doing laundry, making his bed, picking up his clothes, and so forth, however, he noted that she'd probably jump on his back and tell him what to do and really bug him about it. And what would he do? He'd end up taking care of all the chores. His interlocutor observed that it seemed Fran did have a say in the matter, and Cary agreed that she did.

Still others are not so much concerned with demonstrating their competence through displays of knowledge or boasts of their accomplishments as they are with projecting a certain desirable image. David, for example, who, like Joe, is totally naïve about sex and romantic relationships, will often offer lewd comments about passing women, emulating the macho attitudes of his social group. Gene takes every opportunity to remind his listeners how tough he is by talking about fights he has had, displaying his knowledge about military armaments and claiming to have been a member of the Hell's Angels.

In their research with members of the same cohort of mildly mentally retarded adults, Zetlin and Turner (1984) find that, in general, those who are uneasy with their identities as retarded persons see it as especially important to project a favourable image of themselves and do so by emphasizing the differences between themselves and those who are equally or more handicapped. For example, Carl is inclined to use his wife, Maureen, as a foil to display his own competence. He constantly points out her failings, contrasting them with his own abilities. Maureen was telling a researcher about an upcoming trip to Las Vegas, for instance, and mentioned that she had been there when she was 10 years old but couldn't remember it. Carl commented on how bad her memory was; he understood everything at that age, he said, and remembers it well. When they were trying to do some calculations regarding the cost of a party they were planning, Carl asked Maureen how many people were invited. Though she is much better with numbers than he is, her response was not to supply a total, but to enumerate the guests by naming each person invited, a strategy the researcher found helpful. Carl, however, was impatient with her. He said that that was not what he asked for and told her to shut up.

In Jeff's case, this attitude of superiority extends to his circle of mentally retarded friends and acquaintances, with whom he acts as counsellor and critic. He asserts his control over the entire group of more than a half-dozen individuals, turning them against David, for example, when he does something Jeff disapproves of. David is in fact the most frequent recipient of Jeff's criticisms and negative comparisons. Jeff commented once, for instance, that while, like David, he might be a 'slow learner', he is 'not as bad off as David because he can't protect himself'. When David was worrying about how to replace his roommate, Jeff told him that instead of trying to find a new roommate he should move into a board and care home, because 'you can't take care of yourself'. David accepts this, asking Jeff for advice and citing him as an authority in support of his actions or opinions, all of which confirms for Jeff his superior knowledge and judgement.

Arnie, who lives with his wife, Sandy, and their friend, Kent, also bolsters his own self-esteem at the expense of others. Like Carl, he enjoys pontificating and showing off his expertise, and as he is more verbal than either Sandy or Kent, he dominates conversations. He is not content with this, however, and often questions or adds to information that the others might offer. When Sandy mentioned that she had been to see a particular counsellor, Arnie told her that she had seen others, too, though that fact really was not pertinent to the conversation. The same often occurs when

Kent makes a comment or offers a fact. Arnie will usually question it or add to it in some way. The fact that he is often wrong, and that Kent is, though quieter, far more competent in many respects, does not deter him. In another household of three, consisting of a man, his wife and their female roommate, it is the wife, Yvette, who bolsters her own sense of worth at the expense of her friend Lisa's. She constantly criticizes Lisa for her childish behaviour (in which Yvette's husband is often a confederate or instigator), her weight, and her irresponsibility.

Some retarded individuals go so far in their efforts to distinguish themselves from their retarded peers that they effectively isolate themselves. They prefer the company of non-retarded people, with whom they feel they have more in common, but they rarely achieve more than superficial or benefactor relationships which lack reciprocity. When they associate with their retarded peers, it is with an attitude of superiority and condescension which creates resentment. Elizabeth, for example, is chronically lonely. Her attempts to associate with non-retarded people are rebuffed, but she refuses to identify with retarded peers. When she entered an independent living training programme, she quickly alienated the other residents by referring to them as 'kids' and trying to order them around. She preferred to talk to staff members, to whom she was deferential. While they were sympathetic and courteous, they could not offer her the friendship she sought.

(c) Consequences for interaction

The often ineffective efforts of mildly retarded individuals to weave for themselves a 'cloak of competence' are revealing of their cognizance of the stigma of 'stupidity' and their anxiousness about the impression they make on others. They draw attention to the fact that speakers are trying to conceal limitations or assuage damaged self-esteem. Their interlocutors, retarded and non-retarded alike, sensing their vulnerability, are often drawn into a 'benevolent conspiracy', in which they attempt to protect such individuals' fragile self-esteem, either by not revealing that they are aware of their incompetence or by helping them cover up their failings (Edgerton, 1967; Sabsay and Platt, 1985; Turner, Kernan and Gelphman, 1984). For example, one day at lunch in a restaurant, Carl's wife, Maureen, uncharacteristically put him in an embarrassing position by asking him if he had found the grilled cheese sandwich he wanted in the menu. Carl said that he had not really looked yet, but the researcher, realizing that he probably was having difficulty reading the menu, began to casually read aloud the descriptions of several items as if she were herself considering them.

Not everyone, however, is willing to enter into the conspiracy. For some, the attempts that retarded individuals make to present themselves in a better light are simply irritating or embarrassing. For instance, while Joe's efforts to demonstrate expertise on various subjects are often effective in impressing acquaintances and his retarded peers, those who know him well realize the shallowness of his façade and are often irritated by his behaviour. His parents are not terribly patient with him when he tries to pass himself off as an expert on something. At such times, there is a quality of biting sarcasm in their voices. For example, Joe had only recently been persuaded to overcome his fears and go on his first flight in a small plane, an experience he was not entirely enthusiastic about. But one evening soon after, when there was company and the conversation turned to flying, Joe talked at length about the joys of flying in a small plane. His father could sit still for Joe's performance for only so long and eventually undermined him by asking him when he was ready to go up again, a question which Joe did his best to ignore. Of one evening spent in Craig's company a researcher commented:

> I had the feeling during most of this evening that Craig was trying to impress me in various ways. He did this by trying to protect me when we were in Westwood going across the street and worrying that I was going to get my purse stolen. He also tried to impress me with his knowledge of things such as motorcycles and music. He made efforts to show me how 'cool' or 'hip' he was by knowing more of the new rock groups than I did, or by making jokes about drugs, as when I mentioned the light was red: 'Oh, do you have reds?' I don't think he realized how unsuccessful he was in his attempt to impress me nor how transparent, foolish, and eventually irritating the whole thing became. Craig is 25 going on 15. His attempt at arrogance only masks an underlying lack of self-confidence.

10.6 CONCLUSION

For the purposes of this chapter, we have made a conceptual distinction between interactional difficulties which stem from problems with discourse, those which result from inappropriate conduct of social interaction, and those which arise from retarded individuals' attempts to conceal incompetence or create an impression of competence. But in fact the boundaries between intellectual competence and social competence are fuzzy, at best, and in actual interactions the two are often indistinguishable: intellectual incompetence has social consequences, and inappropriate social conduct is often interpreted as intellectual deficit.

We all know people who resemble in some respects the people we have described here. We all know someone like Carl, for example, who is always pontificating about something, even though he really doesn't know what he is talking about and is not really making sense; or someone like Kathy, who obsesses about problems endlessly and pointlessly; or like Maureen, who tells stories in endless, boring detail to make a point that somehow is not really related to the rest of the conversation. We do not mean to suggest that the communicative behaviours we have discussed here are unique to or diagnostic of mildly retarded individuals. Rather it is the occurrence of a constellation of these behaviours, and the frequency with which they are exhibited, that set these people apart from their non-retarded peers. Turner (1984) offers the observation that 'the retarded are just like us, only more so'. It is the tendency to be just a bit 'more so', just a bit more often and in more ways than the rest of us, we suggest, that marks individuals likely to be identified as mildly retarded.

As we have suggested above, the two most important aspects of communicative behaviour on which they are judged are whether they talk in socially appropriate ways and whether what they say is understandable and relevant. And often in the community, as well as in the clinic, they are judged to be wanting in these areas. While many interlocutors are sympathetic, and go to great lengths to prevent or minimize trouble in interactions, others are impatient, frustrated or embarrassed. Regardless of one's attitude, however, the fact remains that mildly retarded individuals are sometimes difficult and unrewarding conversational partners. Yet despite their difficulties, most manage to conduct their affairs in the community successfully and form networks of retarded friends and non-retarded benefactors. All, at least at some time, engage appropriately in a variety of communicative interactions: they are usually polite, greeting people genially, thanking them for visits, assistance and gifts, and congratulating them on birthdays. They hold up their end of a conversation as best they can, attempting to entertain or show interest in their conversational partners.

They also usually make sense. And even when at first they do not, their interlocutors, if they are patient and willing to make some effort, can usually make sense of what they are trying to say. We have, after all, worked with mildly retarded people for a number of years in an attempt to understand their lives, and all that we know about their friendships, their dreams, their work experiences, their sex lives, their problems, their concerns, their failures and their successes, we have learned because they have told us about them.

ACKNOWLEDGEMENTS

The research on which this chapter is based was supported by Grant No. HD 119440-04 from the National Institute of Child Health and Human Development and by Grant NIE-G-80-0016 from the National Institute of

Education. We wish to thank the individuals who have shared their lives with us and allowed us, in a small way, to speak for them. We gratefully acknowledge the contributions of Tom Brauner, Marsha Bollinger, Melody Davidson, Pauline Hayashigawa and David Tillipman to data collection.

REFERENCES

Chafe, W.L. (1976) Givenness, contrastiveness, definiteness, subjects, topics, and point of view in *Subject and Topic* (ed. C.N. Li), Academic Press, New York, pp. 27–55.

Clark, H.H. and Haviland, S.E. (1974) Psychological processes as linguistic explanation in *Explaining Linguistic Phenomena* (ed. D. Cohen), Hemisphere, Washington, DC, pp. 91–124.

Edgerton, R.B. (1967) *The Cloak of Competence: Stigma in the Lives of the Mentally Retarded*, University of California Press, Berkeley, Calif.

Grice, H.P. (1975) Logic and conversation in *Syntax and Semantics. Vol. 3, Speech Acts* (eds. P. Cole and J.L. Morgan), Academic Press, New York, pp. 41–58.

Halliday, M.A.K. and Hasan, R. (1976) *Cohesion in English*, Longman, London.

Kernan, K.T. (1977) Semantic and expressive elaboration in children's narratives in *Child Discourse* (eds. C. Mitchell Kernan and S. Ervin Tripp), Academic Press, New York, pp. 91–102.

Kernan, K.T. and Sabsay, S. (1982) Semantic deficiencies in the narratives of mildly retarded speakers, *Semiotica, 42,* 169–93.

Kernan, K.T., Sabsay, S. and Rein, R.P. (1986) Aspects of verbal behavior cited by listeners in judging speakers as retarded or not retarded, *Mental Retardation and Learning Disabilities Bulletin, 14,* 24–43.

Kernan, K.T., Sabsay, S. and Shinn, N. (in press) Lay people's judgements of storytellers as mentally retarded or not retarded.

Kernan, K.T., Sabsay, S. and Shinn, N. (1988) Discourse features as criteria in judging the intellectual ability of speakers, *Journal of Mental Deficiency Research, 11,* 203–20.

Labov, W. and Waletzky, J. (1967) Narrative analysis in *Essays on the Verbal and Visual Arts* (ed. J. Helm), University of Washington Press, Seattle, Wash., pp. 12–44.

Platt, M. (1985) Displaying competence: peer interaction in a group home for retarded adults in *Social Setting, Stigma, and Communicative Competence: Explorations of the Conversational Interactions of Retarded Adults. Pragmatics and Beyond* (eds. S. Sabsay, M. Platt, J. Graffam and K. Anderson-Levitt), *VI,* 75–94.

Sabsay, S. and Kernan, K.T. (1983) Communicative design in the speech of mildly retarded adults in *Environments and Behavior: The Adaptation of Mildly Retarded Persons* (eds. K.T. Kernan, M.J. Begab and R.B. Edgerton), University Park Press, Baltimore, Md., pp. 283–94.

Sabsay, S. and Platt, M. (1985) Weaving the cloak of competence: a paradox in the management of trouble in conversations between retarded and nonretarded interlocutors in *Social Setting, Stigma, and Communicative Competence: Explorations of the Conversational Interactions of Retarded Adults. Pragmatics and Beyond* (eds. S. Sabsay, M. Platt, J. Graffam and K. Anderson-Levitt), *VI,* 96–116.

Sperber, D. and Wilson D. (1987) *Relevance: Communication and Cognition*, Harvard University Press, Cambridge.

Tannen, D. (1979) What's in a frame? Surface evidence for underlying expectations in *New Directions in Discourse Processing* (ed. R.O. Freedle), Ablex, Norwood, pp. 137–81.

Turner, J.L. (1984) Workshop society: ethnographic observations in a work setting in *Environments and Behavior: The Adaptation of Mildly Retarded Persons* (eds. K.T. Kernan, M.J. Begab and R.B. Edgerton), University Park Press, Baltimore, Md., pp. 147–72.

Turner, J.L., Kernan, K.T. and Gelphman, S. (1984) Speech etiquette in a sheltered workshop in *Lives in Process: Mildly Retarded Adults in a Large City* (ed. R.B. Edgerton), Monographs of the American Association on Mental Deficiency No. 6, American Association of Mental Deficiency, Washington, DC, pp. 43–72.

Zetlin, A.G. and Turner, J.L. (1984) Self-perspectives on being handicapped: stigma and adjustment in *Lives in Process: Mildly Retarded Adults in a Large City* (ed. R.B. Edgerton), Monographs of the American Association on Mental Deficiency No. 6, American Association on Mental Deficiency, Washington, DC, pp. 93–120.

11

Communication in Therapy with Emotionally Disturbed Mentally Retarded Individuals

Douglass R. Price-Williams

In this chapter we are concerned with a precise domain of communicative skills, namely with the communication of emotional states in mentally retarded adult individuals in therapeutic situations. There is an absence of literature on this precise subject, but there is material on related areas. The literature and the state of the art of communication skills in mentally retarded children has been recently well reviewed by Mundy, Seibert and Hogan (1985). In particular, the communication of emotional states in mentally retarded children has been discussed by Emde, Katz and Thorpe (1978), although this and a previous article in the same book by Dante Cicchetti and L. Alan Sroufe (1978) are restricted to Down's syndrome infants. The literature on *adult* emotional expressions is sparse. However it is clear from the article by Mundy, Seibert and Hogan (1985) that communicative skills deficiencies and emotional problems are correlatives:

> It is plausible that the degree to which children cannot interact effectively with peers and adults is related to the tendency to manifest the symptomology of emotional disturbance (e.g. depression or conduct disorder) ... it is reasonable to expect that individual differences in communication skills are related to emotional problems in mentally retarded children. (p. 65)

Although their remarks pertain to children, it may be assumed that they are also valid for adults, and it is this aspect of communicative ability that we shall explore; further relevant literature will be noted in the course of this chapter.

The field of so-called dual diagnosis, that is the study of psychopathology in the mentally retarded is now quite large (see Matson and Barrett, 1982; Syzmanski and Tanguay, 1980; Menolascino and Stark, 1984). The main segments of this field that have been investigated are incidence or prevalence of mental illness, the related problem of diagnosis, the use of instrumentation and the problem of treatment. Within this last heading the question is raised as to the best type of treatment, that is most appropriate for the degree of mental retardation, and most effective in the long run. Whatever type of treatment is employed, whether psychodynamic in origin or that of behaviour modification, the question must arise of communication between the therapist and the dual diagnostic or emotionally disturbed mentally handicapped client. It is not only in treatment that the question of communication becomes a problem; it is also a concern in diagnosis. This is a problem on which there has been little attention paid in the psychopathological literature of mentally retarded persons. The following clinical cases, in which the author is the psychologist, indicate certain kinds of communication problems which involve problems of diagnosis and of reaching a basic understanding with a client. All these cases, with one exception, were with clients from a sheltered workshop in the Los Angeles, California, area. The clients were referred by their counsellors for a variety of reasons, but mainly because the clients' behaviours were interfering with interpersonal relationships or their work. We shall start with two cases which exemplify the difficulty of reaching a diagnostic conclusion due partly to special difficulties of communication.

11.1 DIFFICULTIES OF DIAGNOSIS

The first case whom we will call Boris, is that of a 22-year-old Down's syndrome client. He is caucasian and the last child of a large family. His family are relatively affluent and have a strong religious orientation. For reasons of privacy, the actual religion cannot be referred to, but it is of the philosophical type that encourages the outlook that 'you can do it if you try'. This is the outlook that Boris was socialized into. The client is at the low end of the mildly mentally retarded range; his intelligence tests indicate that he has particular deficiencies in the visual-spatial domain, and in verbal expression. He is myopic, which can be partially corrected by spectacles, which however he does not wear. His presenting problem was that he had the habit of mouthing to the empty air, suggesting he was talking to somebody. Apparently his parents had noted this, had discouraged the habit when Boris was in public, but allowed him to do this in his own room at home. The workshop authorities did not discourage this but the habit concerned them, and that was the reason why he was referred. The client's workshop counsellor noted that the behaviour occurred mostly in times of stress for Boris. The client had never been referred to a psychiatrist and at the time of referral was not on medication. Boris' file indicated that he had been given projective tests two years previously; the only comment had been that Boris had given restrictive responses 'typical of mentally retarded clients'.

Preliminary questioning of the counsellor, the parents and Boris' old high school teacher, and the client himself, revealed that there was an apparent history of imaginary companions. From at least the age of 12, there was an imaginary companion called 'Tran'. Boris' parents had expressed concern at this manifestation and urged Boris to discontinue the practice. A teacher at Boris' high school attempted to eradicate the behaviour by simulating Boris' communications with 'Tran', pretending that he too could hear 'Tran'. Apparently this succeeded, as Boris then proceeded to eliminate 'Tran' in a novel way. At least this is the way in which Boris related the episode to the author. According to him, a young girl, a relative of Boris', also had an imaginary companion. Her imaginary companion was female, 'Tran' was male. Boris then stated that they 'married', and subsequently disappeared. On questioning Boris about this older imaginary companion, it appeared that 'Tran' was always invisible. It was an auditory experience. He heard 'Tran's' voice. This imaginary companion may have thus disappeared, but the behaviour continued under another name. This provides the basis for the present discussion and analysis.

Boris had now, for the past two years, been indicating that there was something which he called Mind Power, which could help him. At first sight, particularly with the reported history of the imaginary companion 'Tran', it might seem that Mind Power had simply replaced the other. However, since Mind Power was a current phenomenon, it could be analysed closely by interrogating Boris. This interrogation indicated the possibility that this wasn't a hallucinatory phenomenon, but a distorted understanding of how the mind works, or very possibly a distorted understanding of how Boris' own mind works — the distortion being due to Boris' manner of communicating ideas. The following excerpts from a tape recorded session indicate the difficulty:

Psychologist: Tell me, Boris, about Mind Power.
Boris: Mind Power is some kind of voice, born in 1964, and my name is
   ...
Psych.: (*interrupting*) You were born in 1964, weren't you?
B.: Yes. My name is ...
Psych.: OK, but tell me about Mind Power.
B.: Mind Power is Down's syndrome. It reads lips to the mind that says when to say something. Mind Power helps me when I help my father. Friday — he tried to fix the TV. And me, my mother and father help. Team work. Mind Power is information sent to the TV. It [*presumably the TV set*] funny, snowing. Talk to Mind Power. When the Mind communicates what I am doing. Team work. It is movement that helps team work.
Psych.: I understand. But do you talk to Mind Power?
B.: Yes.
Psych.: In the same way that you are talking to me?

B.: Not really. The Mind reads lips. Like a deaf person.

While Boris' communication mode appears muddled for the psychologist (and perhaps for the reader), it is nevertheless clear from the last exchange that there is a difference for Boris between talking to a person and talking to Mind Power. It is definitely not the same as if he were talking to an imaginary companion. What seems to be coming through is an attempt at relaying what he has been taught or understands about how the mind works. The mind works, that is *his* mind, like a TV set requiring repair. When he makes an analogy between the 'snowing' of the TV set, it may not be too dissimilar to how he perceives his own mentation. He appears to be grasping the idea that there are two different elements involved: talking and 'mind' or thoughts. He is not sure how these two elements interact, but the reference to a deaf person indicates that Boris is attempting to get over the idea of inference. Boris does not have the cognitive capacity of representing such abstract processes, but he recognizes the processes and concretizes them in this personalistic manner. At any rate, this is a hypothesis which is different from the hallucinatory model.

Nevertheless, it still was not possible to eliminate the hallucinatory model altogether. There was the necessity of finding out the similarity of Mind Power to the older 'Tran'. The questioning continued as follows:

Psychologist: You used to have a friend called 'Tran', right?
Boris: Right.
Psych.: Who was invisible?
B.: Right.
Psych.: Is Mind Power like your friend Tran?
B.: Yes it is.
Psych.: You don't see Mind Power because it is invisible?
B.: That's correct.
Psych.: Does he talk to you?
B.: Yes he does.
Psych.: Can you hear him?
B.: Yes.
Psych.: Is it a him or a her?
B.: It's a him.
Psych.: What sort of voice does he have?
B.: He has — just like mine, I think.
Psych.: Like your own voice?
B.: Yes.

While all this appears to support the hallucinatory hypothesis, Boris then continued to state: 'But not really; the Mind Power listens. When the Mind listens, the Mind is a good team work. It will help my parents, and when

257

my parents say something the Mind communicates ...' In this last statement it is almost as if Boris is saying that he is listening to his own Mind, to his own voice; his statement recalls Piaget's findings that thoughts and voices are intertwined for small children. From a developmental point of view, it is possible that, as with children, the imaginary companion is dying out, and that while there are vestiges of it, Boris is grappling with the notion of how the mind operates. From a clinical standpoint, the course was to discourage the idea of an invisible companion or anything which suggests dissociation, and reinforce the idea that Mind Power is really Boris' mind. The difficulty throughout was to discern the thought processes embedded in the communicatory confusion.

The second case involved the decipherment of reality and fantasy. The problem for the psychologist was whether the client understood that the stories she told were in fact fabrications or whether she was so identified with them that they had become reality. The client was a moderately retarded girl in her early twenties. She had been referred because of interpersonal difficulties both at work and at her group home. She displayed marked negativity with both staff and peers; she appeared depressed and was markedly uncommunicative. During the first few sessions with the psychologist she answered questions in low monosyllables, sitting hunched in a chair with head down and offering little eye contact. The only intervention at this stage was to induce her to sit in a more relaxed fashion in the chair, and to encourage her to make eye contact with the psychologist.

After a month to six weeks of little progress in the sessions, the client (whom we shall call Joan) volunteered an elaborate description of being raped. The account entailed a small, ethnic man called Dr Grey (for reasons of privacy, this too is a pseudonym, but the real name was in fact a colour term). As she said the word 'little', she was asked how tall the man was, and she measured with her hand about 2 ft from the floor. She specified the place where she had been 'raped'; it was in a building adjacent to the workshop. Not convinced that this client understood what was meant by the word 'rape', she was asked to specify in detail what had happened. It turned out that this Dr Grey had taken her clothes off and then stomped all over her body with his feet. Joan went on to say more about her alleged assailant, indicating that his full name was George Grey, and that he was a doctor who had treated her for her bad leg. The interesting part of this account was the way in which she discussed the incident. For the first time in her sessions, she made full eye contact, showed positive affect, laughed and seemed to enjoy the telling of the incident. This was in marked contrast to her previous behaviour. Joan then further elaborated the experience with Dr Grey in blatant symbolical terms. Either on this so-called rape occasion or at another time (it wasn't clear) Dr Grey had injected her with a syringe, which had in it a green fluid. 'I felt great', she reported. This rape fantasy was coupled with Joan's reporting a trip to Honolulu with a male friend at the workshop. Enormous amounts of detail was worked into the story, including the name of the airline, how she got the money, the hotel in Honolulu where they had stayed, and so on.

The rape account was reported to Joan's counsellor at the workshop, and to this writer's surprise, it turned out that there was a Dr Grey, who had in fact treated Joan. He was ethnic also. But of course he was not 2 ft tall, and had not raped the client. However, another client had in fact taken Joan's clothes off, but had not attempted anything sexually. It is also pertinent to mention that grey was this client's favourite colour; everything she wore was of this colour.

It was clear, then, that there was probably a factual basis to Joan's fantasies. It was often difficult for the psychologist to determine what was factual and what was constructed. At another time, Joan gave a rich description of horse riding during the weekend, which the psychologist suspected was totally untrue. However, after enquiry, the account was found to be mainly correct.

Now the question was: to what extent did Joan live in a fantasy world and to what extent were her accounts stylistic? That she was a story-teller was not to be doubted, but her problems of articulation make it difficult to assess the state of mind behind this. An opportunity to test the distinction came spontaneously on the occasion of an obvious fantasy account. There was another young woman, called May, who was a co-member of the home in which Joan lived. May was also a client of this psychologist. Joan had a running feud with May, always criticizing her and saying bad things about her. One day Joan came up with this story about May. May was in a wood in which there lived two blind tree cutters, both with the last name of Green (Joan had a penchant for colours). Both these Mr Greens, being quite blind, cut down a tree near where May stood. They shouted 'timber', but it was too late. The tree felled May in her back. She was rushed to hospital, but it was too late. May died in hospital. Joan finished the story with a flourish, her eyes gleaming: 'May is dead'.

The opportunity to challenge Joan on this story came the following week, as it happened that May preceded Joan for a therapy session. I reminded Joan about her story of the week previously; she remembered it, and in fact told it again. I then told Joan that May had just that moment been in the room for a session. Joan at first looked dismayed and was silent for a moment. Then she looked up, with a somewhat triumphant look as if she had just solved a difficult puzzle. 'Ghost', she said, 'you saw May's ghost'. But she laughed, and could not stop laughing for two minutes. Thereafter, we heard no more about May, but other stories continued with the mutual understanding that they constituted colorations on an otherwise drab and routine life.

259

11.2 FANTASY AND IMAGERY

The case of Joan opens up the larger question of the role of fantasy in the lives of the mentally retarded. It also opens up the possibility of using fantasy deliberately, through guided imagery, in therapy with mentally retarded individuals.

In fact fantasy behaviour has already been investigated with this same workshop population. Turner (1983a), in research on this same population, called attention to what he labelled 'normalcy fabrications'. These were instances when the mentally retarded client exaggerated or distorted normal events into something grandiose or unlikely. Graffam and Turner (1984) cited some examples: 'One man routinely insists that he has been hired either to manage the workshop in some capacity, to manage a television station, or to work as a TV actor. Reports of verifiably fictitious trips to Paris and beyond are relatively common as well' (p. 130). Here one might interpolate cautiously that the investigator needs to be careful in his/her assessment. I had a patient at this workshop who reported consistently that she was going with her husband to France. Judging this as a fantasy, I made enquiries only to find out that her husband was born French and had relatives still there, and that indeed my patient was going there for a vacation. Nevertheless, there are many fantasy stories which, as Graffam and Turner said, are intertwined with normal events. These investigators interpret such examples as, in general, a relief from boredom. The workshop and home schedule is tedious and repetitive. The average client's day is institutionalized to the degree that individual creativity and initiative is absent. From this point of view, the mentally retarded person is no different from any other kind of institutionalized person — like a schoolchild, a patient in a hospital or a prisoner. It is not surprising that fantasy behaviour emerges. As Graffam and Turner make clear, it is not only normalcy fabrications that are manifested. There are a number of other types of fantasy productions enacted, including fantasy identifications. This means taking on the identity of characters played in various movie and television shows; there is no question of any fraudulence. It is just that the client assumes the identity of a well-known character, while admitting at the same time that he/she is who he/she really is. Turner (personal communication, 1984) told me that one client acted out consistently, for months, the identity of Bobby Ewing, a character on the popular television series, *Dallas.* It happened that the production 'killed' off this character, which discomfited the client as he had by this time identified himself not only with the character of Bobby Ewing, but partly with the television actor who played the character, and who of course was still alive.

In clinical work such clear examples of fantasy behaviour (with the exception of the above case of Joan) seldom arose. However, there was one case referred for therapy of a man who had recently displayed such behaviour. He and another male client had taken on the identity of two characters on television that were adolescent detectives, the 'Hardy Boys'. These two clients then acted out their role models on television, by exchanging messages in secret codes, making lists of clues and spying on suspicious characters (Turner, 1983b). Again, this fantasy behaviour persisted over the long period of $2\frac{1}{2}$ years.

This particular client, John, suffered from muscular dystrophy; he was permanently in a wheel-chair. At the time of therapy he was 29 years old. He was considered to be mildly retarded. He was referred for therapy on account of extreme negativity regarding his physical disability, and as regards his attitude towards workshop personnel and parents. He also tended to refuse actions that would have made him less dependent on others. He died about two years after I saw him. At the time of therapy he was extremely lethargic. His psychological attitude was one of extreme bitterness towards parents and colleagues. 'Feel I'm not wanted at home', he complained. He had a sarcastic, almost biting, way of expressing his opinions. He was angry with his doctors, and petulant towards authorities at the workshop. In addition, he adopted a superior attitude towards others; he recounted episodes in which he was depicted as knowing more than other people, or of doing things which resulted in others being discomfited. At this time in therapy, he appeared to have lost interest in his former fantasy behaviour of acting out the 'Hardy Boys', the two young detectives. This may have partly been due to the fact that he had lost his companion in the dual fantasy, who had been transferred to another facility. But his attitude towards his former fantasy behaviour was of interest. John said that he took the part of Joe Hardy. Then he added: 'Actors get paid; I didn't.' Apparently in his mind this seemed to put an end to this play behaviour. By this time of course he was far gone into depression, and it may be that his earlier recourse into fantasy play no longer served as an escape from his difficulties.

The salience of fantasy in the lives of some mentally retarded clients suggests that guided imagery might serve as a useful therapeutic tool. We will now discuss the advantages for communication with clients of using guided imagery as a technique. Two examples are given here. With many mentally retarded clients, sheer verbal communication is difficult, either because of articulation problems or because of poverty of expression. There is also the problem of their long-term exposure to medical and psychological questioning which often results in a reluctance of the client to 'open up'. In order to get round this difficulty the technique of guided imagery was used with several clients. This consisted of providing a client with a description of a setting, and asking him or her to imagine him/herself in this setting and to describe objects, people and events in such an imaginary situation. For example, a setting may be a clearing in the woods. There is a patch of open earth and a spade resting against a tree. The client is given the suggestion that if he/she digs with the spade, something of value may be uncovered. Generally this particular scenario is the opening one in a series. I used it in the following instance. A young man, mildly mentally retarded, was referred because of behaviour disturbance on his work-line in the workshop. He quarrelled a lot with his fellow workers. Also he appeared worried and would not divulge the source of his anxiety to his counsellor. When first interviewed by me, he denied that there was any problem at all (a very frequent phenomenon with such clients). He complained about his fellow workers and about the institution in general, but never revealed anything at all about his own self. After a few attempts at formal interviewing, I introduced the idea of imagery to him. He seemed interested and even enthusiastic, and immediately shut his eyes and began on this first example.

The client first began to describe the type of trees and the nature of the earth. He proved to have a good descriptive ability, replete with details and filling in with shapes and colours. He picked up the spade (shovel) and set to work digging in the earth. He acted out the scene with his hands, all the while his eyes being shut. Then he stopped. 'I hit something', he said. 'What is it?' I asked. 'Can't see it', he answered. I suggested that he dig around the object and clear it from the earth. He acted out this suggestion, and said he had found an iron box, like a treasure chest found in children's stories. (This is usually what is found in this guided imagery example.) I asked him to open it up. He used the spade again and prised the lid open. There was a silence and I asked him what he had found. He replied that it was books. This surprised me as in fact the client could not read. I had expected him to report money or perhaps even gold pieces, in keeping with the treasure chest imagery. I wondered why he would choose books. I asked him to describe the books. They were large, heavy books, ornate with golden clasps, coloured red. I then asked him to open the books and tell me what was inside. He then said there were photographs inside. I probed him further, as he did not immediately indicate what the photographs were. 'Naked girls', he said. This revelation opened the door for this client to be able to talk about his problems with sex. Previously he had never been able to indicate his sexual frustration; the imagery, however, had provided an indirect way of expressing his problem. Henceforth it was not necessary to use imagery when discussing his sexual problems.

Another example of the usefulness of imagery was of a different nature. The client here was an extremely well-articulated young Mexican-American, who again was mildly retarded, but his appearance and verbal fluency would have belied his handicap in ordinary society. He too had problems of sexual frustration, but this was not the issue here. In addition to the diagnosis of mild mental retardation, this client had been diagnosed as schizophrenic. He was currently medicated on one of the phenothiazines. When he arrived for the first interview, he complained of being afraid of the dark and of having nightmares, and of 'seeing spooks', as he put it, and 'hearing funny noises'. This client had heard, from a colleague, that I practised guided imagery, and wanted to do it with me. This was unusual to have a request in this way, but I acceded to the request on account of forming a relationship with the client. To my surprise, he turned out to be really successful at imagery. There was no confusion with him as to the reality status of the images. He did not confuse them with sensory impressions. But he did have extremely well fleshed-out imagery — it involved taste and touch impressions along with visual and auditory ones.

One example of his imagery is provided here. The suggestion was the schematic idea that he would find a wizard, an old man perhaps, who lived on top of a mountain. This wizard would give the client three things that would be of value for him, or important in some way. The excerpt from the tape of the session has the prompts of the psychologist in brackets:

(After the client had shut his eyes for a while: Do you see anything?)
See trees ... at top of mountain. (You've already climbed up?)
Yeah ... Wizard's in a cave ... Good walk in front of me ... Nothing much going on ... (You see the wizard?) No. It's dark in the cave. Pitch black. I can't see nothing ... (Maybe you could get a flashlight, or a lamp? Is there a lamp handy?) Yeah. (OK. Let's pick the lamp up, is it working?) Yeah ... (See anything?) Lots of entrances and tunnels going into different directions. Drawings on the wall. Animals and people. Dinosaurs, birds [*indecipherable*], big flesh-eating animals. No sign of wizard.

(Maybe you should sit down and wait for him?) OK. [*very long pause*] (How do you feel in this cave?) Funny. Scared a little bit, not much. Feel different. Everything is [disorientating]. Sitting on a rock. Big cave. (What is the cave like, etc.?) High walls. Black. [*long pause*] See wizard. He's over by the entrance to one of the tunnels. (Can you describe him?) Big pointed hat on his head with stars on it. Black. He is young man. (Maybe you should say hello to him?) [*To wizard*] Hello. (What does he say to you?) Hi. (Ask him what his name is?) [*To wizard*] What's your name? (What does he say?) Peter ... Peter Willis.

(Remember that he's going to show you something, three things. These things are good for you, or you want to have them, important for you. Ask him to show them to you.) [*long pause*] Too small, can't tell what it is ... little, tiny ... It's a rock. Small rock. Red. (Ask him why he gave you that.) Gave it to me for good luck [*places the rock in his pocket*]. (What's the second thing he has for you?) ... A picture. Small picture. (Can you describe it?) Somebody. A woman. Tall, blonde. Young. She's a beautiful girl. (Does she remind you of anyone?) Looks like some girl I saw in a commercial on TV. (Can you find out her name?) Elizabeth. (Can you find out from the wizard why he gave the picture?) Said he gave it to me so that I could write her and talk to her, be good friends [*places picture in his pocket also*].

(So now there's a third thing?) A pen, to write with. Ball-point. Small. Black. (Did the wizard say that the pen was actually to write with?) Why did you give me a ball-point pen? [*To wizard*] To write letters with. (To whom?) To the girl in the picture. (Do you know her address? Find out from Peter Willis the girl's address.) [*long pause*] He doesn't know her address ... he knows numbers. 14 ... 45, that's all. Street number. (Do you know the street?) Yes. Martin Street. (What town?) Inglewood.

Discussion with this client after this guided imagery gave some associations to the various objects and names in the story, but not all the names could be associated with. He had been to Inglewood when he was a young child, and now remembered shopping-malls and stores. He could not associate to Martin at all. He thought that the blonde Elizabeth came from a shaving-cream commercial. He could not remember a Peter or a Willis. 'Came out of my head, I guess', he commented. (The comment, perhaps, needs to be made that the name Peter Willis has the same initials as the present writer's last name.) The face of the wizard was that of a young blond man. The client thought that he came from Germany; the client had no associations with Germany, but his mother had come from Scandinavia, and his father's family came from Mexico. The numbers 14 and 45 meant nothing to him. The client did keep rocks; he picked up rocks in the workshop garden and took them home. He associated texture, size and colour as indicators of sex in rocks. A pink rock was female, a red rock was male. Male rocks had lines and squares on them; female rocks had deep lines on them. He did own photographs of people.

The use of imagery in this case allowed an entry into this client's more personal world as well as giving an insight into his associations. There was left a suspicion that due to his cognitive inability to express the subtle difference between imagery and hallucinations, he would easily have given the appearance of having hallucinatory material, but there were other symptoms of disturbance that would have been encouraged given his diagnostic label. Placing the locus of control of the imagery firmly and squarely within his reach, by virtue of the guided imagery sessions, allowed him to demarcate what was within and without. In a case like this, it is difficult to establish causation, but at any rate the nightmares stopped, and he ceased to report seeing ghosts and hearing unexplained noises. The point to be made here is that guided imagery served as a means of communication, not just of expressing his internal needs to others, but also of distinguishing for himself a confusion of inner and outer stimuli.

11.3 PROBLEMS OF WITHDRAWAL

Leudar and Fraser (1985) have described some withdrawal strategies in mentally retarded adults. They cite Watzlavick *et al.* (1967) to the effect that withdrawal from communication is an active, complex and inherently paradoxical process. Two cases will be given here that support this statement, in which withdrawal and difficulties of communication were salient features.

The first is a 28-year-old woman, whose IQ was in the lower range of the TMR scale. At the time of referral, she was showing a bizarre behaviour with dolls. She would make paper dolls from the odds and ends of tissue paper, Cellotape and string and cut out pictures from magazines. She also appeared to have an obsession with the faces of clocks and watches, as she would cut out pictures of these from magazine advertisements, and stick them on to the face of the tissue doll. Alice, as she will be called, did not voluntarily communicate with others, and responded only with restricted and telegraphic word responses after persistence by an interrogator. Counsellors and supervisors speculated whether she was hallucinating. Their main concern was that Alice was so completely immersed in this doll behaviour that she was becoming impossible to direct and enter in ordinary communication.

Preliminary interviews supported these reports from her supervisors. Alice was capable of making a few statements — for example, saying 'two months' in response to the question of how long she had been at the workshop. Such statements were rare, and she behaved in the opening sessions in exactly the manner described above.

The initial plan of therapy was to become involved with Alice in the doll construction. This was the only event that she seemed interested in, and it offered the only chance of communication. Thenceforth non-verbal cues of eye contact, gestures and sometimes accidental hand contact were the only avenues of communication. The interesting point was that she was insistent that the therapist construct the doll, not herself. This served as a means of eliciting her interest and to a certain extent the means of getting her out of her withdrawal. Whereas the procedure of asking her questions had only produced a negative affect and withdrawal, making the dolls in the way that she had done it elicited positive affect, and often words. Alice would guide the therapist in the making of the doll. She did this by stating single words as commands: eyes, hat, trousers, and so on. Alice finally called the first doll constructed in this way 'Joe'. It was discovered that this was the name of the bus driver who drove her to the workshop in the mornings. She actually did say also 'but driver'. Alice wanted me to draw the bus driver's badge on the face of the doll. All that could safely be inferred from this exchange was that Joe, the bus driver, was important to her.

The details of the doll-making need to be further described, as any particular act was paid close attention to by this client. Alice was always insistent on adding a watch, and getting numbers and clock hands on to the face of the doll. The numbers need not be in their correct place. Any attempt by the therapist in deviating from this performance made Alice nervous and she would pace up and down, insisting on a particular act — like putting the numbers on the face — until her command was carried out. Once the therapist tried talking to the doll, hoping this would facilitate talking by her, but Alice would have none of this, and forced the therapist to continue constructing the doll. Another time the therapist brought in a doll kit, purchased from a toy store, with removable bits of body parts and clothing. Alice identified correctly all the parts, and indeed placed them correctly on to a cut-out form board for this purpose, but having done this lost all interest in the toy doll and instructed the therapist to resume construction on the tissue doll, Cellotape and cut-outs. While this behaviour could be interpreted as meaning that the client had control over the therapist and that it was basically a communicative strategy of making herself dependent on the therapist, it did allow for verbal interchange to operate somewhat spontaneously, without forcing the issue. The following excerpts from an early conversation with Alice indicate the difficulty of direct questioning and shows the predominance of the patient's internal needs, when she disregards questions and focuses on the doll construction. I was interested to learn whether she related to the doll at all.

Psychologist: Do you ever talk to this doll? [*No answer from Alice or indication that she has heard the question, intent on the doll*] Do you ever talk to this doll?

A.: [*affirmative*] Ummm.

Psych.: What do you say to the doll?

A.: Put hair on the back [*gesturing to doll, a command to the therapist*].

Psych.: [*Puts hair on the back of the doll as ordered*] But do you ever talk to the doll? When you are alone?

A.: [*long pause*] Put circles on doll. Right here [*Gesture to face region of doll*].

Psych.: [*draws circle to represent a face*] Now the doll is beginning to look like ... What does it look like? Looks like a lion to me.

A.: Beetle.

Psych.: Like a beetle. But you call him Joe? [*i.e. the bus driver*] Right?

A.: Put glasses on him.

Psych.: Does Joe wear glasses?

A.: They're broken.

Psych.: What happened to them? Someone step on them?

A.: (*laughs*) Stepped on them. Drive him mad.

Psych.: When did you see Joe last?

A.: This morning.

Psych.: You saw Joe this morning? Did he say 'hello' to you?

A.: He sneezed. Coughed [*simulates cough*]. It doesn't feel too good.

Psych.: What doesn't feel too good?

A.: The way I throw up. [*pause*] Want a drink of water. Go away [*gestures to her stomach, apparently wishing the stomach discomfort would go away or, perhaps, that a drink of water would make the stomach problem go away*].

Psych.: When you go out of here, you can have a drink of water. [*Alice's apparent liking for Joe, the bus driver, provided a motivation for her to sustain a relatively normal conversation with the psychologist in which she displays for the first time normal emotions. The opportunity came when she had asked for the psychologist to make a paper wrist-watch, which she then bound with Cellotape to her wrist, and saying that it is like Joe's, and then adding what sounded like some remark to the effect that he was not well*] Tell me about Joe. Is he all right?

A.: He's thrown up. On the bus.

Psych.: He threw up on the bus, no kidding? What happened?

A.: I don't know (*appears distressed*).

Psych.: Was he very sick today?

A.: I'm worried about him.

Psych.: Why are you worried about him?

A.: I want him.

Psych.: You want him. Where is he now? [*Alice points towards door*] Is he outside somewhere?

A.: He's in the bus.

Psych.: When you say you want him, what do you want him for?

A.: I want him back.

Psych.: Where's he gone?

A.: I don't know [*cries*].

Psych.: You like Joe, don't you? You're very fond of Joe? [*Alice still crying. Answer indecipherable*] Does Joe know that you like him?

A.: No.

Psych.: Oh? Why not? You've never told Joe that you like him? [*Alice crying. Answer indecipherable*] Suppose you told him, what would happen? [*Alice stops crying, looks up. Shrugs shoulders*]

Between the first and second conversations reported here there was a period of two months. Therapy continued in the same manner for nearly one year. The mutual doll construction acted as a vehicle for allowing further conversation, which became more directed as the sessions increased.

The second case to be discussed under this heading was a different type of withdrawal. The patient was seen at a clinic. He was a white 26-year-old male, who worked during the daytime but lived in at a clinic overnight during the period of therapy. Previously he had been living at home. We call him Sam. At age 5 he had been diagnosed as moderately retarded complicated by expressive aphasia and perceptual-motor problems. In conversation, Sam was appropriate in his behaviour — i.e. he attempted to converse with an interlocutor and answer questions, and he did respond in socially appropriate ways. He spoke in one- and two-word utterances, however. He could not repeat (on the Minnesota Test for Differential Diagnosis of Aphasia) sentences at all. He could not read, although he knew most letters. Sam was referred because of conduct problems. His mother reported that often he would return from work and beat on the door. He would then destroy property and tear up his shirts. Initial interviews of the patient revealed a paradoxical picture of loss of control displayed in these temper tantrums and a seemingly overcontrolled withdrawn attitude, which nevertheless was basically co-operative, not hostile and sullen.

Further investigation of Sam's problems revealed that he had been socialized very strictly. This had been done with the best of intentions and in fact great care had been lavished on him by his parents. The fact remained that he had difficulty in expressing his emotional life. This was due to two reasons: first, he had been taught to control to a high degree his feelings and impulses; and secondly, Sam just did not have the verbal ability to express his emotions. When he was frustrated or just simply irritated by an event, there was the tendency to hold in the consequent emotion and the inability to indicate that he was upset. Consequently, when his emotions reached a pitch, he just acted out and began to destroy the environment. The appropriate therapy was first to give him permission — in the face of his previous training — that there were times when expression of emotion was permitted. And then Sam needed to be given some method of expressing such emotions as annoyance in a manner that was both within his linguistic range and indicative for others to recognize that he was upset. Basically this patient was best capable with one-word utterances. A short succinct swear word was appropriate for these occasions, and it was given to him. Sam already knew the word of course, but he had never used it openly, and found it a relief that he was permitted to articulate it on these occasions when he found himself upset. Basically, although other approaches were also used in the therapy of this patient, the method was finding a communicative style for this patient to use in times of frustration and annoyance.

11.4 THE PROBLEM OF APPARENT TRIVIALITY

A particular problem for the psychologist is that of discerning important concerns of mentally retarded persons that are embedded and expressed in apparent trivial events. It is a temptation for the psychologist (or, at least, for this writer) to dismiss these apparent trivialities and proceed with something more important. It took some time before the realization came that, despite the event's seemingly unimportant content *to the psychologist*, it was very important and entirely non-trivial to the client. Consider the case of a 25-year-old mildly retarded man, who had been sexually abused when he was an adolescent, and was now being referred for 'acting-out' behaviour in the workshop with his colleagues and being negative towards his supervisor. There were two instances with this client which exemplified this business of triviality. More or less straightaway, he proceeded to tell me in detail about his practice of buying little cakes from a nearby supermarket. He went into exact specificity about the type of cakes, whether they had currants in them or not, their size, their taste, and how much he paid for them each time — indicating the dollar note he paid over the counter and how much change he received. I learned about the context of how he went to get these cakes, whereabouts in the store the cake section was, who served him, what kind of bag was used to place the cakes, and so forth. This account was given several times, slightly differing each time according to the number of cakes bought and the amount of money needed. From all this I received two important impressions about this client. First, he wanted to tell me that he could act normally like anybody else, that he had the competency to walk into a store and buy something. The second thing was that he nevertheless had some anxiety about the operation. More than once he questioned me whether he had paid the correct amount of money, whether in fact he had been cheated. This client could not express his feelings about the world he lived in, about complicated relationships, about the difficulties of lack of competence, and so on, in any abstract way. However, he could adequately express such matters, with all their nuances and subtleties, in this detailed story of the cakes. The realization of the importance of the cakes and their buying helped with another incident with the same client. This man could read a little, and he had bought three sports almanacs which he kept in a carefully wrapped waterproof parcel, which he carried about with him everywhere. The trait of competency was involved here also. The client did know and remember a great deal of sports trivialities: who played what for which team back in 1972, who came second in the big football championship three years ago, and so on. The client was proud of all this knowledge and wished to express it to the psychologist.

The problem came when he carried the sports almanacs to the workshop and asked for his treasure to be carefully placed in a locker while he was working. This became a nuisance for the workshop authorities and they refused to do it, telling the client to keep the parcel at home. This distressed the client and he lost his temper, resulting in reprimand. It was difficult for the workshop supervisors to understand the complex emotional message this parcel of sports almanacs carried; however, when it was explained to them, allowance was make for him to lock away the parcel and peace ensued.

Similar cases arise with reports of using television. One is struck by clients whose intelligence tests report that they have difficulty with the five digits, forward and backward, rote-memory subtest, yet are fairly proficient in detailing the late afternoon and early evening television guide, with the correct time for each event and the particular channel carrying the programme. Whether or not these clients are always accurate is really beside the point, it is the television world that interests them, and they wish to express that they have the ability of finding the programme that interests them. Again, the psychologist has to sit patiently and hear what is for him/ her trivial details about boring programmes in order to reach some understanding of what the client is trying to express about him or herself.

Graffam and Turner (1984) have remarked under the heading of 'idealistic expectations' that 'elaborate planning goes into what are quite unrealistic expectations for the future' (pp. 131–2). This was encountered in the case of a mildly retarded young man who kept talking about his future marriage. It was difficult to determine whether the actual act of marriage (to another mildly retarded client of the workshop) was unrealistic or not. There was determined opposition to the marriage by the parents of both these young people, but conceivably it was possible. The unrealistic aspect concerned the planning for the wedding and subsequent living together. The male client did considerable planning for the buying of a marriage ring, to the extent of visiting various jewellery stores, putting down financial deposits, designing the ring, and so on. It was often frustrating for this psychologist to be forced to discuss in the therapy sessions the choice of marriage rings, their worth, the size of his fiancée's finger and other details of this nature. Again, it took time to assess that, for this client, quite ponderous emotional issues of bonding, decisions of a lasting nature and doubts about his attachment to this girl were being encoded in the elaborate and lengthy description and discussion of apparent trivialities of fitting a ring to a finger and whether there should be clasps on the ring.

11.5 CONCLUSION

The foregoing material has to be understood under the heading of pragmatics. All of the examples are between two interlocutors: therapist and patient or client. Both interlocutors have their own intentions. In addition, the intention of one, attributed to by the other, may not be the same as the first. For example, although the therapist generally considered that it was the intention of the mentally retarded client to disclose his or her problems, it was sometimes found later to be the case that the client was attempting to manipulate the therapist. This became clear in the case of a young man, who in addition to his mental handicap was also afflicted with a physical handicap. His revelations about feelings of love for a staff member and stories about the liaison were all designed for the therapist to facilitate contact on his behalf. Although such manipulation and indeed other aspects of the therapist–patient relationship are common to other people than mentally retarded individuals, there are certain characteristics of the latter which are focal to this group.

One of these characteristics is that mentally retarded adults have had a long and sustained exposure to being guided, questioned and directed. To a certain extent, they have learned for themselves strategies of coping with this barrage. It is important in therapy for mentally retarded persons to understand that in this situation they are able to dictate selection of what is to be talked about, and overall that the therapy sessions are qualitatively different from being questioned by a psychologist or psychiatrist in test or interrogatory situations. In this respect, Leudar (1981) made an important point when he stated:

> According to Habermas, the communicative structure is free from such constraints only when both participants have an equal chance to select and employ speech acts. This is not the case for the mentally retarded who, with some exceptions (interacting with each other, with their families and friends), find themselves in interactions which are systematically institutionally constrained. (p. 125).

In therapy this tendency becomes a problem because it influences the patient either to be wary in what is reported, or sometimes — as with the young man with the physical handicap — to be manipulative, or in general does not provide the mentally retarded client with the psychological ambience of allowing him/herself to be an equal partner in the speech acts of the sessions. There is also another aspect of the subordinate role in which the mentally retarded person is cast. This is that referral problems (in other words, those problems which are considered to be such and articulated by a supervisor) are not really mental health problems so much as problems to do with obedience, promptness, politeness, deference to superiors, and so on. These types of referral problem become a serious difficulty for the therapist, for he/she is immediately cast into the role of an authority figure if they are dealt with explicitly. But mostly they are complicated problems as the lack of deference, truancy, and the like, often mask a genuine psychological difficulty.

Another problem that is particularly related to therapy with mentally retarded persons is the question of assessment, as has been discussed in the beginning of this chapter. Fraser *et al.* (1986) have stated that:

> Psychiatric assessment of handicapped people is difficult. Their expressive abilities are limited, and many are withdrawn. This poses particular constraints on psychiatric interviews. (p. 50)

271

The difficulty is not only limited to deciding between the occurrence of a specific mental illness syndrome and the possibility of misleading communication, but also deciding whether the *absence* of communication (as in the case of withdrawal tendencies) is due to dynamic processes in personality structure or to sheer difficulty in articulation. This latter difficulty is particularly complicated in those cases where neurological damage is mixed with personality problems. In all these instances of lack of verbal communication or distortions of verbal communication as in semantic aphasia, there has to be greater reliance than is usually the case on non-verbal signals of emotion and intention. This is always difficult for a therapist, or indeed any mental health professional, to assess unequivocally, and requires a good knowledge of the patient or client in different contexts in order to reach a proper conclusion.

One last point needs to be made. The present writer, as well as others, has been impressed by the fantasy production of many mentally retarded clients. Yet when examining the case files of such people, the results and assessments of projective techniques that have previously been given, does not prepare one for the richness of the spontaneous fantasy material. One has the impression that applications of standard projective techniques do not trigger the potential for fantasy behaviour in mentally retarded individuals. However, this is an impression only and it needs to be more carefully pinned down in further research.

In conclusion, it needs to be repeated and emphasized that although most, maybe all, of the communication problems noted in mentally retarded individuals in this chapter are to be observed in intellectually normal people, there do seem to be some communication problems that are likely to occur more often, or in an exaggerated form, among this population. The therapeutic relationship, with its permissiveness for elicitation of expressing emotional problems and its adoption of a non-authoritarian role for the therapist, is an ideal arena for exposing such communication problems.

REFERENCES

Cicchetti, Dante and Sroufe, L. Alan (1978) An organizational view of affect: illustration from the study of Down's syndrome in *The Development of Affect* (eds M. Lewis and L.A. Rosenblums), Plenum, New York, pp. 309–50.
Emde, R.N., Katz, E.L. and Thorpe, J.K. (1978) Emotional expression in infancy: early development in Down's syndrome in *The Development of Affect* (eds M. Lewis and L.A. Rosenblum), Plenum, New York, pp. 351–60.
Fraser, W.I., Leudar, I., Gray, J. and Campbell, J. (1986) Psychiatric and behaviour disturbance in mental handicap, *J. Ment. Defic. Res.*, *30*, 49–57.
Graffam, Joseph, and Turner, J.L. (1984) Escape from boredom: the meaning of eventfulness in the lives of clients at a sheltered workshop in *Lives in Process: Mildly Retarded Adults in a Large City* (ed. R.B. Edgerton), Monographs of the American Association on Mental Deficiency No. 6, AAMD, Washington, DC, pp. 121–44.

Leudar, I. (1981) Strategic communication in mental retardation in *Communicating with Normal and Retarded Children* (eds W.I. Fraser and P. Grieve), Wright, Bristol, pp. 113–29.

Laudar, I. and Fraser, W.I. (1985) How to keep quiet: some withdrawal strategies in mentally handicapped adults, *J. Ment. Defic. Res.*, *29*, 315–30.

Matson, J.L. and Barrett, R.P. (eds) (1982) *Psychopathology in the Mentally Retarded*, Grune and Stratton, New York.

Menolascino, Frank J. and Stark, Jack A. (1984) *Handbook of Mental Illness in the Mentally Retarded*, Plenum, New York.

Mundy, Peter C., Seibert, Jeffrey M. and Hogan, Anne E. (1985) Communication skills in mentally retarded children in *Children with Emotional Disorders and Developmental Disabilities* (ed. M. Sigman), Grune and Stratton, New York, pp. 45–70.

Syzmanski, L.S. and Tanguay, P. (eds) (1980) *Emotional Disorders of Retarded Persons*, University Park Press, Baltimore, Md.

Turner, J.L. (1983a) Workshop society: ethnographic observations in a work setting for retarded adults in *Environment and Behavior: The Adaptation of Mentally Retarded Persons* (eds K.T. Kernan, M.J. Begab and R.B. Edgerton), University Park Press, Baltimore, Md., pp. 147–71.

Turner, J.L. (1983b) Secrets, artifice and semblance: forms and functions of naturally occurring fantasy in the lives of mentally retarded adults, paper presented at Plenary Session, 107th Annual Meeting of the American Association on Mental Deficiency, Dallas, Texas.

Watzlavick, P., Bevin, J.H. and Jackson, D.D. (1967) *Pragmatics of Human Communication. A Study of Interactional Patterns, Pathologies and Paradoxes*, W.W. Norton, New York.

12

Communicative Environments for Mentally Handicapped People

Ivan Leudar

12.1 INDIVIDUALS, ENVIRONMENTS AND COMMUNICATIVE PROBLEMS

Communicative problems are frequent in interactions where at least one participant is mentally handicapped. These problems occur in all aspects of the communication process and may involve (a) *language skills* (i.e. the ability to produce grammatical sentences and use them to represent actual or imagined states of the world); (b) *pragmatic design* (i.e. the production of utterances which are both textually appropriate in discourse and effective in fulfilling speakers' aims); and (c) *socio-emotional function* (which concerns self-presentation, and maintenance or transformation of social structures in communication).

Much research effort has gone into documenting the inadequacies in linguistic skills of mentally handicapped individuals and their developmental and cognitive correlates (O'Connor and Hermelin, 1963; Schiefelbusch, Copeland and Smith, 1967; Schiefelbusch, 1972; Mittler, 1978). With some exceptions (e.g. Price-Williams and Sabsay, 1979; Kernan and Sabsay, 1981; Leudar, 1981; Sabsay and Kernan, 1983; Turner, Kernan and Gelphman, 1984), pragmatic aspects of communication in mental handicap and systematic constraints on communication have attracted much less attention; the interactions of different aspects of communication in generating actual communicative problems have been almost totally ignored. This is unfortunate because it is precisely such interactions which provide us with insight into the communicative processes in mental handicap. Language is the most important source of information regarding whether a person is perceived as mentally handicapped; furthermore, some problems of communication stem from the attempts to appear competent (cf. Eggerton, 1967). Sabsay and Platt (1985) and Kernan and Sabsay (in Chapter 6 in this volume) argue that mentally handicapped persons often design their messages less effectively than they could because they try to present an image of competence. Kernan, Sabsay and Shin (1987) demonstrated that the *labelling* can be based on perceived inadequacies of speech, and on intonation in particular. Sabsay and Kernan (1983) have shown that a mentally handicapped person's inability to articulate clearly results in an increased frequency of 'other initiated other-repair' (i.e. when one clarifies or rephrases unprompted what another person has said) and argue that this affects negatively a mentally handicapped person's self-image. If they are frequent, such repairs, exemplified in section 12.2, can be paradoxical: they are meant to be cooperative, but they reproduce the existence of mental handicap by displaying the participating individuals' different levels of competence and consequently the incompetence of a handicapped person. In fact this type of repair characterizes the speech of adults to children (cf. McTear, 1984, chapter 7). In their case, however, the uneven distribution of repair initiative reflects the complementarity of their relationship and becomes more even, as the children grow up. Not so for mentally handicapped people.

Mental handicap is not an intangible mental phenomenon, but is distributed in the pattern of communication. It may seem provocative and difficult to accept, but according to some researchers (e.g. Brewer and Yearley, 1986) mentally handicapped individuals themselves may cooperate in the process of their own stigmatization. Goffman (1986) also comments on this possibility when he discusses 'acceptance' of a stigma by the stigmatized person: 'Those who have dealings with him fail to accord him respect and regard ...; he echoes this denial by finding that some of his own attributes warrant it' (p. 19). Communications in mental handicap can be deeply problematic in other respects. Leudar and Fraser (1985), and Leudar, Fraser and Jeeves (1984, 1987), investigated the relationship between message design, production of social relationships in institutional settings and emotional needs of withdrawn mentally handicapped people. One of their arguments was that communicative withdrawal can be a matter of asserting personal autonomy in restrictive environments. They also identified some of the withdrawal strategies and have shown how they differed according to how mentally handicapped individuals exercised the control over their communicative environments. Some attempts to control the communicative environment, together with the attempts to achieve autonomy, however, typically lead mentally handicapped people into being seen as behaviourally disturbed and into deepening social problems.

So although the three levels of analysis, given at the onset, are fine conceptually, it is through their interaction that actual communicative disorders are produced, as is, to some extent, mental handicap itself. The argument here will be that one problem has been that researchers have adopted an almost exclusively individualistic perspective and reified communicative disorders. It has been customary to locate communication problems *in* mentally handicapped persons, to assume that they result from their lack of competence and skill and to study these (Leudar, 1981). It would be irrational to deny that mentally handicapped people often lack skills to allow effective and conventional expression, but they also lack opportunities. One should maintain a balanced perspective: there is no need for lack of skill to remain the exclusive focus of research; in fact this is undesirable. We should turn our attention from the shortcomings of competence to the possibility that the communicative environments of mentally retarded people are in some respects unlike those of average individuals and are systematically distorted (cf. Habermas, 1970). Goffman (1986), when discussing stigmatization, writes 'we may perceive his defensive response to his situation as a direct expression of his defect, and then see both defect and response as a just retribution for something he or his parents or his tribe did, and hence a justification of the way we treat him' (p. 16). One should perhaps substitute 'perceive' by 'misperceive'. It seems to us that *individualizing* communicative disturbances overlooks their essential characteristic, namely that a person's competence problems are 'remembered' by his or her audiences and embodied in the structure of institutions; this produces a lasting and non-standard context in which distorted and/or inadequate communicative skills are exercised (cf. Leudar and Fraser, 1985; Leudar, Fraser and Jeeves, 1987). Communicative disturbances do not reside simply in the fact that an individual communicates in a somehow exceptional manner, but also in the fact that this establishes and indeed reproduces a non-standard communicative world. The aim here is to establish some principles to describe communicative environments and to apply them empirically in an investigation of whether what I have said so far about the nature of communicative problems is correct; and whether communicative environments for the mentally handicapped and average individuals do indeed differ from each other.

The central question addressed in this chapter is whether communicative disturbances should be treated as individual or contextual phenomena, or in fact as processes which produce both individuals and their contexts. This question has parallels in other disciplines concerned with communication and cognition. In psychoanalysis 'object relations theory' (e.g. Greenberg and Mitchell, 1983) is specifically concerned with the growth of individuality out of interactions with others, recognizing that 'it is relationships (with others, and with so called internal objects) that build psychic structure' (Alford, 1987, p. 9). In psychology, developing Gibson's framework, Costall (1986) and Costall and Still (1986) proposed *mutualism* which defines meanings as relations between individuals and environments. In philosophy the problem is discussed under the heading *externalism*. Putnam (1975) has argued that meanings of words cannot be exclusively mental entities 'in the head', and McGinn (1983) has elaborated externalism as an approach to the philosophy of meaning. Finally, the findings of research in pragmatics indicate that communicative intentions and the force of communicative acts can be socially distributed and negotiated

(Levinson, 1979; Edmonson, 1981; Leudar and Antaki, 1988; Leudar and Browning, 1988). The increasing consensus in this work is thus that radical individualism hinders research and as an approach to communication has failed. This chapter echoes this trend. Our focus here is on *communicative* environments available for mentally handicapped people and the constraints on both. The aim of the research reported here was to establish dimensions relevant to deciding whether communicative environments differ for handicapped and average populations and how they may be affected by the presence of a secondary handicap of behaviour disturbance. Contemporary pragmatic theory is used to specify the idea of communicative environment and to make the analysis productive and applicable. In section 12.2 we outline some relevant pragmatic concepts, and in section 12.3 we present an account of an empirical study.

12.2 PRAGMATICS, PROBLEMS OF COMMUNICATION AND MENTAL HANDICAP

Three concerns of contemporary pragmatics are relevant here: *intentionality*, *conventionality* and *face*. Most current models of communication are based on the insight that one type of communication, which seems uniquely human, is intention mediated: the speakers' problem is to express their communicative intentions and the hearers' problem is to attribute them correctly (Grice, 1957, 1982; Bach and Harnish, 1979; Recanati, 1986). This is to say that meanings of utterances in dialogues are not the same as their sentence meanings, but correspond to the speakers' purpose(s) in saying something; and the utterances are successful *as communications* if their purpose(s) are recognized (Bach, 1987). The intentional stance on meaning seems appropriate and useful in analysing communications of mentally handicapped people. Their language skills are often particularly affected but all of them, even the severely handicapped, communicate nevertheless (Price-Williams and Sabsay, 1979); this is possible only because clearly articulated and grammatically correct speech is not *necessary* for conveying communicative intent as the following exchanges 1 and 2 illustrate. (These and all the other examples of interactions actually took place in training centres or in hospitals; none are fictitious):

(1)
Psychiatrist: Who you scared of?
P.F.: nki
Psych.: Nobody?
P.F.: nki
Psych.: Nobody
P.F.: mhm.

(2)
Psychiatrist: What's this lady's name?
P.F.: hv gs
Psych.: Say that again
P.F.: hv ges
Psych.: 'Have a guess', is that what you said?
P.F.: Mhm.

While the ability to represent intentions clearly and explicitly in grammatically correct speech is not necessary for communication, there is a price on not being able to do so. Unlike most ordinary cooperative interactions, the process whereby audiences establish their handicapped partners' communicative intentions is foregrounded (Leudar, 1980) and seems to permeate all interaction. The communicative partners of mentally handicapped people often echo even those utterances with clear meaning, as in exchange 3, below. Sometimes it seems as if all expressions of intent by a handicapped person required a validation by their average partners:

(3)
Instructor: Who's going to be putting them [Christmas decorations] up?
Trainee: Lynn H.
I.: Lynn H. [*falling intonation*]
T.: Yeah.

Lack of competence and cooperative efforts to overcome it may have one additional negative consequence. Even in ordinary conversations, communicative intentions are negotiated and the participants need to control the extent to which what they say is subject to interpretation. In exchange 4, for example, K. interprets J.'s preceding move as an indirect request to complain and rejects it, and K. subsequently disowns expressing that intent. J. could have attempted to block the potential interpretation of her move as a request by, for instance, adding, 'don't you think?'

(4)
J.: I really think they should have done it by now.
K.: Why don't phone them yourself.
J.: I didn't ask you to do anything.

It would be interesting to know whether this aspect of communication (i.e. having one's intent reinterpreted by others) is exaggerated for mentally handicapped people. How often, as in exchanges 1 and 2, does the mutually established communicative intention correspond to the one the mentally handicapped person began with and how often does it not?

The second claim common in pragmatics is that communicative intentions are interpretations of utterances against the mutually assumed background of communicative conventions (Grice, 1975; Lewis, 1983). In fact intentional interpretations are based on information of various kinds. It can be specific and reflect experiences two individuals have had together and of each other — they may know, for example, each others' aims, political beliefs, ethical persuasions, attitudes and intellectual strengths and weaknesses. This specific information usually aids conversation but, in some cases, communicative problems may be a reflection of the history of a particular relationship. Normally, however, there is background information which is mutually assumed by participants in cooperative interactions. Most pragmatic approaches hold that ordinarily audiences infer meanings on the assumption that speakers abide by tacit but mutually assumed *communicative conventions*. Figure 12.1 lists some of those which have been put forward.

The figure includes a set of principles formulated by Lewis (1983), according to which we can understand others as rational individuals with beliefs and desires and their utterances as expressions of beliefs and desires. I also include 'maxims for interested speech', formulated by may (1981), to allow interpretation of communications in competitive encounters. However, the focus is on 'maxims of conversation', postulated by Grice (1975); these are shown again in Figure 12.1. Their precise formulation has actually been a subject of much discussion (e.g. Leudar and Browning, 1988; Sperber and Wilson, 1986) but their function seems reasonably clear. Audiences interpret utterances on the assumption that the maxims are in power. If an occasional utterance seems to violate a maxim, it is (re-) interpreted so as to preserve the validity of the maxim. This process is anticipated by the speakers; it constrains their communicative behaviour, but can be also used by speakers to convey indirect meanings — implicatures. The mutual assumption by participants in a conversation that the maxims of conversation are in power is also said to enable the participants to disambiguate what is said ambiguously and to assign to words their intended referents. In other words, the background of maxims expands the meaning potential of utterances and facilitates language processing. The communications of mentally handicapped people, however, often violate maxims of conversation, as do the ones of average individuals interacting with them. In exchange 5, for example, P violates the maxim of relevance; in exchanges 6 and 7, below, the maxim of quality is not assumed by a psychiatrist interviewing a handicapped individual:

(5)
B.: And before that you lived in another hospital. Did you like it there?
P.: [*silence*]
B.: Did you like it there?
P.: I like you as well.
B.: Oh, that's nice, yes.

Figure 12.1: Some of the communicative maxims proposed in the literature.

Maxims of conversation (Grice, 1975)

Quality
Try to make your contribution one that is true
    (i) Do not say what you believe to be false
    (ii) Do not say that for which you lack adequate evidence
Quantity
    (i) Make your contribution as informative as is required for the purposes of the exchange
    (ii) Do not make your contribution more informative than is required
Manner
Be perspicuous
    (i) Avoid obscurity of expression
    (ii) Avoid ambiguity
    (iii) Be brief (avoid unnecessary prolixity)
    (iv) Be orderly
Relevance
Be relevant

Principles of the theory of persons (Lewis, 1983, chapters 8 and 11)

Principle of Charity: '... so far as other constraints allow it, the beliefs and desires ascribed [to another person] should be the same as our own beliefs and desires'
Principle of Rationalization: '[a person] should be represented as a rational agent; the beliefs and desires ascribed to him [...] should be such as to provide good reasons for his behaviour [...]'
Principle of Truthfulness (and trust): '[...] the speaker utters one of the sentences he believes to be true in [a language]; and the hearer (or reader) responds by coming to share that belief of the speaker's (unless he already has it) and adjusting his other beliefs accordingly'

Maxims for interested speech (May, 1981)

Veracity: 'Take plain statements of fact by vulnerable authors at face value'
Best Face: 'Treat the case that is put as the strongest case that can be made'
Normative Partiality: 'When an interested advocate nominates a standard for chosing, assume that the alternative compares favourably with its competitors with regard to that standard'
Empirical Partiality: 'When an advocate furnishes unsolicited information about his preferred product, assume that the information is "positive" in comparative terms for his preferred alternative'
Elision as Concession: 'When an advocate abstains from making a rhetorically pivotal claim, assume that the claim is groundless'

Components of face *(Brown and Levinson, 1978)*

Negative Face: 'the want of every "competent adult member" that his actions are unimpeded by others'
Positive Face: '[...] the want of every member that his wants be desirable to at least some others'

The data on how often maxims of conversation are violated in interactions of 'average' individuals is not available. In fact the focus of the past research has been on violations of communicative conventions by mentally handicapped people rather than by the average individuals interacting with them. Sabsay and Kernan (1983) have shown that violations are frequent for the maxims of quantity and relevance. According to Leudar and Fraser (1985), the violations of the maxim of quantity are particularly frequent in withdrawn individuals, and do not always reflect problems with information processing, but may be a matter of strategy in communication. The communicative consequences of habitual violations of communicative conventions are not clear. Are implicatures not being conveyed? Are the attributions of communicative intentions and beliefs blocked? Do the answers to these questions depend on which maxim is in question?

Can we both assume that a person abides by some of the maxims of conversation and also that he or she is mentally handicapped? It seems to us that this is not the case. First, the evidential clause of Grice's maxim of quality (which allows hearers to assume that speakers have adequate evidence for their assertions) is, in general, in conflict with that being 'mentally handicapped' identifies the labelled individuals as intellectually incompetent. May's maxims and Lewis's principle of Rationalization are formulated on the assumption of 'rationality', that individuals choose as far as possible optimal means to ends — but is such an assumption likely to be made for a mentally handicapped person?

The third important notion is that of *face*. Goffman (1955) sees face 'as the positive social value a person effectively claims for himself [in an encounter]' (p. 223). This corresponds closely to *positive face*, defined by Brown and Levinson (1978) as 'the need [of an individual] to be appreciated by his or her communicative partners'. Brown and Levinson (1978) postulate that people have, in addition, *negative face* (see Figure 12.1). This represents an individual's need to be free of arbitrary constraints. According to them, moves in cooperative conversations are constructed taking into account the participants' mutual need to preserve their face; politeness, in particular, is an attempt to compensate for face-threatening aspects of conversation moves. However, in certain types of dialogue the duty of some participants to consider other participants' face is suspended. One would, for example, be normally apologetic when pointing out somebody's error; but a teacher will not be when correcting a pupil. One usually apologizes for an imposition, but a sergeant does not apologize to a private for ordering him about, whereas the latter had better soften even his requests. Some speech situations are systematically biased with respect to the *face* of others. This is presumably due to the nature of joint activities and the participants' power differentials. In some situations the aim of a move can in fact be to attack the face of another person and devalue them. The interesting point about the notion of face is that it implies that individuality, the self-respect and the value which an individual is attributed by other people arise and are maintained in interactions. The notion of face is obviously crucial in understanding some aspects of communication of mentally handicapped people. It is clear that the face of mentally handicapped people is under constant attack. As I have already pointed out, some communicative problems may be caused by attempts to display competence, i.e. to preserve face. This is, however, not the only problem. Another is whether the communicative partners of a mentally handicapped persons pay the same respect to their *face*. It is my impression that politeness is rarely used to maintain their face especially where the 'threat' reflects the lack of ability. And finally, this chapter is concerned with the extent to which mentally handicapped individuals take face considerations into account in constructing their communications.

12.3 THE NATURE OF COMMUNICATIVE ENVIRONMENTS

(a) Introduction

The empirical research reported here involved the use of questionnaires and is supported by examples of dialogues originating in both naturally occurring and arranged encounters. The aim is as stated above: to consider contextual aspects of communicative disturbances, and to determine whether the communicative backgrounds decribed in terms of communicative conventions differ for the mentally handicapped and the average speaker.

Quantitative and qualitative differences are possible and it is necessary to distinguish them. By qualitative differences, I mean that there could be unique conventions for dialogues in which mentally handicapped individuals are involved. In fact, I do not think that this is so. Maxims of conversation do not summarize the regularities of individuals' actions, but express what is appropriate and rational in cooperative interactions. Leudar and Browning (1988) have argued that different types of communicative situations can be distinguished from each other in terms of which maxims are in force and which are not. It is possible that being a mentally handicapped person and participating in some language games are mutually exclusive. This could arise from constraints on living and work opportunities, but the exclusion from language games could be also directly due to being labelled 'mentally handicapped'. The action of labelling someone mentally handicapped is inconsistent with common human social involvements.

By quantitative differences, I mean that the applicability of the communicative conventions to mentally handicapped speakers is constrained, partly as a result of the label and partly due to their behaviour, and also partly because they do not participate in activities where the conventions are in power. Our prediction was that the communicative backgrounds for both populations would be organized according to the same principles but that there would be quantitative differences: some maxims would be less in force for handicapped individuals.

An additional problem is, however, dual diagnosis — i.e. mentally handicapped individuals often also suffer from emotional, psychiatric and behaviour problems (Koller *et al.*, 1983; Leudar, Fraser and Jeeves, 1984). Leudar and Fraser (1985) argued that many communicative problems are associated with emotional problems of individuals and social aspects of mental handicap rather than reflecting the intellectual retardation, *per se* (Leudar, Fraser and Jeeves, 1987). The empirical study which follows addresses these three points. First, are communicative backgrounds for handicapped and average individuals organized according to the same set of principles corresponding to communicative conventions? Secondly, if so (as it turns out to be), are there quantitative differences in the degree to which these conventions are assumed to be valid for the respective populations? And finally, is the validity of the communicative conventions also constrained by behaviour disturbance?

The information about the communications of mentally handicapped and average individuals was collected by means of questionnaires. Each questionnaire contained statements about communications, each of which either violated or affirmed a communicative convention given in Figure 12.1. The rationale is that the statements violating and affirming a particular convention 'would go together', but of course only if that convention was an aspect of the rated person's (or population's) communicative background. If a convention is not an aspect of the communicative background, no such grouping of statements would be observed. Factor analysis was used to decide which statements in the questionnaires 'went together', i.e. constituted independent factors. In accordance with the above analysis, the prediction was that the same factors would summarize the data for the mentally handicapped and average populations.

(b) Technical details

Questionnaires

These consisted of 110 statements about communication (Figure 12.2), each of which was accompanied by a five-point rating scale labelled 'never', 'rarely', 'occasionally', 'often' and 'very often'. The statements were presented to the informants typed in three different random orders and the instructions were to rate to what extent each statement was true of the rated person. The statements about communication were chosen such that each communicative behaviour (or a characteristic) singled out either violated or affirmed at least one of the postulated communicative conventions. The item 'Breaks promises', for example, violates the quality maxim. Ratings on the item convey the degree to which the ratee is seen to abide by the quality maxim or to violate it.

The raters

Some of the raters were instructors at adult training centres in Cupar, Kirkaldy and Leven or nurses at Lynebank and Gogarburn Hospitals, all in Fife. They were asked to complete the questionnaires for mentally handicapped individuals in their care, whom they had known for at least three months. They were also asked to complete the questionnaires for exactly as many non-handicapped acquaintances. They were asked to include not only spouses and friends, but also people with whom they did not get on that well. The intention was to use these individuals as controls and their data as baselines. It turned out, however, that our informants were quite ready to complete the questionnaires on their mentally handicapped charges but not for the non-handicapped acquaintances, despite the fact that both would remain anonymous. In fact, some of them flatly refused to do this, and it seemed as if it was acceptable and appropriate to reflect on the communicative relationships with mentally handicapped but not those with the average acquaintances. It was therefore necessary to extend the control group by asking individuals unconnected with health care to complete the questionnaires on their (non-handicapped) acquaintances. These additional informants were chosen as widely as possible and they ranged from academics to policemen to bar-attendants. In all 40 informants took part.

The rates

The questionnaires were distributed for 200 mentally handicapped individuals and 157 came back completed. The handicapped individuals either lived in the two hospitals or worked in the training centres and lived either at home or in a variety of community facilities. The average age was 29 years, the range being 16–45 years; 75 ratees were men, and 82 were women. The IQ of all the participants could not be assessed, but the available scores from hospital/ATC records indicate the range 25–70; in other words, the sample included mildly, moderately and severely retarded individuals. All the participants were native speakers of English, and 200 questionnaires were distributed for non-handicapped individuals and 160 of them returned; 75 individuals were women and 85 men. The age was between 15 and 62 years, mean being 30 years. We attempted to make this group of subjects as varied as possible and the background of subjects varied widely: the sample included nurses, ATC instructors, students, policemen, academics, retired persons, building workers, etc. All spoke English as their first language.

Statistical analysis

The inter-rater reliability of the questionnaire was established by having the questionnaire completed for 10 individuals (five handicapped and five non-handicapped) twice, by two independent raters. A correlation $r = 0.837$ was obtained ($p < 0.001$).

The questionnaire data for the two populations was analysed separately, using factor analysis. Since this technique is open to criticism that the factors are artefacts of the mathematical methods employed, several methods of factor extraction (principal components method and principal factor method) and rotation (varimax and quartimax) were used and the results compared. Different methods of analysis yielded the same factors and the principal component factoring and varimax rotation solution is reported here. Kaiser's criterion (eigen value larger than 1) was used to select the statistically significant factors. The significance of the rating scales' loading on factors was determined using the Burt-Banks formula (Childs, 1970).

(c) Results

Factors are ordered sets of items and they can be interpreted as produced by a psychological process or a property. The factors are here said to be 'produced' by communicative conventions in the following sense. Each convention distinguishes the behaviours which affirm it from those which violate it, and in so doing produces a dimension, at the one pole of which cluster behaviours which violate a maxim and at the other are those which affirm it. If the communicative backgrounds for our two populations contain the same conventions, then the same factors should be obtained for both. However, if a convention is not assumed for the handicapped population, the corresponding factor should be absent. The prediction was that for each factor for one population, there would be a factor for the other population, composed of the same items in approximately the same order. With minor, but significant, exceptions this was the case. Figure 12.2 reports the pairs of corresponding factors; the loadings for the handicapped population in the first column, those for the average population in the second column.

The analysis of the questionnaires for average individuals yielded 11 factors which together accounted for 68% of variance. For the mentally handicapped population there were 12 significant factors, which together accounted for 70% of variance. I have defined, above, the sense in which a factor can be produced by communicative conventions; and this seems to have in fact happened. The factors obtained closely correspond to postulated communicative conventions, and the factors are labelled below accordingly.

Six of the factor pairs seem to be produced by 'maxims of conversation' (Grice, 1975). The first pair is produced by the 'maxim of quality'. This has two clauses: first, the sincerity clause forbids claiming what one knows to be false, and the second, evidentiality, forbids making claims without

Figure 12.2: Structure of communicative background for mentally handicapped and average populations (factors and factor loadings).

	handicapped population	average population
Quality		
What he/she says can be trusted	−0.67	−0.66
He/she is sincere	−0.58	−0.73
Can be trusted to carry out promises	−0.53	−0.72
Lies when he/she could be telling truth	0.55	0.61
Breaks promises	0.53	0.70
He/she is insincere	0.51	0.81
Tells tales about himself/herself		0.59
Tells 'tales' about others		0.58
Attempts to mislead others without having to		0.57
Makes claims without any evidence for their truth		0.59
Irrelevance		
He/she finds it difficult to relate to the topic of conversation	0.66	0.63
What he/she says is often not relevant to what others are talking about	0.60	0.52
The contributions he/she makes to conversations are usually relevant	−0.63	−0.63
He/she usually picks up the topic of and what he/she says is relevant	−0.75	−0.81
Quantity		
Bores people by stating obvious	0.67	0.57
Repeats the same statement several times in a short period of time	0.65	0.55
Asks the same question several times in a short period of time	0.62	0.57
Repeats what others say without an apparent reason	0.59	0.57
He/she has a tendency to state the obvious		0.59
Manner – Prolixity		
Tends to say more than is needed	0.80	0.84
His or her replies to questions are too detailed	0.72	0.79
When he/she explains something he/she goes into unnecessary detail	0.71	0.82
Talks too much	0.68	0.67
His/her conversations tend to wander		0.54
Does not explain himself/herself in enough detail	−0.52	
Tends to say less than is needed to be informative	−0.55	
Manner – Incoherence		
Contradicts himself/herself within a short period of time	0.81	0.88
He/she says one thing one moment and another the next	0.71	0.85
He/she expresses contradictory beliefs in a short period of time	0.57	0.77
He/she jumps from topic to topic incoherently	0.50	0.74
He/she seems to verbalize whatever comes into his/her head	0.53	
What he/she says is often ambiguous	0.52	
Manner – speech impediment		
It is difficult to work out what he/she means from the words he/she uses	0.82	0.71
His/her speech is so indistinct that it is difficult to understand	0.82	0.61
He/she has a speech impediment which makes understanding difficult	0.82	0.59

He/she has difficulties in finding words to express what he/she wants	0.71	0.72
What he/she says is vague and imprecise in meaning	0.55	0.70
What he/she says is often ambiguous		0.52

Indirectness

Does not say what he/she means, but rather expresses himself/ herself in a roundabout fashion	0.68	0.72
Gives clues as to what he/she wants rather than expressing it directly	0.65	0.77
Is indirect in expressing what he/she wants others to do	0.56	0.73
He/she hints rather than making his/her point directly	0.56	0.76
He/she tends to 'call a spade a spade'	−0.50	

Disclosure

Keeps things to himself/herself	0.73	0.60
Refuses to divulge information	0.55	0.57
He/she is secretive	0.53	0.60
Talks only to some people	0.52	
He/she is unwilling to talk to strangers	0.50	
It is difficult to fashion what he/she feels	0.49	0.49
Recounts personal experiences spontaneously	−0.50	−0.60
He/she is a chatter-box	−0.50	
Talks to strangers as if he knew them well	−0.55	
Reveals information spontaneously	−0.65	
He/she is an open person	−0.68	−0.59

Communality

Helps others without being asked	0.72	0.70
Notices and attends to needs, interests and wants of others	0.71	0.66
Makes positive comments about others	0.70	0.73
Makes nice comments about work or actions of others	0.64	
Makes effort to be understood and appreciated by others	0.63	0.67
He/she cares about being appreciated by others	0.60	0.55
Tells others they are clever, nice, pretty, etc.	0.60	0.66
Tries to be friendly	0.59	0.63
Seeks agreement	0.59	
Pays no attention to needs and interests of others	−0.51	

Hostility

Talks about others behind their back	0.75	
Makes negative comments about others when they are not present	0.73	
Makes negative comments about work and actions of others	0.69	
Makes negative comments about the personalities of others	0.58	
Tells others they are stupid, ugly, silly, etc.	0.60	
Picks up arguments with others	0.73	
Is often in conflict with others	0.64	
Disagrees with other people for the sake of disagreement	0.62	
He/she is argumentative	0.58	
Tries to make others to adopt the beliefs as he/she holds	0.62	
Makes claims without any evidence for their truth	0.60	
Attempts to mislead others when he or she has to	0.58	
Exaggerates in describing events	0.58	
Tells tales about others	0.56	
Attempts to mislead others without having to do so	0.52	
He/she insinuates about others	0.50	
He/she is sarcastic	0.52	

Uncooperativeness

Refuses to do what told	0.76	0.60
Refuses to carry out reasonable requests	0.75	
He/she is uncooperative	0.70	0.43
He/she has to be forced into doing what he/she does not like	0.69	0.68
It is almost impossible to make him/her do something if he/she does not want to	0.63	0.67
Refuses to answer questions	0.54	0.45
Gives in to commands only grudgingly		0.72

Conflict/conflict avoidance

Picks up arguments with others		0.74
He/she is argumentative		0.72
Tries to make others to adopt the same attitudes and beliefs as he/she holds		0.66
He/she is often in conflict with others		0.62
He/she disagrees with other people for the sake of disagreement		0.56
Side-steps conflict if possible	0.68	−0.68
Avoids disagreement	0.63	−0.60
He/she avoids conflict	0.68	−0.55
Withdraws when he/she meets conflict	0.61	−0.45
He/she is submissive	0.55	
Makes negative comments about work/actions of others		0.47
Makes negative comments about the personalities of others		0.43
Tells others they are stupid, ugly, silly, etc.		0.42

adequate evidence. The sincerity clause allows one to assume that the speaker believes what he or she says. The evidentiality clause allows one to conclude (bearing the evidential standards of the dialogue in mind) that what a person claims is actually true and to treat the person as a competent source of evidence. The first pair of factors shown in Figure 12.2 is clearly produced by this maxim. It is bipolar and the items which violate the maxim are opposed to those which affirm it. One difference between the 'average population' and the 'handicapped' versions of the dimension is that an evidentiality item ('Makes claims without adequate evidence') appears only for the average population. For the handicapped population it contributes to the dimension 'hostility' (see below). This could mean that the maxim of quality for the handicapped population has only the sincerity clause: we do not assume that the mentally handicapped are a competent source of evidence or at least are less ready to do so! However, the present evidence, by itself, does not quite warrant this conclusion. The item 'Tells tales about others' which violates the sincerity clause is for the handicapped population also a part of the dimension 'hostility'. It seems that some (untrue) statements by the mentally handicapped, irrespective of which clause of the quality maxim they violate, are interpreted in the first place as signs of hostility. The two possibilities are, of course, not exclusive. That

288

the maxim of quality is often not assumed for handicapped persons is made clear in interactions such as exchange 6, which took a place between a female instructor and a mentally handicapped woman 'chatting':

(6)
R.: So have you saved up any money for Christmas?
K.: Yeah.
R.: Have you?
K.: Yeah.

The reply to the question is not taken as sufficient evidence on which to base the conclusion that K. has saved money for Christmas. Possibly, the second reply is. The question 'Have you?' introduces the possibility that K. is either lying or does not know what she has done. The similar thing happens in exchange 7, but there it is the validity of the evidentiality clause which is brought into doubt:

(7)
Instructor 1: [*to another instructor*] Where is John?
Trainee: Gone shopping.
Instructor 1: [*addressing the other instructor*] Is John gone shopping with P.?
Instructor 2: Yeah.

Moreover, the average participants often seem to find it necessary to validate even those mentally handicapped person's claims which are obviously true, as in exchange 8, a practice which ordinarily would not be allowable:

(8) [*Playing dominoes*]
Instructor: How many dots do you need?
Trainee: Five.
Instructor: Five, that's right.

This sequential organization (initiation–response–feedback) has been reported as typical for dialogues in classrooms by Sinclair and Coulthard (1975). Such structures are typical when participants in dialogues are asymmetrically empowered (knowledge being one form of power).

There are really two problems involved. One is that the speaker may produce communications which violate the maxim of quality and thus be insincere or unreliable. Secondly, the maxim may not be applied even to communications which abide by the maxim and their verity thus brought into question. The difference is between sincerity and competence on the one hand, and trust and respect on the other. Is this also possible for the maxim of relevance and can a relevant contribution to a conversation be

COMMUNICATIVE ENVIRONMENTS

deemed irrelevant? The second pair of factors is in fact produced by the 'maxim of relevance.' It is bipolar and the items which refer to communications which violate Relevance are opposed to those which abide by it. It seems easy to find examples of mentally handicapped being irrelevant but not as easy to find examples of an apparently relevant contribution being treated as a *non sequitur*. This is possibly because relevance is in the first place a textual relation, and only in the second place a convention (cf. Sperber and Wilson, 1986).

The third pair of factors reflects violations of the clause of the 'maxim of quantity', which states that one's contributions to conversation should not be more informative than required. All the items refer to communications in which the speaker volunteers information already known to his or her audience as in exchange 9:

(9) [*A group of handicapped trainees watch a video recording taken of them at a disco*]
J.: [*addressing P.*] That was me there, that was me.
P.: [*responding to J.*] Yeah, that was you.
J.: [*addressing S.*] I am on the tele ...
S.: [*responds to J.*] We know.
T.: Oh get him [*i.e. J.*] to shut up.

The next three pairs of factors all seem to be produced by the 'maxim of manner'. The fourth pair contains behaviours relevant to the clause which specifies that the speaker should be brief and avoid unnecessary prolixity. The difference between the factors obtained for mentally handicapped and average populations is that for the former the factor is bipolar, with the negative pole items indicating laconicity and at the positive pole the items indicating verbosity. The factor for the average population contains only the items indicating 'verbosity'.

The fifth pair of factors is produced by the two clauses of the maxim which specifies that speakers should avoid ambiguity and be orderly. All the behaviour scoring on the factor violate this dictate in one way or another. Finally, the sixth pair of factors brings together violations of the clause which specifies that the speaker should avoid obscurity of expression. All the items in the factors refer to utterances whose meaning is difficult to work out for one reason or another.

The items which constitute the seventh pair of factors refer to indirect acts of communications, in which the speaker does not put on record his or her communicative intention, which thus seem to violate Lewis's principle of manifestation (Figure 12.1). The reason for indirectness can be either the lack of competence — the speaker is not able to represent his/her communicative intent in words — or possibly strategic (Leudar, 1981). Thus the seventh pair of factors can be referred to as indirectness.

290

So far the questionnaire data are consistent with the view that interactions on the whole proceed against the background of maxims of conversation. All the four maxims of conversation produced the same factors for both populations, with some qualifications which we will return to below. The remaining factors seem to be produced less by assumptions about information content and form of messages than by assumptions about the social and interpersonal impact of messages.

The eighth pair of factors reflects the extent to which the individual is willing to share his/her beliefs and feelings with others. The factor is bipolar: at one pole there are behaviours which are secretive and reflect unwillingness to share information, beliefs, feelings, as in exchange 10; the behaviours at the other pole reflect readiness to exteriorize one's propositional attitudes:

(10)
R.: Are you going to any parties?
K.: I can't say.
R.: Pardon?
K.: I can't say.
R.: You can't say, why are they a secret, your parties.
K.: I keep it to meself.
R.: Oh you keep it to yourself.
K.: Yep.

In this exchange, K. declines to reveal to the instructor the plans for her holidays; the refusal becomes the topic of conversation and it is by the way re-established that R. has a right to request information and K. has a right to deny it. In fact the refusal to share information and withdrawal strategies, in general, are complex (Leudar and Fraser, 1985). Withdrawal is sometimes the only way in which an otherwise powerless person can exercise control in a conversation. The withdrawn person's aim in conversation may well be to differentiate themselves from their communicative partners, rather than achieve consensus and mutuality because this would be oppressive to them.

The next two dimensions seem to be related to politeness and respect for one's communicative partners' *face* and its lack. The ninth pair of factors subsumes items which refer to behaviours which maintain the addressees' 'positive face' (see Figure 12.1) (see also Brown and Levinson, 1978). The items include preferences for consensus, positively evaluating others and their actions and paying attention to the needs of others. I have labelled this dimension 'communality'. Another way of looking at the dimension is as reflecting a strategy of invoking what Lewis subsumed under the principle of charity — in this case, that the mentally handicapped speaker is like his or her 'normal' counterpart in conversation.

The next dimension, *hostility*, has been obtained only for the handicapped population. It comprises behaviours which violate both the positive face and the negative face of one's communicative partners. Included are negative evaluations of others and their actions, argumentativeness and violations of the maxim of quality. The argumentative behaviours for average individuals are subsumed in the non-cooperativeness factor. Does this mean that the lack of cooperation by mentally handicapped people is interpreted as hostility?

Not all dialogues are cooperative and based on actual or prospective mutuality of beliefs, feelings and intentions. Some dialogues involve conflict and the final pair of factors is related to conflict. The factor for average population is bipolar. One pole is constituted by conflict behaviours, at the other pole are the behaviours of conflict avoidance. The corresponding factor for the mentally handicapped population has, however, only one pole which is constituted by behaviours of conflict avoidance. It will be remembered that the conflict behaviours for the handicapped population were subsumed in the dimension 'hostility'.

As pointed out above, communications are successful as communications if one conveys to one's audience one's communicative intent. For requests this means that the speaker conveys to his/her audience how he/she wants it to act, and expects that if possible, the audience will do so by the way of cooperating with the speaker. If the speaker requests something he or she expects, then unless there is a good reason not to, the addressee will carry out the request. The ninth pair of factors reflects systematic violations of this expectation. The behaviours on this dimension are those in which the individual refuses to cooperate with speech acts intended to regulate his or her behaviour.

These results indicate that, with some exceptions, the dimensions of the communicative background are the same for the handicapped and average populations. However, it remains possible that the maxims of conversation may not be in power to the same extent for conversations in which mentally handicapped persons participate: some of the maxims may be more often violated by mentally handicapped speakers and some may not be applied to their communicative actions by their partners in interactions, or both. So the second problem addressed is whether there are quantitative differences in the degree to which the maxims of conversation are in power for the two populations. This made it necessary to analyse the questionnaires for both populations using the same standards. A common set of 11 main dimensions which closely corresponded to those obtained in the factor analysis was used. The score for each dimension was calculated as an unweighted mean of the ratings on the relevant items of the questionnaires. In this way, each person's questionnaire was transformed into a profile in the same way, irrespective of whether the rated person was mentally handicapped. The means and standard deviations for the two populations are given in Table 12.1. The differences between the means were tested for significance using t-tests.

The table shows that, as a group, mentally handicapped individuals *are reported* to produce significantly more communications which violate maxims

Table 12.1: Average scores of handicapped and average populations on communicative ground scale

Dimension	Handicapped individuals (mean)	(s.d.)	Average individuals (mean)	(s.d.)	t(315)	p
Quality	1.6	0.7	1.4	0.7	3.1	0.002
Speech impediment	1.3	1.0	0.5	0.6	8.0	0.001
Irrelevance	1.9	0.8	1.4	0.5	6.5	0.001
Indirectness	1.4	0.9	1.0	0.9	3.3	0.001
Incoherence	1.5	1.1	0.8	0.8	5.9	0.001
Conflict avoidance	1.9	1.1	1.7	0.9		
Uncooperativeness	1.6	1.1	1.6	0.9		
Hostility	1.7	0.9	1.6	0.9		
(negative evaluation)	1.6	1.0	1.5	1.0		
(argumentativeness)	1.8	1.0	1.7	0.9		
Communality	2.0	0.7	2.0	0.7		
(consensus)	2.2	0.8	2.3	0.6		
(positive evaluation)	1.7	0.9	1.7	0.8		
Disclosure	2.0	0.9	1.9	0.8		
(secretiveness)	2.0	1.0	1.6	0.9	3.6	0.001
(openness)	1.9	1.1	1.9	1.0		
Quantity	1.8	0.9	1.9	0.8		
(verbosity)	1.5	1.2	1.3	1.1		
(laconicity)	1.8	1.0	1.5	0.8	3.5	0.001

Scale: 0, never; 1, rarely; 2, occasionally; 3, often; 4, very often.

of conversation. According to the informants, it is more often difficult to make out what the mentally handicapped individuals mean, and furthermore what they say is less likely to be true, relevant and coherent. The information they convey is often insufficient. These social representations of mentally handicapped individuals' communications are consistent with the findings of Sabsay and Kernan (1983), who have shown that narratives by mentally handicapped people *actually* lacked coherence and violated maxims of quantity and relevance. Another quantitative difference concerns the maxim of quality. The mentally handicapped speakers are *seen* as less constrained by this maxim. This either means they are perceived as less sincere about what they believe or less able to satisfy standards of evidence needed for the maxim to apply. Unfortunately the data does not allow us to distinguish these two possibilities.

It is also important that there are *no differences* between the two populations in other respects. They are not reported as more hostile and uncooperative or less seeking mutual ground. Obviously these features are not general communicative extensions of mental handicap. They are, however, associated with behaviour disturbance.

12.4 COMMUNICATIVE GROUND AND BEHAVIOUR DISTURBANCE

So far we have seen that the communicative environment of both mentally handicapped and average populations is structured by the same conventions, and I argued that this is so because these conventions reflect organization of social interactions rather than the character and dispositions of individuals. There were some quantitative differences between the two populations which suggest a tendency for the maxims of conversation being less likely to be assumed for the handicapped population. The more interpersonal dimensions of the communicative background were, however, not in general affected by the handicap.

The second problem I raised in the introduction concerned the relationship between behaviour disturbance and the communicative background. The Behaviour Disturbance Scale (Leudar, Fraser and Jeeves, 1984) was used to determine the subjects' disturbance profiles. The scale was completed for every handicapped person, as appropriate, either by a nurse in a hospital or by an instructor at a training centre. This was done at about the same time as the questionnaire on communication was completed, but we asked for both to be completed by different informants. The Behaviour Disturbance Scale measures intensity of a behaviour problem along six dimensions: aggressive conduct, emotional disturbance, communicativeness, anti-social conduct, idiosyncratic mannerism and self-injury. The aim here was to investigate whether each of these aspects of behaviour disturbance is associated with typical changes in communicative background. For statistical analysis multiple regression was used, correlating separately the scores for each dimensions of disturbance with the 11 communicative background scores. Figure 12.3 gives the results. There is a strong relationship between behaviour disturbance and communicative background; between 6% and 64% of variation in the former is explained by variations in the latter (Figure 12.3, final column). Each dimension of behaviour disturbance is associated with a distinct communicative background.

Quality maxim violations are particularly characteristic of anti-social conduct, as is uncooperativeness. Incoherence and irrelevance are characteristic of individuals scoring highly on 'idiosyncratic mannerisms'. As one would expect, withdrawn individuals score low on the dimensions 'quantity' and 'disclosure'; this simply rephrases the fact that they are withdrawn. The low disclosure is, however, also associated with emotional disturbance. This supports the contention by Leudar, Fraser and Jeeves (1984) and Leudar and Fraser (1985) that communicative withdrawal is an accompaniment of mood disturbance. The violations of 'cooperativeness' are particularly characteristic of aggressive individuals and of emotionally disturbed individuals. Leudar, Fraser and Jeeves (1984) and Leudar and Fraser (1985) argued that behaviour disturbances should not only be perceived from the point of view of their causes, but can be also understood as communicative problems in terms of

Figure 12.3: Relationship between dimensions of communicative background and behaviour disturbance (percentage of variance shared and β).

		Incoherence	Irrelevance	Speech impediment	Quantity	Uninformativeness	Disclosure	Communality	Quality	Directness	Hostility	Uncooperativeness	Conflict avoidance	Total
Aggressive conduct	%								2.3		4.5	29.6	11.3	47.7
	β								0.2		0.2	0.3	−0.3	
Emotional disturbance	%	6.9					3.7				3.2	20.4		34.2
	β	0.3					−0.3				0.2	0.2		
Communicativeness	%	2.1			3.4		35.1	8.0			4.3	3.7		56.6
	β	−0.2			0.3		0.2	0.2			0.3	−0.2		
Anti-social conduct	%			3.0						38.8		3.0		44.8
	β			−0.2						0.5		0.3		
Idiosyncratic mannerisms	%	22.7	3.4										6.3	32.4
	β	0.4	0.2										0.3	
Self-injury	%						5.9							5.9
	β						−0.2							

their extensions into social contexts. The strong relationship between behaviour disturbance and communicative background supports their argument.

In section 12.3 we have seen that the communicative background may vary depending on whether the person is mentally handicapped; here we see that it may be also affected by behaviour problems. The findings unfortunately open the possibility that the differences between handicapped and average populations were, at least in part, due to the relative prevalence of behaviour disturbance in the mentally handicapped population. It is not possible to separate these in the present study, as the information on mental age of individuals was not available. The issue clearly requires a further research, and it would be advisable to study the communicative background for individuals free of behaviour disturbance. However, this may be difficult because the frequency of behaviour disturbance is correlated to mental age.

12.5 DISCUSSION AND CONCLUSION

The main point of this chapter was to investigate backgrounds against which mentally handicapped individuals communicate and compare them to those for the average individuals. We found that the communicative backgrounds for both populations were constituted by the same tacit conventions; there were no unique ones for interpreting the talk by mentally handicapped persons. Two possible but important exceptions to this were that the maxim of quality for mentally handicapped persons has possibly only the sincerity clause, not the evidentiality one. The example of interactions we considered documented that even obviously true or indisputable sentences by mentally handicapped individuals were treated as needing validation. This change in the communicative background is possibly a direct reflection of being labelled 'mentally handicapped'. The second exception was that the dimension 'hostility' was only obtained for the mentally handicapped population. This may mean that some communications of mentally handicapped people in which they refused to cooperate and involving conflict were interpreted, in the first place, as expressions of hostility. We found further that although the backgrounds for both populations are qualitatively the same, mentally handicapped persons were *reported to* violate maxims of conversations more often than the average persons. This finding can be interpreted in two ways. First, it is possible that some mentally handicapped people actually violate maxims of quality, quantity and relevance more frequently than their average partners. This may be so, but it is important to bear in mind the reasons for such violations. They are not necessarily caused by the lack of skill. The second possibility was that such maxims are assumed to be in power only in certain interactions, in which mentally handicapped people cannot take part on account of being labelled 'handicapped'. In fact some of the research actually supports this possibility: it seems that the average individuals adopt a didactic stance to their mentally handicapped partners, even when this is inappropriate (Vogel, 1987). Such restriction in communicative opportunities for mentally handicapped people should be investigated thoroughly.

We also found that each dimension of behaviour disturbance was associated with a distinct pattern of violations of communicative conventions. In this the results support the argument by Leudar, Fraser and Jeeves (1984) that behaviour disturbances are not just individual phenomena, but have extensions into the social environment which may keep disturbed behaviours from extinction after their initial causes have been removed. Our study does not do justice to the complexities of the relationships between low intelligence and lack of ability, behaviour disturbance and the changes in communicative background. It does suggest, however, that the clarification of the relationship will lead to understanding mental handicap as both a social and individual phenomenon. I interpret our results to mean that communicative environments for mentally handicapped people are systematically distorted and do not provide the same opportunities as those for average persons.

ACKNOWLEDGEMENT

Some of the research reported in this chapter was supported by SHHD grant K/MRS/50/C330. I am grateful to Fife Regional Council, to the staff at Gogarburn, Lynebank and Strathmartine Hospitals and to the staff of

Dalgairn, Leven, St Clair and Woodland Adult Training Centres for all their assistance and cooperation.

REFERENCES

Alford, C.F. (1987) Habermas, post-Freudian psychoanalysis, and the end of individual, *Theory, Culture and Soc.*, *4*, 3–29.

Bach, K. (1987) On communicative intentions: a reply to Recanati, *Mind and Language*, *2*, 141–54.

Bach, K. and Harnish, R.M. (1979) *Linguistic Commun. and Speech Acts*, MIT Press, Cambridge, Mass.

Brewer, J.D. and Yearley, S. (1986) Stigma and conversational competence: a conversational analytic study of the mentally handicapped, paper presented at BSA Conference on Erving Goffman, University of York, July.

Brown, P. and Levinson, S.C. (1978) Universals in language use: politeness phenomena in *Questions and Politeness: Strategies in Social Interaction* (ed. E. Goody), Cambridge University Press, Cambridge, pp. 56–311.

Childs, D. (1970) *The Essentials of Factor Analysis*, Holt, Rhinehart and Winston, London.

Costall, A. (1986) The psychologist's fallacy in ecological realism, *Teorie & Modelli*, *III*, 37–46.

Costall, A. and Still, A. (1986) *Cognitive Psychology in Question*, Harvester Press, Brighton.

Edmonson, W. (1981) *Spoken discourse: a model for analysis*, Longman, London.

Eggerton, R.B. (1967) *The Cloak of Competence: Stigma in the Lives of the Mentally Retarded*, University of California Press, Berkeley, Calif.

Goffman, E. (1955) On face-work: an analysis of ritual elements in social interaction, *Psychiat.*, *18*, 213–31.

Goffman, E. (1986) *Stigma. Notes on the Management of Spoiled Identity*, Harmondsworth, Penguin.

Greenberg, J. and Mitchell, S. (1983) *Object Relations in Psychoanalytic Theory*, Harvard University Press, Cambridge, Mass.

Grice, H.P. (1957) Meaning, *Phil. Rev.*, *66*, 377–88.

Grice, H.P. (1975) Logic and conversation in *Syntax and Semantics 3: Speech Acts* (eds P. Cole and J.L. Morgan), Accademic Press, New York, pp. 41–58.

Grice, H.P. (1982) Meaning revisited in *Mutual Knowledge* (ed. N. Smith), Cambridge University Press, Cambridge, pp. 223–43.

Habermas, J. (1970) On systematically distorted communication, *Inquiry*, *13*, 205–18.

Kernan, K.T. and Sabsay, S. (1981) Towards an ethnography of the mildly retarded, a paper presented at Eighty-ninth Annual Meeting, APS, Los Angeles, Calif. USA.

Kernan, K., Sabsay, S. and Shin, N. (1987) Discourse features as criteria in judging the intellectual ability of their speakers, *Discourse Processes* (forthcoming).

Koller, H., Richardson, S.A., Katz, M. and McLarren, J. (1983) Behaviour disturbance since childhood among a 5-year cohort of all mentally retarded young adults in a city, *Am. J. Ment. Defic.*, *88*, 21–7.

Leudar, I. (1980) Some aspects of communication in Down's syndrome in *Language: Social Psychological Perspectives* (ed. H. Giles *et al.*), Pergamon, Oxford, pp. 247–53.

Leudar, I. (1981) Strategic communication in mental retardation in *Communicating with Normal and Retarded Children* (eds W.I. Fraser and R. Grieve), Wright, Bristol, pp. 113–29.

Leudar, I. and Antaki, C. (1988) Completion and dynamics in explanatory conversations in *Analysing Lay Explanation: A Casebook of methods* (ed. C. Antaki), Sage, London, pp. 148–55.

Leudar, I. and Browning, P.K. (1988) Maxims of communication and language games, *Language and Commun.* (forthcoming).

Leudar, I. and Fraser, W.I. (1985) How to keep quiet: some withdrawal strategies in mentally handicapped adults, *J. Ment. Defic. Res., 29*, 315–30.

Leudar, I., Fraser, W.I. and Jeeves, M.A. (1981) Social familiarity and communication in Down syndrome, *J. Ment. Defic. Res.,* 25, 133–42.

Leudar, I., Fraser, W.I. and Jeeves, M.A. (1984) Behaviour disturbance and mental handicap: typology and longitudinal trends, *Psychol. Med., 14*, 923–35.

Leudar, I., Fraser, W.I. and Jeeves, M.A. (1987) Theoretical problems and practical solutions to behaviour disorders in retarded people, *Health Bull., 45*, 347–55.

Levinson, S.C. (1979) The essential inadequacies of speech act model of dialogue in *Possibilities and Limitations of Pragmatics* (eds H. Parret, M. Sbissa and J. Verscheuren), J. Benjamin, Amsterdam, pp. 473–92.

Lewis, D. (1983) *Philosophical Papers,* Oxford University Press, Oxford, Vol. 1, chapters 8 and 11.

McGinn, C. (1983) *The Subjective View: Secondary Qualities and Indexical Thoughts,* Clarendon Press, Oxford.

McTear, M. (1984) *Children's Conversation,* Blackwell, Oxford.

May, J.D. (1981) Practical reasoning: extracting useful information from partial informants, *J. Pragmatics, 5*, 45–9.

Mittler, P.J. (1978) Language and communication in *Mental Deficiency: The Changing Outlook* (eds A.M. Clarke and D.B. Clarke), Methuen, London, pp. 258–321.

O'Connor, N. and Hermelin, B. (1963) *Speech and Thought in Severe Subnormality,* Pergamon, Oxford.

Price-Williams, D. and Sabsay, S. (1979) Communicative competence among severely retarded persons, *Semiotica, 26*, 35–63.

Putnam, H. (1975) Meaning of meaning in *Mind, Language and Reality,* Cambridge University Press, Cambridge, Vol. 2.

Recanati, F. (1986) On defining communicative intentions, *Mind and Language, 1*, 213–42.

Sabsay, S. and Kernan, K.T. (1983) Communicative design in the speech of mildly retarded adults in *Environments and Behaviour: The Adaptation of Mentally Retarded Persons* (eds K.T. Kernan, M. Begab and R. Edgerton), University Park Press, Baltimore, Md., pp. 283–94.

Sabsay, S. and Platt, M. (1985) *Weaving the Cloak of Competence,* Working Paper No. 32, Socio-Behavioural Group, University of California, Los Angeles, Calif., USA.

Schiefelbush, R.L. (1972) *Language of the Mentally Retarded,* University Park Press, Baltimore, Md.

Schiefelbush, R.L., Copeland, R. and Smith, J. (eds) (1967) *Language and Mental Retardation. Empirical and Conceptual Considerations,* Holt, Rinehart and Winston, New York.

Sinclair, J.M. and Coulthard, R.M. (1975) *Towards an Analysis of Discourse: The English Used by Teachers and Pupils,* Oxford University Press, London.

Sperber, D. and Wilson, D. (1986) *Relevance: Communication and Cognition,* Basil Blackwell, Oxford.

Turner, J.L., Kernan, K.T. and Gelphman, S. (1984) Speech etiquette in a sheltered workshop in *Lives in Process: Mildly Retarded Adults in a Large City* (ed. R.B.

Edgerton), Monographs of American Association on Mental Deficiency No. 6, American Association on Mental Deficiency, Washington, DC.

Vogel, S. (1987) Dialogues with the mentally handicapped: the effect of type of interaction and audience on conversation, unpublished ms., University of Manchester.

Subject Index

Author Index

Koenig, M.A. 218, 219
Kogan, K. 219
Kohlberg, L. 86
Koller, H. 283
Kologinsky, E. 59
Konstantareas, M. 60
Korblum, S. 41
Krupski, A. 118
Kuczaj, S.A. 12
Kurtz, B. 91

Labov, W. 231
Lackner, J. 96, 97
Lambert, M.J. 6, 9
Lamberts, F. 122
Langness, F. 118, 124
Laskey, E. 205
Leeming, K. 36
Lehay, M. 52
Leifer, J. 115, 218, 220
Lemperle, G. 38
Lennenberg, E.H. 38, 42, 92
Leonard, L.B. 35, 94, 102, 114, 115, 196
Leri, S.M. 37
Leudar, I. 147, 228, 265, 271, 274–9,
    281–3, 290, 291, 295, 296
Levin, J. 131
Levine, H. 118, 124
Levinson, J. 130
Levinson, S.C. 160, 277, 280, 281, 291
Lewis, D. 279, 280
Lewis, M. 115, 208, 218, 220
Li, A. 129
Libergott, J. 125
Libkuman, T. 88
Liebert, A. 118
Lieven, E. 222
Light, P. 57–61, 64, 67
Lincoln, A. 121
Lloyd, L.L. 39
Lobato-Barrera, D. 61
Lobb, H. 121
Logan, D. 83
Looney, P. 129
Lord, C. 190
Lovaas, O.I. 41, 187
Lowe, M. 129
Lozar, B. 6, 9
Ludwig, R. 121, 123
Luftig, R. 58
Lunzer, E. 93, 114
Luria, A. 74, 85
Lyle, J.G. 5, 8, 10, 11, 218
Lyons, J. 22

MacDonald, J. 125, 129, 157, 181, 204,
    206, 210
MacKenzie, H. 5, 9, 94, 98, 104

MacMillan, D. 120
MacNamara, J. 122
Mahler, A. 130
Mahoney, G. 94, 114, 189, 196, 199, 218
Maisto, A. 117
Manolson, A. 125
Manolson, H. 205
Mar, H. 120, 125
Marcell, M. 123
Marr, H.H. 27
Marshall, N. 196, 218, 219
Martin, H. 196, 201
Masterson, J. 9, 81, 221, 222
Mastropieri, M. 131
Masur, E.F. 172
Mathews, J. 38, 41
Matson, J.L. 254
May, J.D. 279, 280
McArthur, K. 159
McCauley, C. 13, 26, 27, 90, 104, 117, 118,
    130
McConachie, H. 223
McConkey, R. 44, 159, 196, 201, 204,
    207–8, 212
McCune-Nicholich, L. 114, 129, 130
McDade, H. 123
McDonald, L. 195, 197
McGinn, C. 276
McKenzie, H. 93
McLaughlin, J. 85, 124
McLean, T.E. 39, 76, 119, 125, 187, 188,
    197, 222
McManis, D. 117
McNerney, C. 126, 128
McNutt, J.C. 37
McTear, M. 275
Meador, I. 117, 119
Mein, R. 5, 6–11
Meltzoff, A. 113
Menolascino, F.J. 254
Mercer, C. 119, 144
Merrill, E. 120, 122, 125
Mervis, C.B. 4, 8, 12–16, 115, 132, 218,
    219, 222
Middleton, D. 145
Milgram, N. 7, 8, 83, 85
Miller, A. 67
Miller, E. 67
Miller, J. 83, 104, 105, 113, 114
Miller, J.F. 5, 9, 93–8
Mitchell, S. 223, 276
Mitler, P. 40, 122, 147, 149, 157, 186, 274
Moerk, E.L. 201
More, K. 113
Morehead, A. 112
Morehead, D. 112
Mosley, J. 88, 118, 119
Mundy, P.C. 254

307

Woodward, M. 93, 115, 117
Woolbridge, P. 121, 122
Wooton, A.J. 155, 160, 182, 199
Wulz, S.V. 40, 44, 45, 52

Yearley, S. 275
Yeates, K. 84–9

Yellin, A. 121
Yoder, D. 83, 97, 105, 125, 126

Zacks, R. 118
Zeaman, D. 91, 92, 119
Zetlin, A. 118, 248
Zigler, E. 83–5, 87, 88, 117